GANDHI IN INDIA'S LITERARY AND CULTURAL IMAGINATION

This book engages with the socio-cultural imaginings of Gandhi in literature, history, visual and popular culture. It explores multiple iterations of his ideas, myths and philosophies, which have inspired the work of filmmakers, playwrights, cartoonists and artists for generations.

Gandhi's politics of non-violent resistance and satyagraha inspired various political leaders, activists and movements and has been a subject of rigorous scholarly enquiry and theoretical debates across the globe. Using diverse resources like novels, autobiographies, non-fictional writings, comic books, memes, cartoons and cinema, this book traces the pervasiveness of the idea of Gandhi which has been both idolized and lampooned. It explores his political ideas on themes such as modernity and secularism, environmentalism, abstinence, self-sacrifice and political freedom along with their diverse interpretations, caricatures, criticisms and appropriations to arrive at an understanding of history, culture and society.

With contributions from scholars with diverse research interests, this book will be an essential read for students and researchers of political philosophy, cultural studies, literature, Gandhi and peace studies, political science and sociology.

Nishat Zaidi is Professor of English at Jamia Millia Islamia, New Delhi. A scholar, critic and translator, she is the recipient of several prestigious grants and has conducted collaborative research with the Centre for Indian Studies in Africa, University of Witwatersrand, SA, South Asia Institute, Heidelberg University, Germany, and Michigan State University, USA. Her publications include her monographs, *Makers of Indian Literature: Agha Shahid Ali* (2014), *Ocean as Method: Thinking with the Maritime* (with Dilip Menon et al. 2022) and *Terrains of Consciousness: Multilogical Perspectives on Globalization* (Wurzburg University Press, 2021, co-authored with Zeno Ackermann et al.) and her translations and edited books, *Day and Dastan* (2018, with Alok Bhalla) and *Between Worlds: The Travels of Yusuf Khan Kambalposh* (2014, with Mushirul Hasan), among others. Her forthcoming work is *Karbala: A Historical Play* (translation of Premchand's Play *Karbala* with a critical introduction and notes) to be published in 2022.

Indrani Das Gupta is Assistant Professor in the Department of English, Maharaja Agrasen College, University of Delhi, India. Currently pursuing her PhD from Department of English, Jamia Millia Islamia, India, in the area of Indian Science Fiction. She is engaged in the examination of the interface of science fictionality with the paradigms of nation state and the social variables that constitute the ontological human existence. Her research interests include science fiction studies, crime fiction, children and young adult narratives, utopia/dystopia, sports culture, popular culture and postmodern narratives. She is the non-fiction editor of *Mithila Review: An International Journal of Science Fiction and Fantasy*.

GANDHI IN INDIA'S LITERARY AND CULTURAL IMAGINATION

Edited by
Nishat Zaidi and Indrani Das Gupta

Routledge
Taylor & Francis Group

LONDON AND NEW YORK

Cover credit @gettyimages

First published 2022
by Routledge
4 Park Square, Milton Park, Abingdon, Oxon OX14 4RN

and by Routledge
605 Third Avenue, New York, NY 10158

Routledge is an imprint of the Taylor & Francis Group, an informa business

British Library Cataloguing-in-Publication Data
A catalogue record for this book is available from the British Library

Library of Congress Cataloging-in-Publication Data
A catalog record for this book has been requested

ISBN: 978-0-367-68887-5 (hbk)
ISBN: 978-0-367-70284-7 (pbk)
ISBN: 978-1-003-14547-9 (ebk)

DOI: 10.4324/9781003145479

Typeset in Bembo
by Apex CoVantage, LLC

CONTENTS

PART II
Consumptions of Gandhi: Articulations or
Disarticulations?

PART III
The Construction of Self: Experimental Site of Praxis
and Its Discursive Limits

PART IV
Gandhian Presence in Intimate and Public Spheres:
Reflections on Corporeality, Ethicality and Society **209**

FIGURES

NOTES ON THE CONTRIBUTORS

Bharti Arora is a faculty member of the Department of English, Tagore Government Arts and Science College, Pondicherry. She has completed her PhD in English from Jamia Millia Islamia, New Delhi. Her areas of research interest are Indian writings in English and in translation, women writing, gender studies, nation and region. Bharti's book, based on her PhD thesis, titled *Writing Gender, Writing Nation: Women's Fiction in Post-independence India* was published in 2019.

Dhritiman Chakraborty received his doctoral degree on "Postcolonial Political" from the Center for Studies in Social Sciences, Kolkata, India (CSSSC), where in his dissertation, he adopted a phenomenological methodology to offer a different narrative of dissent in India. He has published parts of this research in various anthologies and in journals. In his postdoctoral engagement, he is exploring paradigms around which the postcolonial political can be rethought from a non-Western perspective.

Bhaswati Chatterjee is an alumna of Presidency College, Kolkata, and presently Associate Professor in History, Vidyasagar College, Kolkata. She is a teacher and researcher in gender, politics and social history of Bengal in colonial and postcolonial period. She was awarded her doctoral thesis on the second social reform from the University of Calcutta, 2017. She has published on women's autobiography, gender, politics and social reform on colonial and postcolonial periods. She is currently co-editing *Her Story*, a Festschrift on Professor Geraldine Forbes.

Indrani Das Gupta is working as Assistant Professor in the Department of English, Maharaja Agrasen College, University of Delhi, India. Currently pursuing her PhD from Department of English, Jamia Millia Islamia, India, in the area of Indian Science Fiction. She is engaged in the examination of the interface of science fictionality with the paradigms of nation state and the social variables that constitute the ontological human existence. Her research interests include science fiction studies, crime fiction, children and young adult narratives, utopia/dystopia, sports culture, popular culture and postmodern narratives. She is also the non-fiction editor of *Mithila Review: An International Journal of Science Fiction and Fantasy*.

Baran Farooqi is a Professor of English literature at Jamia Millia Islamia. Besides Shakespearean and Modern European drama, her interests include women's studies, gender and Urdu literature and culture. She is also a well-known translator of Urdu into English.

Nishat Haider is a Professor of English at Jamia Millia Islamia, New Delhi, India. She is the author of *Tyranny of Silences: Contemporary Indian Women's Poetry* (2010). She has served as the director at the Institute of Women's Studies, University of Lucknow. She is the recipient of many academic awards including the Meenakshi Mukherjee Prize (2016), C. D. Narasimhaiah Award (2010) and Isaac Sequeira Memorial Award (2011). She has lectured extensively on subjects at the intersection of cinema, culture and gender studies. Her current research interests include postcolonial studies, translation, popular culture and gender studies.

M.H. Ilias is a Professor at the School of Gandhian Thought and Development Studies and Dean, Faculty of Social Sciences, Mahatma Gandhi University, Kerala. His recent publications include *Arabi-Malayalam: Linguistic-Cultural Traditions of Mappila Muslims of Kerala, Off-Campus Orientalism: Western University Branch Campuses in the Gulf* and *Space Memory and Jewish National Identity*. He has been the recipient of Ford Foundation Fellowship for Postdoctoral Research (2007) at Oxford University and Postdoctoral Visiting Research Fellowship (2008) at the Centre for Modern Orient, Berlin.

Aishwarya Kumar is presently pursuing his doctoral studies in English at School of Letters, Ambedkar University Delhi. His research interest focuses on the linkages between literature, philosophy and ethics. His M.Phil. dissertation closely analyses fictions of J. M. Coetzee and investigates claims about its ethical character. In his current doctoral project, he intends to study the origin of storytelling and the form of novel, to understand the relationship of philosophy and fiction.

Vinay Lal is a cultural critic, writer, blogger and Professor of History and Asian American Studies at the University of California, Los Angeles (UCLA). His intellectual and research interests include South Asian history, comparative colonial histories, the Indian diaspora, cinema, cultures of sexuality, the global histories of non-violence and the thought of Mohandas Gandhi. His 18 books include the two-volume *Oxford Anthology of the Modern Indian City* (2013); *Deewaar: The Footpath, the City, and the Angry Young Man* (2011); *Political Hinduism* (2009); *Of Cricket, Guinness and Gandhi* (2005) and *The History of History* (2003). His most recent book is *The Fury of Covid-19: The Politics, Histories, and Unrequited Love of the Coronavirus* (2020). He blogs for ABP and at vinaylal.wordpress.com and has an academic YouTube channel called, <u>dillichalo.</u>

Aparna Pathak has completed her M.Phil. in English from the Department of English, Jamia Millia Islamia, New Delhi. Her research interests include comic book studies and she has worked on Joe Sacco's comics journalism for her M.Phil. dissertation. She intends to continue her research in the same field by working on comic books and visual culture through the theoretical lens of posthumanism. She has completed her M.A. in English from MCM DAV College, Chandigarh, and B.A. Hons. from Kalindi College, University of Delhi.

Disha Pokhriyal is a PhD candidate in the Department of English, Jamia Millia Islamia, where she is working on contemporary South Asian memoirs by women. Her areas of interest include life writing, translation, theories of self and visual arts. She is also engaged as an assistant professor of English in Satyawati College (Evening), University of Delhi.

Haris Qadeer teaches at the Department of English, University of Delhi. His research interest areas include literatures and cultures of South Asian Muslims, refugee narratives, postcolonial studies, cultural studies, translations and South Asian writings in English. He was a visiting fellow at the Potsdam University, Germany (2019). He has a special issue of *Thesis Eleven* on postcolonial world literature. His recent publications include *Sultana's Sisters: Gender, Genre, and Geneology in South Asian Muslim Women's Fiction* and *The Silence that Speaks: Short Fiction by Indian Muslim Women.*

Barnali Saha is Assistant Professor at the School of English Studies, Vivekananda Institute of Professional Studies, New Delhi, India. She has obtained her PhD in English from the GGS Indraprastha University, New Delhi, India. Her doctoral work investigated the articulation of the Partition from a literary and cultural point of view. As a research scholar, she has published several papers and has attended and presented at many national and international conferences. Apart from her academic work, she enjoys writing short stories and translating short fiction from Bengali and Hindi to English.

Lakshmi Subramanian, currently a Professor of History at Humanities and Social Science Faculty in BITS Pilani Goa campus, has had a long and distinguished teaching and research career. She is best known for her work on maritime history and the social history of music in South India. Her recent publications include *Singing Gandhi's India Music and Sonic Nationalism* (2019) and *The Sovereign and the Pirate Ordering Maritime Subjects In India's Western Littoral* (2016).

P. Rajitha Venugopal is Assistant Professor in the Department of Humanities and Languages, Flame University, Pune. She completed her PhD from the Department of English, Jamia Millia Islamia on the works of Barbara Kingsolver, with a special focus on ecocritical perspectives. Her M.Phil. research was on the short stories of Narayan, the first published Adivasi writer in Malayalam literature. Her areas of interest include ecocriticism, American literature, postcolonial literature, writings from the margins and regional literature.

Ruchika Wason Singh is a visual artist, independent researcher and art educator based in Delhi, India. She holds degrees in B.F.A. Painting (1997) and M.F.A. Painting (1999) from the College of Art, New Delhi. She has been a U.G.C. Junior Research Fellow at University of Delhi from 2001 to 2006. She received PhD in 2008. Parallel to her studio practice, she is involved in the research project *A.M.M.A.A. – The Archive for Mapping Mother Artists in Asia*. She has been an associate professor in the Department of Painting, College of Art (2012–2017) and a Visiting Faculty at Ashoka University, Sonipat, India (2019, 2020).

Nishat Zaidi is a Professor of English at Jamia Millia Islamia, New Delhi. She has taught at Aligarh Muslim University and Vasanta College for Women, Varanasi, before joining Jamia Millia Islamia. Her publications include *Makers of Indian Literature*: *Agha Shahid Ali* (2014); *Day and Dastan* (translation, 2018); *Between Worlds: The Travels of Yusuf Khan Kambalposh* (2014); *A Voyage to Modernism: Sir Syed Ahmed Khan*, translated and edited by Mushirul Hasan and Nishat Zaidi (2011). Her forthcoming work is *Karbala: A Historical Play* (translation of Premchand's Play *Karbala* with a critical introduction and notes) to be published in 2022.

ACKNOWLEDGEMENTS

This book has its inception in the seminar organized by the Department of English, in collaboration with Gandhi Smriti and Darshan Samiti on "Gandhi in India's Literary Imagination: Rethinking History Culture and Society," on 21–22 October, 2019, to mark the celebration of 150 years of Mahatma Gandhi. We would like to thank Jamia Millia Islamia, New Delhi, and Gandhi Smriti and Darshan Samiti, New Delhi, for supporting the seminar. The debates and discussions initiated at the seminar allowed us to conceptualize the book in its present shape. The editors would like to acknowledge the following for providing permissions pertaining to the papers included in the volume and the images and illustrations used by contributors:

- To the publishers of *Frontline* and *Marg* for permission to publish revised versions of papers by Vinay Lal and Lakshmi Subramanian.
- To Adwaita Gadnayak, Director General, NGMA, New Delhi, for granting permission to publish the work of Mr Upendra Maharathi titled *Gandhi and People Gathering*; to Vajpeyi, Managing and Life Trustee, The Raza Foundation, New Delhi, for permission to publish the work of Mr S.H. Raza titled *Shanti*; to Atul Dodiya for permission to publish his works *Lamentation, Bapu at Rene Block Gallery, New York* and *Broken Branches*; to Iranna G.R. for permission to publish his work *NAVU (We Together)*; to Indrapramit Roy and Ram Rahman (Founder Member, SAHMAT) for publishing the work of Mr Indrapramit Roy titled *Post Card for Gandhi*; and to Krishen Khanna and Radhika Chopra for publishing the work of Mr Krishen Khanna titled *News of Gandhiji's Death*, in Ruchika Wason Singh's chapter.
- To *The Internet Archive* for access to the image *In the Untouchable Quarters* by Kanu Desai and to *World Digital Library* for access to the work of Nandalal Bose titled *Netaji Subhas Chandra Bose and other patriots trying to liberate Mother*

India from outside India published in the Constitution of India, to Argha Kamal Ganguly, Assistant Curator, NGMA, New Delhi, and Karan Khanna (son of Mr. Krishen Khanna) for their observations, support and assistance in Ruchika Wason Singh's chapter.

• To James Pach for permission to use "Diplomat Cartoons"; to Yusuf Munna for copyright permission to use his cartoons published in *Cartoon Mirror*, and Professor Frances Pritchett for permission to use the cartoon – "Gandhi in the Lap of Bharatmata," in Barnali Saha's chapter.

We would like to appreciate all our contributors for their cooperation and timely revisions.

Finally, both Indrani and Nishat would like to acknowledge the support of family and friends for their patience and support.

Nishat Zaidi
Indrani Das Gupta

INTRODUCTION

Nishat Zaidi

Inquilab aaya, nayi duniya, naya hungaama hai
Shahnaamah ho chuka ab daur-e-Gandhinaamah hai
The revolution has begun, a new world, a new uprising is here,
Gone are the days of chronicles of Kings, the chronicle of Gandhi is here.[1]

With this couplet, the iconic Urdu poet Akbar Illahabadi (1846–1921) announced the arrival of Gandhi on the political scene, ushering in a new world order in which the imperial structures would have no place. Veritably, ever since his emergence on the political canvas in the early decades of the twentieth century, Mohandas Karamchand Gandhi (1869–1948), Father of the Indian Nation, has dominated politico-philosophical ideas and socio-cultural formations across space and time. Gandhi had become a legend in his own lifetime; his figure sparked popular imagination, and hundreds of folksongs that circulated in different parts of India during the peak of the nationalist movement presented him in different personas (Chauhan 2019; Kushwaha 2009). He inspired poets and writers in almost all Indian languages. Printmakers and cartoonists in the British and Indian press were never tired of engaging with his political, cultural and philosophical ideas. In Raja Rao's novel *Kanthapura* written by the author in the 1930s when Gandhi was still at the peak of his political career, Jayaramachar, the Harikatha man in a small village of South India, narrates the story of the birth of incarnation of Shiva thus:

> In the great heavens, Brahma, the self-created one, was lying on his serpent, when the sage Valmiki entered . . . 'Oh, learned sire, what brings you to this distant world?' asked Brahma . . . 'I have come to bring you sinister news. Far down on the earth you chose as your chief daughter Bharatha, the goddess of wisdom and well-being. . . . O Brahma, you who sent us the prince

DOI: 10.4324/9781003145479-1

propagators of the holy law and sages that smote the darkness of ignorance, you have forgotten us so long that men have come from across the seas and the oceans to trample on our wisdom and to spit on virtue itself. They have come to bind us and to whip us, to make our women die milkless and our men die ignorant. O Brahma, design to send us one of your gods so that he may incarnate on earth and bring back light and plenty to your enslaved daughter . . . ' 'O sage' pronounced Brahma, 'is it greater for you to ask or for me to say "yea"? Siva himself will forthwith go and incarnate on earth and free my beloved daughter from her enforced slavery. Pray seat yourself; the messengers of heaven shall fly to Kailas and Siva be informed of it.' And lo, . . . there was born in a family in Gujarat a son such as the world has never beheld.!

(17–18)

Interestingly, written in Gandhi's lifetime, the novel enacts the transformation of Gandhi from an individual to an idea, translocating him from the living present to a hoary past and elevating him from the quotidian to the mythic stature. The Gandhi myth informs the actions of villagers in the novel, transmuting their ritual and institutional practices and redrawing their spatial and temporal contexts.

Moving beyond the dominant perceptions of myth as "primitive science," manifesting projections of unconscious desire (Freud, 1900), or "cultural reflectors" (Boas, 1910), B. Malinowsky called for a shift in focus to the society that produces these myths and the function they serve in the society. In his study of the interrelation between myth and social organization, Malinowski has argued that myths are to be viewed as charters for social institutions. He noted, for example, that for the Trobrianders, the myths are closely tied to their social structures. The function of myths can be detected in their pursuits, and myths govern and control "their moral and social behaviour." In other words, Malinowski demonstrates "an intimate connection exists between the word, the mythos, the sacred tales of a tribe, on the one hand, and their ritual acts, their moral deeds, their social organization, and even their practical activities on the other" (96). To Malinowski, myth was "not merely a story told but a reality lived" (100). By this logic, the past continuously impinges on the present, with the social and cultural institutions moulding themselves under its exigencies. Past appears as an agentive tool in the present. The view of the cognitive system as socially determined has been further iterated by scholars as varied as Levi Strauss (1962), Geertz (1973), etc.

In transplanting the Gandhian text to a mythic past, the author of *Kanthapura* was undergirding the enormous influence exerted by Gandhi on sociopolitical frames. Iqbal Narain and Asha Kaushik have argued "as an incessant dialectic of idea and action, Gandhian philosophy exemplifies praxis" (204). However, in this urging to interpret the influence of the Gandhi myth on the political, cultural and aesthetic practices of the people in terms of "operational category" rather than "conceptual paradigm," the question arises as to whether the past is "an infinite and plastic symbolic source wholly susceptible to contemporary purposes"? (Appadurai

201). Has the Gandhi myth evolved as a mirror open to manipulation of ideologies of all hues reflecting their own specificities, without any form or pattern to it? These questions gain currency and relevance in the face of the multiple iterations of Gandhi, and the free-flowing manner in which the idea of Gandhi has informed the quotidian for millennials and postmillennials growing up seven decades after his assassination.

At a time when one thought that Gandhi was no more than a hollow symbol and a series of empty platitudes, his wide-ranging presence in print and digital cultures in the twenty-first century has proven otherwise. Gandhi's sustained representation, adaptation and consumption within popular culture suggest that Gandhi is now part of our folkloric imagination. If the iconic portrayal of Gandhi in Attenborough's *Gandhi* used a grand narrative, there has been a range of engagements with Gandhi in the realms of visual, sonic and popular culture that have made multifarious forays into the Gandhi narrative, renewing it every time, re-politicizing him in the contemporary context, some even questioning his anointment as the Mahatma discounting the diverse responses that Gandhi's politics invoked in his lifetime and after his death. From filmmakers and playwrights to cartoonists, painters, artists in the digital space, all have responded to the idea of Gandhi. The graphic novel *Gandhi: My Life is My Message* (2013) by Jason Quinn (illustrated by Sachin Nagar) endeavours to de-mystify Gandhi by presenting his humane side. In theatre, a dance drama named "Gandhi – The Musical" written and directed by Danesh Khambata, the many performances of the Hindi play *Godse@ Gandhi.Com* by Asghar Wajahat, a Gujarati play *Yugpurush* depicting Gandhi's relationship with his spiritual mentor Shrimad Rajchandraji, to name a few, have been popular. Cinema scape in the post-millennia decades too has been abuzz with Gandhi straddling the ideological frames of both left and right. This is evidenced by a series of films on Gandhi, delving into the personal, political and ideological dimensions of his life. For instance, Kamal Hassan's *Hey Ram* (2000), Jahnu Barua's *Maine Gandhi Ko Nahi Mara* (2005), Rajkumar Hirani's *Lage Raho Munnabhai* (2006), Feroz Abbas Khan's *Gandhi My Father* (2007), Rakesh Ranjan Kumar's *Gandhi to Hitler* (2011) and A. Balakrishnan's *Welcome Back Gandhi* (2012/2014). Gandhi's image has been both venerated and trivialized, memefied and lampooned and idolized and poked fun at. Gandhi's ubiquity itself has been subjected to both adulation and mockery with artists commenting upon the sociopolitical scenario through their delineation of his figure. Gandhi has been transformed into an aesthetic subject worthy of artistic investment spanning a wide range of media such as painting, sculpture, video installation works and digital productions.

At once fascinating and frustrating, Gandhi defied political thinkers and historians back in his day and continues to do so even in current times. The year 2019 witnessed a large-scale celebration of 150 years of the birth anniversary of Gandhi. The institutional patronizing of Gandhi across the geographical locations and political dispensations is in conjunction with the great adulation Gandhi has inspired among the political leaders the world over. Nelson Mandela, for instance, claimed that Gandhi's tactics offered "the best hope for future race relations" (qtd.

Mishra); Dr Martin Luther King, Jr, and more recently, Barack Obama have held him up as their inspiration. Statues of Gandhi adorn squares, parks and buildings all over the world including the one in Parliament Square, London; Gandhi's birthday, 2 October, has been called the International Day of Nonviolence.

As the long shadow of Gandhi has only grown larger in the present symbol-driven globalized political economy, Gandhi has been the subject of intense scholarly enquiry across the world. Scholars of various hues have engaged with aspects of his incredible life and his vast body of work, interpreting it, critiquing it and even appropriating it. Faisal Devji's seminal reading of Gandhi in his 2012 book *The Impossible Indian: Gandhi and the Temptations of Violence* pitches Gandhi as the most astute political thinker of our times. Through his nuanced arguments and intricate analytical moves, Devji sees *Satyagraha* as Gandhi's gesture to put a limit to the ideologies of liberal modernity founded on the calculus of interest. He argues that Gandhi's privileging of friendship over brotherhood, and his rejection of territorially defined nation state emanated from his faith in the superiority of the spiritual and the moral over the material. This, Devji further argues, shaped Gandhi's understanding of non-violence and *Satyagraha* and his emphatic espousal of self-sacrifice.

There have been several publications in the last decade on Gandhi's biography and theoretical debates on his philosophical and political thought (Tridib Suhrud, *The Diary of Manu's Gandhi, 1943–44*, 2019); books charting his journey as a practising lawyer in South Africa and his numerous trials and experiments to actualise his vision of an egalitarian society in India (Ramchandra Guha's *Gandhi: The Years That Changed the World, 1914–48*, 2018); elaborating the relevance of his ideas across a broad spectrum of disciplines (Judith Brown, Anthony Parel edited *Cambridge Companion to Gandhi*, 2011); showcasing the applicability of his thought to material life (Shruti Kapila and Faisal Devji edited *Political Thought in Action: The Bhagwad Gita and Modern India*, 2013); enacting the networks between his dietary regime, food habits and slavery, indentured labour and capitalism (Nico Slate's *Gandhi's Search for the Perfect Diet: Eating with the World in Mind*, 2019) and reading his ideas within the folds of philosophy (Akeel Bilgrami's essay "Gandhi as Philosopher" from his book *Secularism, Identity, and Enchantment*, 2014 and his edited book *Marx, Gandhi and Modernity: Essays Presented to Javeed Alam*, 2015; Shaj Mohan and Divya Dwivedi edited *Gandhi and Philosophy: On Theological Anti-Politics*; 2018). In short, recent works on Gandhi have sought to read him and theorize his ideas in myriad and even divergent ways.

All along, the enormous admiration and enigma invoked by Gandhi is counterbalanced by his several disavowals the world over. Perry Anderson, in his book *The Indian Ideology* (2012), views Gandhi's "intense religious belief" coming in the way of his "intellectual development" (52). Ashwin Desai and Goolam Vahed, two prominent South African academics of Indian origin, in their book *The South African Gandhi: Stretcher-Bearer of Empire* (2015), cast him as a white supremacist who spewed hatred against native Africans during his time as a lawyer in South Africa between 1893 and 1914. From the vandalization of his statue in 2015 in South Africa, which was Mohandas Gandhi's home from 1893 to 1914, to the online campaign with the hashtag #Ghandimustfall which forced the University of Ghana to dismantle Gandhi's statue from its campus, Gandhi has been as much an object of disdain as veneration. He has been interpreted in terms of environment, climate change, direct action movements, conflict resolution, sanitation, religious tolerance, social justice, consumption-led growth, sustainable development, prohibition, vegetarianism, small-scale industry, economic models and so on in a large number of conferences, seminars and symposia held in the last decade. Based on these paradoxes, Arundhati Roy in her scathing critique of Gandhi, "The Doctor and the Saint," says, "Gandhi has become all things to all people. . . . He is the Saint of the Status-Quo" (2014, n.p.).

Verily, read and cast within diverse discourses, Gandhi has continuously occupied the centre stage of historical and social value systems concerning "the meanings of modernity, the historical and the epistemological" principles of our world (Rudolph and Rudolph 4). Even as the engagement with Gandhi, both as an individual and as an idea, has never waned, the terms of engagement have been mostly constant, namely Gandhian ideas and their efficacy. A shift in the frame of reference from the man to his multimodal representations lands us with a different set of questions, such as how the historical personage and his ideas have been continually reclaimed for affective articulations that are both private and collective? How does the iconicity of Gandhi encompassing people belonging to different castes, classes, locations, artistic mediums, ideologies and actions often conceal fissures and gaps behind the veneer of currency? In what ways does the referential promiscuity of Gandhi promote interests of certain social groups and their politics while marginalizing others? What are the ideological leanings and contexts of the coterie of artists, writers and other creative people involved in producing the iconicity of Gandhi? In a world and a polity beset by self-interest and violence at various levels, what makes Gandhi's message of peace and justice still a part of popular discourse? In their consumption of images of Gandhi highlighting his quest for social cohesion founded on principles of non-violence and self-sacrifice, do people caught in the thralls of aggressive individualism and consumer culture perceive a possibility of transcendence to the sacred collectivity? How, with an astonishingly vast recall value, Gandhi as a brand name par excellence has been deployed in the service of the same capitalist economy that he so forcefully and relentlessly opposed during his lifetime?

Arjun Appadurai, in the context of his study of south Indian temples has argued that past is not necessarily a "bounded resource" available without any limits or regulating principle, but rather "a rule-governed, therefore finite, cultural resource" (218). Appadurai writes that

> The anthropological assumption that the past is a boundless canvas for contemporary embroidery represents the confluence of two historically distinct lines of argument. The first, inspired by Malinowski, simply derives from observation of the rhetorical invocation of the past (as "charter") in

contemporary social organisation, and the tacit conclusion that such charters have no inherent limits, except those of expediency. The second, inspired by Durkheim (1954), carried through by Evans-Pritchard (1940), Hallowell (1937) and Lee (1959) and most recently revived by Geertz (1966), makes a subtler and further-reaching relativist case. In this latter view, concepts of time (and indeed, the perception of duration itself) are fundamental cultural variables. The joint consequence of these two arguments is to render the past a boundless resource in particular cultures, as well as infinitely variable cross-culturally.

(200–1)

Appadurai, on the other hand, argues in favour of "the existence of culturally variable sets of norms whose function is to regulate the inherent debatability of the past" (201). The essays in this volume navigate various cultural and literary texts to unearth the patterns regulating the way the Gandhian past is construed, constructed and in turn impinges on the present. They work upon the assumption that our lives are "a network of lived and narrated stories, practices, strategies, fantasies, negotiations, and exchanges that along with the surviving aural, tactile and visual traces, fashion our experiences of the past, of others, and of ourselves" (Greenblatt 218).

One of the most dedicated scholars and translators of Gandhi, Tridip Suhrud ruefully admits, "[t]he term Gandhian today invokes stylised caricatures" (2005, 1491). Marking a departure from the already available enormous body of scholarship exploring and critiquing Gandhi's philosophy and praxis of satyagraha, non-violent civil disobedience, this volume proposes to unpack the various figurations and configurations of Gandhi, based on multiple articulations and disarticulations, to arrive at an understanding of history, culture and society. Echoing Tridib Suhrud, the volume wishes to probe whether the pervasiveness of the iconic/mythic Gandhi indicates "the failures of Gandhian imagination; if not a failure of the Bapu himself" (2005, 1491) or should it be evinced in a more positive light as an emblem of the profound influence of the Mahatma? The chapters approach these questions from diverse theoretical paradigms and critical standpoints. Together, they underscore the ambivalences that have surrounded Gandhi since the time of his emergence on the horizon of world polity. A muse to many artists, a prime influencer for many activists, an icon to many political leaders, the more Gandhi is invoked, the more elusive he becomes. No matter how adulatory or scathingly critical these invocations are, they lay bare fractures and fragmentations of contemporary thought as much as the chasm between the individual and the idea.

The section titled "Inhabiting Gandhi in Sonic and Visual Practices: Enunciations of 'Darsan' and Activism" engages with the medium of print, music and painting to fathom their use of Gandhi as an idiom. The first chapter in the section "Gandhi's Image and Images of Gandhi: The Culture and Politics of Visual Representations" by Vinay Lal explores how the vast visual representational apparatus contributed to the promotion of nationalist sentiments by transplanting Gandhi to the mythic imagination. Lal focuses on the nationalist prints of Gandhi produced primarily in Kanpur and, more particularly, in the workshop of Shyam Sundar Lal. Through this, Lal raises some seminal questions that the contemporary scholarship on Gandhi must grapple with, namely, how in Gandhi's espousal of non-violence, violence was continually embedded as a force to be confronted; how the gestures of *Asahyoga* or non-cooperation towards the British contained within them a deferred promise of cooperation among different communities in India; how, in a nation where literacy levels remained pitiably low, Gandhi attained an enormous popularity. Lal argues that it's the printmakers rather than the vast body of literary writers or painters, who contributed to firming up the iconicity of Gandhi, which in Asian history, as Lal aptly points out, only the Buddha can match. Besides, as they evinced a considerable familiarity with Gandhi's life, the prints circulated by the printmakers are much more than portraits; they undergird the multiple layers of interpretive possibilities such as the dialectical relationship between the Gandhian non-violence and the violence espoused by the Garam Dal leaders like Bhagat Singh who enjoyed huge popularity among the masses. Lal further argues that the extraordinary demonstration of playfulness and ease with which printmakers transformed the Indian mythic material into the nationalist narrative deserves a close scholarly enquiry.

Lakshmi Subramanian's chapter traverses the largely uncharted terrain of music, prayers and chants as the site of the nationalist struggle. Subramanian reads Ashram Bhajanavali "a collection of 253 devotional verses that formed part of the Ashram's quotidian prayer in Sabarmati" drawn from several languages and multiple religious traditions as one of the major archival sources to examine how music, the space of the Ashram and prayers coalesced to facilitate the idea of *swaraj* and political regeneration of nation. If the idea behind the institution of Ashram formed by Gandhi was to create a community that "affirmed itself by its quest for an ethical society where each individual had the possibility of knowing the *svadharma*" (Suhrud 1491), music played a key role in forging this community. Like spinning, Subramanian argues, singing was also a "habitual exercise to be learned and perfected" and Gandhi's choice of hymns represented his lifelong refusal to frame the devotional and sacral in narrow religious terms.

Ruchika Wason Singh's chapter complements Vinay Lal's chapter as it examines Gandhi's mass political appeal generated through the representational practices in High Art. Through a close reading of the paintings of artists like Nandalal Bose, Ramendranath Chakroborty, Dhiren Gandhi, MF Husain, Atul Dodiya and SH Raza, Singh examines how artistic perception of Gandhi and his relationship with his mass followers has evolved through the nationalist, post-independence and post-liberalization phase. If to artists like Nandalal Bose, Gandhi inspired ideas of friendship, cooperation and collectivity among his followers, the contemporary artists in post-liberalization India can imagine his loneliness at the sight of a changing world. These artists in their nuanced and complex portrayals of Gandhi transmuted Gandhian ethos and philosophical ideas and contributed to the visual iconicity of Gandhi as a global mass leader. Singh further argues that a close reading of the paintings exposes artists' perception of Gandhi as a force to negotiate and navigate internally fractured spaces of the nation and the colonial encounters.

The following section titled "Consumption of Gandhi: Articulation or Disarticulation?" deals with the multiple crisscrossing of popular cultural productions, circulation and assimilations centred on Gandhi. Haris Qadeer's chapter "Mahatma in Memescape: Making of Gandhi in Participatory Digital Culture" responds to the multiple symbolic imageries invoked by the netizens within the meme-space's participatory digital culture. In doing so, it underlines how Gandhi is continuously constituted, refracted and remade for readers rather than being out there for us to discover. Dwelling on two critical facets of Gandhian philosophy, fasting and non-violence, Qadeer's chapter contends that the many "Gandhis," constituted and reconstituted in the digital medium, serve as a source of contested meanings that both sustain and, in the process, unravel the mythification of Gandhi for contemporary readers.

The subsequent two chapters by Barnali Saha and Aparna Pathak turn to the popular mediums of cartoons and comic books to argue that in representing contrarian positions within the same medium, the artists suggest a cultural horizontalization that marks the making of an icon. Barnali Saha explores the political scenario of 1946–1947 through the representations drawn in editorial cartoons on Gandhi published by the Nationalist (I.N.C. perspective) Press, the Muslim and the British Press. Saha's chapter reads cartoons as core cultural narratives to establish a dissonance in Gandhi's articulations and disarticulations in cartoons with divergent ideological perspectives. Aparna Pathak in her essay "Intersections of the Popular and the National: A Study of Biographical Comic Books on Gandhi" focuses on comic books to explore how Gandhi's persona and ideologies get represented in a comic book medium. She undertakes an analysis of two comic books: *The Gandhi Story* by SD Sawant and SD Badalkar (1966) and the twin-book series of Amar Chitra Katha, *Mahatma Gandhi I: The Early Days* and *Mahatma Gandhi II: Father of the Nation* published in 1989 (reprinted in 2008). Pathak's essay unravels the strategies that enable comic books to straddle the contradictory domains of history and myth to constitute a nation.

The next two chapters on cinema delineate the Indian cinema's ceaseless fascination with Gandhi. M.H. Ilias, in his chapter "Gandhi, the New Divine: Gandhi Ethos in the Malayalam Socials of 1950 and 1960s," deploys Ashis Nandy's idea of four afterlives of Gandhi that reverberates in literature, culture and public affairs. The paper emphasizes one type of "afterlife" of Gandhi which is of a mythic figure evocative of idealistic values that resist oppression and various injustices that beset society. Focusing upon "social films" drawn from Malayalam cinema of the 1950s and 1960s, Ilias' essay argues that the "invisible" Gandhi used as a floating signifier in these films allowed the entry of the marginalized into mainstream culture and facilitated the transformation of the existing societal codes.

Interrogating visual culture's capacity to comprehend Gandhi and his paradoxical legacy, Nishat Haider's chapter "Framing Gandhi" charts the evolving revisions and alterations of Gandhi "within the ongoing debates on presentist regime of historicity, memory as well as the politics of mnemonic practices." As the spectre of Gandhi continues to haunt the Hindi cinema, Haider situates contemporary Hindi cinema's engagement with Gandhi and his alternative politics of ethics in the gap between politics and ethics. Haider argues that by involving spectators as active interpreters, the films develop a cinematic language that wrenches "ruptures and silences" from the "unconscious realm," thereby combining aesthetics and entertainment with morality and ethics.

Alluding to Akbar Illahabadi's popular couplet about the transformative influence of Gandhi on the ordinary oppressed people of his country, "*Buddhu Mian bhi Hazrat-e-Gandhi ke saath hain/Go Musht-e-khak hain magar Aandhi ke saath hain*" [Buddhu Mian, a proverbial commoner, is with Gandhi; though a mere speck of ash, he is with a storm which lends him strength to rise], historian Irfan Habib explains:

> What was earlier the role of Buddhu Miyan or the Ordinary Man in Indian history? Nothing! He was nowhere. He is now brought into history. And as more and more ordinary peasants, ordinary women, joined the national movement, India became more and more of a nation. Because there is no nation unless the larger number or mass of the people feel that they should be independent and they should rule themselves.
>
> *(2015)*

Most descriptions of Gandhi's tours across the length and breadth of the country are replete with reports of the groundswell of peasants at railway stations forcefully stopping the train carrying Gandhi in their quest for darshan. Gandhi's travels across the country became the "tour of mass conversions to the new creed" (Tendulkar 78) with the circulation of a large number of anecdotes about ominous events visiting those who uttered bad words for Gandhi and newspapers like *Swadesh* printing reports testifying the miraculous power of the Mahatma (Amin 291). However, this "Boundless love" (Mahadev Desai; qtd. Amin 290) of the masses was transformed through the political intervention of the educated elites, as Shahid Amin argues:

> It is worth stressing here that the Gandhi darshan motif in nationalist discourse reveals a specific attitude towards the subalterns – the sadharan janta or ordinary people as they are referred to in the nationalist Hindi press. To behold the Mahatma in person and become his devotees were the only roles assigned to them, while it was for the urban intelligentsia and fulltime party activists to convert this groundswell of popular feeling into an organized movement.
>
> *(291)*

The section "The Construction of Self: Experimental Site of Praxis and Its Discursive Limits" comprises chapters that explore how the self is made and unmade under the spectre of the Gandhian symbol. Simultaneously, they discuss the interface of Gandhian politics and Marxism, subaltern activism and conceptual understanding of secularism to explore the limits of democratic institutions. In their own ways, the chapters assert the need to revisit the Gandhian schema through genres like testimonials, autobiographies and realist texts for one of the salient features of the sign of an icon is that it allows the universal to conflate with the personal.

Dhritiman Chakraborty focuses on unfolding the "postcolonial political" premised on a comparative reading of the non-sovereign, non-autonomous understanding of the self as elucidated by Michel Foucault and Gandhi. A close reading of Mulk Raj Anand's novel, *Untouchable* (1935), is used to enunciate and explain this argument. Bhaswati Chatterjee's chapter testifies how the mass-mobilization programmes initiated by Gandhi changed the dynamics of public space and simultaneously brought about a transformation in the private domain's precincts. Bhaswati's chapter reads three autobiographies of twentieth-century Bengali women and a monograph on the Noakhali incident – Renuka Ray's *My Reminiscences: Social Development During the Gandhian Era and After (2005)*; Ashoka Gupta's *In the Path of Service: Memories of a Changing Century (2005)*, Phulrenu Guha's *Elomelo Mone Elo* (Haphazard Recollections) (1997) and the monograph *Noakhalir Durjoger Dine* (Turbulent Days of Noakhali) (1999) to unpack the discursive space that dismantles the boundaries between private and public space/identities, individual versus the world and fictional versus historical. Aishwarya Kumar in "Examining Gandhi's Disavowals and Rethinking His 'Experiment' in *The Story of My Experiments with Truth*" reads Gandhi's autobiography in terms of "disavowals" as a literary strategy to pose a self that is not idealized as a Mahatma. Instead, it is vulnerable to changes and modifications in accordance with historical factors.

P. Rajitha Venugopal's chapter "Gandhian Environmentalism and Its Limits: A Reading of C. K. Janu's 'Autobiographical Testimonio' *Mother Forest*" undertakes a textual analysis of CK Janu's political struggle and the autobiographical narrative *Mother Forest: The Unfinished Story of C.K. Janu* (2004), combined with Janu's "unfinished" efforts to reclaim her land and ecosystem for her community. In examining Gandhian environmentalism refracted through a subaltern critical lens, Rajitha's essay presents a crisscrossing of resistance methods situated in Kerala's contemporary context vis-à-vis the famous Gandhian modes of resistance namely fasting and non-violence.

The four essays in the section "Gandhian Presence in Intimate and Public Spheres: Reflections on Corporeality, Ethicality and Society" analyse literary texts to examine various iterations of Gandhi. Indrani Das Gupta's chapter, through its analysis of Shrilal Shukla's Hindi novel, *Raag Darbari* (1968; translated into English by Gillian Wright, 1992) dwells on the somatic politics of Gandhi's views of *brahmacharya* and dietary regimes, to track its downfall in the politico-ethical values of Nehruvian postcolonial nation-state. Body, which was the site of embodied ideal in the Gandhian ethics–politics and which served as a key signifier in the anti-colonial struggle, is divested of its sacrality in the postcolonial nation-state. This renders hollow the Gandhian idiom of body. In their essay, Baran Farooqi and Disha Pokhriyal undertake a close reading of Saadat Hasan Manto's short story "Swaraj Ke Liye" (For Freedom's Sake), published in 1950. Through this, they attempt to counter Gandhi's observations on celibacy and abstinence in marital relationships as a means to espouse political commitments. Bharti Arora's chapter "Gandhi and Peasant Organizations in Colonial India: A Reading of Satinath Bhaduri's *Dhorai Charit Manas*" examines *Dhorai Charit Manas* (1949–65/2013). The chapter endeavours to illuminate Gandhi's role and influence in peasant insurrection in colonial India, while simultaneously highlighting the fault lines in Congress's ideology concerning peasant organizations. Gandhi's support for the cause of peasants' rebellion against the British rule is well etched in popular imaginary. However, Bhaduri's text exposes the limits of Gandhian politics by highlighting Gandhi's appeasing tone towards zamindars, a narrative also supported by the Congress to maintain the balance of power between peasants and zamindars. The chapter further argues that Bhaduri's text refutes the form and rubric of the nation-state as being limited and confronts the debilitating nature of the epistemology of freedom.

In a poem that W. H. Auden wrote upon hearing the death of Sigmund Freud, titled "In Memory of Sigmund Freud" (1939), Auden described the near-mythical influence of Freud, thus, "to us he is no more a person /now but a whole climate of opinion // under whom we conduct our different lives" (1991, 275). The manner in which Gandhi's charismatic figure has assumed new hues, figurations and positionalities over the years (Rudolph and Rudolph 4), Gandhi too has become a "whole climate of opinions." But more importantly, Gandhi has emerged as a frame story, describing and explaining multiple stories and diverse narratives which require deep and intense investigation as narratives encapsulate worldling by structuring the meanings that sustain culture (Cohan and Shires 1; Sinfield 23).

This volume contains several stories in which the "representations" of Gandhi serve to throw light on contemporary culture and society. "Representation" has been theorized as a mechanism to connect meaning and culture, involving language, signs and images, a process that engages with description, elucidation of the stated object as well as participates in constructing the object through varied use of language and other assorted signs (Stuart Hall 15–16; Hannah F. Pitkin 5). Adapting from Linda Åhäll, this anthology reads Gandhi as "a cultural grammar, a value that informs stories" (136). It grounds itself as a representational frame to understand Gandhi both as a text that informs other narratives or representations, and as a micronarrative undermining grand narratives. Douglas Allen argues that "[t]here is not one static, essential, universal, ahistorical, noncontextualized, absolutely true view of Gandhi's philosophy and its relevance for the twenty-first century" (viii). In consonance with this spirit, essays in the volume study the multifarious re-imaginings, reformulations and refashioning of Gandhi and his ideas in literary and cultural texts, not merely as metaphors but as "complex, active, embodied . . . figures inhabiting distinctly everyday features" (Hall 11).

Additionally, as this volume reveals, the numerous afterlives of Gandhi highlight the use of Gandhi as the icon that can sustain our ideological pretence and hegemonic narratives. The representations of Gandhi in print, electronic and digital media, and in newer disciplines and cross-disciplinary genres invoke strong emotional responses. In consequence, they are further subjected to multiple remediations across the media genres, some like memes manipulating the original images and investing them with new connotations. Gandhi, who dared to criticize the mechanics of Western civilization as early as in 1909 (*Hind Swaraj*) when its influence was universally being put in place, continues to dominate the popular imagination at the end of the century and beyond when in the wake of globalization, those same mechanics are firmly ensconced in the global theatre of politics and culture. But it is in this surge of affective density that one may trace the iconicity of Gandhi, for "iconic consciousness" does not depend so much on cognitive understanding as it does on understating "by contact, by the 'evidence of senses' rather than the mind" (Alexander 782). Even as the actions of writers, artists and designers, consumers have played a significant role in elevating Gandhi to a mythic status, the inherent appeal and enigma of Gandhi transcends the materiality of the icon. His unfulfilled task of making a free nation and a free man and his non-violent resistance as an illustration of agency and potency cast in ethical practice continues to haunt both his detractors and his admirers. The iconicity of Gandhi is centred on the need to address the absences and silences in our post-industrial society exemplified by today's political and social dissonances.

It is not that the literary and cultural engagements with Gandhi and his vision have not been studied before. As a case in point, one may mention works like Snehal Shingavi's reading of the 1930s novel about Gandhi and the nationalist agitation as marked by a deep ambivalence in his *The Mahatma Misunderstood: The Politics and Forms of Literary Nationalism* (2014), Sumathy Ramaswami's erudite study of works by modern artists from India who turned to Gandhi as their muse, in her book, *Gandhi in the Gallery: The Art of Disobedience* (2020), Lakshmi Subramanian's study of Gandhi and sonic nationalism in her book *Singing Gandhi's India: Music and Sonic Nationalism* (2020), or Lisa N Trivedi's *Clothing Gandhi's Nation: Homespun and Modern India* (2007) and Peter Gonsalves' *Khadi: Gandhi's Mega Symbol of Subversion* (2012). These and other similar works have studied how Gandhi has remained at the helm of political iconography in India and how various signifying practices of the culture industry have turned to him for the articulation of views of varied hues. But most of these readings have been genre-specific, giving us a little sense of how these representations have negotiated with each other to collectively produce the icon. One such cross-genre study was undertaken by the art magazine *Marg* when it brought out a special issue in December 2019, *Gandhi and Aesthetics* by Tridip Suhrud. But the focus was once again Gandhi's own conceptual understanding of art and not the other way round.

Drawing from the title of Gandhi's autobiography, this book can be viewed as an exploration of multiple experiments with and about Gandhi. Furthermore, the book examines the inconsistencies in Gandhian politics and philosophy in its interface with environmentalism, lived experiences and the construction of "self." The book engages with how these are refracted through their literary and artistic disarticulations. It focuses on the modality of consumption that continually keeps on churning a Gandhi for the contemporary readers attuned to new technologies and the various media productions. Given that the new media technologies read, subvert, resist and adapt Gandhi in their engagement with their immediate milieu, the book attempts to initiate conversations across the multiple disciplines. The sign of Gandhi, located at the cusp of the sublime and the mundane, emerges in these conversations as a politico-ethical arbiter deliberating on social and historical issues. The book seeks to interpret competing processes and transactions embedded in the "management of meaning" (Cohen and Comaroff). It hints at the post-Gandhi society trying to encapsulate its role in the quotidian practices of a global world order, which is seeking a cure for a literal virus as well as viruses of factionalism, communalism, racism and the looming economic crisis, by channelizing the Gandhian past. Gandhi, both in his life and after his death, in his thoughts and the resistance they invited, remains the touchstone to interpret the *longue duree* of subcontinent's history and its culture and society across the spectrum of space, time, gender, class and caste permutations. In investigating creative responses to Gandhian philosophy of swaraj, satyagraha and non-violence as literal and figurative truths that expose the fractured and fragmented consciousness of our violent and uneasy times, this volume aims to afford new possibilities to engage with the contemporaneity of the Gandhian past.

Note on Translation and Transliteration

The chapters in the volume draw upon a wide range of literary and cultural texts in different Indian languages. As a result, no uniform pattern of transliteration has been used. Mostly, basic English phonetic approximation is used to make the texts easily accessible to the twenty-first-century international readers. While some of the material used by the authors is available in English translations/subtitles and the authors have used them, they have also had to contend with the task of translating some of it for their readers. In such cases, fidelity to the SL text has been the prime consideration.

Note

1 " انقلاب آیأ ، نئ دنیا نیأ بنگامہ ہے
شأبنامہ ہو چکأ اب دورے گأندھی نامہ ہے " (see *Gandhinama* by Akbar Illahabadi with Introduction by Mohd Naimur Rahman, Allahabad: Kitabistan. 1948. P 2).

Works Cited

Åhäll, Linda. *Sexing War/Policing Gender. Motherhood, Myth, and Women's Political Violence.* Routledge, 2015.

Alexander, J. C. "Iconic Consciousness: The Material Feeling of Meaning." *Environment and Planning D: Society and Space*, vol. 26, 2008, pp. 782-94.

Allen, Douglas. "Introduction: Key Issues and Overview of Gandhi's Philosophy for the Twenty-First Century." *The Philosophy of Mahatma Gandhi in the Twenty-First Century*, edited by Douglas Allen, Lexington Books, 2008, pp. vii–xviii.

Amin, Shahid. "Gandhi as Mahatma: Gorakhpur District, Eastern UP, 1921–2." *Selected Subaltern Studies*, edited by Ranajit Guha and Gayatri Chakravorty Spivak, Oxford UP, 1988, pp. 288–351.

Anderson, Perry. *The Indian Ideology. 2012*. Verso, 2013.

Appadurai, Arjun. "The Past as a Scarce Resource." *Royal Anthropological Institute of Great Britain and Ireland*, vol. 16, no. 2, 1981, pp. 201–19. *JSTOR*, www.jstor.org/stable/2801395.

Attenborough, Richard, director. *Gandhi*. Goldcrest Films, 1982.

Auden, W. H. "In Memory of Sigmund Freud." *Collected Poems*, edited by Edward Mendelson, Vintage, 1991, pp. 273–76.

Balakrishnan, A., director. *Welcome Back Gandhi*. Ramana Communications, 2012.

Bilgrami, Akeel, editor. *Marx, Gandhi and Modernity: Essays Presented to Javeed Alam*. Tulika Books, 2015.

———. *Secularism, Identity, and Enchantment*. Harvard UP, 2014.

Boas, F. *Kwakiutl Tales*. Columbia University Contributions to Anthropology, 1910.

Brown, Judith, and Anthony Parel, editors. *The Cambridge Companion to Gandhi*. Cambridge UP, 2011.

Chauhan, Dipshikha. "Influence of Gandhi on Bhojpuri Folk Songs." *Journal of Arts, Culture, Philosophy, Religion, Language and Literature*, vol. 3, no. 2, May–Aug. 2019, pp. 167–70.

Cohan, Steven, and Linda M. Shires. *Telling Stories: A Theoretical Analysis of Narrative Fiction*. Routledge, 1988.

Cohen, A. P., and J. L. Comaroff. "The Management of Meaning: On the Phenomenology of Political Transactions." *Transaction and Meaning: Directions in the Anthropology of Exchange and Behavior*, edited by B. Kapferer, Institute for the Study of Human Issues, 1976, pp. 87–107.

Desai, Ashwin, and Goolem Vahed. *The South African Gandhi: Stretcher-Bearer of Empire*. Stanford UP, 2015.

Devji, Faisal. *The Impossible Indian: Gandhi and the Temptations of Violence*. Harvard UP, 2012.

Freud, S. "The Interpretation of Dreams." *The Standard Edition of the Complete Psychological Works of Sigmund Freud*, edited by J. Strachey, Hogarth, 1900/1953, Vols. 4–5.

Gada, Uttam. *Yugpurush: Mahatma Na Mahatma*. Directed by Rajesh Joshi. *YouTube*, Uploaded by Shrimad Rajchandra Mission Dharampur, 6 Dec. 2016, https://youtu.be/tC_cxVmJeWM.

Gautam, Vinayshil. "Some Aspects of Folklore as an Agent of Nationalism in Bhojpuri Speaking Area: 1917–1942 – A Case Study." *Essays in Indian Folklore*, edited by L. P. Vidyarthi, Indian Publications, 1973, pp. 180–90.

Geertz, Clifford. *The Interpretation of Cultures: Selected Essays*. Basic Books, 1973.

Gonsalves, Peter. *Khadi: Gandhi's Mega Symbol of Subversion*. Sage Publications, 2012.

Greenblatt, Stephen. "Psychoanalysis and Renaissance Culture." *Literary Theory/Renaissance Texts*, edited by Patricia Parker and David Quint, John Hopkins UP, 1986, pp. 210–24.

Guha, Ramchandra. *Gandhi: The Years That Changed the World, 1914–1948*. Penguin Books, 2018.

Haasan, Kamal, director. *Hey Ram*. Raaj Kamal Films International, 2000.

Habib, Irfan. *Building the Idea of India*. Lecture at Aligarh Muslim University, 7 Sept. 2015, http://jaiss.org.in/Publications/Building%20the%20Idea%20of%20India_Prof.%20Irfan%20Habib.pdf. Accessed 24 Nov. 2020.

Hall, Stuart. "The Work of Representation." *Representation: Cultural Representations and Signifying Practices*, edited by Stuart Hall, Sage Publications, 1997, pp. 13–74.

Hirani, Rajkumar, director. *Lage Raho Munna Bhai*. Vidhu Vinod Chopra Productions, 2006.

Jahnu, Barua. *Maine Gandhi Ko Nahi Mara*. Anupam Kher, 2005.

Kapila, Shruthi, and Faisal Devji, editors. *Political Thought in Action: The Bhagavad Gita and Modern India*. Cambridge UP, 2013.

Khambhata, Danesh R. "Gandhi – A Musical." *YouTube*, Uploaded by NCPA Mumbai, 3 May 2017, https://youtu.be/grw-mm_IYdw.

Khan, Feroz Abbas, director. *Gandhi, My Father*. Anil Kapoor, 2007.

Kumar, Rakesh Ranjan, director. *Gandhi to Hitler*. Amrapali Media, 2011.

Kushwaha, Subhash Chandr, *Lokrang*. Vol. I. Agora Prakashan, 2009.

Lévi-Strauss, C. *The Savage Mind*. *1962*. Translated by George Weidenfield and Nicholson Ltd. Garden City Press, 1966.

Malinowski, Bronislaw. "The Role of Myth in Life." *Magic, Science, Religion and Other Essays*. *1948*. Doubleday Anchor Books, 1954.

Mishra, Pankaj. "Gandhi for the Post-Truth Age." *The New Yorker*, 22 Oct. 2018, pp. 1+.

Mohan, Shaj, and Divya Dwivedi. *Gandhi and Philosophy: On Theological Anti-Politics*. Bloomsbury Publishing, 2018.

Narain, Iqbal, and Asha Kaushik. "Charisma, Ideology, and Politics: Gandhi in Indo-Anglian Novels." *Indian Journal of Political Science*, vol. 49, no. 2/4–6, 1988, pp. 204–20. *JSTOR*, www.jstor.org/stable/41855367.

Paranjape, Makarand. *The Death and Afterlife of Mahatma Gandhi*. Penguin Random House, 2018.

Pitkin, Hanna Fenichel. *The Concept of Representation*. U of California P, 1967.

Quinn, Jason. *Gandhi: My Life Is My Message*. Illustrated by Sachin Nagar. Penguin Random House, 2013.

Ramaswamy, Sumathi. *Gandhi in the Gallery: The Art of Disobedience*. Roli Books, 2021.

Rao Raja. *Kanthapura*. *1938*. Orient Paperbacks, 2008.

Roy, Arundhati. "The Doctor and the Saint." Introduction. *Annihilation of Caste*, by BR Ambedkar, edited and annotated by S Anand, Verso, 2014. *Z-Library*, https://covers.zlibcdn2.com/covers/books/72/78/0d/72780dea49826bfac3f78dce51f6c66b.jpg. Accessed 8 Aug. 2021.

Rudolph, Llyod I., and Susanne Hoeber Rudolph. Preface. *Postmodern Gandhi and Other Essays: Gandhi in the World and at Home*. Edited by Llyod I. Rudolph and Susanne Hoeber Rudolph, U of Chicago P, 1967, pp. vii–x.

Shingavi, Snehal. *The Mahatma Misunderstood: The Politics and Forms of Literary Nationalism in India*. Anthem Press, 2013.

Sinfield, Alan. *Literature, Politics, and Culture in Postwar Britain*. U of California P, 1989.

Slate, Nico. *Gandhi's Search for the Perfect Diet: Eating With the World in Mind*. Orient BlackSwan, 2019.

Subramanian, Lakshmi. *Singing Gandhi's India: Music and Sonic Nationalism*. Lotus Collection/Roli Books, 2020.

Suhrud, Tridib. "Dandi March and Gandhi's Politics." *Economic and Political Weekly*, vol. 40, no. 15, 9–15 Apr. 2005, pp. 1491–92. *JSTOR*, www.jstor.org/stable/4416456.

———. *The Diary of Manu's Gandhi, 1943–44*. Oxford UP, 2019.

Tendulkar, D. G. *Mahatma: Life of Mohandas Karamchand Gandhi*. Vol. ii, (1952). Publications Division, M/O Information & Broadcasting, Govt. of India, 2016.

Trivedi, Lisa N. *Clothing Gandhi's Nation: Homespun and Modern India*. Indiana UP, 2007.

Wajahat, Asghar. *Godse@ Gandhi.Com*. Bhartiya Jnanpith, 2014.

PART I

Gandhi in Sonic and Visual Practices

Enunciations of "Darsan"
and Activism

1

GANDHI'S IMAGE AND IMAGES OF GANDHI

The Culture and Politics of Visual Representation[1]

Vinay Lal

There is but no question that Mohandas Karamchand Gandhi was the pre-eminent public face of India to the rest of the world for more than three decades, shortly after his return to India from South Africa in January 1915. This is all the more remarkable in view of the fact that at this time he was far from being a household name in his native country, just as India in the second decade of the 1900s was not bereft of political leaders of immense stature, among them Annie Beasant, Bal Gangadhar Tilak, Chittaranjan Das, Bipin Chandra Pal, Lala Lajpat Rai and Mahadev Govind Ranade. Indeed, their names would continue to reverberate for many years thereafter: as a school-going boy in the 1960s and 1970s, I remember vividly having to memorize the contributions of the triumvirate known simply as "Lal Bal Pal." Yet, it is indisputably true that Gandhi eclipsed everyone else, and around the world, India came to be practically synonymous with his name. In India itself, as the eminent literary critic Harish Trivedi noted in a brief account of the voluminous representations of Gandhi in fiction, poetry and cinema, he held a place in the literary canon that staggers the imagination. The poet Harivansh Rai Bachchan, Trivedi wryly comments, "was no Gandhian," and yet felt inspired to pen 204 poems in a tribute to the Mahatma. There is also the example of another Hindi poet, Bhavaniprasad Mishra, who wrote 13 poems in 13 days following the assassination of Gandhi, and on his birth centenary in 1969, he published a collection of 500 poems on Gandhi. "It may be doubted," Trivedi unsurprisingly avers, "whether any historical and fully documented human being of our age or any other was ever acclaimed in such superhuman and indeed divine terms, especially in his own lifetime, and indeed from a relatively early stage of his life" (201).

Hindi was far from being the only language, or even necessarily the principal one, in which the epic life of Gandhi was being framed even as the Mahatma was,

DOI: 10.4324/9781003145479-3

so to speak, constantly rewriting the script. In the mid-1990s, the compilers of the Sahitya Akademi's *Encyclopedia of Indian Literature* required some 20-odd pages just to enumerate some of the literary portrayals of Gandhi in 15 Indian languages. In literature, as in politics, the stamp of "the Gandhi era" was ineradicable, even if, though this is far outside the scope of the present chapter, not all his contemporaries in the middle class were enamoured of him—not even in Ahmedabad, a city where he earned his stripes and where until the Dandi March in 1930 he made his "home" (to the extent that he had one) but to which he paid his last visit in November 1936 (Suhrud 6 December 2019). The critical question before us is a rather different one: if literary representations of him were prolific, does that sufficiently convey how his name and teachings circulated in India and to what effect? In 1931, to follow the decennial census from that year, the literacy rate for British India as a whole was 9.5 percent and a mere 2.9 percent among women. The literacy rates for Burma and Ceylon, which were considerably higher—36.8 and 33.7 percent, respectively—disguise the extent of illiteracy in the heartland, which is better approximated by the 10.8 percent literacy rate in the Bombay Presidency and the corresponding rate of 5.5 percent in the United Provinces (Hutton). Even allowing for the fact that some people may have heard poems of Gandhi being recited, most Indians would not have accessed literary representations of Gandhi. So just how did ideas of "the Mahatma" circulate and become part of the public sphere?

The burden of the recent scholarship on Gandhi, which shows little signs of diminishing even as it has taken new turns in recent years, has been to critique, complicate and, indeed, defang the hagiographic readings of the Mahatma and to suggest that there were multiple Gandhis. One of the intellectually more engaging attempts to move away from the received view is encountered in the historian Shahid Amin's complex reading, to put it simply, of Gandhi from below (1984). Drawing upon local newspapers, pamphlets and other forms of what we may call little literatures, he argued that common people did not always subscribe to the authorized image of Gandhi; sometimes they even committed violence in his name. Amin takes the occasion of Gandhi's visit to Gorakhpur in 1921, where he addressed a "monster meeting" to probe just what villagers and dwellers of small towns thought of the Mahatma, and how his charisma "registered in peasant consciousness": he appears not merely as a leader of his people, a divine soul, but as a miracle-monger, sorcerer, wielder of divine chastisement, vocal (and sometimes unwelcome) advocate of temperance, stern task-master and much else (Amin 18).

Large as is the archive that Amin drew upon, there are still larger bodies of material shaped around Gandhi which are only now, albeit rather slowly, receiving some scrutiny. Gandhi appeared in thousands of prints, oil paintings, watercolours, sculptures, cartoons and advertisements: this extraordinarily rich and varied archive suggests that the representational apparatus played a significant role in generating a public persona of Gandhi and transforming him into the Mahatma, a world-historical figure, the "messiah of ahimsa" and much else. If the oil painting stands at the higher end of the visual representational apparatus, cartoons and nationalist prints most likely brought Gandhi into humbler Indian homes and the public sphere. I shall turn my attention here to a small set of nationalist prints produced in black and white. Christopher Pinney has, on several occasions, characterized, though on what grounds is far from being clear, S. S. Brijbasi & Sons, based in Karachi, as the most important printmaker in pre-independence India. Printmakers were active in many of the larger cities, among them Karachi, Lahore, Delhi, Allahabad, Bombay and Calcutta. But the most important centre of nationalist printmaking may yet have been Kanpur (colonial-era Cawnpore), however surprising this may appear to someone whose impression of Kanpur is that of a city that is indescribably filthy and which for decades appears to have had none of the attractions of a metropolis while retaining all of its drawbacks. It is all too easily forgotten that Kanpur was once dubbed "the Manchester of the East": Bombay's textile mills are the stuff of common lore, but Kanpur's Elgin Mills, set up in 1862, antecede Bombay's Swadeshi Mills by 25 years. Chitra Joshi, one of the few historians to have trained her gaze on Kanpur, says of the city that it "became an important centre of the textile and leather industry in north India in the nineteenth century" ("On De-Industrialization" 160).

Kanpur was, of course, one of the principal sites of the Rebellion of 1857–1858: it is here that the rebel leader, Nana Saheb, was alleged to have committed atrocities against the British, thus calling forth the full force of British vengeance and cruelty. The revolt had a transformative effect on Kanpur, which the British, having turned it into one of their strongholds in north India, retained as a colonial outpost from where they outsourced police and army personnel for the rest of the country. Indeed, it is largely owing to the heavy police and military personnel that a demand arose for woollens, canvas clothes and shoes. A new textile production unit called Muir Mills would come up in 1882. The First and Second World Wars, according to Joshi, "were major phases of expansion" of the city, "with the Kanpur factories taking bulk orders for the British armies." Throughout the first half of the twentieth century, a large part of which coincides with "the Gandhi era," Kanpur remained a hub of small-scale manufacturing as well, and "a host of small cottage units producing nuts, bolts, bearings, leather goods, furniture, and packing cases supplied materials to the large factories." Other ancillary businesses catering to the needs of workers—tea stalls, tobacco and betel nut shops, stores for provisions—came into being, and on any day, hundreds of workers could be seen milling around: "Business was brisk" (ibid.).

However, there is something possibly yet more germane in understanding the place of Kanpur in the history of nationalist printmaking. The city's residents warmly embraced the non-cooperation movement that had been launched by Gandhi. The 40th annual session of the Congress in 1925 convened in Kanpur under the leadership of Sarojini Naidu; moreover, over the course of the decade, most of the principal stalwarts of the nationalist movement, among them Lala

Lajpat Rai and Madan Mohan Malaviya, visited the city to drum up support for the Congress. In 1913, the promising young journalist, Ganesh Shankar Vidyarthi, founded the journal *Pratap*, which would become a vehicle for nationalist opinion as much as a voice for the working class. The *Pratap* under Vidyarthi was vocal in its advocacy of the rights of the working class. Vidyarthi was, it might be said, a little unusual in his ecumenical political views in that he was supportive of Gandhi and the Congress as much as he was of those who stood for armed militancy. By the early 1920s, Vidyarthi had assumed a place in the local leadership of the Congress; and in 1929, he was elected President of the Uttar Pradesh Congress Committee. Vidyarthi was imprisoned in 1930 when thousands of Congressmen were taken into custody in consequence of the Salt Satyagraha and only released after the Gandhi-Irwin Pact in early March 1931. He died just days later, stabbed to death as he made a heroic attempt to stem communal rioting in Kanpur. Vidyarthi's death would occasion a flowering tribute from Gandhi in his weekly *Young India*: "His blood is the cement that will ultimately bind the two communities. No pact will bind our hearts. But heroism such as Ganesh Shankar Vidyarthi showed is bound in the end to melt the stoniest hearts, melt them into one."

The city also had a large Muslim population and many of its Muslims stood behind Gandhi's Khilafat campaign, even if some had become alienated from the Congress movement. That some bad blood had developed recently between the two "communities" is hinted by the aforementioned riot of 1931. What is more germane is that Kanpur's singularity lay still perhaps in something else, as a city which was hospitable to both the mainstream nationalist movement and the armed revolutionaries whose exploits made them household names in much of north India. It is in Kanpur that the Communist Party of India had its inaugural meeting in December 1925. On the British view, its industrial character gave birth to "a large number of persons of very desperate character—a factor not to be found in any other city of UP"; communist activists, on the other hand, saw in Kanpur a fertile field for trade union activity (Joshi, *Lost* 268–69). In a few years, Kanpur would emerge, alongside Delhi and Lucknow, as one of the three principal sites for the organizational activities of the Hindustan Socialist Republican Army (HSRA) (Maclean 2015). The young Bhagat Singh even served a short stint as a journalist for Vidyarthi's *Pratap* (Dogra September 2016). Working-class militancy by the 1930s had created panic that is captured, says Chitra Joshi, in contemporary cartoons and "in popular discourse, the city came to be known as "Red City" (*Lal Kanpur*)" (Joshi, "On De-industrialization" 162).

It is in such a city that Shyam Sundar Lal came to be established as a "Picture Merchant" with an office at the Chowk.[2] Though a few scholars have over the course of the last decade or two drawn attention to popular prints, little is known about Shyam Sundar Lal and how his business originated, and much the same can be said for most other major publishers of prints from the 1920s to the 1940s.[3] According to his grandson, who still manages the business, Sundar Lal opened his shop and publishing venture in 1923 (Aggarwal January 2018).[4] We similarly have very little idea how these prints were used or circulated. Just how many copies of each design were printed? Were they put up in the marketplace, or affixed to walls in other public spaces, to goad, inspire and provoke people into political action being torn down by orders of the police? Were these prints framed and prominently displayed in homes where nationalist feelings ran high? No mention of them is found in any memoir or autobiography of those days, as far as I am aware. Is it possible that they were passed from one hand to another at political meetings?

Writing of the images of armed revolutionaries, one scholar avers that many can be traced to Kanpur, "and of these, a disproportionately large number appears to have been published by one press: Shyam Sundar Lal" (Maclean 126). Radhe Lal Agarwal, most likely a member of the family, is mentioned on some prints as the "sole agent" in Uttar Pradesh. Shyam Sundar Lal could apparently rely upon several printers in Kanpur—among them Job Press, Coronation Press, Misra Press, National Press, Ramdass Press and the Central Press—as well as printers in Allahabad, primarily Krishna Press and Bhargava Press. Just exactly how many artists were commissioned or employed at his workshop, provided he had one, is also uncertain; in the nationalist prints, at least, the names of Roop Kishore [Rup Kishor] Kapur, on whom Pinney has lavished some attention, and Prabhu Dayal predominate among the artists. The images were copyrighted, suggesting that Sundar Lal was not averse to acquiring profits; indeed, as other prints from his publishing company, such as those of wrestling champions suggests he was not inspired solely by nationalist sentiments (Thomas).

Nevertheless, Sundar Lal must have been aware that in publishing material that was in some cases in open defiance of press regulations and other measures taken by the government to check seditious activity, he ran the risk of having his business shuttered and being hauled into jail. On 13 April 1940, the police finally pounced upon him: descending upon his shop with a search warrant, they found "in his shop a number of pictures for sale, publication or distribution, such pictures coming under the category of unauthorized news sheet"—the latter a term defined in the Indian Press (Emergency Powers) Act of 1931.[5] The martyrs featured in such prohibited posters, postcards and calendars included Chandrasekhar Azad, Bhagat Singh and Jatin Das. The case came to trial on 6 June 1940 in the court of Rama Kant, Magistrate of Kanpur, who declared himself convinced that the "objectionable" material found in Sundar Lal's shop fell well within the definition of "unauthorized" and that the defendant therefore was guilty as charged.

It is Gandhi, however, rather than armed revolutionaries who was by far the most common subject for printmakers and whose life and work generated an extraordinarily diverse array of narratives. The enterprise of putting into question the received teleology of Indian nationalism, in which Gandhi figures as the high priest, commenced neither with Subaltern Studies nor with Dalit scholars. The first generation of Marxist commentators, such as M. N. Roy and the young Soumyendranath Tagore, was by the 1920s already writing of Gandhi and the Congress in a highly critical vein; and we may say that later the historians of the Subaltern School brought a certain sophistication to their critique not only of imperialist but, more significantly, of nationalist schools of historiography, seeing them as joined at the hip with their emphasis on elites and the uncritical adulation of the idea of the nation. Christopher Pinney, quite possibly the most engaging, and certainly the most influential, scholar to have launched forays into the vast visual archive of Indian popular culture, has extended the critique yet further. He has argued, putting it rather plainly, that Bhagat Singh and his cohorts loomed much larger in the political imaginary of what is termed "the freedom struggle" than the sanctioned official historiography will allow. If his argument had gone thus far, it would scarcely be exceptional; after all, Nehru had admitted as much in Gandhi's own lifetime. "Jatin Das's death," wrote Nehru of the revolutionary who died of a prolonged hunger strike in protest against prison conditions, "created a sensation all over the country." The "popularity that the man achieved," he wrote in a similarly effusive language for Bhagat Singh, "was something amazing"; at one point, Nehru was to add in his autobiography of 1941, Bhagat Singh had eclipsed Gandhi in popularity (Nehru 134–44; Lal, "Phenomenon" Sept. 2019; Lal, "Bhagat" [forthcoming]; Moffat 2019).[6] Indeed, the historian Manmath Nath Gupta, who over several decades vigorously championed the "revolutionaries" as the true if unheralded architects of Indian independence, was as early as 1939 calling into question what he took to be the hegemonic nationalist narrative and its strategies of occlusion (Gupta *History; They Lived Dangerously*).

Pinney's claim is rather more striking, namely that popular culture is much less observant of the pieties of official nationalism and can barely be contained. Thus, on his reading, even Gandhi, however loath he may have been to allow revolutionaries who had resorted to violence a place in the emerging history of the nation, perforce had to concede that the nation stood in deep debt to the patriotism of martyred young men and women. His pièce de résistance for this argument is a print from around 1931 where "Gandhi reveals his true allegiances to B. K. Dutt": "Just as Hanuman, the monkey-god tears his chest to reveal his allegiance to his master, the god Ram, so here Gandhi tears his (inferior) peaceful existence to reveal his faith in revolutionary struggle," a reference to the print's representation of Gandhi baring his chest before Bakuteshwar Dutt—the revolutionary most famous for exploding two bombs alongside Bhagat Singh at the Central Legislative Assembly on 4 April 1929—to reveal an image of the holy trio of the martyred Bhagat Singh, Sukhdev and Rajguru (Pinney, *Photos* 136). Popular opinion, it would seem, impels Gandhi towards the disguised truth; his secret self triumphs over the self shaped by manufactured consent.

To bolster Pinney's argument, it may be said that we do not have a similar image of Bhagat Singh tearing open his chest to reveal an image of Gandhi. However, this image lends itself to a great many more interpretations and questions than Pinney, who seems a bit too eager to join those contemporary commentators who have thought it fit both to diminish Gandhi's role in the struggle for independence and take the shine off him, is willing to allow. As Pinney recognizes, viewers of the print would at once have thought of Ram and Hanuman. Should we then simply affirm that Hanuman is to Ram as Gandhi is to Bhagat Singh? Could such a view have had any traction at all to the viewers? That hardly seems possible: howsoever much Bhagat Singh was valorized, there is absolutely nothing else to suggest that Gandhi in the common imagination was held to be his *bhakta*. We might ask what relationship the image has to the written word: in other words, do the newspapers, pamphlets and broadsheets of the day at all support such a reading which establishes Gandhi in the role of a bhakta to Bhagat Singh? How far does the analogy with Hanuman and Ram extend considering that Bhagat Singh was known to be a committed atheist and derived at least some of his following from those who held him up as an example of a revolutionary inspired not by Ram's victory over Ravana but by the writings of Marx and the tactics of insurgency pioneered by Lenin? Could the printmaker have only been suggesting that Gandhi, whose own relentless commitment to ahimsa was a matter of public knowledge, had enough of largesse in him that he was willing to embrace Bhagat Singh? It appears to be just as plausible to argue that the print was calculated to make Bhagat Singh acceptable to Gandhi's followers and bring Bhagat Singh, lionized as a patriot, to the door of divinity—if only by sheer proximity to Gandhi.

Those who would like to unsettle the old hierarchies of Indian nationalist biography and install Bhagat Singh and the HSRA "revolutionaries"—a word, let it be noted in passing, that is scarcely ever critically analysed in these contexts—as somehow more authentic specimens of an uncompromising politics will do what they will but it is indubitably the case that however one positions oneself with respect to Gandhi, he still predominates in the visual imaginary of nationalism. Bhagat Singh appears with a fedora, in the jail cell, with the hangman's noose around him and his companions, as the inheritor of the tradition of militant resistance that nationalism came to associate with Maharana Pratap Singh and Shivaji, or as the forerunner of Subhas Bose: it is largely within this world that he is circumscribed. But Gandhi overwhelms with his presence in nearly every domain of life, extending for the printmaker the representational apparatus in myriad ways—as a world historical figure, a modern-day Krishna, the architect of satyagraha, the instigator of local struggles, the weaver alike of yarn and epic narratives, the custodian of the country's moral integrity, the exemplar of yogic discipline, an ardent social reformer, the mariner who brings the boat safely to shore, sometimes just as an ashram dweller. It is striking as well, and deserving of detailed consideration elsewhere, that Gandhi is singularly alone among modern Indian figures in sharing with the Buddha a history of aniconic representation.

In the series of prints to which I now turn for an all too brief discussion, most from the publisher Shyam Sundar Lal, we commence with Gandhi and Kasturba side-by-side (Figure 1.1): the caption describes him as "Shanti ke devta" [The God of Peace], and at the bottom, he is identified as "Mahatma Gandhi." She is named "Dharmapatni Mahatma Gandhi," his lawful or dutiful wife; strikingly, the caption above her portrait, "Mateshwari Kastur Bai," characterizes her as akin to Parvati, the consort of Shiva (Mateshwar). Gandhi appears in a pensive mood, bare-chested: though he is already the Mahatma, he is pondering the course of action he might adopt to lead the nation. This is the Gandhi who has just been launched on to the national stage. The print is just as unadorned as Gandhi and Kasturba themselves. The same photograph of Gandhi sans Kasturba appears in a print (Figure 1.2), also from the workshop of Shyam Sundar Lal, bearing the caption "Rashtra Ke Sutradhar"—the weaver of the country's destiny, the stage manager charged with guiding the country to a new future. Quite possibly, the same photograph may exist with yet other captions, pointing to the mental agility of the printmaker, who is cognizant of the fact that Gandhi appeared attractive to some as a messenger of peace, to others as the arbiter of the country's fate, and yet to others in one of his many other guises. Or was the printmaker already attuned to the stratagems of marketing?

FIGURE 1.1   Kapur, Roop Kishor. "Shanti Ke Devata; Mateshwari Kastur Bai." Published by Shyam Sundar Lal, Picture Merchant, Chowk, Cawnpore

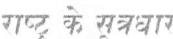

FIGURE 1.2   Artist unknown. "Rastra Ke Sutradhar: Mahatma Gandhi." Published by Shyam Sundar Lal, Kanpur.

It is literally as the *Sutradhar* that Gandhi appears in another undated print from Sundarlal's workshop (Figure 1.3). Here Gandhi sits beside the *charkha*: he is looking into the camera, obliging his interlocutor. The top of the print bears a caption "Azaadi Ke Paigamber ki Ghoshna" or "An Announcement from the Divine Messenger of Freedom"; below Gandhi's image are printed his "Eleven Demands," which, though the print is undated, can be traced to the demands that Gandhi put forward before Lord Irwin in late January 1930 (*Collected Works* 48: 271). Gandhi had called for total prohibition; reduction of the land revenue,

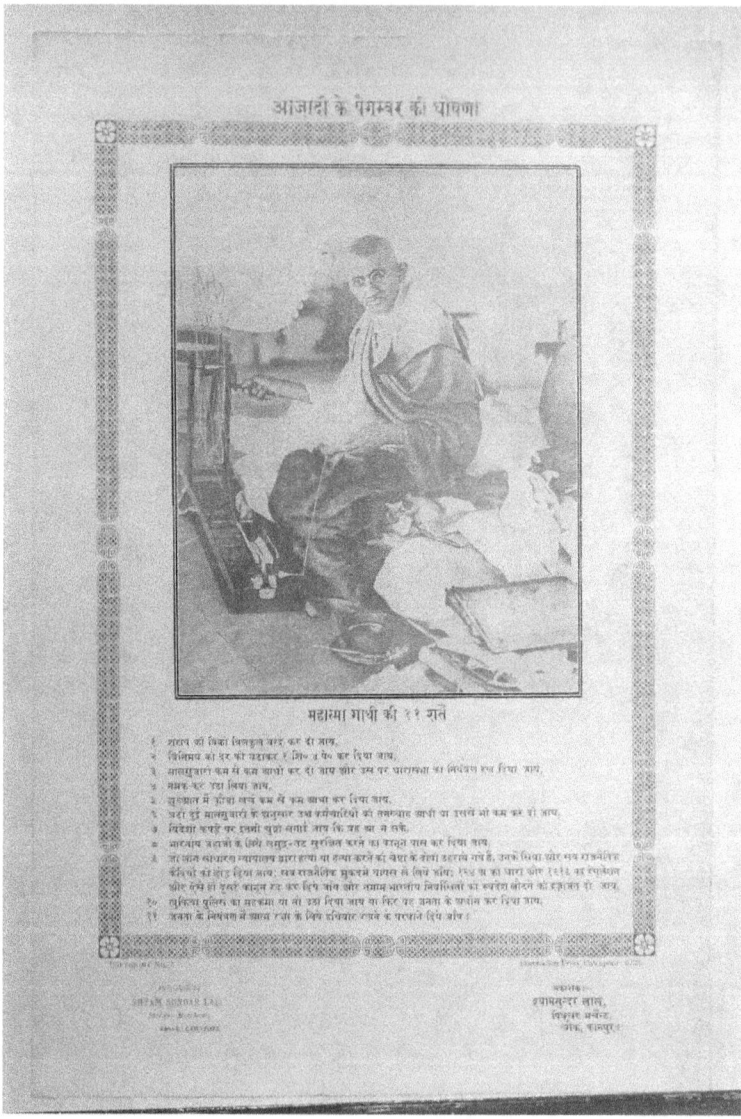

FIGURE 1.3 Designer unknown. "Azaadi Ke Paigamber Ki Ghoshna." Published by Shyam Sundar Lal, Kanpur.

and similarly of military expenditures, by at least 50 percent; a protective tariff on imported clothes; and, among other things, the elimination of the salt tax. The constituency at which the print was most likely aimed is suggested by the use of a somewhat elevated or Sanskritic Hindi. We have already encountered the characterization of Gandhi as "Devta," as the "Prophet" of Freedom; at the same time, in the public imagination Gandhi was indelibly linked with the cause of the charkha: he could be found spinning at his ashram and in public forums, in and out of jail. Print after print points to how these two representations would be

भगवान की तकली

महात्मा गांधी (जेल में)

FIGURE 1.4 Dayal, Prabhu. "Bhagvan Ki Takli." Published by Shyam Sundar Lal, Kanpur.

conjoined, as the artist Prabhu Dayal (Figure 1.4) amply suggests. The thread passes through Gandhi's supple fingers; the caption says it all: "Bhagwan Ki Takli." And yet it doesn't: the accent on Gandhi's hands is still more pronounced here than in the previous print. In South Africa, he worked in the printing press with his own hands: we see the potter's hands; indeed, there is no potter without his hands, but we do not ordinarily see the hands with which Gandhi sought to weave both the dignity of physical labour and the materiality of the body into the swaraj of the soul.

Sabarmati Ashram, where Gandhi eventually made his home after a brief spell at Kochrab Ashram before finally embarking from it for Dandi more than a decade later, was in many respects the centre of his universe. Ashram dwellers were bound to a set of observances; much as anyone else, Gandhi partook of most of the activities that dominated ashram life, but he also devoted a portion of his day to reading, writing and keeping up with his correspondence (Figure 1.5).

It is at this ashram that, on 10 March 1922, shortly after the publication of a number of his pieces that were deemed seditious, Gandhi was taken into custody. The police party arrived late at night, and Gandhi was sent word that he could take time to bid farewell to friends and the ashram inmates and collect a few belongings. The drama of that night is captured in a print called "Arrest of Mahatma Gandhi,"

FIGURE 1.5 Artist unknown. "Gandhi Ashram, Sabarmati." Published by Shyam Sundar Lal, Kanpur.

published by Arorbans Press, Lahore (Figure 1.6). Gandhi was awoken from his sleep; a police officer bends towards him, a paper—presumably the arrest warrant—in his outstretched right hand, while another police hovers just behind him. The beam of the flashlight illuminates the warrant, the dark night and a portion of Gandhi's face.

There is yet more attention to detail, suggesting more than just the printmaker's familiarity with some elements of Gandhi's life: for instance, the alarm clock on a little night table just behind Gandhi's bed reminds the viewer of the demands on Gandhi's time, his punishing schedule and his strict adherence to punctuality. The disciplined life

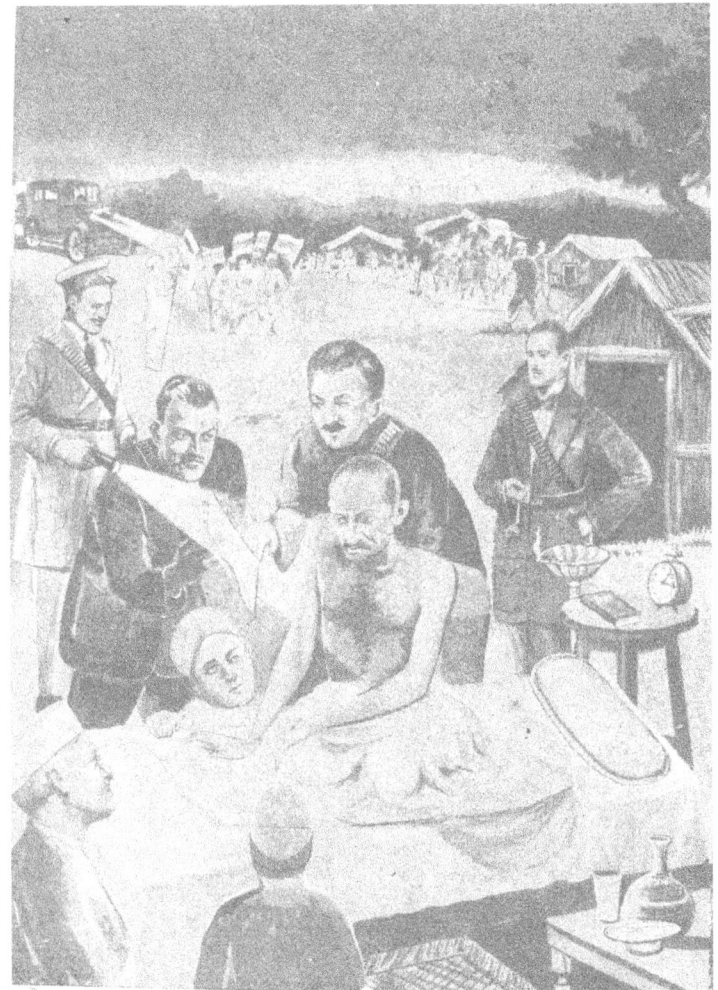

Arrest of Mahatma Gandhi

Arorbans Press, Lahore.

FIGURE 1.6   Artist unknown. "Arrest of Mahatma Gandhi." Published by Arorbans Press, Lahore.

is evoked also in the artist Prabhu Dayal's print for Sunder Lal called "Satyagraha Yoga-Sadhan" or the achievement of satyagraha by means of yoga (Figure 1.7). Gandhi is centre stage, flagged at either end by Motilal and his son Jawaharlal: he sits meditatively on a bed of thorns, reminiscent perhaps of the dying Bhishma as he lay upon a sheaf of arrows and delivered a last set of teachings on the duties of the king and the slipperiness of dharma. There are no rose bushes without thorns; there is no freedom without restraint and discipline: indeed, if Patanjali may be paraphrased, the freedom of spiritual

FIGURE 1.7 Dayal, Prabhu. "Satyagraha Yoga-Sadhan." Published by Shyam Sundar Lal, Kanpur.

integrity is experienced in the act of discipline itself, which is ultimately rendered superfluous by the reality that its practice discloses. The sun of "Purna Swaraj" shines upon the three—the resolution demanding "full independence" had been passed in December 1929 by the Congress, at the annual meeting in Lahore presided over by Jawaharlal. A little more than a year later, Gandhi was one of the pallbearers at the funeral of Motilal Nehru. Sunder Lal's printmaker captured the last journey of this great soul: the funeral procession emerges from the ancestral Nehru home, Anand Bhavan, the men ranged on one side and the women on the other side (Figure 1.8). The caption confers the epithet of "tyagmurti" on Pandit Motilal but he is, I would argue, the most obvious but by no means the only figure of sacrifice. Gandhi, long since the Mahatma, and by now the leading figure in the struggle for freedom, leads the pallbearers; he is himself a figure of sacrificial discipline and devotion.

It is with the idea of non-cooperation, *asahayoga*, that Gandhi had first stirred the nation and helped to transform the Congress into an organization capable of spearheading a movement of mass non-violent resistance. The non-cooperation movement lasted from 1920 until early 1922 when, after an incident at Chauri Chaura which led to the outbreak of what Gandhi characterized as "mob" violence—a description that has been critiqued by some historians and commentators as an indication of his bourgeois sensibility and his inability to countenance the idea of a "real" revolution—he called for its suspension (Guha 69–120). In the complex prints that I bring to the fore here, the trope of non-cooperation figures prominently— but not exclusively so (Figs. 1.9–1.12). Krishna had lifted Govardhan to save the inhabitants of Vrindavan from the wrath of Indra, who, offended that the villagers

FIGURE 1.8   Lal, Shyam Sundar. "Tyagamurti Pandit Motilal Nehru Ki Antim Yatra." Published by Shyam Sundar Lal, Kanpur.

were no longer willing to render him puja, decided to flood the land and submerge it under water. In a print from Calcutta, entitled "Asahayoga Govardhan" (Figure 1.9), Gandhi, ably assisted by C. R. Das, the Ali Brothers, Motilal and Lajpat Rai, makes of non-cooperation a mountain under which one might expect Ram Rajya to flourish. Elsewhere, Gandhi, Motilal and Jawaharlal, who together embody the virtues of courage, endurance, shrewdness and heroism, are rendered by Prabhu Dayal as the three skilled boatmen ("teen chatur mallaha") who can steer the boat of non-cooperation through a frightful storm to safety (Figure 1.10).

The idea of non-cooperation receives yet greater elaboration in a print published by the Bombay-based Joshi Brothers with the title "Ramayana Asahayoga Setu Bandhan," rendered into English on the print itself as "Non-Co-operation Setu Bandhan" (Figure 1.11). The print plays with multiple narratives, almost dividing into several

FIGURE 1.9 Artist unknown. "Asahayoga Govardhan." Published by Kunjanlal Singhania, Calcutta.

FIGURE 1.10   Dayal, Prabhu. "Asahayoga Nauka Ke Teen Chatur Malaha." Published by Rashtriya Chitra Prakashan, Cawnpore.

FIGURE 1.11   Artist unknown. "Ramayana Non-Cooperation Setu Bandhan." Published by Joshi Brothers, Bombay.

panels in each of which the viewer is witness to a story. Gandhi is at the forefront of a group of political leaders astride a bridge across which the letters "NON CO-OP ERAT" are seen; a portion of the bridge, presumably bearing the letters "ION," has perhaps fallen into the water, or has not yet been put up. Non-cooperation was never a narrative only of how Gandhi induced the nation to cease cooperating with the British and thereby sap the very foundations of colonial rule; it was also a narrative, at a time when the Congress was divided between "moderates" and "extremists," of cooperation and rapprochement among Indians of different political persuasions. The Ali Brothers and Motilal Nehru among others are arrayed besides Gandhi—or are they behind him, since he is perhaps the first among equals? He holds aloft the banner of swaraj. Hanuman set fire to Lanka as he made good his escape after meeting with Sita: here satyagraha, imprinted lightly on a captive Hanuman, his hands tied behind his back, seems to have lit a fire that cannot be domesticated by the British. A print such as this one calls for considerable interpretation: the bridge to Lanka brings Rama closer to Sita even as it takes him into the fortress of the enemy. Non-cooperation always holds out the promise of a cooperation that is deferred; violence is inescapably present to every advocate of ahimsa.

The non-cooperation movement of 1920–1922 gave way to the "Constructive Programme," activity by armed revolutionary groups, and, moving into the next decade, the Dandi March and the salt satyagraha (Figure 1.12) and widespread civil disobedience (Figure 1.13). Printmakers were alert in giving recognition to Gandhi's view, to which he was deeply committed until the end of his life, that political emancipation from colonial rule was wholly insufficient unless one could also articulate a vision of economic, cultural and social freedom for the masses. Gandhi remained a staunch advocate of prohibition, as is conveyed in a print entitled "Destruction of Palm-Trees" (Figure 1.14), though the zeal with which the toddy trees are being felled suggests at least a touch of violence.

"The Way to Swaraj" for Gandhi lay in rural reconstruction, the revitalization of the village economy, adherence to swadeshi and a respect for manual labour (Figure 1.15): though he has not been seen this way, Gandhi was also, as I have previously hinted, the theorist of the "handmade" and always mindful of the unmatched integrity of the hand. The singularity of Gandhi is evident in many of the prints, as we have seen, but printmakers were always animated by larger considerations. The economic exploitation of India had been a subject for Indian nationalists since at least the late nineteenth century and would become the subject of famous studies by Dadabhai Naoroji and Romesh Chunder Dutt; but printmakers were not far behind, as is evident in the print, also from Shyam Sunder Lal's publishing house, called "Sampatti Haran," or "Looted by the Foreigners" (Figure 1.16). Gandhi appears here, at the extreme left centre of the print; he is dwarfed by the figure of a despondent Bharat Mata, as though to suggest that, in some respects, even a Gandhi could only be on an onlooker to the immense economic tragedy unfolding in India.

What is most striking about nationalist prints, and worthy of a far more detailed analysis than is possible at this juncture, is the manner in which printmakers worked Indian mythic material—stories and characters from the Ramayana and

FIGURE 1.12 Artist unknown. "Dandi Mein Namak ki Loot." Published by Shyam Sundar Lal, Kanpur.

FIGURE 1.13 Dayal, Prabhu. "Bardali Vijaya." Published by Shyam Sundar Lal, Kanpur.

FIGURE 1.14 Dayal, Prabhu. "Destruction of Palm–Trees." Published by Shyam Sundar Lal, Kanpur.

FIGURE 1.15 Artist unknown. "Way to Swaraj." Published by S. S. Brij Basi & Sons, Karachi.

FIGURE 1.16 Kapur, Roop Kishor. "Sampatti Haran." Published by Shyam Sundar Lal, Kanpur.

the Mahabharata, and the vast store of Puranic lore—into the nationalist narrative. "Asahayoga Govardhan" (Figure 1.9) may once again be recalled in this context, though two further examples, with which I close, will suffice for our purposes. The story of young Markandeya being saved from Yama, the Lord of Death, who comes astride a bull would serve Prabhu Dayal with the template in "Bharatuddhar": Yama

Raja now appears in the guise of a colonial police official, Bharat Mata substitutes for Markandeya, and Shiva is transmogrified into Gandhi (Figure 1.17). "The Meeting of Krishna and Gandhi" (Figure 1.18) is extraordinary in its deceptive simplicity. The left-hand column narrates incidents from Krishna's life, and the right-hand column offers a parallel narrative of Gandhi's life. This is far from being the only print where Krishna's *bansuri* has taken on new life as Gandhi's spindle. But where else, except in the marvellously fecund world of these nationalist prints, would one expect the butter thief ("maakhan chor") to meet his match in the salt thief ("namak chor")?

FIGURE 1.17 Dayal, Prabhu. "Bharatuddhar." Published by Shyam Sundar Lal, Kanpur.

FIGURE 1.18   Artist unknown. "Krishna Gandhi Milan." Published by Lala Sant Lal Jain, Chowk, Cawnpore.

Notes

1 The earlier version of this essay was published in *Frontline* in late April 2018.
2 Some of the prints bear the name "Shyam Sundarlal Agarwal"; yet others "Shyam Sunderlal." Sundar also appears frequently with a variant spelling, "Sunder."
3 One notable exception is the account of the publisher S. S. Brijbasi furnished by Christopher Pinney, *Photos of the Gods,* 2004, though even here we are from having a full-fledged understanding of this publisher's activities. Similarly, Pinney has a brief discussion of the printmaker Rup Kishor Kapur (1893–1978), but nothing in the discussion approximates what could be called even a brief biographical account. See Pinney, "Iatrogenic Religion and Politics," 2009, pp. 50–54.
4 Phone interview with Kedar Nath Aggarwal, 14 January 2018. I am grateful to Rahul Rajora of Delhi for putting me in touch with Mr. Aggarwal.
5 Case No. 507, "Judgement" of 6 June 1940 in the court of R. S. Rama Kant, Magistrate 1st Class of Cawnpore. Rahul Rajora kindly shared the text of this judgement, which to the best of my knowledge has received no previous mention in the scholarship, with me.
6 Jawaharlal Nehru, *Toward Freedom: The Autobiography of Jawaharlal Nehru,* 1941. I have discussed this briefly in "The Phenomenon of Bhagat Singh", *ABP Blog,* 28 Sept. 2019, and at greater length in "Bhagat Singh: The Afterlives of an Icon," forthcoming in *Cultural Critique.* For the most extended scholarly treatment of Bhagat Singh's popularity, see Chris Moffat, *India's Revolutionary Inheritance: Politics and the Promise of Bhagat Singh,* 2019.

Works Cited

Aggarwal, Kedar Nath. Phone Interview. Conducted by Vinay Lal, 14 Jan. 2018.

Amin, Shahid. "Gandhi as Mahatma: Gorakhpur District, Eastern UP, 1921–22." *SubalternStudies III: Writings on South Asian History & Society,* edited by Ranajit Guha, Oxford UP, 1984, pp. 1–61.

"Clearing the Issue." *Young India.* 30 Jan. 1930. *Collected Works of Mahatma Gandhi,* 100 vols, Government of India, Publications Division, 48: 271.

Dogra, Bharat. "Bhagat Singh: A Media Role Model." *The Hoot,* 27 Sept. 2016, www.thehoot.org/media-watch/regional-media/bhagat-singh-a-media-role-model-9669. Accessed 6 Sept. 2017.

Guha, Ranajit. "Discipline and Mobilize." *Subaltern Studies VII: Writings on South Asian History and Society,* edited by Partha Chatterjee and Gyanendra Pandey, Oxford UP, 1993, pp. 69–120.

Gupta, Manmath Nath. *[Bharatiya krantikra Andolan ka itihasa, 1939]. Bhagat Singh and His Times.* Lipi Prakashan, 1977.

———. *History of the Indian Revolutionary Movement. 1939.* Somaiya Publications, 1972.

———. *They Lived Dangerously: Reminiscences of a Revolutionary.* People's Publishing House, 1969.

Hutton, J. H. *The Census of India, 1931: Volume 1: India; Part I: Report.* Manager of Publications, 1931, https://archive.org/details/CensusOfIndia1931/mode/2up.

Joshi, Chitra. *Lost Worlds: Indian Labour and Its Forgotten Histories.* Anthem Press, 2005, pp. 268–69.

———. "On 'De-industrialization' and the Crisis of Male Identities." *International Review of Social History,* vol. 47, no. 10, 2002, pp. 159–75. *JSTOR,* www.jstor.org/stable/44735350.

Lal, Vinay. "Bhagat Singh: The Afterlives of an Icon." *Cultural Critique,* forthcoming, 2022.

———. "The Phenomenon of Bhagat Singh." *ABP Blog,* 28 Sept. 2019, https://news.abplive.com/blog/opinion-the-phenomenon-of-bhagat-singh-1082432. Accessed 6 Sept. 2017.

Maclean, Kama. *A Revolutionary History of Interwar India: Violence, Image, Voice and Text*. Oxford UP, 2015.

Moffat, Chris. *India's Revolutionary Inheritance: Politics and the Promise of Bhagat Singh*. Cambridge UP, 2019.

Nehru, Jawaharlal. *Toward Freedom: The Autobiography of Jawaharlal Nehru*. Beacon Press, 1941, pp. 134–44.

Pinney, Christopher. "Iatrogenic Religion and Politics." *Censorship in South Asia: Cultural Regulation From Sedition to Seduction*, edited by Raminder Kaur and William Mazzarella, Indiana UP, 2009, pp. 50–54.

———. *Photos of the Gods: The Printed Image and Political Struggle in India*. Reaktion Books, 2004.

Suhrud, Tridip. "Inconvenient Truth: How Gujarat Forgot Gandhi." *Mint*, 6 Dec. 2019, www.livemint.com/news/india/inconvenient-truth-how-gujarat-forgot-gandhi-1549474968445.html. Accessed 6 Sept. 2017.

Thomas, Rosie. "An Aladdin's Cave of 1950s B-Movie Fantasy." www.tasveergharindia.net/cmsdesk/essay/103/index_3.html. Accessed 7 Sept. 2017.

Trivedi, Harish. "Literary and Visual Portrayals of Gandhi." *The Cambridge Companion to Gandhi*, edited by Judith M. Brown and Anthony Parel, Cambridge UP, 2011, pp. 199–218.

2

MUSIC FOR THE CONGREGATION

Assembling an Aesthetic for Prayer

Lakshmi Subramanian[1]

On 2 October 2018, a video featuring Gandhi's favourite bhajan, "*Vaishnav Jan to*," went viral. The rapidity with which the sonic image circulated brought home to many the power of simultaneity that the internet and social media commanded in India. What the images did not convey was the context in which the bhajan had, by 1915, become the Mahatma's message or its import within his scheme of politics and social regeneration. What was it about the lyrical content and musical arrangement about Narasingh Mehta's bhajan that made it iconic? How did it feature as part of the Ashram's congregational service? What did Gandhi seek in putting together a repertoire of devotional songs that came out formally as the Ashram Bhajanavali? The Ashram Bhajanavali, or the hymnal, was a collection of 253 devotional verses that formed part of the Ashram's quotidian prayer in Sabarmati. These verses were in several languages and drawn from Hindu, Muslim and Christian traditions. Gandhi translated them while confined in Verawada Jail in 1930.

What was the rationale behind the Bhajanavali, indeed, behind the self-conscious braiding of song and prayer? What was its underlying social and aesthetic idea, and how was this formed? These are some of the questions that will be addressed in this chapter. It takes its cue from the centrality of prayer that Gandhi espoused in his private and public life, testing it first within the Sabarmati Ashram's precincts in India and then extending it outside its portals to public meetings. For Gandhi, the overriding imperative behind his aesthetic choices was to facilitate the salience of music and sung prayer in cohering a community of satyagrahis, of moral subjects, to embark upon the struggle for swaraj. All other considerations were secondary. This forming of a community of satyagrahis is not to suggest that Gandhi did not appreciate the value of good music and musical renditions or that he did not value the importance of trained teachers in leading the congregation or providing the necessary instruction to the residents in the Ashram.

DOI: 10.4324/9781003145479-4

Indeed, he was personally moved by the passionate voices of contemporaries like M.S. Subbulakshmi (1916–2004)[2] or Dilip Roy (1897–1980),[3] he was receptive to the artistic interventions of musicians like Vishnu Digambar Paluskar (1872–1931),[4] but by the same measure, he was alert to the functions that music could play in catering to the immediate requirements of the small community that he built up in the Ashram at Sabarmati.

Between Gandhi's sojourn in South Africa, where he experimented with the Tolstoy farm[5] (1910–1911) and his return to India (1915), where he immediately set about organizing the Ashram in Sabarmati,[6] his ideas on music and prayer as the guiding principle for moral self-improvement and political action had crystallized. Gandhi was not especially musical in his childhood. However, in all probability, he might have been exposed to the standard chants and musical sermons expected in a typical Vaishnav household. We do not hear of his acquaintance with any form of art music. His voyage to England and his stay there when he attempted to play "the English gentleman" and, along with that, the violin for a few months was significant, for it was here that he listened to church music and was deeply moved by the experience. Gandhi's exchanges with several Christians and theosophists pushed him into thinking more deeply about his religion and spiritual inheritance. The invocation of the well-known Surdasi hymn "*Nirbal ke bal ram*" (Help of the helpless, the strength of the weak) embodied his inner turmoil and struggles in reconciling his faith and combating counter narratives from other religious traditions.

The setting up of the Tolstoy Farm (1910) in the wake of the suspension of the first phase of passive resistance in South Africa coincided with Gandhi's decision to give up his career in law and experiment with both education and an expanded articulation of the idea of Satyagraha and its preconditions of self-improvement and character building. Whether it was the emphasis on manual training or spiritual training, the idea was to live correctly, embrace discipline and restraint, and accommodate diverse religious faiths by imbibing their essence (Hunt 89). Music was seen as a positive aid in this experiment; religious hymns, chants and songs were freely used in the service. Several residents in the farm volunteered to sing; in this connection, Gandhi's nephew Prabhudas Gandhi mentioned how his mother Kashibehn had a melodious voice that Gandhi was partial to (Snodgrass 53). Gandhi could not have been unaware of the power commanded by the sonic in ritual settings; consequently, he emphasized the need to compile an appropriate selection of hymns, prayers and songs and enlist a trained teacher's services in providing proper lessons and training. However, what is important to stress here is that Gandhi's aesthetic choices were subordinated to his preoccupation with prayer's centrality, which could never be confused with the temporary seduction of a song or the compelling lure of a melody. Prayer, as he observed, "was a longing of the soul, a daily admission of one's weakness" (qtd. Brown 7) and was crucial to the refinement of the self. It could thus never be mechanical or tedious, nor could it be entertaining. However, to make it efficacious, music and singing were proper props, for these had the power to make prayer a joyful experience.

The songs chosen in South Africa and subsequently in India were mixed and inter-faith; he oversaw translations of hymns such as "Lead Kindly Light" and saw no contradiction in singing these alongside the Ramdhun. One consideration behind his selection of songs was that ritual utterances and prayers were not always intelligible, and therefore, he had to take recourse to simple and sweet bhajans from those saints who had creatively devised an ideal medium to convey the essence of the Hindu religion. In his correspondence, during these years (1910–1914), he stressed the value of music in inculcating good habits in facilitating body and mental discipline – the key to any programme of self-purification and political struggle.

Gandhi returned to India in 1915 to take charge of the nationalist struggle that had languished in the years following the swadeshi agitation. Even before he met leaders and publicists, he decided to establish an ashram in Ahmedabad to train satyagrahis and devise an appropriate curriculum for them. Music and devotional chanting occupied pride of place, and as he set out designing service for the newly found Ashram, he was able to dip into a pool of new ideas and symbols that had already found currency in the emerging musical and literary culture in India. By the closing decades of the nineteenth century, the music of the courts and salons had moved into cities and urban centres, where a politically conscious and educated middle class emerged as listeners, sponsors and publicists. Reforming courts also played a role in the changing context of patronage, due to which questions of relocating music practice within a middle class, extending its democratic access by addressing issues of respectability and pedagogy were keenly debated. The emerging discourse was complex and accommodated several strains – reformist and revivalist – associated with figures like V. N. Bhatkhande (1875–1935)[7] and V. D. Paluskar respectively (Bakhle). Both these men had emerged as significant figures of reform and regeneration of Indian music, bringing the practice of music before a wider public domain and amidst a new middle-class constituency. Paluskar, in particular, stressed the need to decouple music from "ustadi" hands to emphasize its devotional aspects that would make its practice and pursuit respectable among the middle class and, therefore, focused almost entirely on teaching bhajans. Paluskar's work coincided with the proselytizing agenda of Arya Samajists and other Hindu revivalist initiatives,[8] including notably the founders of the Gita Press[9] that helped create and consolidate a Hindu identity in the literary and the musical domain. Other reformers did not share Paluskar's agenda; those in Bengal and Western India who were appreciative of the Indo-Islamic musical legacy had intimate connections with their "ustadi" teachers whose aesthetic understanding was decoupled from religious and identity politics. However, in terms of available acoustic choices, the more excellent circulation of music performances in the wake of concerts and musical drama did have the important effect of creating a shared sonic community that responded to a palette of tunes, melodies and songs.

Gandhi, by temperament, was not interested in any form of musical entertainment. He had no time for theatre; he was unambiguously critical of entertainment that he saw as tawdry and irrelevant for the times and instead preferred to instil in his following a deeper appreciation of good habits that alone could orient the subject to a moral cause. Nevertheless, he was not unmindful of the value and power of good music – he was determined to get a good teacher for his newly created Ashram and, with his help, refine an aesthetic for congregational singing and craft a community of devotees. Gandhi was, or at least projected himself to be a perfectionist and, therefore, insisted on expertise and talent when it came to leading the service. This perfectionism was as much an expression of his discerning listening habits as it was of his moral agenda that emphasized the importance of disciplined and mindful labour in the constitution of the truth-seeking subject.

The Ashram at Sabarmati that Gandhi founded with his associates and donors in 1915 was, as Gandhi said on one occasion, neither an infirmary nor an orphanage (Snodgrass 255); instead, it was meant for volunteers who dedicated themselves to realizing a spiritual goal through manual labour and moral cultivation. In fostering the spirit of Swaraj, manual labour was obligatory just as adherence to dietary regulations and daily prayers accompanied by singing were to constitute a self-conscious set of actions for personal immersion. This self-conscious set of regulations meant that the repertoire had to be scripted to resonate with the broader community as an acoustic and as a literary resource. The repertoire was built up over the years, and the final form was a condensed set of chants (shloka), songs (bhajan) and recitation (mantra). In 1930, Gandhi began translating the hymnal for the benefit of his English readers. The songs were set to tune by a trained musician Pandit Narayan Moreshwar Khare, who also led the service. Not all the songs were suitable for congregational and choral singing; barring the simple *ramdhun* that everyone could join in, most other songs were reserved for leading singers with identified talent. Thus, both lyrics of a song and how they were rendered in diction and musical communication were vital considerations. These were reiterated time and again by Gandhi as he urged his followers to pay due attention to enunciation and diction, drawing their attention to some superb recitation he happened to encounter in his visits to South India (Kalekar Letters 1952, letters 13/6/27 and 11/7/27).[10]

Therefore, to speak of the musical aesthetic and its articulation for the Sabarmati congregation is to locate it in the larger context of Gandhi's agenda for satyagraha and the availability and circulation of musical idioms he encountered and to which he responded. As far as the prayer service was concerned, Gandhi's intended to go beyond the dogmatic and doctrinal aspects of Hinduism and communicate the experiential dimensions of faith that he saw as inclusive and capacious. Musically, what mattered was the availability of a form that was easy to identify with, resonated with older forms of musical communication and reception. In a sense, Gandhi found the bhajan to be a ready-made reconstituted musical idiom that had already been popularized thanks to the interventions of Vishnu Digambar Paluskar and of publishing initiatives such as the Shri Venkateshwara press in Bombay that had brought out versions of the Hanuman Chalisa and Vishnu Sahasranam for regular recitation and singing. It was not surprising, therefore, that Gandhi approached the Gandharva Maha Vidyalaya, a teaching institution established by Paluskar in Lahore and Bombay, to train teachers as well as to disseminate devotional music among a wider public. Gandhi was familiar with the school's reforming agenda and endorsed it when he sought to enlist a trained practitioner like Pandit Khare and then give him a free hand to order and organize the songs that would subsequently become the ashram hymnal or Bhajanavali.

Narayan Moreshwar Khare joined the Ashram around 1918, primarily to teach music to the residents and compile along with others like Kaka Kalelkar, a hymnal that could be used as part of the daily prayer service. The project began modestly and grew over time; in his preface to the Hindi version of the Bhajanavali, Khare writes how from small beginnings, it grew and integrated songs and verses in other languages and how even melodic arrangements changed. Khare reaffirmed how the message was God's inherent unity and how the Ashram took care to continually expand its prayer as time went by, thus making for a dynamic collection (Ashram Bhajanawali). There seems to have been token deference to the convention in morning and evening ragas or melodies. The Gujarati bhajan of Narasingh Mehta, "*Vaishnav Jana To,*" held the pride of place followed by Sanskrit shlokas from the Upanishads, the Gita, with expositions and explanations of the same in Gujarati and English, small invocatory hymns to Ganapati, a medley of Hindi bhajans, mostly of Tulsidas, Surdas, Kabir, Nanak, Premanand, Rangdas, Biharidas and Mirabai, of Gujarati bhajans, as well as Bengali songs primarily composed by Tagore, English hymns and finally the national song or Vande Mataram (Ashram Bhanawali). In all probability, Khare would have remained faithful to Paluskar's lucid and communicative style specially adapted for singing devotional songs.

As a collection drawn from diverse sources, the Bhajanavali embodied Gandhi's personal preferences and what he saw as preconditions of an effective congregational repertory. Like many of his contemporaries, Gandhi found the bhajan an effective medium to convey personal devotion distributed around a larger collective and create that ambient atmosphere to enhance prayer. Aligning music to prayer was, therefore, the driving rationale. In practical terms, this meant treating music lessons and singing akin to spinning – a habitual exercise to be learnt and perfected. Thus, Gandhi often spoke about the disciplined habits needed for learning a song – the attention to diction, rhythm, melody and the appreciation of exercise to aid prayer and not as a substitute for it. This necessarily meant that aesthetics for Gandhi was about pedagogy best suited for the constitution of a moral subject. In a letter to Pandit Khare dated 7 October 1924, he confessed that he had come "to look upon music as a means of spiritual development" (*Complete Works* 223) and requested him to ensure that all of the residents sang bhajans with a correct understanding of their content. Such an emphasis meant that Gandhi's reflections were about refining the efficacy of prayer through song and not about music per se. As he expressed his sentiments in a letter to Narandas Gandhi, "if we strive for truth, we would not be content merely to attend prayers but would try to concentrate our attention on them. We would try to follow songs and the discourses, be punctual in attending the prayers and respond to them as a fresh experience every day. The freshness does not consist in the variety of bhajans or other recitations, but should result from the increasing purity of our heart" (*Complete Works* 21).[11]

That Gandhi's enthusiasm for music as part of Ashram practice and as an integral part of his views on National Education had several takers is without a doubt. Many among his following expressed their desire for learning music earnestly and were encouraged to do so. Gandhi exhorted women residents to overcome their shyness and sing boldly and in public. Others like Rehana Tyabji (daughter of well-known judge Abbas Tyabji and a Gandhian), a close confidante and follower with an eclectic bent of mind, responded to his call more creatively. Not only did she see herself as a Vaisnavite devotee of Krishna and sing bhajans with great feeling, she even integrated a section of the "kalma" into the prayer repertoire, keeping in synch with Gandhi's appreciation of sung prayer as a necessary condition of self-realization, with his call for unity of religions. Gandhi was wholesome in his praise of Rehana's melodious rendering as he was later of M. S. Subbulakshmi, whose bhajans profoundly impacted him. He did not have the technical language to explain their appeal, but it is evident that a combination of emotionalism or bhava, of heightened devotional dimensions that characterized the Ashram aesthetic, was what he responded to and attempted to replicate.

What stands out about Gandhi's reflections on music is its centrality in his discourse on ethical action that was not confined to the Ashram but extended to every facet and arena of activity. The Ashram and the experiments conducted therein were a microcosm of the public domain that Gandhi intervened in during the nationalist struggle. The emphasis was on attentive listening and immersive participation in any task that was undertaken. Every task was to be treated as a prayer, which alone could prepare the social body to undertake Swaraj and Satyagraha's challenges. From morning prayers in the ashram, to prayer meetings in public, from spinning in silence or singing the national song with genuine emotion, the message was on discipline and commitment. Gandhi was clearly after an aesthetic that did not negate the significance of affect but involved a disciplining and privileging of specific affective structures. He partially followed Paluskar's agenda, wherein the devotional and the sacral were foregrounded with one crucial difference, namely his life-long resistance to frame devotion in narrowly Hindu terms. Uncannily, he had found in the domain of music, inclusive acoustic and emotional elements that could be brought together purposefully to allow for an experience, where the song "Lead Kindly Light" resonates with the Zend Avesta, the Kalma and the Ramanama. His understanding, however, did not convince his detractors who found him either inadequately Hindu or too Hindu with the result that his cry for Ramanama was stilled by three fatal bullets fired on him on 30 January 1948. The idealized Vaishnav remains a dream and the bhajan that moved the Mahatma, a sonic trace of man and a failed mission.

Notes

1   First published in *Gandhi and Aesthetics*, edited by Tridip Suhrud, Marg, vol. 71, no. 2, December 2019.
2   Madurai Shanmukhavadivu *Subbulakshmi, the Carnatic singer from Madurai, was the first musician to be awarded Bharat Ratna, India's highest civilian honour.*

3 Dilip Kumar Ray, was awarded the *Sangeet Natak Akademi Fellowship* for his contribution to music. He was also a poet and essayist.
4 Vishnu Digambar Paluskar is credited with having sung the popular bhajan, 'Raghupati Raghav Raja Ram' and is also believed to have arranged the music for the National Song of India, *Vande Mataram*. He founded the *Gandharva Mahavidyalaya* on 5 May 1901.
5 Tolstoy Farm, established in 1910 in Transvaal, South Africa, was the first Ashram organized by MK Gandhi, and which served as the headquarters to initiate the satyagraha campaign against the discrimination faced by Indians in South Africa.
6 Sabarmati Ashram, the place where Gandhi and his wife Kasturba lived from 1917 to 1930, was the epicenter of many political movements introduced by Gandhi – for instance, the Salt satyagraha of 1930. The Ashram was also the leading site where manual labour, agriculture, and many literary initiatives were undertaken.
7 Vishnu Narayan Bhatkhande was the first musicologist who wrote the modern treatise on Hindustani Classical music. It was he who provided a structure to the largely oral traditions of Hindustani Raag Music.
8 Arya Samaj (Noble Society) was established by Dayananda Sarasvati (1824–1883) in 1875 in Bombay. Arya Samaj was premised on studying the four Vedas, considered by Sarasvati the "original source of revelation" (Snodgrass 39). Sarasvati, was "openly opposed to the Brahminic and British controls over society." His idea of reform was intertwined with his advocacy for a greater presence of Hindu nationalism [with]in [the] public space" (ibid.). Other Hindu revivalists included Paramahansa Ramakrishna (1836–1886 – a mystic devoted to the Goddess Kali and Swami Vivekananda (1863–1902) whose speech at World Parliament of Religion became immensely popular.
9 Gita Press, established in 1923 was a unit of the Gobind Bhawan Karyalaya, Kolkata, registered under the Societies Registration Act, 1860 (presently governed by the West Bengal Societies Act, 1960). The prime mission of Gita Press was to inculcate and nurture the spiritual and ethical side of human civilization globally through literature.
10 *The Complete Works of Mahatma Gandhi* (Internet edition) Vol. 25, Entry No. 177. Letter to Pandit Khare dated 7 October 1924.
11 *The Complete Works of Mahatma Gandhi* (Internet edition) Vol. 45, Entry No. 25 Letter to Narandas Gandhi dated 18.12.1930.

Works Cited

Ashram Bhajanavali. Compiled by Narayan S. Khare, Navjivan Prakashan, https://archive.org/stream/in.ernet.dli.2015.540325#page/n1/mode/2up https://archive.org/download/in.ernet.dli.2015.319832/2015.319832.Aashram-Bhajnawali.pdf). Accessed 14 Oct. 2020.

Bakhle, Janaki. *Two Men and Music Nationalism and the Making of an Indian Classical Tradition.* Oxford UP, 2005.

Gandhi, M. K. *The Complete Works of Mahatma Gandhi,* Internet ed. Vol. 25, p. 45.

Hunt, James D. "Gandhian Experiments in Communal Living – the Phoenix Community and the Tolstoy Farm in South Africa." *Peace Research,* vol. 30, no. 1, Feb. 1998, pp. 83–95.

Kalelkar, Kaka, editor. *Bapu's Letters to Ashram Sisters.* Navjivan Publishing House, 1952.

Snodgrass, Cynthia. "The Sounds of Satyagraha. Mahatma Gandhi's Use of Sung-Prayers and Ritual." Diss. U of Stirling, 2007.

3

VISUALIZING GANDHI

The Icon and His People

Ruchika Wason Singh

MK Gandhi remains an enduring figure in Indian art, society and politics. From the early twentieth century, when Gandhi entered the political arena to our present-day times of escalating influence of digital technologies, Gandhi's image and teachings have served as a dependable icon for the premodern, modern and contemporary Indian artists to voice India's socio-political ethos. In form, ideology and philosophy, Gandhi has continually functioned as a firm foundation for Indian artists to construct their artistic response to India's fluid social and political landscape.

In this chapter, the interest lies in framing Gandhi as a visual resource and an ideological reference used by artists to define their response to the socio-political landscape of India. The chapter will route this enquiry through the illustration of the relationship between Gandhi and his followers. A visual mapping of selective responses of Indian artists will be done through three different stages – Gandhi's political trajectory spanning from the 1920s to 1940s (nationalist phase), Gandhi's visual representation in post-independence India, and the deconstructive approach of artists to Gandhian philosophy underpinning the Indian socio-cultural life in post-liberalization phase of the 1990s.

If we look at Gandhi and his mass followers as social actors weaving the socio-political fabric of the nationalist phase together, we can find different vantage points to understand their relationship. It is political, interpersonal and social. What is peculiar about the nationalist Indian art of this phase is that it reveals – what this essay would term as the making of a "socio-political collective." We see Gandhi as the guide, anchor, philosopher and leader situated among the young and the old, men and women, children, political leaders, freedom fighters, artisans, musicians, gardeners, farmers, household keepers and *harijans* (children of God).[1] The interactive situations within which the visual representations of Gandhi and his followers are framed include images of protest marches and historical events like non-cooperation movement and the iconic Dandi March, devotional meetings

DOI: 10.4324/9781003145479-5

for prayers and walks, sermons/speeches, exhortations to the masses to participate in the freedom movement and involvement in social events organized for/by the *harijan* community. These artistic works are sourced from either real-life narratives that often seem to be drawn, painted, or sculpted copies of historic photographic images or inspired by the artists' imagination. Either way, they serve as subjective visualization of Gandhi with the masses contributing in India's nation-making project.

Within the scope of this chapter, it is pertinent to ask, what does the visual depiction of the "socio-political collective" offer to our understanding of the geopolitical landscape of colonial India? Also, how are these geopolitical concerns challenged by the socio-political works of Indian artists in postcolonial India? To explore these ideas embedded in Gandhi's relationship with the ordinary Indian public, the chapter focuses on three aspects found in artistic renditions – dependence, solidarity and reverence. In the subsequent sections of the essay, the relation of Gandhi with the Indian social collective shall be explored through these three dimensions represented in Indian artistic works spanning from the early twentieth century to contemporary times, and, accordingly, highlight the changing socio-cultural and political ethos of India.

Gandhi's Political Trajectory During India's Freedom Struggle

In works such as *In the Untouchable Quarters* (Desai pre-1932) and *Gandhi and People Gathering* (Upendra Maharathi 1947) Gandhi is shown seated, standing or moving among a group of people.[2] Gandhi and his followers' compositional arrangement follows either linear or semicircular/circular formation. This linearity or circularity creates visual patterns of political ideology, which can be seen in many other compositions.[3] Linear formation represents Gandhi leading the masses in a march and the people following him. While semicircular/circular formation is when Gandhi is seen standing or seated in a group, surrounded on all sides or partially. The flocking, converging, blind-following formations of political congregation defined by a multitude of identities from different social categories depict the masses' dependence on the "Mahatma" for political leadership and guidance. It posits Gandhi as a non-hierarchical value of significance amidst the collective based on veneration and trust, towards whom the masses offer their solidarity.

In this artistic reproduction of solidarity, the most celebrated image is *Bapuji* by Nandalal Bose (1930; National Gallery of Modern Art), who rose to champion both Gandhi and nationalism in his art. His iconifying of Gandhi as the slightly forward bending figure, marching ahead, holding a stick, an almost photographic image of the Noakhali Gandhi is depicted in several of his works and has become an emblematic figure of the Indian nationalist struggle. Bose also created the painting *Dandi March* (1930s; *Livemint*) with the iconic figuration of marching Gandhi, flanked by several figures of the local farmers behind him. In these works, Gandhi is seen participating in political, historical events of immense importance. He is equally engaged in mass mobilization for political goals, giving a sermon under a tree as seen in *Gandhiji at Dandi* by Ramendranath Chakraborty (late 1930s; Tuli 14). Likewise, in *Gyarah Murti* by Devi Prasad Roy Chowdhury (*probashionline* 2016), one can see Gandhi's followers manifesting varied emotions of a nationalist nature trying to keep pace with the swiftness of their leader. This desire to join Gandhi is also portrayed imaginatively in the drawing – *Gandhiji, and People Gathering* (1947) by Upendra Maharathi, who creates the head of Gandhi as a rising sun and numerous heads of mass followers can be seen moving towards him. In all of these works, a scenario of united political participation and social intermingling emerges suggesting the formation of a common collective bound together by the unified goal of freedom – with Gandhi as the pivot that supports this formation.

The inclusivity created by Gandhi's secular nationalist vision characterizes the nature and relationship of the collective. It also becomes the artistic vantage point from where the artists draw their stand.[4] Gandhi's inclusive approach towards the masses is taken up emphatically by Nandalal Bose, whose admiration of the Gandhian egalitarian ethos can be further seen in the *Haripura Posters* (National Gallery of Modern Art and The Heritage Lab 1937). Created on Gandhi's invitation to decorate the *Haripura* Session held between 19 February and 22 February 1938, Bose produced these posters with his students in Shantiniketan. In these works, the social actors of the collective become the primary subjects, and the posters move beyond decoration and display to appear more like a celebration. Raman Siva Kumar elaborates,

> Called the *Haripura Posters*, this collection of over 90 paintings represented rural performers and artisans at work, peasants engaged in daily chores, and animals they were familiar with in their quotidian lives. Done in a style that invoked the simplicity of folk art and yet infused with the refined sensibilities of an individual master; they were the work of a modern artist responding to and harmonizing his sensibilities with that of village India. And, therefore, accessible at once to the informed art connoisseurs and the common man. To Nandalal, Haripura was also an exercise in total designing that brought art, architecture, and crafts and the personal and the collective – together in a single continuum.
>
> *("From Swadeshi" 4–5)*

In *Wool Spinning*, *Paper Making* and the *Blacksmith* (1937; National Gallery of Modern Art) and *Wrestlers*, the *Farmer*, the *Female Musician* and the *Woman Milking the Cow* (1937; The Heritage Lab), we see not only images of masses in different contexts but also an abiding presence of the Gandhian value system. The masses emerge as metaphors of the Gandhian vision that secures a communitarian spirit. Furthermore, these images illustrate the influence of Gandhi's belief in self-reliance, social equality and the simple values of life in fostering a sense of community among people of diverse castes, classes and groups. These Haripura subjects also share an interpersonal relationship with Gandhi encapsulated in the figuration of his caregivers, well-wishers and admirers, who are seen surrounding Gandhi in his sickness and mourning his death a decade later. In *Love – The Sustainer* (1943; D. Gandhi), a fragile, weak and bare-chested Gandhi is seen sitting apparently on a hospital bed. In the monochrome black and white work, he is the centre of attention. He is being fed by a woman sitting next to him. The pair is surrounded by a group of people visible only in their bodily contours, but their silent presence is no less suggestive of their admiration and concern for the Mahatma. In the coming years, this emotional bonding of the people with Gandhi is tested to the core as they learn about the death of their leader and mourn his loss.

In *News of Gandhiji's Death* (1948, oil on canvas) by Krishen Khanna, many people are seen standing under the street light and reading newspapers.[5] In this otherwise dark composition, the white and bright newspaper stands out to convey significant news. This stark painting of the newspaper depicts the assassination of Gandhi by the right-wing religious extremists. With a slightly bent stance, the readers seem involved in the reading of this tragic news and overcome by grief. As suggested by their headdresses, these people belong to both Hindu and Muslim communities and also from other sections of the society. The painting represents a moment of despair, shock and bereavement. Khanna's representational approach of depicting (mourning of) the death of Gandhi is significant as it presents the role the masses play in polity. Sumathi Ramaswamy has called the death of Gandhi as "a camera-free death" (129), which "in the absence of any photograph or film, in the works of art . . . is recalled in various ways" (125). However, instead of visualizing the body of Gandhi in the ghastly event, Khanna chooses to portray the passing away of Gandhi in its aftermath, through the very people in whom Gandhi found solidarity, and who in return found a sense of nationalistic belonging in him.

In both the images – *Love – The Sustainer* and *News of Gandhiji's Death*, the masses are portrayed as passive recipients. Nevertheless, their commitment to Gandhi cannot be underestimated. Their controlled emotions get overtly expressive and dramatic in some of the works. In *Fate of Three Great Men – Gandhi, Buddha, Christ* (Maharathi, National Gallery of Modern Art), physical dramaturgy is employed as a visual tool by the artist to express the magnitude of this loss. Women holding a bleeding Gandhi is dramatically imaged to enhance the immediacy of the situation. In *Bloody Sunset* (National Gallery of Modern Art), Maharathi paints a grim picture showing blood dripping with tears flowing and becoming rivulets to foreground the violence and the loss engendered by Gandhi's assassination. Sumathi Ramaswamy has highlighted this dramatic, imaginative depiction of Gandhi's death as a by-product of the absence of photographic documentation of the event. She views it as an opportunity to see "how the artist can give free rein to his or her imagination to visualize that murderous moment" (Borges, Interview 4 October 2020). Even in death, the socio-political collective demonstrates its solidarity with their leader, and their sense of dependence is now tested evermore shaped by emotions of fear and evocation of chaos.

The Years Following the Independence of India and the Remaking of History

The near simultaneous occurrence of momentous historical events – death of Gandhi and the independence of India – directed the transformation of Gandhi and the masses' artistic visualization by Indian artists in both form and context. From here on, the artists could not draw upon real life as Gandhi's death put an end to new events, and those in history became vital stories to be recreated through existing photographs, imagination or looked up to, for hope and strength.

Perhaps, the most crucial framing of Gandhi with his people and his values for a nationalist imagination invoked post his death can be seen in his illumination of India's *Constitution*.[6] Once again, it was Nandalal Bose, the creative champion, who was invited for this purpose.[7] Even as Bose exemplified his nationalist fervour through his aesthetic practice, his illumination of Gandhi in the Indian Constitution needs to be seen as more than just illumination. *Netaji Subhas Chandra Bose and other patriots trying to liberate Mother India from outside India* (Figure 3.1) provides excellent illustration of a pattern of a visuality found in the *Constitution*. In this image devoted to Gandhi, we see the marching icon with the people, and his words quoted to support Subhas Chandra Bose's image. In this and other related visualizations,[8] Bose embeds Gandhi in solidarity with people. R. Sivakumar also has highlighted the significance of selecting these images and asks, "what is the significance of the narrative scheme?" (Kumar, "From Swadeshi" 12).

In *The Constitution*, the section on the Indian Freedom Movement in its two forms – naram dal and garam dal – is represented by the images of Gandhi and

FIGURE 3.1   Bose, Nandalal. *Netaji Subhas Chandra Bose and Other Patriots Trying to Liberate Mother India From Outside India.* Part XIX "Miscellaneous," *The Constitution of India*, World Digital Library.

Subhash Chandra Bose. Incidentally, Gandhi and Bose are the only two prominent nationalist leaders whose signatures do not appear in the Constitution. As an associate and admirer of Gandhi, Nandalal Bose makes him the central figure to represent the period of nationalist struggle. Gandhi is represented twice – first, in a miniature copy of Bose' own iconic representation of the *Dandi March* painting and second, Gandhi's image as the peacemaker at Noakhali. The first presents him as a grand galvanizer of the Indian people into a non-violent moral force. The second shows him bravely struggling to soothe India's communal fault lines, a double image as it were of our potential strength and inherent weakness as a nation. Netaji ostensibly represents the revolutionaries among the freedom fighters but by quoting a part of his radio broadcast of 6 July 1944 in the painting, Nandalal Bose redirects our attention to Gandhi. The representation of Subhas Chandra Bose addressing Gandhi as "Father of the Nation" and seeking his blessings as depicted in this image underscores Gandhi's pre-eminent presence in Indian history and his emblematic position within the newly formed Indian state (Kumar, "From Swadeshi" 13).

Nandalal Bose's illustrations were created by using indigenous painting techniques and stone colours that complemented the artistic style of the famous calligrapher, Prem Bihari Narain Raizada (Saxena The Heritage Lab). Chakraborty informs us that the "choice of paper and its supplier for the Indian Constitution was (also) a well-thought decision as the institute – The Handmade Paper Institute draws from the values of the Swadeshi Movement" (*Sahapedia* 30 January 2020).[9] But their visual significance lies in the nature of the book – a Constitutional document, on which Nandalal Bose's works reiterate the spirit of collectivism. In this sense, the works create a visual legitimacy underscored in the very first page of *The Constitution of India*, bearing the words justice, liberty, equality and fraternity as the core of the preambles. With India becoming independent and Gandhi being visually installed into the Constitution in the early decades of India's nation-making project, representation of Gandhi and his supporters' kept surfacing in various artistic imagination and artistic practices. At the time of independence, Gandhi conveyed the same values he preached throughout his lifetime, and his image is considered resolving the anxieties, if any, of the ordinary people in new India.

Postindependence, we see Indian artists remembering and eulogizing history by painting actual historical events in various artistic forms and styles. These paintings are the following: *Gandhiji visiting political prisoners at DumDum Jail in 1947* (1960; Tuli 222–23) and *Gandhiji with Khan Abdul Ghaffar Khan and Others in Northwest Frontier Province in 1938* (1960) by Pandit Somnath Khosa (Tuli 199), *Gandhiji with Sardar Patel* (1969; Tuli 198) and *Morning Walk with Gandhiji, Khan Abdul Ghaffar Khan & Jawaharlal Nehru* (1969) by KM Adimoolan (Tuli 201). In all these paintings, the sociopolitical actors remain the same, but the change is visible in the psychological implications of painting as memory and repossession, and possibly documentation. Gradual artistic liberty in the subject matter also begins to surface in the works of this period. In *Gandhiji: Harmony of Religions* (1970) by Badrinath Arya (Tuli 242), the eulogy and reverence continue but the artist embeds within the iconic forms, symbolic objects and metaphors suggestive of inclusivity. Arya places Gandhi against a crucifix with a large *chakra* behind his head. He stands on a large cloud and it is evident that his location is not earthly. The floating cloud makes his movement and presence seem omnipresent. Arya's eight-armed Gandhi is holding prayer beads, a wooden stick, a bird cage from which a white bird is shown as released and about to join the flock, and also a paddle with a sea anchor lying near his feet. This personification of the leader with emblems of hope provides much solace to the three earthly human figures who face him and are seated near his feat. Their identities are also created in contrast through hieratic scaling with a much larger than life figure of Gandhi facing three tiny figures, idolizing him, and seeking his blessings enunciated in gestures made by extended hands. The central figure among them is, with its back towards viewers, reading from a prayer book and is flanked by a figure of *pandit* (Hindu priest) drawn on the left and by a figure of *maulvi* (Muslim priest) on the right. This imaginative and representative idolization continues the Gandhian saga marked by dependence, solidarity and reverence of the people for their leader. Arya takes Gandhi out of the political and social spaces, imagines him in a free space, from where he can continue to retain his relationship with the people as a spiritual guide. However, the artist has another visual ploy. He portrays Gandhi holding two small children, possibly newly born in his front-most hands. The children facing Gandhi are dramatized in the colour of their skin and their class status. One child is dark-complexioned, wearing tattered clothes, and the other is light-complexioned and fully clothed. This subtle insertion of differences in the social identities and yet been treated equally with love and affection by Gandhi completes the picture of solidarity. Arya successfully reinstates the ethos of the socio-political collective from both ends, and the work dated 1970 shows the continuity of Gandhian values instilled well into the newly formed nation.

In later years, as modernist approaches took roots in Indian art, we can find shifts in the manner in which Gandhi and his collective are imagined. Through metaphors and metonyms, absence of human figures, codified forms and the artists creating a mystery about the identity of the actors in the collective, the Gandhian collective imagination is re-constructed. Most important, the works also show the deconstruction of the dependence, solidarity and reverence that had previously marked the collective. Simultaneously, these works also challenge our perception of the revered icon, in whose re-imagination lie the fears and anxieties of postcolonial India.

The 1990s and Beyond: Deconstruction of Gandhian Philosophy in Indian Life

Though MF Husain in his works such as *Autobiography XIV – "Madrasa Hismania"* (1989) and *Great Men of the Twentieth Century* (1992) situates Gandhi in nationalist frame within the quotidian existence and global politics, in *The Attenborough Panels/ Untitled* (1983; "After Gandhi"), signs of imbalance can be seen emerging. Just like

Arya portrays continuity, Husain's figuration of discontinuity or destabilizing of Gandhian values is apparent in the imbalance of Gandhi's physical stance. Husain's figuration represents almost a break in our perception of Gandhi as intently strong, forward-marching icon (present also in works such as *Dandi March* or *Bapuji*). In these six panels, barring the first one where we also see a flock of goats, Gandhi is seen alone. If Nandalal Bose iconized Gandhi as an emblematic figurehead of India's freedom struggle; in these panels, Gandhi's aloofness does not suggest strength, leadership, firmness, balance and focused action. In every panel, a faceless and at times headless Gandhi is framed in a space with a door behind him, against which he is unable to find himself a comfortable place. In none of the frames is Gandhi seen seated or standing with composure. These images mark a shift from the pre-independent period representations of Gandhi discussed earlier. Possibly, Husain brought for us the early signs of challenges to the Gandhian vision. As Gandhi struggles to find his feet on the ground and the imbalances in the body suggest lack of control, the work opens new patterns of imagination/representation. This new representation begins to emerge through Gandhi's contextualization in new socio-political conflicts of the times.

If the singular Gandhi in *The Attenborough Panels* created for us a mental platform on which the new realities of postcolonial India is set out, to frame our perceptions of the Gandhian ideologies, the 1990s opened new contextual and visual paradigms in which Gandhi is either present or absent. In the day-to-day lives of people, Bose's institutionalization of Gandhi within the illuminations of the *Constitution* seems to waver at times. With the demolition of the Babri Masjid in December 1992, the masses who once formed the sociopolitical collective with Gandhi now are seen dispersing into independent pockets of sectarian identity.

Art and imagination are as much shaped and deliberated by challenges to Gandhi's inclusive nationalism as it inspires the artists to respond to this mass leader. The right-wing political ideologies and multiple acts of divisiveness thwart the responses of artists. In 1995, *Postcards for Gandhi*, a major art project and a seminal art exhibition, was organized by SAHMAT, a Delhi-based artist collective to re/imagine Gandhi in contemporary times as a social actor and a visionary.[10] The project and the exhibitions that followed it are significant from three different vantage points – they create the artists as "the new socio-political collective of Gandhi," encourage the artists/masses to practise the use of postcards as a simple medium of communication[11] and retain the faith in the symbols and philosophy of Gandhi amidst the politics of sectarian turmoil in the country. This postcard idea which developed as an extension of a linocut art workshop organized by Gulam Mohammed Sheikh at MS University, Baroda, was used by Vivan Sundaram, Ram Rahman and Shamshad Husain to engage the artists across the country to respond to the humble postcard, to transform it into an object of interest. The trio invited 100 artists from different parts of the country to participate in this mobilization project. Each artist was asked to create six postcard-sized works. The underlying idea was to usher them to visualize their subjective understanding of Gandhian values and philosophy in contemporary times and to create solidarity and reclaim the same collective energy as exemplified in the pre-independent era. The difference was that here the artist was both the participant and visual respondent. Each work was a part of one large set of postcards, which were grouped to be exhibited (in six different exhibitions) in six different cities in India, all on the same day, on 2 October. *Postcards for Gandhi* also lent to contemporary Indian art, the expansiveness of public art practice and art collection, embedding the Gandhian values of equality. The low-uniform-selling price of each original postcard broke the hierarchy of artistic elitism. The mass production of these postcards further extended their availability for the public. These strategies in planning the project became significant in the envisioning of *Postcards for Gandhi* as a project, an event and a participatory agenda.

Creating Gandhi has also been what Sumathi Ramaswamy has suggested as "rites of passage" for Indian artists.[12] Anupam Sud says the participation in the project was a detour from her involvement with interpersonal human relations in her artistic practice. The invitation to participate evoked her childhood memory of drawing Gandhi on the school blackboard. Sud decided to use nostalgia to re-start her engagement with Gandhi in her adult years and thus, paved way for the creation of the postcards. The dormant experience embedded in her memory came back in present-day times.

In the subjective imagination of the artists, Gandhi surfaces as a symbolic expression of hope and anguish. Indrapramit Roy created a postcard *Untitled (Post Card for Gandhi-1* 1995) (Figure 3.2). In this simple yet evocative work, the artist has played with the contours of Gandhi's head and created multiple forms which are similar and resemble the stamp of Gandhi. Roy also uses new and used stamps of Gandhi. In 16 equal-sized small boxes fitted within the postcard-sized work, there is play and exploration through which the presence and absence of Gandhi are suggested. There is visibility and camouflage, appearance and disappearance, life and death, all attributed to Gandhi's figuration. Through black charcoal marks, layerings of paint and burning the paper to make holes looking like bullets marks, Roy's work exemplifies the anxieties of living in times where Gandhian values are at stake.

There is a shift in the positioning of Gandhi etched by Atul Dodiya, who portrays Gandhi retreating with his back facing the audience in *Lamentation* (1997; Figure 3.3), Gandhi as a witness in *Bapu at Rene Block Gallery, New York 1974* (1998; Figure 3.4), and Gandhi camouflaged amidst the remnants of communal violence in *Broken Branches* (2002). After Nandalal Bose, it is Atul Dodiya who has considered Gandhi as his muse and in his diverse projects used Gandhi to communicate his ideas on the Indian socio-political scenario.[13] Dodiya's art draws inspiration from postmodern aesthetics to portray Gandhi. His borrowings from art history translated into the present-day create unique visual experiences, which generate curiosity to embody newer meanings and simultaneously encapsulate a mystery leaving a space for the viewer's interpretation. In *Lamentation* (1997; Gallery Chemould), a retreating Gandhi is seen with his right hand on a young boy's shoulder, walking towards a railway platform. The two, along with other camouflaged figures of people, are placed towards the canvas's right. On the

FIGURE 3.2 Roy, Indrapramit. *Post Card for Gandhi*. 1995, Collage and Painting on Paper, 5 3/4″ × 3 ½″, *Postcards for Gandhi* – SAHMAT project. *Postcards for Gandhi: 125 Years of Mahatma Gandhi: 1869–1994*, by Indrapramit Roy & Ram Rahman, SAHMAT, New Delhi.

FIGURE 3.3   Dodiya, Atul. *Lamentation.* 1997, Oil and Acrylic with Marble Dust on Canvas, 69″ × 96″, Gallery Chemould, Mumbai.

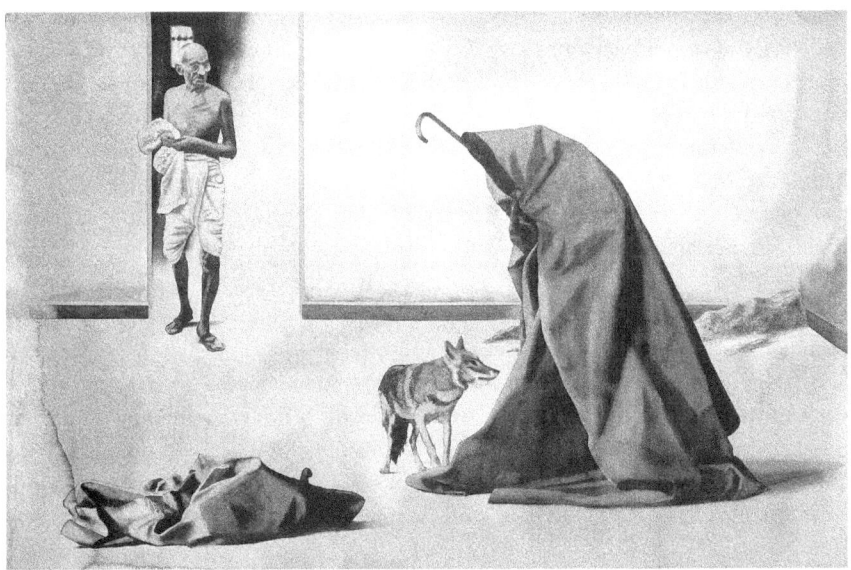

FIGURE 3.4   Dodiya, Atul. *Bapu at Rene Block Gallery, New York.* [1974]1998, watercolour on Paper, 45″ × 70″, Archer Art Gallery, Ahmedabad.

left are painted two large figures of a mother and a young daughter borrowed from Picasso's *Mother and Child [First Steps]* (1943; artsy.com). The mother is teaching her daughter to walk. These figures are surrounded by angels crying and lamenting the situation. The angels are reminiscent of Giotto's lamenting angels from Giotto's Fresco di Bondone *Lamentation of the Death of Christ* [1304–13] (Wikiart). Dodiya's intertextual references and their invested meaning and his forms of Gandhi with the masses challenge our imagination of the relationship between the two.

Gandhi resurfaces in *Bapu at Rene Block Gallery, New York 1974* (1998; Figure 3.4), where Dodiya portrays him as a witness to a situation and not as the key actor of an event or a leader. He chooses to bring Gandhi (who died decades back) into contemporary times, to observe the artist's present socio-political times.[14] Almost as if Dodiya was himself curious to know as to what would have been Gandhi's reaction to India's different social identities struggling to claim space, he situates Gandhi at a distance, in a moment of thoughtful observation. Gandhi watches a coyote and a man wrapped mysteriously in a large felt cloth with only a stick popping out. The two actors are in a performance, which is suggestive of a confrontation. Dodiya borrowed the symbolism of the coyote from the American Indians who consider the coyote as a sacred animal. And the covered shepherd as the mysterious controller from the 1974 performance by Joseph Beuys, *I like America and America likes Me* (performed at Rene Gallery in New York). Dodiya uses it to mark his method of communication with the viewer. In these works, the social actors replaced by Dodiya evoke new routes we can embark in our imaginings of Gandhi.

With the crippling communal violence in 2002, these new routes become more emphatic in their emotive impact that Dodiya recreates by using fragmentary objects in *Broken Branches*. He replaces human figures with metaphoric and metonymic imagery such as billboard paintings, used prosthetic limbs, hand-coloured framed photographs and objects and instrumental tools for human use (Figure 3.5), which are curated by the artist in arrangements within locked museum cabinets. The people are conspicuous by their absence, but their presence is felt in the fragments, which reveal the lives of a nation experiencing conflict, grief, fear, struggle and hope. Amidst the several cabinets arranged within the room, two chairs and a table were also placed as a seating arrangement. The audience becomes a temporary inhabitant of the room and a witness to Gandhi's photograph placed inside the cabinet, which is somewhat not the focus amidst the assemblages of curious objects. These are times of chaos and dissonance performed by the very people, for whom Gandhi devoted his life. In the works discussed above, the collective is questioned. There is also hope of resurgence.

The rewriting of history with a desire for sociopolitical solidarity surfaces in *Naavu* (2012) by Iranna G.R. (Figure 3.6). The artist has exploited metonymy as a tool of communication with the Gandhian *khadaun* (wooden slippers) as central focus of the painting. The multitudes in the work takes us back to Dandi March and the formation of the collective and to its desire for progression and

FIGURE 3.5   Dodiya, Atul. *Broken Branches* (detail image). 2002, Mix Media Installation, Asia Art Archive, Hong Kong.

FIGURE 3.6   Iranna, GR. *NAVU (We Together)*. 2012, wood, metal and found objects, acrylic, 15" × 60." *Our Time for a Future Caring*, India Pavilion at the 58th International Art Exhibition, 11 May 2019–24 November 2019, Curated by Roobina Karode, La Biennale di Venezia. Kiran Nadar Museum of Art.

egalitarianism as depicted in the diverse participations found in the *Haripura posters*. The gigantic assemblage on the wall shows *khadaun* hung on the wall facing right. Each footwear is carrying with it objects such as musical instruments, cooking vessels, tools, notifying the marcher's identity. The work provokes us to find Gandhi in the people or the people in Gandhi.

Perhaps the most abstract, philosophical and transcendent imagining of Gandhi and his people has been by SH Raza, in whose works the Gandhian ethos, philosophy of life and values find a resolved attainment. In what is called "the seven paintings" of Raza concerning his works on Gandhi created in 2013, there is a distilled expression of visual and conceptual solace. In *Hey Ram* (2013), *Satya* (2013), *Shanti* (2013; Figure 3.7), *Peed Parai* (2013), *Sanmati* (2013), *Swadharm* (2012) and *Thoughts of Gandhiji* (2012), Raza incorporates within its simplicity not just his concern for the Gandhian principles but the knowledge of the entire universe.

Raza's use of the *bindu* with the painted text *Shanti* in Hindi, as in *Shanti* (acrylic on canvas, 2013), shows a black hole in the centre with girdles around it. These are symbols from his oeuvre, signs of peace, into which he infuses Gandhi's words. The other paintings also show a similar visual and conceptual strategy. In *Hey Ram*, *Satya* and *Peer Parai*, the brushstrokes in subdued, muted colours of paint unmark the areas through diagonal or horizontal divisions. These spaces painted with empathic strokes are meditative, and their lack of accompaniment of a physical form is compensated with the inclusion of texts. Raza juxtaposes with/superimposes upon the strokes words/concepts popularly associated with Gandhi. This is his artistic ploy, marking a sharp contrast to the ushering of our visualization by Dodiya. Through the associated text, thoughts on Lord Ram, meditation on truth and peace, and understanding the pain of the others seem to echo in our imagination. Raza creates in our minds, a visual realm to decode the contextual abstraction in the works. Both Gandhi and his people are absent as figurative, metaphorical or metonymical representations but are evoked in our imagination. These works also provide the viewers a free space to revive the ideas of the Gandhian ethos beyond the boundaries of time and space. In a way, reading the text in the painting becomes an act of remembering, reaffirming and imagining the Gandhian values.

The universal element is reiterated in *Shanti*, where a large black dot in the centre with girdles gradually circling it stands out as the *bindu* (a point). It is a significant symbol from his oeuvre. The *bindu* is centre of the universe, a simple and yet an all-encompassing a symbol. The *bindu* is the point of culmination of our imagination, the acceptance of our faith and point of surrender to the universe. By juxtaposing the word *Shanti* in the painting with the use of *bindu*, Raza extends the Gandhian concept within the larger context of universal time, space and energy. It appears as if Raza wishes to understand Gandhi's relationship with his people through the propagation of peace. The core that is the *bindu* along with the insertion of the text becomes Raza's suggestive methodology. This is also seen in *Sanmati* (good judgement 2013), where

FIGURE 3.7   Raza, SH. *Shanti*. 2013, acrylic on canvas, 150″ × 120″, Visual Arts
Gallery, India.

geometrical forms suggesting sacred and spiritual connotations are paired with
words sourced from a popular devotional song. The unique characteristic of
the visualization of Gandhi which emerges in these paintings is the pairing of
text (that has an obvious meaning for us) with coloured, flat spaces within a
single frame without any forms. This contextual abstraction of Raza makes the
visualization on the part of the viewer elastic. Text as a form and viewing as a
cognitive act enabled through reading becomes obvious in *Swadharm* (religion
of the self 2012) and *Thoughts on Gandhiji* (2012). In *Swadharm*, Raza uses words
of Vinoba Bhave and in *Thoughts on Gandhiji* the words of Gandhi spread across
the canvas. Painted in black, over layers of brush strokes, the text becomes

an exercise in meditative painting. Raza's works re-install hope. The seemingly simplified abstraction withholds the complexities of a chaotic world, in which both the icon and his people have lived. Raza ushers us to believe that the world envisioned by Gandhi is a possible one. He makes us search for it in his works.

In the trajectory of the works of art discussed in this chapter, it can be seen that the referential dependence on Gandhi has been a constant in artistic engagements with the themes of sociopolitical narratives. We see subjective approaches by artists in thought and in form. This is apparent in their selection of an ideological concern or a life segment of Gandhi adapted in their works. The artists' perception of Gandhian ideologies remains undiluted. But, in light of the changing participation of the other actors of the sociopolitical collective, the visualization and contextualization of Gandhi undergoes changes. His ideologies earlier revered, are later challenged and deconstructed. In this course, Gandhi the leader also becomes a witness to the times in which the artist lives. In the hands of the artists as the "new socio-political collective," Gandhi is resurrected and his ideologies are institutionalized through art. Under the umbrella of what these works offer to our understanding of Gandhi, one can ask, if Gandhi can at all be seen in isolation? Even in his solitary figure, his "aloneness" itself appears as a metaphor of strength for the masses across times. In the imagination of the Indian artists, Gandhi, his people and his ideologies coalesce to form the subjects of artistic meditation. The coding and decoding of the layers of their relationship prompted through their representation in visual formats serve as documentation of our times.

Notes

1 The word *harijan* was a title given by Gandhi to the marginalized people of the lowest social category in the Hindu caste system. However, this term has been mired in controversy with the marginalized sections considering *harijans* as a condescending term and instead, preferring the more political term, Dalit.
2 See *In the Untouchable Quarters,* Drawing in Pen and Ink, Pre-1932, The Internet Archive, Retrieved from, https://archive.org/details/mahatmagandhiske00desa/page/66/mode/2up. Accessed 6 September 2020 and *Gandhi and People Gathering*, 1947, Drawing in Pen and Ink, Virtual Exhibition: Bapu, National Gallery of Modern Art, New Delhi, http://ngmaindia.gov.in/virtual-tour-of-bapu.asp. Accessed 18 November 2020.
3 See also the artworks – *Gandhiji at Dandi* by Ramendranath Chakraborty (Tuli 184), *Gyarah Murti* by Roy Chowdhury (probashionline 2016).
4 This perspective of cohesiveness in social diversity becomes a challenge as right-wing politics in post-independent India sought to contain art. However, as exemplified by SAHMAT, this censorship is countered by art.
5 See *News of Gandhiji's Death,* 1948, Oil on canvas, 85.1 × 85.1 cm (33.5 × 33.5 inches), Haus der Kunst, Munich. Retrieved from, https://postwar.hausderkunst.de/en/artworks-artists/artworks/news-of-gandhijis-death-die-nachricht-von-gandhis-tod. Accessed 10 October 2020.
6 The drafting committee of the *Constitution* was appointed on 29 August 1947. The assembly chaired by Dr BR Ambedkar consisted of 389 members, and it took them almost three years to draft the preambles of the *Constitution*. Finally, after being signed by

all the members of the Constituent Assembly, the *Constitution* came into implementation on 26 January 1950.

7 Siva Kumar mentions that it was sometime in October 1949 that Nandalal was invited to illuminate the Constitution. This was followed by invitation to PBN Raiza to write the Constitution in calligraphy.

8 See also *Portrait of Father of the Nation (Gandhiji's Dandi March)* (Bose Part XVII "Official Language" *The Constitution*) *Bapuji the Peace-Maker – his tour in the riot affected areas of Noakhali* (Part XVIII "Emergency Provisions" *The Constitution*).

9 S Chakraborty states that scientist KB Joshi . . . was working in an oil mill in Newasa, Maharashtra, in the 1930s when he met with Gandhi. According to CV Puntambelkar, who worked with HMPI for 39 years, Joshi was already working on paper produced from cotton linters and rags, and which he showed to Gandhi as an alternative to the paper being imported at the time. The latter, averse to machines being used for paper production, encouraged Joshi to work on handmade paper instead (qtd. S Chakraborty *Sahapedia*, 30 January 2020).

10 Sahmat, founded in 1989, is a group of artists championing an egalitarian socio-political system in India by involving different visual and performance artists and theoreticians in their projects.

11 Postcards were Gandhi's favoured medium of communication to reach out to the masses. As an inexpensive means of dialogue, Gandhi believed that the power of the postcard was far-reaching and the choice of using it was an egalitarian act.

12 Ramaswamy stated "[o]ne of the things that got me really intrigued in the course of this project is the fact that drawing, painting, sculpting Gandhi is almost a rite of passage with artists of India – and not just in Gandhi's lifetime but especially since the 1990s. Both the most famous of artists, and then newest have produced at least one work on him" (IANS 15 October 2020).

13 This is just one of the Gandhian projects by Atul Dodiya. In his series of works titled *Re-Imagining the Mahatma,* Dodiya has chosen to paint historical events. However, in the context of this paper, I have selected only some of his works for discussion.

14 However, Dodiya's symbolic forms suggest the conflicting times are not India specific. This lack of specificity also makes his works universal in appeal.

Works Cited

Adimoolan, K. M. *Gandhiji with Sardar Patel. 1969*, Black Ink & Wash, 56.2 X 66.5 cms, Curated Exhibition and Auction Catalogue, Osian's -Connoisseurs of Art Pvt. Ltd., 2002. *A Historical Epic: India in the Making 1757–1950: From Surrender to Revolt, Swaraj to Responsibility*, edited by Neville Tuli, Osian, 2002, p. 198.

———. *Morning Walk with Gandhij, Khan Abdul Ghaffar Khan & Jawaharlal Nehru.*1969, Pen & Ink, 72.7 X 57.3 cms, Curated Exhibition and Auction Catalogue, Osian's -Connoisseurs of Art Pvt. Ltd., 2002, *A Historical Epic: India in the Making 1757–1950: From Surrender to Revolt Swaraj to Responsibility*, edited by Neville Tuli, Osian, 2002, p. 201.

Arya, Badrinath. *Gandhiji: Harmony of Religions.* 1970, Watercolour & Wash on Board, 101.0 X 65.5 cms, Curated Exhibition and Auction Catalogue, Osian's-Connoisseurs of Art Pvt. Ltd. *A Historical Epic: India in the Making 1757–1950: From Surrender to Revolt Swaraj to Responsibility*, edited by Neville Tuli, Osian, 2002, p. 242.

Beuys, Joseph. *I Like America and America Likes Me.* 1974, Performed at Rene Gallery, New York.

Bondone, Giotto di. *Lamentation (The Mourning of Christ).* 1304–13, Fresco, 200 x 185 cm. Scrovegni (Arena) Chapel, Padua, www.wikiart.org/en/giotto/lamentation-the-mourning-of-christ-1306-1.

Borges, Jane. "Gandhi Was Master Choreographer of His Own Image." *Mid-Day*, 4 Oct. 2020, www.mid-day.com/articles/gandhi-was-master-choreographer-of-his-own-image/23024222. Accessed 12 Oct. 2020.

Bose, Nandalal. *Bapuji 12.4.1930*. 1930, Linocut Print, *Virtual Exhibition: Bapu*, National Gallery of Modern Art, http://ngmaindia.gov.in/virtual-tour-of-bapu.asp. Accessed 10 Oct. 2020.

———. *Babuji the Peace-Maker – His Tour in the Riot Affected Areas of Noakhali, The Constitution of India*. World Digital Library, p. 315, www.wdl.org/en/item/2672/view/1/315/. Accessed 11 Oct. 2020.

———. *Dandi March -1930*. 1930, Tempera on Wood. Photos – *The Art of Being Gandhi*.

Chakraborty, Ramendranath. *Gandhiji at Dandi*. Late 1930s. "Curated Exhibition and Auction Catalogue, Osian's -Connoisseurs of Art Pvt. Ltd." *A Historical Epic: India in the Making 1757–1950: From Surrender to Revolt Swaraj to Responsibility*, edited by Neville Tuli, Osian, 2002, p. 184.

Chakraborty, Shruti. "The Indian Constitution: Not Just Any Piece of Paper." *Sahapedia*, 30 Jan. 2020, www.sahapedia.org/indian-constitution-not-just-any-piece-paper. Accessed 15 Oct. 2020.

Chowdhury, Devi Prasad Roy. *Gyarah Murti* (Sculptures). "Man Who Has Left a Mark on the Indian Currency Note." *Sudipto Sengupta*, 13 Feb. 2016, www.probashionline.com/deviprasad-roychowdhury/. Accessed 30 Sept. 2020.

Collection HindSwaraj; JaiGyan, Digitizing Sponsor Public. Resource.Org, Contributor Public Resource.

Gandhi, Dhiren. *Love- The Sustainer*. 1943, Woodcut Print, 36 x 27 cm, Collection of Anil Relia. "Reducing Myself to Zero: The Art of *Aparigraha*." Sumathi Ramswamy, *MARG Gandhi & Aesthetics*, vol. 71, no. 2, Dec. 2019, p. 7, https://marg-art.org/reader/?order-id=T3JkZXI6Nzgx&line-id=T3JkZXJMaW5lOjEyNzg=. Accessed 10 Oct. 2020.

Husain, M. F. *Autobiography XIV: 'Madrasa Hismania' Boarding School in Baroda, Nationalist Leader Abbas Tyabji Its patron. On Gandhi Jayanti Day I Did a Sketch of Gandhi on Black Board. Our School Uniform Was Gandhi Topi. Medium of Instruction Gujarati, Urdu and Arabic. Maulavi Akbar Taking the Class. I am Sitting Holding a Fan Next to My Life-Long Friend Arshad (specs)*, 1989, Acrylic on Canvas. From Rashda Siddiqui, *In Conversation with Husain Paintings*, Books Today, 2001.

———. *The Attenborough Panels/Untitled*. 1983, Acrylic on Canvas, 90 x 32 inches. x 6 Nos, "After Gandhi." www.aiconcontemporary.com/exhibitions/m-f-husain-the-attenborough-panels/selected-works. Accessed 10 Oct. 2020.

———. *Great Men of the Twentieth Century*. 1992, "Mahatma Gandhi MF Husain Painting 15." https://webneel.com/daily/15-mahatma-gandhi-mf-husain-painting. Accessed 6 Oct. 2020.

Khosa, Pandit Somnath. *Gandhiji with Khan Abdul Ghaffar Khan and Others in Northwest Frontier Province in 1938*. 1960, Oil on Bromide Paper pasted on Board, 73.5 X 98.0 cms, Curated Exhibition and Auction Catalogue, Osian's -Connoisseurs of Art Pvt. Ltd., Mumbai, 2002, *A Historical Epic: India in the Making 1757–1950: From Surrender to Revolt, Swaraj to Responsibility*, edited by Neville Tuli, Osian, 2002, p. 199.

———. *Gandhiji Visiting Political Prisoners at DumDum Jail in 1947*. 1960, Oil on Bromide Paper pasted on Board 75.8 x 100.9 cms, Curated Exhibition and Auction Catalogue, Osian's -Connoisseurs of Art Pvt. Ltd., 2002, *A Historical Epic: India in the Making 1757–1950: From Surrender to Revolt Swaraj to Responsibility*, edited by Neville Tuli, Osian, 2002, pp. 222–23.

Kumar, Raman Siva. "From Swadeshi to the Constitution – Nandalal Bose and the Nationalist Project." *History for Peace: A Seagull Foundation Initiative 2020*, www.academia.edu/44047503/From_Swadeshi_to_the_Constitution_Nandalal_Bose_and_the_Nationalist_Project. Accessed 10 Sept. 2020.

"Listen in Episode XVII, Gandhi and Me: A Conversation with Atul Dodiya." *YouTube*, Uploaded by Sunaparanta -Goa Centre for the Arts, 4 Oct. 2020, www.youtube.com/watch?v=Nwx2QCfaaQs&t=1844s. Accessed 8 Oct. 2020.

Maharathi, Upendra. *Bloody Sunset*. Tempera on Paper, *Virtual* Exhibition: *Bapu*, National Gallery of Modern Art, http://ngmaindia.gov.in/virtual-tour-of-bapu.asp. Accessed 10 Oct. 2020.

———. *Fate of Three Great Men, Gandhi, Buddha, Christ*, Water Colour Painting, *Virtual* Exhibition: *Bapu*, National Gallery of Modern Art, http://ngmaindia.gov.in/virtual-tour-of-bapu.asp. Accessed 10 Oct. 2020.

"Mahatma Gandhi Was a Master Choreographer of His Own Image." Interview, by IANS, 15 Oct. 2020, https://newsd.in/mahatma-gandhi-was-a-master-choreographer-of-his-own-image-ians-interview/. Accessed 12 Oct. 2020.

Mann, Jon. "When Joseph Beuys Locked Himself in a Room with a Live Coyote." *Artsy.net*, 3 Nov. 2017, www.artsy.net/article/artsy-editorial-joseph-beuys-locked-room-live-coyote.

Moss, Jessica, and Ram Rahman. "Tribute to Gandhi: 1994–1995-Postcards for Gandhi." *The Sahmat Collective: Art and Activism in India Since 1989*. Smart Museum of Art, U of Chicago P, 2013, p. 134.

"Nandalal Bose: The Man Who Illustrated the Constitution of India." *The Heritage Lab*, 25 Jan. 2018, www.theheritagelab.in/nandalal-bose-art/. Accessed 5 Oct. 2020.

Picasso, Pablo. *Mother and Child (First Steps)*. 1943, Revised Summer 1943, Oil on Canvas, 130.2 × 97.1 cm, www.artsy.net/artwork/pablo-picasso-mother-and-child-first-steps. Accessed 5 Oct. 2020.

Postcards for Gandhi: 125 Years of Mahatma Gandhi: 1869–1994. Postcards for Gandhi (a New Set of 100 Postcards, 2018) 150 Years of Mahatma Gandhi: 1869–2018. SAHMAT, Ram Rahman, "Thematic Ad-Portfolio: Postcards for Gandhi. MARG." *Gandhi & Aesthetics*, vol. 71, no. 2, Dec. 2019, pp. 1–9, https://marg-art.org/reader/?order-id=T3JkZXI6Nzgx&line id=T3JkZXJMaW5lOjEyNzQ=. Accessed 5 Oct. 2020.

Prakar, Akar. *Gandhi in Raza*. 2017, Bose et al. In Association with Raza Foundation in Association with Mapin Publishing, Ahmedabad.

Ramaswamy, Sumathi. *Gandhi in the Gallery-The Art of Disobedience*. Roli Books, 2020.

Ramaswamy, Sumathi, and Katie King. "Growing Up to Paint Bapu." *B Is for Bapu-Gandhi in the Art of the Child in Modern India*, https://sites.duke.edu/bisforbapu/about-the-project/growing-up-to-paint-bapu/. Accessed 7 Oct. 2020.

Raza, S. H. *Hey Ram*. 2013, 23.5" x 23.5", Acrylic on Canvas. *Gandhi in Raza*, Akar Prakar, 2017, in Association with Raza Foundation and Mapin Publishing, Ahmedabad, p. 15, https://issuu.com/mapin/docs/gandhi_in_raza. Accessed 28 Sept. 2020.

———. *Peed Parai*. 2013, 59" x 59", Acrylic on Canvas. *Gandhi in Raza*, Akar Prakar, 2017, in Association with Raza Foundation and Mapin Publishing, Ahmedabad, p. 21, https://issuu.com/mapin/docs/gandhi_in_raza. Accessed 28 Sept. 2020.

———. *Sanmati*. 2013, 59" x 59", Acrylic on Canvas. *Gandhi in Raza*, Akar Prakar, 2017, in Association with Raza Foundation and Mapin Publishing, Ahmedabad, p. 23, https://issuu.com/mapin/docs/gandhi_in_raza. Accessed 28 Sept. 2020.

———. *Satya*. 2013, 59" x 47.25", Acrylic on Canvas. *Gandhi in Raza*, Akar Prakar, 2017, in Association with Raza Foundation and Mapin Publishing, Ahmedabad, p. 17, https://issuu.com/mapin/docs/gandhi_in_raza. Accessed 28 Sept. 2020.

————. *Swadharm*. 2013, 59" x 59", Acrylic on Canvas. *Gandhi in Raza*, Akar Prakar, 2017, in Association with Raza Foundation and Mapin Publishing, Ahmedabad, p. 25, https://issuu.com/mapin/docs/gandhi_in_raza. Accessed 28 Sept. 2020.

————. *Thoughts on Gandhiji*. 2013, 59" x 47.25", Acrylic on Canvas. *Gandhi in Raza*, Akar Prakar, 2017, in Association with Raza Foundation and Mapin Publishing, Ahmedabad, p. 27, https://issuu.com/mapin/docs/gandhi_in_raza. Accessed 28 Sept. 2020.

Somak Ghoshal, *Livemint*, 2 Oct. 2020, www.livemint.com/mint-lounge/features/photos-the-art-of-being-gandhi-11601612229797.html. Accessed 10 Oct. 2020.

————. *The Farmer* 1937. "Nandalal Bose: The Man Who Illustrated the Constitution of India." *The Heritage Lab*, 25 Jan. 2018, www.theheritagelab.in/nandalal-bose-art/. Accessed 10 Oct. 2020.

————. *The Female Musician* 1937. "Nandalal Bose: The Man Who Illustrated the Constitution of India." *The Heritage Lab*, 25 Jan. 2018, www.theheritagelab.in/nandalal-bose-art/. Accessed 10 Oct. 2020.

————. *Haripura Posters*. 1937. Tempera on Paper. "Nandalal Bose: The Man Who Illustrated the Constitution of India." *The Heritage Lab*, 25 Jan. 2018, www.theheritagelab.in/nandalal-bose-art/. Accessed 10 Oct. 2020.

————. *Haripura Posters*. 1937. Tempera on Paper. *Papermaking* 1937, *Wool Spinning* 1937, *Blacksmith* 1937, *Virtual* Exhibition: *Bapu*, National Gallery of Modern Art, http://ngmaindia.gov.in/virtual-tour-of-bapu.asp. Accessed 10 Oct. 2020.

————. *Netaji Subhas Chandra Bose and Other Patriots Trying to Liberate Mother India from Outside India*. *The Constitution of India*. World Digital Library, p. 327, www.wdl.org/en/item/2672/view/1/327/. Accessed 10 Oct. 2020.

————. *Portrait of Father of the Nation (Gandhiji's Dandi March)*. *The Constitution of India*. World Digital Library, p. 305, www.wdl.org/en/item/2672/view/1/305/. Accessed 10 Oct. 2020.

————. *The Woman Milking the Cow* 1937. "Nandalal Bose: The Man Who Illustrated the Constitution of India." *The Heritage Lab*, 25 Jan. 2018, www.theheritagelab.in/nandalal-bose-art/. Accessed 2 Oct. 2020.

————. *The Wrestlers* 1937. "Nandalal Bose: The Man Who Illustrated the Constitution of India." *The Heritage Lab*, 25 Jan. 2018, www.theheritagelab.in/nandalal-bose-art/. Accessed 2 Oct. 2020.

PART II

Consumptions of Gandhi

Articulations or Disarticulations?

4

MAHATMA IN MEMESCAPE

Making of Gandhi in Participatory Digital Culture

Haris Qadeer

"I should slip out of the public gaze," Mohandas Karamchand Gandhi expressed his desire to Polak in May 1911 (Lelyveld 93). Though, as mentioned in Joseph Lelyveld's *Great Soul: Mahatma Gandhi and His Struggle with India*, Gandhi might have had a momentary desire to escape the public eye and devote his time to farming and educating people, but it will not be gainsaying that he is one of the few political personalities in the world whose public and private life has been unremittingly subjected to repeated scrutiny, both during his life and after his assassination. He was not only a national leader of India and an icon of protest but also a Mahatma (great soul) for his followers. According to the historian Shahid Amin (1988), Gandhi's deification and unofficial canonization started after visiting the Gorakhpur district in the 1920s. Public gaze played an indispensable role in the deification, and it may be speculated that Gandhi was aware of the power of the public gaze as he openly exhorted people to observe him. Dipesh Chakrabarty claims that Gandhi invited a public gaze on himself and shunned the idea of privacy: "'Watch me closely' was his instruction to those who wanted to study him" (61). He was observed by people who venerated him as divine and saintly – they waited for hours to have his *darshan* (religious viewing of sacred idols and saints). He was scrutinized by the people who ridiculed his appearance and his way of life. It is well known that Winston Churchill once disparagingly dubbed him a "half-naked seditious faker" (Tayyebulla 92). However, it was not only Churchill but also various other politicians who were consumed by the Gandhian myth. Sean Scalmer (2011) shows how the imagination of English intelligentsia was preoccupied with Gandhi's half-naked body.[1]

The multiplicity of the gazes that Gandhi received might be one of the probable reasons for his polyphonic representations: his life has been widely discussed, debated, hailed, assailed, derided, but never ignored. While he was alive, a complex iconography celebrating his life began to evolve, and in his afterlives,

DOI: 10.4324/9781003145479-7

he continues to be a part of our culture – he is re-invoked in various forms of official documentation and represented through public memorials. Rudolph claims that the renewed interest in Gandhi's image and Gandhism "began to recuperate in the 1980s when a postmodern Gandhi began to take shape" (32). The author credits Richard Attenborough's film *Gandhi* (1982) for rekindling the interest and explains how a "newly remembered Gandhi" began to "inspire and legitimize a burgeoning civil society of social and political movements and not-for-profit, non-governmental and voluntary organizations" (32). Cartoonists, painters, performers and film-makers have presented their subjective interpretations of Gandhi over the last few decades. In an interesting study, Rachel Dwyer throws into relief Gandhi's substantial presence in various documentary footages of the Indian freedom movement, which were later edited into various documentaries. She also demonstrates how "Gandhi appears as a character in many historical costume dramas (fictional stories set in historical times) about the freedom struggle, where his ideas play a key role in the salvation of the hero/heroine" (350).

Though most of the visual artists and film-makers have emphasized the spiritual stature of Gandhi, the gaze of cartoonists, to a great extent, has neutralized the spiritualized portrayal of Gandhi by depicting him as a commoner.[2] In the genre of graphic satire, most of the cartoonists – from English cartoonists such as Leslie Gilbert Illingworth (1902–1979) and David Low (1891–1963) to Indian cartoonists such as RK Laxman (1921–2015), OV Vijayan (1930–2005) and NK Ranga (1925–2002) – have repeatedly reworked "the image of Gandhi to develop strategies of protest that interrogate state formation, the marginalization of the masses, and emergent capitalisms" (Devadawson 1).

Given the enormous attention that Gandhi, "the Saint of Status Quo" (Roy 18), has received from the visual artists worldwide, he could rightly be regarded as the visual icon of India. Recent studies on Gandhi's iconographies by scholars such as Seema Bawa (2018) and Gayatri Sinha (2013) demonstrate the preoccupations of various visual artists with Gandhi and Gandhism. Bawa explores how postcolonial history has imagined the powerful persona of Gandhi. She notes "the imagery of Gandhi created through his iconography itself carries a symbolic power for audiences, especially the masses" (55). Sinha studies the images of Gandhi circulating in popular culture and the contemporary art, and she emphasizes how "as a visual monument, the space that Gandhi occupies is between the mythical and the narrative of nationhood, a symbol of immanence and mobility" (113). However, most of the studies that deal with the representations of Gandhi in the visual cultures have ignored his iconography in the internet's virtual sphere.

This essay seeks to address the gaps in the scholarships and explore multiple representations of Gandhi in the digital sphere of the internet. The focus of this chapter is on the portrayal of Gandhi and Gandhism in the mass-mediated genre of internet memes which are "now present in the public sphere not as sporadic entities, but as enormous groups of texts and images" (Shifman, "Cultural Logic" 341). It also examines how, in the absence of formal gatekeeping, a reverse process of "de-Mahatmafication" (decanonization and de-spiritualization) is being attempted in the participatory digital culture – a culture driven by hyper-mimetic logic.[3] It investigates Gandhi memeplex (primarily photo-based memes) to explore temporal transition in his iconic photos and analyse how his memes become a contested site of meanings altered and repurposed by prosumers (a contraction of the words producer and consumer) according to their specific ideologies. While analysing the representations of Gandhi in the virtual sphere, one may begin by asking the following questions: Why is it essential to examine Gandhi's virtual iconographies? What might be the purpose behind his resurrection in the memescape? What kind of gaze is cast upon him by internet users? How are his ideas and philosophies discussed and debated in the vernacular discourses of netizens?

The essay proceeds in four stages: it begins with a brief discussion on the internet memes, and in the second section, it examines Gandhi's memes through content, form and stance and speculates on the reasons for his presence in the virtual sphere. The last two sections of the essay dwell upon Gandhi's fasting and non-violence, the two crucial aspects of his philosophy, to understand how internet users are reinterpreting Gandhian values in the digital age activism. The primary source of the study is based on the online archives of Gandhi memes available on various meme aggregators, social networking sites and other online platforms. Given the enormous numbers of memes circulating on Gandhi, the memes analysed in the present study are neither exhaustive nor conclusive in representing how Gandhi is depicted in the memescape. A few representative memes related to the central arguments have been examined in the paper.

Memes and Memescape

Internet memes, shortened as "meme," now have become common currency in the digital world, but they were debated long before the internet era. The evolutionary biologist Richard Dawkins coined the term in *The Selfish Gene* (1976). The etymology of the word meme can be traced to the Greek word *mimema*, signifying something which is imitated. Dawkins clipped the word to rhyme with gene and used the term to describe gene-like spreadable units of culture that spread from person to person. He described meme as: "a unit of cultural transmission, or a unit of *imitation*. 'Mimeme' comes from a suitable Greek root, but I want a monosyllable that sounds a bit like 'gene'" (192). He explains:

> Examples of memes are tunes, ideas, catch-phrases, clothes fashions, ways of making pots or building arches. Just as genes propagate themselves in the gene pool by leaping from body to body via sperm or eggs, so memes propagate themselves in the meme pool by leaping from brain to brain via a process which, in the broad sense, can be called imitation. If a scientist hears, or reads about, a good idea, he passes it on to his colleagues and students. He mentions it in his articles and lectures. If the idea catches on, it can be said to propagate itself, spreading from brain to brain.

(192)

Like genes, memes are replicators that undergo variation, competition, selection and retention. Thus, for Dawkins, memes are analogous to genes in their capability to transmit information, and like them, they can survive in a competitive environment through "longevity, fecundity, and copying-fidelity" (194). Though most scholars credit Dawkins for coining the term, there are some disagreements.[4] The term meme through postulated by a biologist was subsequently adopted and adapted by scholars of various academic disciplines such as anthropology, folklore, literature, linguistics, philosophy and psychology. In a recent short video by the advertising agency Saatchi & Saatchi, Richard Dawkins explains how the term meme has mutilated and evolved and has been "hijacked" (Vincent) by internet users. In the video, Dawkins' voice transmogrifies into an auto-tuned song about internet memes – a song about the appropriation of the term meme in netizen's vernacular discourses.

In his essay "The Language of the Internet," Patrick Davidson gives an "academic definition" of the term and postulates: "an internet meme is a piece of culture, typically a joke, which gains influence through online transmission" (122). Like Davidson, Börzsei, too, focuses on humour as the most important element of memes; she describes internet meme as "a form of visual entertainment" (5) present in many different formats such as a still image, an image with a phrase/quote/movie catchphrases or humorous slogan, an animated GIF (Graphics Interchange Format) or even an edited video. Developing Dawkins's idea, Susan Blackmore in *The Meme Machine* (1999) emphasizes imitation as the main feature of the meme, arguing that "a meme is whatever it is that is passed on by imitation" (43). Internet memes can spread in their original forms by the users, through "likes" and "share" options provided by different online platforms such as Twitter, Instagram and Facebook, or they can be created via software available on different websites and smartphones. While referring to memes as a conceptual troublemaker, Shifman identifies three main characteristics of memes: (i) share common characteristics of content, form and/or stance; (ii) created with awareness of each other; and (iii) circulated, imitated and transformed via the internet by multiple users ("Digital Culture" 367).

Davidson and Börzsei trace the genealogy of memes in the digital sphere to the rise of emoticons in the 1980s. According to Davidson, "emoticons come from the Internet's childhood" (125) and were created by Scott E Fahlman, a user of text-based social network USENET, to avoid "misinterpreted humour" in virtual communication. He added an emoticon of a smiling face, a symbol that he lifted from the pre-internet time. The emoticons' primary purpose was to inform (pass the non-verbal, non-textual information) and entertain members who were part of the network. The smiley faces gained popularity in many other online communities. Davidson observes "this practice of contextualizing one's written messages with an emoticon to indicate emotional intent has become widespread. Today there are countless other pseudo-pictograms of expressions and objects which are regularly added to typed communication. Emoticons are a meme" (124). From emoticons and internet jokes, memes have metamorphosed into an important way of interaction in the virtual sphere. Like many Web 2.0 applications, memes spread from person to person and represent the general mindset of the users. Interestingly, Gandhi's digital iconographies appear to follow a reverse cycle of metamorphosis on the internet – the Gandhi memes were trending years before the advent of his emoticon avatar founded by Twitter India in 2018 to celebrate his 150th birthday.[5]

Virtual Sphere, Participatory Culture and Gandhi's Resurrection

For Habermas (1991), the public sphere is a domain of social life in which public opinion is formed. As an idea, it can be understood as open and democratic social spaces and public spaces in which public opinion is formed out of the rational public debate. The idea of public sphere is based on the notion of participatory culture and public opinion. With the advent of participatory Web 2.0, views and opinions are being actively articulated on many online platforms. Various scholars have advocated the application of Habermas' formulations to the digital sphere. Jones maintains "cyberspace is promoted as social space because it is made by people, and thus as a "new public space" it conjoins mythical traditional narratives of progress with the strong modern impulses towards self-fulfilment and personal development" (22), whereas Papacharissi thinks, "a new public space is not synonymous with a new public sphere. . . . A virtual space enhances discussion; a virtual sphere enhances democracy" (14). Application platforms mark the Web 2.0 spaces for facilitating user-generated content, and it has given rise to a culture of participation. The culture is akin to Henry Jenkin's idea of the participatory culture postulated in his book *Textual Poachers* (1992).[6] While differentiating between participation and spectatorship, Jenkins examines the process by which fans respond to popular media – they are not merely the passive consumers of the popular texts but "become active participants in the construction and circulation of textual meanings" (24). The creative process of participation involves remixing and appropriation of the original material. Instead of merely consuming the information, fans participate in the cultural exchanges as producers or prosumers. Similar trends can be observed among the Indian internet users who form the second-largest group of active internet users worldwide. A surge can be seen in the penetration of the internet among the rural and the urban masses in India from the last decade. According to a report published by the internet and Mobile Association of India, 451 million active internet users are in India (India 2013). Web 2.0 has enabled people to consume, produce and disseminate information on the virtual sphere. On the one hand, it empowers people to voice their opinions through digital activism, but on the other hand, it is also misused by various individuals as well as groups for hate politics, trolling and propaganda.

In the last few years, Gandhi appears to have become a favourite of the meme enthusiasts. A simple google search on 11 April 2020 showed more than 2,24,00,000 results for the keyword "Gandhi memes," though most of them were based on MK Gandhi, some others were on the Gandhi family. Apart from 9GAG, Reddit and

4Chan, there are online groups created explicitly for memes on Gandhi. Such groups and pages can be found on Facebook, Twitter and Instagram, and they play a crucial role in demonstrating how Gandhi and his values are perceived by the people who consume and produce such content. The internet memes can also be read as (post)modern folklores as they narrate stories about contemporary culture.[7] In the early twentieth century, various folk narratives in different Indian languages played a vital role in constructing Gandhi's image as Mahatma among the masses. Thus, it can be argued that internet memes, as web narratives, are now recasting the image of Gandhi in the virtual sphere.

Along with his iconic photos and quotes, many doctored images and fake news on Gandhi are circulating on the internet. Interestingly, Gandhi himself was appalled by the fake news and the propaganda circulating during his time. He believed "false news is a crime against humanity" (Gowda, n.p.). Various fact-checking websites in India are combating the false propaganda and hate circulating against Gandhi in the cybersphere. On 2 October, Alt-News, a news portal, published an investigative report on how Gandhi's photo with Nehru clicked on 6 July 1946, at the All-India Congress Committee meeting in Bombay, India, was doctored and circulated (Chaudhuri). Discussions on fake and doctored photos have gained impetus recently. However, Gandhi was perhaps the first Indian personality whose photo was tampered within the early twentieth century. In November 1931, Indian delegates participating in the Round Table Conference were invited to Buckingham Palace to meet King George. Speculations were doing the rounds in the British Press and in the conference circles about the dress that Gandhi would wear. He was discreetly advised to wear a regulation court dress for the occasion; however, Gandhi refused to shun his Indian attire. An American mock-up, *Experiment with Mahatma Gandhi* morphed Gandhi's photo.[8] The photo depicted the dress that he would not wear to the palace. Though morphing photos was a complicated and expensive affair in the pre-internet days but now, as Hany Farid observes in *Fake Photos*, "powerful and low-cost digital technology has made it far easier for nearly anyone to alter digital images" (1).

Memes trends in response to the words and the actions of living persons and contemporary public events are no novelty but memes on Gandhi, who is dead for more than 70 years, problematize the understanding of the process of production and dissemination of memes. Why is he being resurrected in the memescape? What could be the hyper-memetic logic behind hundreds of memes that make derogatory references to Gandhi's private life? The circulation of the fake news and doctored Gandhi's images may be regarded as hyper-memetic logic behind the spread of umpteen derogatory memes on Gandhi. At this juncture, it could be mentioned that Gandhi's attitude towards gender and sexuality is a matter of long-standing debate among scholars. However, the memes on Gandhi do not mirror the complexities of the issue; they are rather conclusive in their depictions. Such kinds of memes appear to be a part of some political propaganda against Gandhi and his ideas. Pratik Sinha, the founder of Alt-News and the author of *India Misinformed: The True Story* comments "it is often said that the practice of social media to mislead the populace at large for political propaganda had already began in India in 2012–13" (Sinha 1). Sinha's claim appears to be valid for several memes as they categorically target Gandhi's private life and public life, though the same cannot be said for the entire Gandhi memeplex.

Online meme generator websites and mobile phone apps have half-finished templates for creating memes on Gandhi. Interestingly, these templates resonate with the format of Gandhi's original pictorial quotes (an original quote by Gandhi along with his photograph). By imitating the form of the pictorial quotes, often memes create a momentary illusion of an original quote from Gandhi's writings. The format of many Gandhi memes appears to be inspired by the poster format "Demotivator" (a black frame with white text and an image). The poster is traced back to the satirical and parody version posters of the 1990s inspirational posters produced by Despair, Inc. The solemnity of images of their posters was contradicted by the inclusion of written text in them. Similar contradictions are an indispensable part of a majority of memes on Gandhi. The layout of most of the Gandhi memes templates can be divided into three parts: a monochrome photograph of smiling, bespectacled Gandhi, a display/reaffirmation of his canonized identity (*Mahatma*) and a black space. This blank-black space, in the template, is the actual site of contestations – the space used by the prosumers for the "acts of vernacular creativity" (Burges 29), a space that is used by the meme creators to articulate their subjective opinions regarding Gandhi. These templates are almost like half-solved puzzles; they beckon the users to fill up the gaps, appropriate the context or give a new meaning to the depiction of Gandhi, and this willingness to complete the incomplete enhance the spreadability of the memes.

The prosumers of Gandhi memes are active agents who play a crucial role in the dissemination of memes. They alter the meaning according to their ideologies and, to use Rosaira Conte's idea, they can be "viewed as 'vectors' of, rather than actors behind, cultural transmission" (95). An analysis of a group of memes on Gandhi would reveal a polyphony of opinions, and the multiplicity of views coming together through satire, humour, social and political commentary is akin to Ryan Millar's idea of " 'polyvocality' of memes" (2013). Gandhi memes can be analysed through three dimensions that constitute them: content, form and stance (Shifman). Content of the specific text refers to the ideas or ideologies carried by the memes, the form is the encoding of the messages – the users perceive the message through their senses –and stance relates to the information memes convey about their communication. For Shipman, all these three dimensions of memes are potentially mimetic, and users can decide to imitate any one of them while recreating memes. The following analysis is based on a group of Gandhi memes template available on mgflip.com.[9] *Content*: humorous/satirical/offensive interpretation of Gandhi and his words. *Form*: bespectacled Gandhi, iconic monochrome photographs – dressed in Khadi – and reclamation of spiritual status (Mahatma). *Stance*: Saintly, smiling, peaceful and poised.

With hundreds of memes created and disseminated by the users, the dimensions mentioned above may vary with different versions of memes on Gandhi. For instance, one may find animated or doctored images of Gandhi in a variety of memes. In these memes, Gandhi is portrayed as presenting his opinions on a wide-ranging topic, and an investigation of the texts of memes would reveal a contradiction between Gandhian values and the texts of memes. Most of the versions of memes exploit his iconic photos – they are either used in their original form or morphed as per the imagination and capabilities of meme enthusiasts. The choice of his iconic photos accelerates the spreadability of the memes. Gandhi's iconic photos are an important part of the history and the politics of India and the world – these photos depict crucial moments in history and are also the medium through which histories are narrated. For Shifman (2014), the contemporary culture challenges the earlier notion of photography, he notes "while iconic photos emerged as a cultural category in an era in which a rhetoric of truthfulness was strongly associated with photography, in contemporary participatory culture, wherein individuals are expected to create personal versions of popular images, the 'iconization' of single photos may be challenged" (348). Thus, it can be inferred memes offer challenges to the ways in which Gandhi's photos are iconized.

Preoccupied with the "Mahatma" image of Gandhi, in almost all the memes, the users portray him in his white *Khadi*, the homespun "sacred" clothes, which stands for his simplicity, his resistance and his struggle.[10] The saintly, poised and smiling face of Gandhi and non-serious, comic texts present a strange blend of contradictory elements. It may produce humour, a major component of memes as Knobel and Lankshear (2007) observed in their study.[11] As a matter of fact, humour is the major component of all the successful memes (most liked and shared) on Gandhi. It could be analysed from the theory of incongruity of humour, according to which humour and laughter arise because of a strong comic juxtaposition between the familiar and the invented. A Kantian perspective can also help in understanding the humour in memes. In the *Critique of Judgement*, Kant observes that humour consists of a clash of two disparate elements and a resolution. He also emphasized "surprise" as an essential component, for him "laughter is an affect arising from a strained expectation being suddenly reduced to nothing" (161). In Gandhi memescape, the unexpected connection between the text and the image surprises the consumers resulting in the production of humour. Contradictory to the popular depictions of Gandhi in the print and the popular culture, the meme prosumers attribute imagined, unpredicted statements to Gandhi – most of which contradict his perceived divine and saintly personality. The memes' consumers, to use Munro's words, find "the inappropriate within the appropriate" (351). From Bollywood and Bigg Boss TV show to pizza and pork, in the memescape, the figure of Gandhi is deployed to articulate his opinions about mundane as well as serious topics. In the following two sections, two important Gandhian ideals and the responses of meme enthusiasts have been examined.

Fasting/Feasting

Consumption of food and its rejection occupies a crucial place in Gandhian politics. His moral and political outlook is represented by his choice of vegetarianism and his practice of fasting. Along with using them as a means of resistance against the British hegemony, they have also played an important role in his iconization. His diet, which was a combination of his religious beliefs and dietary and nutritional theories, was an integral part of the austere lifestyle he advocated for his followers. After briefly engaging with Gandhi's choice of vegetarianism and his fast, the essay examines the depiction of Gandhi's eating habits and fasts in memescape.

Gandhi was a staunch supporter of vegetarianism; Henry Salt's *A Plea for Vegetarianism* (1886) had a strong influence on his food habits. He admitted in his autobiography that his choice of vegetarianism before reading Salt's book was purely personal.[12] Salt's book persuaded Gandhi to read more books on dietetic studies; he devoured, as he mentions in his autobiography, "all the books available on vegetarianism" (44). Gandhi's embrace of *Ahimsa* (non-violence) began with his vegetarianism. Leela Gandhi demonstrates how during his stay in London, Gandhi was profoundly influenced by the culture of fin de siècle animal welfare, which shaped "the complex etymology of Gandhian ahimsa" (18). Gandhi joined the London Vegetarian Society during his student days and was elected subsequently as its secretary. In 1931, when he visited England for the Round Table Conference on India, he was invited to deliver a speech by Dr Oldfield, the society's president. On 20 November 1931, in his speech titled "The Moral Basis of Vegetarianism," he emphasized the need to explore the moral consequences of vegetarianism and the relationship between health, body and eating habits. The secret of healthy living was to "eat sparingly and now and then fast" (Gandhi 20). He also disseminated his belief in a moderate vegetarian diet throughout his life through his autobiography, correspondences and journalistic pieces that he published in *Harijan*, *Young India* and *Hind Swaraj*. His moral and philosophical dietary outlook emphasized quantity, quality and prohibition of certain food items. During his life span, he engaged in at least 13 major fasts and undertook fast unto death because for him fasting was a potent weapon in the Satyagraha armoury. He saw it both as a means of self-purification and penance.

In the virtual sphere, there are hundreds of memes on Gandhi's consumption and rejection of food. These memes, like most of the photo-based Gandhi memes, use his iconic black and white photos. One ubiquitous, iconic photo of Gandhi, which has been used in many memes, is his photograph at the telephone booth of the Sevagram Ashram, 1940. It has been exploited by many users to comment on Gandhi's fasting and feasting. Interestingly, the telephone booth and the original photo have been preserved by the Sevagram Ashram, India, and are available for public viewing. The same photo is also available for remixing and appropriation as meme template on various online meme generators such as imgflip.com and indianmemetemplates.com. An examination of the original photograph's temporal–spatial setting demonstrates it to be an amalgamation of indigenous modernity and colonial modernity. Gandhi, a representative of passive resistance, standing at the Sevagram Ashram (translated as the village of service),[13] conversing over the telephone, a mechanical invention, a representative of colonial modernity.

The image/text relationship in the two image micros (photos superimposed with text) memes reproduced here present two very "un-Gandhian" images of Gandhi – the binary opposite of everything that Gandhi practised and preached. In the derivative reproductions, the act of Gandhian *Seva* (serving) has been given globalized and urbanized twist. He is not "serving" but "ordering" food over his telephone, most probably, after his fasts.

In the first image-micro picture, Gandhi's imagined telephonic call to the contemporary-urban consumerist service of the home-delivery of "two" pizzas from "Domino's," a global chain of pizza outlets, contradicts his primary belief in the agro-based economy of rural India. These memes consist of several other elements: first, as opposed to Gandhi's discouragement of food-fetishism, to put in his own words, "to cut down the quantity of your food, and reduce the number of meals" ("Moral Basis"), he has been depicted as a glutton ordering a large quantity of food for himself – "Two" pizzas with his hand gesture (two raised fingers) accompanied

FIGURE 4.1 *Two Cheese Pizzas With a Liter of Root Beer.* Meme. ImageFlip.com[14]

by words to suggest he has not eaten for ages. Second, the desire to relish pizzas, a foreign food item contradicts Gandhi's idea of swadeshi (Homegrown). In fact, in all his food writings, he advocated Indian food items; he mentions consumption of a limited quantity of cheese or Indian paneer, which is quite different from the types of cheese used for pizza toppings. In another meme that also makes use of the telephone booth photograph, Gandhi is portrayed as ordering foods and drink that are forbidden and discouraged in the Gandhian food politics: the topping of "meat" on two pizzas, and the topping of cheese, along with a litre of "root beer." Though Gandhi ate meat for a brief span of time, as he mentions in his autobiography,[15] in the meme, he is depicted as a connoisseur of the meat pizzas and an aficionado of beers.

Attempt to place Gandhi in a globalized and consumerist world could be seen in other memes on his fasts and eating habits. In a photoshopped meme, first posted by the user @theyashbhardawaj on Twitter, on 2 October 2015, Gandhi is depicted as uninstalling Zomato, a food application software from his cell phone, before going on fast. In another meme, a MacBook is superimposed in Gandhi's photo, and he is portrayed as posting photos of his food on Instagram

FIGURE 4.2 *Food for Thought.* Meme. ImageFlip[16]

In most of the memes on food and fast, urban and consumerist culture forms the background, and the figure of Gandhi in these memes mirrors the complexities of the current young generation. He, as depicted by internet users, perhaps, could be termed as "the Millennial Mahatma."

The Nuclear Gandhi and Militarized Masculinities

Satya (Truth) and Ahimsa (non-violence) are two guiding forces behind Gandhi's philosophy. His views on Ahimsa were the result of his study of different religions of the world as he stated "If I am a follower of Ahimsa, I must love my enemy" (Gandhi and Dalton 40). His idea of Ahimsa has made him a global icon of peace, however, in the world of internet memes, Gandhi's views on Ahimsa rarely find a place. It is substituted by the imagined ideas of destruction and violence. As depicted in most of the memes, Gandhi is not peace-loving or a believer of Ahimsa, but a violent and aggressive man who is not a lover but a destroyer of his enemies. Such representations of Gandhi may shock many, but the association of Gandhi with aggression and violence is rare but not unprecedented in the visual cultures. Gandhi II, in Weird Al' Yankovic's *UHF* (1989), an unmade sequel to Richard Attenborough's *Gandhi*, portrays him as an action hero of Hollywood cinema of 1980. The hyper-masculine Gandhi's meme-avatar consumes meat, uses weapons and punches his enemies. This *"Himsak"*(violent) image of Gandhi has crept its way into pop-culture with multiple jokes, memes and webcomics. In the short story, "[b]ecause Thou Lovest the Burning-Ground" from *Alternate Warriors* (1993) by Mike Resnick, Gandhi, failing his university exams, turns into a violent warrior. He is depicted as a modern warrior holding a rocket launcher on the cover page of the book.[17]

A recent graphic novel, *Gandhi: The Beast Within* (2017), written by Jason Michalski and illustrated by Antonio Rojo, portrays Gandhi as a Hulk-like superhero who fights with tyrants such as Hitler. The most intriguing inversion of Gandhi's revered pacifist image is Sid Meier's *Civilization*, a turn-based video game series. The nuke-hungry, hyper-aggressive, warmonger, fictional Gandhi is a stark contrast to the peace-monger, real counterpart. In September 2010, *Critical Miss*, a webcomic, published a comic comparing real Gandhi with his aggressive portrayal in the *Civilization* video game series, which was later uploaded on Reddit. A series of internet memes has erupted in response to Gandhi's violent representations, and most of the memes made use of the images from the texts mentioned above. These memes have been termed as "The Nuclear Gandhi" memes by 'Know Your Meme,' an international meme database with the website www.knowyourmeme.com that documents memes and other internet phenomena. The "Nuclear Gandhi" memes replicate Gandhi's aggressive avatar, reinstate explicit connection between him and nuclear wars as depicted in the *Civilization* series and generously borrow the catchphrases and the animated images of Gandhi from the series.

"The World is the problem; the atomic bomb is the answer"[18] is one such meme that uses an iconic photograph and takes a jibe at Gandhi's views on wars and nuclear weaponry. Though it is well known that his advocacy of non-violence against the colonial authority had created a curiosity in the world, he publicly articulated his opinion about atomic weapons in his speeches, articles and interviews.[19] The meme imagines Gandhi as a global leader who has found the final solution to all the worlds' problems – not in Ahimsa but the destruction of the world through nuclear weapons.[20]

In the second meme, which is a remix of the nuclear Gandhi from the *Civilization* video game series, Gandhi's face is superimposed on the body of the Canadian rapper, Drake. The reaction image, in the form of four panels, known as "Drakeposting" in the vernacular discourse of meme-makers is used to express love and disgust or liking and disliking for something and is taken from the music video of the rapper's 2015 hit single "Hotline Bling." The meme format has a striking resemblance with the format of the Rage comics, a genre of an amateur-looking four-panel comic about the Rage guy, which began to be shared on various online platforms in 2008. However, in the Drake memes, the panels show two contradictory positions. Following the meme's format, the Nuclear Gandhi meme is expressing his disgust for the "Nuclear non-proliferation" global policies and other symbols of peace. The reference is to the Treaty on the Non-Proliferation of Nuclear Weapons (NPT),[21] denoted by the text and two symbols – a scroll with a tick mark and a dove with an olive branch, the universal symbol of peace. In the second panel, Gandhi expresses his liking for nuclear weaponry and war: represented by symbols of an animated missile, an atomic nucleus, an explosion and an international ionizing radiation trefoil. In the other "Nuclear Gandhi" memes, an unsettling liaison between Gandhi and nuclear arms can be noticed. True to the coined self-contradictory term "Nuclear Gandhi," the memes bring together two binary ideas – Gandhi and the imagery of violence and destruction of the world. The militarized masculinities are an integral part of the character of Nuclear Gandhi, and such distorted representations of Gandhi often produce dark humour.

Conclusion

In this essay, multiple representations of Gandhi in the memescape in the virtual sphere of the internet has been analysed. The study moves away from many established researches of Gandhi's depiction in the visual cultures where most of the time, Gandhi's spiritual stature becomes the focus of attention. It is argued that in order to understand all the dimensions of Gandhi's image in the visual cultures, his iconographies in the virtual sphere need to be explored and investigated. The discussion on the memes and the online sphere in the first and second sections of the essay established the important role that new technologies play in forming views and opinions about Gandhi. His autobiography, speeches, interviews and other writings have been compared with meme's text and form to explore the incongruities between Gandhi and his meme avatars. Given the maverick and iconoclastic personality of Gandhi and countless memes on him, it is a herculean task to dwell upon the representation of every aspect. Thus, a group of memes based on Gandhi's eating, fasts and the idea of non-violence was selected for the analysis. It was also demonstrated how the circulation of memes on Gandhi is not just for entertainment but also serves a strong social function. Through memes, internet users often cast a wary eye on Gandhi and Gandhian values. When the users create, share, like or remix Gandhi memes, they are either in agreement or in disagreement with the meme's content. Thus, like other memes, Gandhi memes are also a site of contestation of collective identity "the arena where the hegemonic meets the alternative, and the public chooses the winner by clicking 'like' or 'dislike', and, most importantly, 'share'" (Anastasia 10). Gandhi's depiction in memes is opposite to the real counterpart, or to use Devji's and Birla's phrase, "the Gandhi who is enjoying a revival in public life today does not appear to be a historical character" (266).

Notes

1 Sean Scalmer mentions many English observers who quote and misquote Churchill's statement. Gandhi was also dubbed as 'Naked Fakir' and 'The Little Naked Man of India' in Europe. See Scalmer 16–17.
2 For the depiction of Gandhi and the tradition of graphic satire, see Devadawson and Khanduri. For Indian artists' preoccupation with Gandhi, see Sumathi Ramaswamy, *Gandhi in the Gallery: The Art of Disobedience*, Roli Books, 2020.
3 According to Shifman, the contemporary media's landscape is governed by a *hypermemetic* logic where "almost every public event sprouts a stream of memes". See Shifman, "Digital Culture," p. 04.
4 Shifman notes that Ewald Hering, an Austrian sociologist, had coined the phrase *Die Mneme* (from the Greek word *mneme*, meaning memory) in 1870, and Richard Simon, a German biologist, used the phrase as the title of his book *Mnemischen Empfindungen in ihren Beziehungen zu den Originalempfindungen* (1904), and an English translated of the book was published in 1914 as *The Mneme*. See, *Memes in the Digital World*, p. 363.
5 https://economictimes.indiatimes.com/tech/internet/twitter-india-unveils-gandhi-emoji/articleshow/66040165.cms?from=mdr.
6 Participatory culture for Jenkin is a "culture with relatively low barriers to artistic expression and civic engagement, strong support for creating and sharing one's creations, and some type of informal mentorship whereby what is known by the most experienced is passed along to novices. A participatory culture is also one in which members believe their contributions matter, and feel some degree of social connection with one another (at the least they care what other people think about what they have created" (3).
7 Foote demonstrates how the internet can create lived culture; she also states: "all folklore is made up of memes, but not all memes are folklore" (31).
8 See, *Experiment with Mahatma Gandhi*. Sketch. Gandhi through Sketches, https://gandhi.gov.in/cartoon.html. Accessed 15 April 2020.
9 The template is available on the following link: https://imgflip.com/memegenerator/116217190/Mahatma-Gandhi-Rocks. Accessed 15 April 2020.
10 Khadi, for Gandhi, was much more than homespun clothing material. Emma Tarlo explains how in the early decades of the twentieth century, upon returning from South Africa, Gandhi adopted Indian style dress as a means of political protest and identification with the marginalized group. His choice of "*Kathiawadi* peasant dress [which] visually challenged the well-established hierarchies that elevated Western over Indian, urban over rural and elite over popular" (2).
11 The analysis of the memes created between 2000 and 2005 reveals humour to be the significant component of all the successful memes.

12 Gandhi writes how Salt's book influenced his choice of vegetarianism. He takes a vow before his mother to abstain from meat. At the same time, he wishes that every Indian should be a meat eater. He believes that the propagation of vegetarianism was his mission (Gandhi, *An Autobiography*, 41).

13 Gandhi believed that villages are the foundation of nation-building. The establishment of Ashrams at Champaran, Sevagram, and Warda bespeak of his faith in rural India. In his various writings and speeches, he vociferously spoke in the favour of villages. See Divya Joshi.

14 Retrieved from, https://imgflip.com/i/2vuh3c. Accessed 19 March 2020.

15 Though Gandhi promised his mother that he would never consume meat, his friend persuaded him to try goat meat. Gandhi became a meat eater for almost and year in which he enjoyed "not more than half a dozen" meat feasts (Gandhi, *An Autobiography*, 16–21).

16 Retrieved from, https://imgflip.com/i/122sll. Accessed 19 March 2020.

17 The cover page of the *Alternate Warriors* is available on the link: https://www.reddit.com/r/badscificovers/comments/diqkyd/alternate_warriors_edited_by_mike_resnick/

18 The dank meme can be found on the following link: https://en.dopl3r.com/memes/dank/the-world-is-the-problem-the-atomid-bomb-is-the-answe-mahatma-gandhi/83516. Accessed 15 April 2020.

19 On the day of Gandhi's assassination (30 January 1948), Margaret Bourke-White, an American journalist, questioned him about his views on nuclear weapons: "How would you meet the atom bomb with nonviolence?" Gandhi answered, "I will not go underground. I will not go into a shelter. I will come out in the open and let the pilot see I have not a trace of ill-will against him. The pilot will not see our faces from his great height, I know. But the longing in our hearts – that he will not come to harm – would reach up to him and his eyes would be opened." See, *Gandhi on Nuclear Arms*.

20 *Drakeposting Gandhi*. Meme, Warmonger Gandhi, FaceBook, Retrieved from, https://m.facebook.com/WarmongerGandhi/photos/a.618505194835308/2338710562814754/?type=3&source=48. Accessed 19 March 2020.

21 NPT's goal is "to prevent the spread of nuclear weapons and weapons technology, to promote cooperation in the peaceful uses of nuclear energy and to further the goal of achieving nuclear disarmament and general and complete disarmament." See, *Treaty*.

Works Cited

Amin, Shahid. "Gandhi as Mahatma: Gorakhpur District, Eastern UP, 1921–2." *Selected Subaltern Studies*, edited by Ranajit Guha and Gayatri Chakravorty Spivak, Oxford UP, 1988, pp. 288–350.

Bawa, Seema. "Power and Politics of Portraits, Icons and Hagiographic Images of Gandhi." *Economic and Political Weekly*, vol. LIII, no. 5, 2018, pp. 54–61.

Birla, Ritu and Faisal Devji. "Guest Editors' Letter: Itineraries of Self-Rule." *Public Culture* 23 (2), edited by Faisal Devji and Ritu Birla, 2011, pp. 265–68.

Blackmore, Susan. *The Meme Machine*. Oxford UP, 1999.

Börzsei, Linda K. "Makes a Meme Instead: A Concise History of Internet Memes." *NewMedia Studies Magazine*, Mar. 2013, https://works.bepress.com/linda_borzsei/2/.

Brisbane, Australia, 2007, https://eprints.qut.edu.au/16378/1/Jean_Burgess_Thesis.pdf. *Civilizations V: Beyond Earth*, Window Version, Firaxis Games, 2010.

Burgess, Jean. *Vernacular Creativity and New Media*. Queensland University of Technology.

Chakrabarty, Dipesh. *Habitations of Modernity: Essays in the Wake of Subaltern Studies*. U of Chicago P, 2002.

Chaudhuri, Pooja. "Photoshopped Image Showing Mahatma Gandhi With a Woman Shared on Social Media." *Alt-News*, 2 Oct. 2019, www.altnews.in/photoshopped-image-showing- mahatma-gandhi-with-a-woman-shared-on-social-media/.

Conte, Rosaria. "Memes Through (Social) Minds." *Darwinizing Culture: The Status of Memetics as a Science*, edited by Robert Aunger, Oxford UP, 2000.

Davidson, Patrick. "The Language of Internet." *The Social Media Reader*, edited by Michael Mandiberg. New York UP, 2013, pp. 120–34.

Dawkins, Richard. *The Selfish Gene: 30th Anniversary Edition*. Oxford UP, 2006.

Denisova, Anastasia. *Internet Memes and Society: Social, Cultural, and Political Context*. Routledge, 2019.

Devadawson, Christel R. "Strategies of Protest: Gandhi in Contemporary Cartoons." 2013, www.aags.org/publications/2013-proceedings?tmpl=%2Fsystem%2Fapp%2Ftemplates%2Fprint%2F&showPrintDialog=1.

Dwyer, Rachel. "The Case of the Missing Mahatma: Gandhi and the Hindi Cinema." *PublicCulture* 23–22, edited by Faisal Devji and Ritu Birla, 2011, pp. 349–76.

Farid, Hany. *Fake Photos*. MIT Press, 2019.

Foote, Monica. "Userpicks: Cyber Folk Art in the Early 21st Century." *Folklore Forum*, vol. 37, no. 1, 2007, pp. 27–38.

Gandhi, Leela. "Ahimsa and Other Animals: The Genealogy of an Immature Politics." *Rethinking Gandhi and Nonviolent Relationality: Global Perspectives*, edited by Debjani Ganguly and John Docker, Routledge, 2007, pp. 17–37.

Gandhi, Mahatma and Dennis Dalton. *Gandhi: Selected Political Writings*. Hackett Publishing, 1996.

Gandhi, Mohandas K. "*Gandhi on Nuclear Arms*." Gandhian Institutions-Bombay Sarvodaya Mandal & Gandhi Research Foundation, www.mkgandhi.org/articles/NuclearArms.htm.

———. *The Moral Basis of Vegetarianism*. Navajivan Mudranalaya, 1959.

———. *An Autobiography: My Experiments with Truth*. Translated by Mahadev Desai. Penguin Books, 2012.

Gowda, Rajeev. "Mahatma Gandhi 150th Birth Anniversary: What Would Gandhi Say About the Indian Media?" *The Hindu*, 2 Oct. 2019, www.thehindu.com/opinion/op-ed/what-would-gandhi-say-about-the-indian-media/article29568704.ece.

Habermas, Jurgen. *The Structural Transformation of the Public Sphere*. Translated by Thomas Burger with the Assistance of Frederick Lawrence. MIT Press, 1991.

Indian Internet, 2019. Internet and Mobile Association of India, Neilsen, https://cms.iamai.in/Content/ResearchPapers/d3654bcc-002f-4fc7-ab39-e1fbeb00005d.pdf.

Jenkins, Henry. *Textual Poachers: Television Fans & Participatory Culture*. Routledge, 2002.

Jones, Steve. *Virtual Culture: Identity and Communication in Cybersociety*. Sage, 2002.

Joshi, Divya. *Gandhi on Villages: Selected and Complied with an Introduction*. 2002, www.gandhiashramsevagram.org/pdf-books/gandhi-on-villages.pdf.

Kant, Immanuel. *Critique of Judgement*. Translated by James Creed Meredith, revised, edited, and introduced by Nicholas Walker. Oxford UP, 2007.

Khanduri, Ritu Gairola. "Gandhi and Satyagraha of Cartoons: Cultivating a Taste." *Caricaturing Culture in India: Cartoons and History in the Modern World*, Cambridge UP, 2013, pp. 68–92.

Knobel, Michele, and Colin Lankshear. "Online Memes, Affinities, and Cultural Production." *A New Literacies Sampler*, edited by Michelle Knoebel and Colin Lankshear, Peter Lang Publishing Inc., 2007, pp. 199–239.

Lelyveld, Joseph. *Great Soul: Mahatma Gandhi and His Struggle With India*. Harper Collins, 2011.

Milner, Ryan M. "Media Lingua Franca: Fixity, Novelty, and Vernacular Creativity in Internet Memes." Selected Papers of Internet Research 14.0, 2013, Denver, USA.

Monro, D. H. "Theories of Humor." *Writing and Reading Across the Curriculum*, edited by Laurence Behrens and Leonard J. Rosen, Foresman and Company, 1988, pp. 349–55.

Papacharissi, Zizi. "The Virtual Sphere: The Internet as a Public Sphere." *New Media &Society*, vol. 4–1, Sage Publications, 2002, pp. 09–27.

Resnick, Mike. *Alternate Warriors*. Tom Doherty Associates, 1993.

Roy, Arundhati. *The Doctor and The Saint: The Ambedkar-Gandhi Debate: Caste, Race, and Annihilation of Caste*. Penguin, 2017.

Rudolph, Lloyd I., and Susanne Hoeber Rudolph. *Postmodern Gandhi and Other Essays: Gandhi in the World and at Home*. U of Chicago P, 2006.

Scalmer, Sean. *Gandhi in the West: The Mahatma and the Rise of Radical Protest*. Cambridge UP, 2011.

Shifman, Limor. "The Cultural Logic of Photo-Based Meme Genres." *Journal of Visual Culture* 13–13, Sage Publications, 2014.

———. *Memes in Digital Culture*. MIT Press, 2013.

———. "Memes in a Digital World: Reconciling with a Conceptual Troublemaker." *Journal of Computer-Mediated Communication*, vol. 18, 2013, pp. 362–77.

Sinha, Gayatri. "The Afterlives of Images: The Contested Legacies of Gandhi in Art and Popular Culture." *South Asian Studies*, vol. 29, no. 1, 2013, pp. 111–29.

Sinha, Pratik. *India Misinformed: The True Story*. Harper Collins, 2019.

Tarlo, Emma. "Khadi." www.soas.ac.uk/south-asia-institute/keywords/file24807.pdf.

Tayyebulla, Md. *Beyond the Symbol and the Idol at Last*. Allied Publishers, 1964.

Treaty on the Non-Proliferation of Nuclear Weapons (NPT), United Nations, www.un.org/disarmament/wmd/nuclear/npt/.

Vincent, James. "Video: Richard Dawkins Attempts Memedom via Saatchi and Saatchi." *Independent*, 26 June 2013, www.independent.co.uk/life-style/gadgets-and-tech/video-richard-dawkins-attempts-memedom-via-saatchi-saatchi-8674875.html.

5

MAHATMA IN ANTIPHONY

Gandhi in Indian Nationalist, Muslim and British Press Cartoons, 1946–1947

Barnali Saha

Introduction

The Partition of India in 1947 that resulted in the death and displacement of millions of people continues to inhabit the consciousness of the people of South Asia as a historical phenomenon identified with violence. Although the legacy of the Partition is palpable in frequent episodes of contemporary religious tensions, discourses on minority belonging or lack of it, the continual deliberations and discussions on secularism, the idea of nation and nationalism in India, the critical exploration of the phenomenon of Partition as a tension-ridden historical episode has largely been restricted. Partition's limited critical examination is mainly because the multiplicity of discourses on Indian national struggle leading to the momentous event of freedom at midnight have sought to elide the Partition as the price paid for autonomy, resulting in an apparent historiographical lacuna. Nevertheless, despite its limited representation, India's Partition and the politics that led to it have continued to dwell in Indian cultural discourse as an alternative episode to the glorified incident of Indian independence from the British. Scholars and creative writers have undeniably explored "the possibilities offered by literary fiction and 'high art' to narrativize the violence" (Misri 8) of the Partition. In the process, these scholars have constructed a "minor canon of literary texts" (Misri 8) dedicated to problematizing the phenomenon, and one cannot help but wonder if "literature [is] the most representative form in every cultural context" (George 224).

In this respect, works of feminist historiography, especially by Urvashi Butalia, Ritu Menon and Kamala Bhasin, have been categorical in rising above the cultural asymmetries and positioning the unheard memories and testimonies of actual victims and witnesses of Partition violence within the heart of the archive. Nevertheless, even their efforts are largely textual rather than visual, stylistic rather than performative. Therefore, recognizing the importance of other forms of cultural

DOI: 10.4324/9781003145479-8

expressions apart from the literary/verbal text to constitute a cultural archive of the Partition and its politics, this paper expands beyond the literary spectrum by turning to the domain of political cartoons from the English language press (colonial, nationalist and Muslim press) and media to consider their engagement with the politics of 1946–1947. The paper solely concentrates on examining Mahatma Gandhi's figure, as an epitome of cultural iconography and a central political figure of the time, in the editorial cartoons published in 1946–1947.

Gandhi and the World of Representation

The cartoon published in the *Avadh Punch* (Figure 5.1) in 1936 is a sarcastic take on the politics of the Indian National Congress and relies on wit to represent the figure of Mahatma Gandhi and his ubiquitous *Charkha*. The cartoon shows Lady Congress stamping on the *Charkha* and a flock of pigeons (symbol of sacrifice/peace) surrounding the lady. Lady Congress disrupted the peace that hitherto prevailed and had unequivocally disinclined to sacrifice herself at the "altar of Gandhiji's jokes," as the hook-nosed Mr. Punch puts it. Addressing the lady, he says, "Your survival in itself is a miracle. Who likes to roost on the base of the spinning wheel? Live long!" Punch's address suggests the Congress' dependency on the aura of Gandhi, both as an individual, spiritual and ascetic, and as a political patriarch of the party effecting the circuit of its moves with the whirr of his spinning wheel. The *Avadh Punch* did not subscribe to the Congress' political model and wished Lady Congress a new life away from the repressive mass of Gandhi's machine. Since a machine "is at work everywhere . . . with all the necessary couplings and connections" (Deleuze and Guattari 1), and the Congress' machinery, it seems, according to the cartoon, at least, "is plugged into" Gandhi's, its "energy-source-machine" (Deleuze and Guattari 1). The *Punch* wishes to break this coupling by featuring Lady Congress as an independent "organ-machine," interrupting the connection violently. Her violent action of dismantling the stagnant set-up has shaken the anorexic Gandhi, who is consternated. With his mouth open, Gandhi gapes at the destruction of his finely tuned machine by someone whose servitude he seems to have taken for granted. The cartoon is an example of how politics, wit and humour grants cartoons a fundamental identity wherein the recoding of information directly affects its consumption.

Since its inception as the typified expression of political aesthetic, the Gandhian image has ruled the world of representation in unequivocal terms. One may, in this regard, direct one's attention to the Gandhian iconography grafted in early political cartoons from South Africa. In this context, mention may be made of the cartoon titled "Passive Resistance in the Transvaal" published in 1906 (see Figure 5.2).

The cartoon evokes Gandhi's position as a passive resister in the Transvaal Closer Union Society meeting, where he spoke against indentured labour. The cartoon depicts Gandhi as a mahout astride the elephant that is labelled "Indian Community." The South African colonial secretary, who opposed Gandhi's views, is seen steering

FIGURE 5.1 "Lady Congress and the Sacred Birds." *Avadh Punch*. 5 January 1936. From Personal Collection of Author.

the vehicle. Nevertheless, his efforts prove abortive, as suggested by the line accompanying the original cartoon in *Sunday Times*: "The Elephant 'sat tight': the steamroller exploded" (The Steamroller v. the Elephant, *Sunday Times*, South Africa). As the capable mahout, Gandhi is a predominant force, and the cartoon illustrates how a pressing political scenario can be depicted through wit and humour.

The Steam Roller v. The Elephant. (The Elephant 'sat tight'; the Steam Roller exploded.)   Sunday Times

FIGURE 5.2   "Passive Resistance in Transvaal." *Sunday Times*, 1906.

The "Steam-Roller" cartoon, as well as others published in South Africa, direct our attention to two things: first, that Gandhi has, since his induction into the political scenario, been a significant political and cultural force whose non-violent/passive-resistant ideology was time and again problematized in editorial cartoons. Second, by deconstructing the visual syntax of political cartoons on Gandhi, one would notice that, more often than not, in these early cartoons, Gandhi is depicted a lone individual – a representation of an ultimate force. This strategy ultimately led to several editorial cartoons from the nationalist press and other representations that showcase Gandhi as a lone figure contesting the hegemonic powers. His goodness and the force of his ideology make it impossible to place him besides other (lesser) mortals.

By 1931, Gandhi had become the "Mahatma-the Great Soul" (Khanduri 88), but the minority press continued to depict Gandhi as a mortal being and not as a divine from 1946 to 1947 which reveals the tremendous political tension that accosted some sections of the minority community who feared complete political and cultural erasure in the times to come at the hand of a majority community. The cartoons encapsulated their anxiety of annihilation. Nevertheless, the code of affront ingrained in the Gandhian cartoons from the minority press when compared with works of literature like Mulk Raj Anand's *Untouchable* (1935), Raja Rao's *Kanthapura* (1938), R.K. Narayan's *Waiting for Mahatma* (1955) allows for interesting observations to emerge. These novels, which problematize political events like non-cooperation movement, the Quit India Movement, the Civil Disobedience Movement helmed by Gandhi, show the power of ideology as a representational modality to reach an audience. Popular Gandhian songs like "*Gandhi ke bhagat bano rasiya, /des prem hori khelo, /rang swadeshi rangaaon badhiyaan*" (popular Gandhi bhajan by Bhawani Prasad Misra "[b]ecome Gandhi's devotee, dear friend/Play the patriotic colours of *Holi*/Let the colours of nationalism overwhelm you") further underline the troubling construction of Gandhi. Gandhi's representation as a being and a non-being, as a visual idiom whose charisma allows instant recognition, and also grants him a metonymized space along with the likes of Buddha and Christ can be found in various scenarios, including the narrative of cartoons.

Gandhi's spiritual, almost mythical existence (the kind the *Punch* cartoon as mentioned above criticized) illustrated in the Indian nationalist press, his framing as an obsessive inflammatory tool with which to attack the Congress and its politics showcased in the Muslim press and his representation as a mainly human image of victimhood represented in the British press unequivocally suggest his presence as a unique cultural icon. From being depicted as the son of Bharatmata (See Figure 5.4), the gendered anthropomorphized icon of Indian nationalism [see *Bharat Mata* by Erwin Neumayer and Christine Schelberger (2008), *The Goddess and the Nation: Mapping Mother India* by Sumathi Ramaswamy (2010) and Sugata Bose's *The Nation as Mother: And Other Visions of Nationhood* (2017)] to being the mascot of India's Clean India campaign,[1] as a god in a dedicated temple in Odisha (See Figure 5.3) and a metaphor often employed to criticize the rising trend of communalism in India, the Mahatma's historical and political legacy remains immutable. Like his *Charkha*, the pair of his glasses and his slight bone-evident frame are also important coordinates extending from him that have been universally domesticated into a pedigree of prospective props in a cartoonist's lexicon, as the Mahatma continues to haunt the global political and popular cultural scene.

Political Cartooning and the Figure of the Mahatma

Benedict Anderson suggested an elevation of newspaper cartoons from their caricaturing stance and proposed a problematizing of the genre as "symbolic speech" (qtd. in Khanduri, "The Times of R. K. Laxman: Acche Din [Good Days]" 2016), generating public consciousness. "For Anderson, not merely the content but the form of the cartoon – distribution of light and dark, the characters and use of space was crucial for interpreting the cartoon's message" (Khanduri, "The Times" 2016). Suggesting a move beyond the familiar constellation of lampooning, humour and leisure-time-reading that triangulates cartooning, Anderson sought to look at cartoons as affecting the public's relationship with the political "where the public

FIGURE 5.3   *The Mahatma Along With the Gods.* Gandhi being worshipped in the
Mahatma Gandhi temple, Sambalpur Odisha. Personal photograph.

had access to modern political communication but did not have "political muscle"
(qtd. in Khanduri, "The Times" 2016).

Therefore, cartoons as chronicles of sociopolitics are a template of popular
culture "shaping public opinion" (Khanduri 49). It is the confluence of "caricature,
prose, topical content and a dash of humor" that makes cartoons "a critical form of
political journalism and a special category of news" (Khanduri 2). Talking about the
"raw history" and "historical potential" of photographs, Elizabeth Edwards directs
our attention to their pictorial authority that not only facilitates the "production
of photographs but also the opportunity to interpret" (Khanduri 30) to "give
voice to images and through them to insert the human voice" (Edwards 235).
Cartoons follow a similar trend as their interpretative ingenuousness places their
"visual sovereignty coevally with [their] ethnographic potential" (Khanduri 30). As
for debates, cartoons articulate lines of instability that often remains indiscernible

भारतमाता की गोद में महात्मा गांधी

MAHATMA GANDHI

FIGURE 5.4   "Mahatma Gandhi in the Lap of Bharat Mata." Print from the 1940s

under the garb of mythical solidarity of a myriad of political ideologies. Hence, the idea of a "public in a cultural form" is invoked by the genre of cartoons that construct "publics and counterpublics – interpretative communities bound by a visual experience" (Khanduri 30). Thus, cartoons, especially political cartoons, can be seen as "highly complex 'modern' attempts to formulate visual identities under specific historical and political conditions" (Pinney 96) that resonate with the reading public.

Gandhi in the Muslim Press, 1946–1947

Editorials from English dailies that supported the Muslim League's ideology direct our attention to its "embattled relationship with the Congress and the nationalist press" (Khanduri 98). A narrative of victimization and "persecution" of the minority press (*Dawn*, 28 March 1947) and, by extension, the Muslim identity, in general, is a leitmotif ubiquitous in Muslim dailies of the years 1946–1947. The narrative presents Muslims as the "weakest in the triangle," "who have to fight for survival against far two stronger parties" (*The Star* 10 January 1947) and frequently have "handicaps and restrictions" (*Dawn* 10 May 1947) placed on them. The Muslim press that has always been a "fount of communal goodwill" (*The Star*, 28 June 1947) is "specially gagged" (*Dawn*, 10 May 1947) by the "nationalist press" (Kamra 99) identified as the "Hindu Press" (*The Star*, 7 January 1947) in the pursuit of its "duty of propagating truth, justice, or fair-play without fear or favour" (*The Star*, 12 May 1947). The narrative, therefore, of the nationalist press "guilty" of "debasing journalism" (*The Star*, 12 May 1947), "manufacturing downright lies" (*The Star*, 18 April 1947) and "dishonest propaganda" (*The Star*, 31 March 1947) spills over into the discourse propagated by the political cartoons published at the time. Like the editorials, the cartoons too broadcasted an account of Muslim "victimization . . . [ultimately] leading to a righteous anger . . . [resulting in] large-scale (justified) violence" (Kamra 99) and the "establishment of a nation through sacrifice and much suffering" (Kamra 99).

That the fundamental function incumbent upon the Muslim-League supporting press of 1946–1997 was to censure the Congress' policies is evident in the cartoon titles "Try it!" published in *Dawn* in 1947; this cartoon is said to have deeply offended Nehru because of its offensive content. The cartoon seemed to channel and regulate the widespread Muslim displeasure at the Congress by using visual syntax to belittle the Indian National Congress' operation and its stalwarts as irrational and archaic in opinion and thus unfit for modern politics. An ailing Congress in the cartoon ("Try it") is surrounded by the familiar constellation of Gandhi and Nehru, who instead of administering modern medicine resort to sorcery as a curative measure. Gandhi is portrayed as a shaman with a skull hat while Nehru says that sorcery is the "last straw to save" the Congress. The dialectic of political rivalry is inseparable from the discourse the cartoon structurally establishes. The Congress' political policies are ridiculed and reduced to dark sorcery. The cartoon depicts Congress' policies not only as vulgar but also as demonic and dangerous as well.

The cartoon titled "Indelible Writing on the Wall"[2] shows Gandhi, Nehru, Patel and Azad, the stalwarts of Indian politics trying to expunge the writing – "Pakistan" from the wall. They are aided in their effort by the "Atlee Minorities Exterminator." Nevertheless, the inscribed letters prove ineradicable. Victory is ultimately accomplished notwithstanding "[t]he powerful resources and ceaseless machinations of those who wanted to keep the Muslim nation of India under the perpetual subjection of a hostile and alien majority" (Editorial, *Dawn*, 4 June 1947).

The cartoon inculpates both the British and the majority community's political leaders to persecute the Muslim minorities by denying them their fundamental right to a land of their own.

The political investment in the formulation and the intensification of a discourse of the differentiated treatment of minorities relentlessly operates in the Muslim press' editorial cartoons, rendering many of them as complex examples of sarcastic ingenuity. A unique cartoon titled "Taj by Mission Light," published in *Dawn*,[3] depicts the problematic relationship between the Cabinet Mission members and the Indian National Congress and its all-imposing patriarch, Gandhi. The superimposition of Gandhi's head in place of the central dome of the Taj Mahal, an icon of Oriental culture to the British, is meant to produce humour and question the over-imposing paternalism of Gandhi as the representative of the Congress.

The cartoon suggests that the aura of Gandhi's ideology (mostly favouring the majority community) might have unduly influenced the Cabinet Mission resulting in minorities being deprived of any possible solution to unsatisfactory political representation.[4] Having established by the iconography that the question of discrimination is fundamental to Congress politics, the lines by William Morris from his poem "The Earthly Paradise" that accompany the cartoon: "Nor did they think that they might long draw breath; In such an earthly paradise as this; But looked to find sharp ending of this bliss" – become suggestive. "Morris designed 'The Earthly Paradise' as an examination of two integrally related quests: the external search for a terrestrial Eden without change or death and the psychological quest for the paradise within, the experience of perfect love unmarred by fate and death" (qtd. in Silver 27). As Morris says, "dark vision reaches its climax in . . . [the creative piece], we are persuaded that the chance of gaining paradise through love" (qtd. in Silver 27) is impossible, if not improbable. The cartoons communicate the idea that the Cabinet Mission's encounter with Gandhi is a stimulus that will set in motion a neurotic journey of political dissension, which will ultimately thwart the latent good intentions of the Cabinet Mission.

What is interesting in the editorial cartoons of 1946–1947 of the nationalist and the Muslim-League supporting press are their warped reduction of all political contingencies to the two figures of Jinnah and Gandhi respectively. In their eyes, they are readily discernible vertices of a triangulated political rigmarole in which their corresponding ideology becomes the fountainhead of the other community's misery. As such, what we notice in the political cartoons from 1946 to 1947 is a strategic dismembering and dissolution of their humanity followed by an adaption of their figures as leitmotifs of egomaniacal despotism. The creative, seldom tangential, belittling of Jinnah and Gandhi carries the code of Poetic Justice for the righteous minorities resulting in a deluge of cartoons portraying them in various iniquitous situations. Two cartoons are especially illustrative in this respect:, the first one published by *The Diplomat* shows Jinnah as a nautch girl, while the second shows Gandhi as a toddler, a Benjamin-Button like figure oscillating between somatic ageing and ideological puerility.[5]

In this context of problematizing the political cartoons, it is crucial to consider that the subject of many of these cartoons, both in the nationalist press and in the Muslim press, is the unending tussle between the Congress and the League/India and Pakistan/Hindus and Muslims. This struggle is worth bearing in mind because it is by this "endless struggle against one another that transforms them [The Congress and the League/Hindus and Muslims] from an undifferentiated collection of beings into two cohesive, if warring, communities" (Collins 62). It is the conflict between the two binary opposites that constructs and sustains political discourse, not only through the myths that they produce but also through the mimetic nature of the tropes, the figures of speech, and themes that present them as "an undecidable case of twins" (Girard quoted in Collins 64). Further, the cartoons advocate a derivative enmity of sorts that accounts for a kind of god/demon struggle (with the *other* unequivocally posed as the demon). Consider, for example, an untitled cartoon by Ajmal published in *Dawn*. The cartoon shows several Congress leaders eavesdropping on the All India Muslim League Council Meeting. Their slyness is suggested by the unsanctioned imbibing of the proceedings that they anxiously and stealthily intercept. While Maulana Azad is depicted as listening at the keyhole, Nehru is seen peeping into the chamber hoisted by his comrade, while a confused and perturbed Gandhi is lost in thought. The suggestion is that although the Congress and the Muslim League are two separate political entities, the Congress is obsessed with the latter and never ceases to observe it to be abreast of the goings-on in the other's camp and be ready for any contingency that might present itself. Moreover, it does not matter considering their innate cunning if such information is unlawfully intercepted.

Since it is the ideological conflict that defines the Congress and the League, it can be argued that the press supporting the respective parties used visual rhetoric to escalate tensions between them and, by extension, the people supporting them. Although separate, the nationalist press and the Muslim press never "cease observing one another" (Collins 62) and comment on important events and observations made by the *other* party's stalwarts. In "Oh, Yeah,"[6] published in *Dawn*, we see Gandhi pointing with one hand and caressing the head of a goat with the other. Although his stance is obsequious, head bowed, figure bent and hand exposed, his intention is violent. Several other goats are tied to a post, while another, marked Muslim, stands next to a representative of the British Empire observing the proceedings. A dog marked Congress dominates the scene with its ominous presence. The comment at the bottom reads: "[i]n the eyes of Congress, Hindus, Muslims, Sikhs and Christians were all Indians and entitled to its care – Mr. Gandhi." The title "Oh, Yeah," unwilling to give credence to Gandhi's secular assertion on behalf of the Congress, is evidently sarcastic. The visual syntax reinforces the idea that Gandhi's words are a sham, and he, despite his avowals of non-violence, is just another violent crony of the Congress propagating their vicious agenda.

The illustration conflates the plot by invoking a truncated account of sacrifice. The idea of scapegoating the people, suggested by the literal presence of goats as the animals of sacrifice, makes the illustration grotesque and presents the Congress and Gandhi as partisans in the murder of their kin for the sake of political control. One cannot escape noting the similarity between the Congress hound and eponymous hound of Arthur Conan Doyle's novel *Hound of the Baskervilles* (1901). A comparison of Sidney Paget's illustration of Conan Doyle's hound of hell (see Figure 5.5) and the menacingly large quadruped in the cartoon suggests a similarity that serves to reinforce the idea that the Congress is a vile and vicious agency ready to devour its victim irrespective of its religion.

FIGURE 5.5 "The Hound of the Baskervilles." Victorian Web.

The beleaguered rapport between the Congress and the Muslim League[7] is perhaps the most favourite subject of the Muslim press, where the need to valorize the League goes hand in hand with the necessity to demean Congress politics as naïve, illogical and vile. In this context, no special privilege is meted to the Muslim politicians who do not subscribe to the League's ideology. The suspect nature of this failing of Muslims, who the Muslim press supporting the League's policies and the demand for Pakistan naturally considered brothers, is criticized in no uncertain terms as a betrayal to one's religion.

In general, the importance of the Muslim press's political cartoons seems to be: first, constant reinforcement of the narrative of unethical persecution of minorities by the majority which acts as a refrain in the illustrations. Consider, for example, the cartoon titled "Vulture's Harvest" (*Dawn*, 6 February 1947). Focusing on two hanged men, the cartoon is grotesque in every possible way and, therefore, unequivocally befitting in its semantics, at least, to suggest the victimization of the innocent Muslims by the majority community-led Congress. The hanging bar is labelled "Congress Sincerity" while the bodies that dangle with their necks broken bear the inscription "Muslim Rights in Bihar" and "Muslim Rights in U.P.," respectively. A third noose labelled "Reserved for Muslim National Freedom," ominously waits for its victim. The cartoon which seems to illustrate the following news: "Following news that the Muslim League Parties in Bihar and U.P. Assemblies have decided to boycott sessions of legislatures where their views are stream-rolled by the Congress party, comes the news that Mr. Gandhi has asked Muslims to put the 'sincerity' of the Congress majority in the Constituent Assembly to 'test'" (*Dawn*, 6 February 1947).

The negation of Muslim representation by Gandhi and the "steam-rolling" of their "views" in legislative sessions have been regarded as a precise instance of minority oppression by the Congress. Gandhi, the vulture in the cartoon, is the majority's spokesperson who wishes death for the innocents who support the League's political ideology. The discourse of righteousness thwarted and the empty noose reserved for the body of the "Muslim National Freedom" suggests the instability of the minority position and the inherent danger that lurks (notice Gandhi as vulture waiting to devour the corpses of the innocent) in the shape of the Congress.

Gandhi in Indian Political Cartoons, 1946–1947

Considering the superseding objective of political cartoons as "symbolic speech" (as noted by Benedict Anderson) intended to generate public opinion, they tap into "familiar cultural constructs" (Edwards xiv) to bring home a point. Indeed, it is the shared cultural context between the reader and the writer that enables the former to decode the message the writer wishes to convey, often symbolically or covertly. Hence, stereotyping and repetition of ideas, symbols or motifs inform the genre of political cartooning in no uncertain manner.[8]

Consider, for example, the cartoon "Sawing Through a Woman"[9] which problematizes the Partition through its visual syntax. The cartoon is unique in many respects, not just in locating the people of India in the embodied "gendered form of Mother India" (Kamra 76) but also in refraining from inculpating Jinnah as the singular (communal) force responsible for India's Partition. The cartoonist appears to desist such a simplistic denunciation of Jinnah and includes Nehru in the picture to prove his point that as far as Partition was concerned, both Jinnah and Nehru, representatives of the Muslim League and the Congress, respectively, were equally culpable. The two leaders are illustrated as stage magicians standing opposite to one another and performing the magic trick of "Sawing Through a Woman" (*Pioneer*, 9 July). We know that "[a] human magician blends science, psychology and performance to create a magical effect," (Williams and Owen, n.p.) and "[m]agical effects are all in some form based on hidden mathematical, scientific, or psychological principles; often the parameters controlling these underpinning techniques are hard for a magician to blend to maximize the magical effect required. The complexity is often caused by interacting and often conflicting physical and psychological constraints that need to be optimally balanced" (Williams and Owen, n.p.). Generally, this *tuning* is done by repeating of activity time and again with complete coordination between the actors till it is perfected. In the illustration, however, the tuning is faulty, as suggested by the remarks of the profusely perspiring and tensed John Bull standing in the background. As Jinnah and Nehru vigorously saw through the box marked Pakistan on one side and Hindustan on another, Bull addresses his remark to the protruding head of the woman (Mother India, presumably) whose body is hidden in the box that Jinnah and Nehru (both depicted as stage magicians in the cartoon) saw through: "I only 'ope that nothing goes wrong madam," he says. Bull's anxiety is palpable, and so is the tenseness in Gandhi's features, who also stood in the background witnessing the performance. The cartoon, therefore, translates the Partition as akin to one of the "magicians' misdirection techniques [that] could be used to induce . . . misperception" (Tompkins, Matthew L et al. 2016) among people (of India, in this case) for the (political) benefit of the magicians (Jinnah and Nehru). The vulnerability of Mother India is suggested by her role as the magicians' female assistant performing the part of the victim who is sawn. As a "national iconic signifier for the material, the passive, and the corporeal, to be worshipped, protected and controlled by those with . . . power" the "essential woman" (Kaplan et al. 10), Mother India, is illustrated as a subaltern victim unable to control the vanguards of her honour that now tear her apart. The cartoon accuses both the political leaders of matricide, an eventuality that seems more than possible, if not probable, given that the two magicians performing the trick are at loggerheads and any attempt at ideological harmonization between the two is bound to fail.

The nationalist press, in adorning Gandhi's iconography with mysticism and spirituality, as seen, for instance, in the cartoon depicting Gandhi as a Bhakti saint in *Janmabhoomi*, fails to situate him, as Kamra points out, at the core of the political rigamarole of the nationalist movement. Forever marginalized, Gandhi is often depicted as a lone figure; his goodness marginalizes his political appeal. Consider, for example, the cartoon titled "Danger Signal,"[10] which confirms this tautology. Extracted from a plethora of leaders of national importance and superimposed on the scene as the singular face both dominating and auxiliary to the political scenario, the vegetal leitmotif of Gandhi as innocence personified is exemplified in this representation. Magnified as the only person who can adjudge the contingency of the Partition as an impending catastrophe, Gandhi is seen as waving a flag of warning at the locomotive as it makes its way towards a divergence of the railway track into Hindustan and Pakistan. Thus, the cartoon privileges Gandhi's position as the voice of sanity, asking people to be aware of the anathema that might befall them if the Partition becomes a reality.

The cartoon that appears to dramatize Gandhi's request to Jinnah that he is allowed to stay in Pakistan for a while is perhaps one of the very few of the political cartoons of the time that features him as a mortal. Titled "Till Death Do Us Part,"[11] in the cartoon Gandhi is depicted as an unruly guest who threatens to board in the Hotel Pakistan permanently, establishing his spatial right as India's representative in Pakistan's newly independent domain. That Gandhi's request perplexed Jinnah is evident by his depiction as a beleaguered hotel manager tearing out his hair in desperation not knowing how to evict Gandhi's moral force.

Gandhi in the Colonial Press Cartoons

The deluge of the archetypal image of Gandhi working at his *Charkha* that we find in illustrations by David Low, Leslie Illingworth, Raven Hill and other cartoonists from the British press in the politically turbulent years of colonial politics (1930–1947) proves the media's consideration of Gandhi an irresistible subject of caricature. Consider, for example, the cartoon titled "The Elusive Mahatma" by Leonard Raven Hill (*Punch*, 26 August 1931), which problematizes the magnetism of the Gandhian agency.

The enigma of Gandhi's personality receives a concerted subscription in colonial cartoons during the 1930s. David Low said that "the British people had grown a conscience about India by the nineteen-thirties" and "old imperialism was wearing out" (Low qtd. in Khanduri 88). Although the Gandhian politics of non-violence was disregarded as "passive resistance" (Low qtd. in Khanduri 88) by colonial officials, cartoons on Gandhi found many receptive audiences in Britain and India correspondingly. He was considered as a signifier of revolutionary nationalist politics. In the cartoon by Raven Hill, we see Britannia pining for the elusive Mahatma. Accompanied by only a portrait of the great man, the lady looks out like a transfixed lover yearning for the loved one's return. However, the discourse of equanimity demonstrated by the *Punch* cartoon changes in the later years of tumultuous political drama of India's nationalist struggle to suggest turmoil. One may refer to the cartoon titled "Free India" by Leslie Illingworth published in the *Daily Mail* on 20 May 1947 to substantiate the argument.

In May 1947, the British Cabinet acquiesced to Lord Mountbatten's proposal for India' partition into a Hindu and a Muslim state. With the contingency of the

Partition in the vicinity, the noted cartoonist Leslie Illingworth published a cartoon titled "Free India" to depict the ground reality of the tumultuous socio-political scenario of the time. The cartoon portrays a group of protesters all demanding the British leave India. In the cartoon, the Gandhian demand for Swaraj or home rule for India mingles with the cry of the U.S. sympathizer calling out British reign as "tyranny." In the background, however, are the victims of violent communal rioting. The illustration of the bird of prey locating its food among the dead is a trope Illingworth used to invoke the brutal massacres following Jinnah's speech in August 1946 asking Muslims to take direct action in support of their demand for a separate Muslim state. The Great Calcutta Killings or the Direct-Action Day Riots on 16 August 1946 was one of the most disturbing communal riots between Hindus and Muslims, killings hundreds of thousands of people (see Saha 2018). As pictures following the riots of dead bodies littered in the streets were published, people realized the enormity of India's communal problem that ultimately resulted in India's Partition the following year. Illingworth's invocation of the chilling image of dreadful riots by using the carrion bird's visual trope suggests how in his view, political leaders and protesters were oblivious to the real suffering of people who were ultimately the faceless victims of religious riots. Through his cartoon, he provides a powerful critique of the bigotry of the politicians whose ambition and ideology eventually resulted in the outbreak of unprecedented violence, making the Partition of India one of the bloodiest instances of communal intolerance in the history of the world. Illingworth squarely inculpates these politicians and their supporters for the despicable state of India. The disconsolate female figure in the picture with a child is supposedly the Indian subcontinent, *Bharat Mata*, who was the muse of the national independence movement. The mother nation whose bounty and grace were eulogized by the poet Bankim Chandra Chattopadhyay in his poem *"Vande Mataram" (Hail, the Mother)* now genuflected to the political whims of her sons. Her stooping posture, holding her young close to her to avoid harm, signifies the Indian politicians' failed efforts to protect her.

The narrative suggests the absence of a heroic saviour of spiritual purity to safeguard the Indian nation. In the riot-torn scene of communal intolerance, the British are conspicuous by their absence because political bigotry has driven them out of the Indian subcontinent, and they can no longer save the weak and the poor even if they search for them. From the cartoon, the reader receives the impression that Indian independence in the British eye was a travesty. It is interesting to note that as far as colonial politics is concerned, the British press more often than not abstained from serious criticism. Consider, for example, the cartoon titled "The Indian 'Working Party'" published in the *Punch* in 1946 which censures the unprofessional ineffectuality of a working party meeting deciding India's fate. The negotiating parties are sitting on the back of an elephant that looks despondently unsure of its role as a bearer of political prowess. As a national symbol, the elephant is the representative of the mute populace marginalized in political discussions that might affect them the most. The outdoor meeting spot and the Taj Mahal in the background add a touch of orientalism and render the whole idea of important negotiations in the open as more entertaining than a serious business. The puerile nature of the engagement is suggested by the title of the caption as well. British press did not abstract or marginalize Gandhi from the political party as was seen in Muslim Press.

Conclusion

A discussion of the political cartoons on Gandhi suggests that though subjective and ideologically apparent, these cartoons form a lasting discourse of Gandhian historiography. The visual syntax and symbols that animate the cartoons interpret the contours of politics subtly surrounding Gandhi and, in doing so, initiate debate and manipulate public consciousness. Apart from being cultural representations that through their epistemological and pedagogical constituent visualize Gandhi as a combination of a mystic and a human, a quack and a political figure, the plethora of cartoons studied in this chapter also problematize spatial politics by reading how the discursive location of the cartoonist determines his narrative. Furthermore, despite their ideological overtness, the political cartoons on Gandhi analysed in the chapter deftly foreground the significance of the narrative lens of cartoons, allowing us to apprehend the political history of the anti-colonial nationalist struggle. Thus, although deeply problematic and circumscribed by ideological binaries, this visual legacy of Gandhi in cartoons enables us to engage with the history of the subcontinent via his representation and use that critical understanding to confront our past of violent communalism, territorial conflict and problematic nationalism for better insights into the present.

Notes

1 Sanitation and hygiene in every Indian home were essential to the Gandhian ideology. To him, "Sanitation [was] more important than independence" (Gandhi qtd. in Sampath) and he made people pledge that they should never litter nor allow another to do the same. Keeping in mind Gandhi's attributes on cleanliness as next to godliness, the Swachh Bharat Abhiyan or the Clean India Campaign inaugurated by the current Indian Prime Minister Narendra Modi invokes Gandhi's morality by using his image and the image of his spectacles, as the insignia for the mission. This adds Gandhi's essential patriotic decent to the governmental campaign and equates the present government's political position in terms of public welfare with that of Gandhi, popularly believed as the greatest national leader India has ever begat.

2 "Indelible Writing on the Wall." *Dawn*, 23 March 1946. Retrieved from, www.euaca demic.org/UploadArticle/4401.pdf. Accessed 4 May 2020.

3 "Taj by Mission Light." *Dawn,* 14 April 1946. Retrieved from, www.bl.uk/britishli brary/~/media/subjects%20images/south%20asia/ior%20pdfs/chevening/3_parti tion_1947_cartoons.pdf. Accessed 4 May 2020.

4 In the 1920s and 1930s, Gandhi became the icon of nationalist politics in India working under the aegis of the Congress Party, which he led during that time. His noncooperative nonviolent movement and his protests against the Rowlatt Acts of 1919, the famous Salt March of 1930 and his other acts of civil disobedience were performed as a member of the All India Congress Party. Therefore, the view that Gandhi was the personification,

the physiognomized version of the Indian National Congress' popular ideology, was well established. Cartoons like "Try it" by Ajmal published in *Dawn* which shows Gandhi as a sorcerer trying to recuperate an ailing Congress represent the aforementioned idea. Several cartoons published in *Dawn* propose this point of view. Other works like *Pakistan Or the Partition of India: What Congress and Gandhi Have Done to Untouchables* by Dr. BR Ambedkar (1946), *Mahatma Gandhi: The Congress and Partition of India* by DC Jha and *Mahatma Gandhi: Congress and Leadership* by S. R. Bakshi (1997) are important works that equate Gandhi as synonymous with the Congress Party and by extension its ideology that he imbibed and proliferated.

5 "Jinnah as a Nautch Girl." National Herald, 1945, Cartoon. Retrieved from https://thediplomat.com/2017/08/the-shadow-of-doubt-india-pakistan-and-vulgar-cartoons-in-1947/. Accessed 4 May 2020. And "Second Childhood." Dawn, 1946, Cartoon.

6 "Oh, yeah." Dawn 21 June 1946, Courtesy of the Dawn archive, Accessed 4 May 2020. Retrieved from, www.bl.uk/britishlibrary/~/media/subjects%20images/south%20asia/ior%20pdfs/chevening/3_partition_1947_cartoons.pdf, Accessed 4 May 2020.

7 Popular non-nationalist newspapers like *Dawn* and *Star* dedicated their editorial pages to underscore the persecutions endured by the Muslims at the hands of the Congress. While nationalist dailies like *Hindustan Times* vilified Jinnah and his politics, the non-nationalist English dailies used similar strategies, tropes and metaphors to valorize the self and demonize the Congress. As such like Jinnah occupying the position of the demonical *other,* we see Gandhi, Nehru and Patel in synonymous situations. The cartoon titled "Consolation" published in *Dawn* on 19 February 1947 cartoon titled "Consolation" shows Gandhi looking in disquiet at a Muslim outside his window. Behind him Khan Abdul Ghaffar Khan, the Pashtun independence activist also known as 'Frontier Gandhi' speaks with Gandhi through an A.I.R. microphone. In his hand, we notice a newspaper with the headline "Muslim League Victory in Mardan." The comment accompanying the text seems to answer Gandhi's (read Congress') concern at the sight of the remnant Muslim League figure (a relic of the Muslim League politics) in the vicinity. It reads, "It is only an optical illusion, Mein Mahatma. I have killed the League [Muslim League] in the Frontier with my short-wave, medium-wave and long-wave." The idea that Gandhi and the "Frontier Gandhi" as members of Congress representing the party are colluding in Muslim League Party's extinction is problematic. Also, the equating of Gandhi as Hitler (Mein Mahatma) incorporated the same warped cultural logic that the Congress supporting nationalist dailies like the *Hindustan Times* and *The Leader* used in cartoons like "Heavenly Blessings" (*The Leader*, 25 August 1947) where Jinnah's ideology was paralleled with that of Hitler. The Congress and India seemed to have occupied the exact location in the non-nationalist Muslim Press that Jinnah held opposite the nationalist press and the Congress.

8 See Free India and its Patriarch, Mahatma Gandhi. Cartoon. *Amrita Bazar Patrika.* *https://artsandculture.google.com/asset/amrita-bazar-patrika-volume-79-issue-227–15th-august-1947-page-1/JQFIutm5U-GH7Q.*

9 "Sawing Through a Woman." Pioneer, 9 July 1947, Accessed 18 October 2018. https://blog.uvm.edu/imorgens-rel195a/2015/12/04/saving-the-bharat-mata-what-was-at-stake-for-her-children/.

10 "Danger Signal." National Herald, 28 May 1947, Accessed 18 October 2018. www.agefotostock.com/age/en/details-photo/danger-signal-hindustan-times-may-1947-model-release-not-available/DPA-MKG-33555

11 "Till Death Do Us Part." *Pioneer*, 9 August 1947.

Works Cited

Ambedkar, B. R. *Pakistan or the Partition of India: What Congress and Gandhi Have Done to Untouchables*. Samyak Prakashan, 2016.

Bakshi, S. R. *Mahatma Gandhi: Congress and Leadership*. Anmol Publications Pvt. Limited, 1997.

Bhaba, Homi K. "The Other Question: The Stereotype and Colonial Discourse." *Twentieth-Century Literary Theory*, Palgrave, 1997.

Bose, Sugata. *The Nation as Mother and Other Visions of Nationhood*. Penguin Random House, 2017.

Burt, Jonathan. *Animals in Film*. Reaktion Books, 2002.

Collins, Brian. *The Head Beneath the Altar: Hindu Mythology and the Critique of Sacrifice*. 1st ed. Michigan State University Press, 2014.

Deleuze, Gilles, Félix Guattari, Michel Foucault, and Gilles Deleuze. *Anti-Oedipus: Capitalism and Schizophrenia*. Penguin Classics, 1983.

Edwards, Elizabeth. Raw Histories: Photographs, Anthropology and Museums. Berg, 2001.

Edwards, Janis L. "Political Cartoons in the 1988 Presidential Campaign: Image, Metaphor and Narrative." *Garland Studies in American Popular History and Culture*, Garland, 1997.

George, Rosemary Marangoly. "Feminists Theorize Colonial/Postcolonial." *The Cambridge Companion to Feminist Literary Theory*, edited by Ellen Rooney, pp. 211–31. Cambridge UP, 2006.

Harrison, Randall. *The Cartoon, Communication to the Quick*. Sage, 1981.

Jha, D. C. *Mahatma Gandhi: The Congress and Partition of India*. India Research Press, 2004.

Kamra, Sukeshi. *Bearing Witness: Partition, Independence, End of the Raj*. U of Calgary P, 2002.

———. "The War of Images: Mohammed Ali Jinnah and Editorial Cartoons in the Indian Nationalist Press, 1947." *Ariel*, vol. 34, 2003.

Kaplan, Caren, Norma Alarcón, and Minoo Moallem. *Between Woman and Nation: Nationalisms, Transnational Feminisms, and the State*. Duke UP, 1999.

Khanduri, Ritu Gairola. *Caricaturing Culture in India: Cartoons and History in the Modern World*. Cambridge UP, 2014.

———. "The Times of R. K. Laxman: Acche Din (Good Days)." *Cambridge University Press*, 10 Feb. 2016, www.cambridgeblog.org/2016/01/the-times-of-r-k-laxman-acche-din-good-days/. Accessed 10 Jan. 2020.

Layard, George S. *Shirley Brooks of Punch: His Life, Letters, and Diaries*. Henry Holt, 1907.

Misri, Deepti. *Beyond Partition: Gender, Violence, and Representation in Postcolonial India*. U of Illinois P, 2014.

Neumayer, Erwin, and Christine Schelberger. *Bharat Mata: India's Freedom Movement in Popular Art*. Oxford UP, 2008.

Pinney, Christopher. *Camera Indica: The Social Life of Indian Photographs*. U of Chicago P, 1997.

Psalm 58:3–5 (KJV). Bible Gateway, www.biblegateway.com/passage/?search=Psalm 58:3-5&version=KJV. Accessed 13 July 2019.

Ramaswamy, Sumathi. *The Goddess and the Nation: Mapping Mother India*. Duke UP, 2010.

Rovin, Jeff. *The Illustrated Encyclopedia of Cartoon Animals*. Prentice Hall, 1991.

Rowland, Barry. *Herby and Friends: Cartoons in Wartime*. Natural Heritage, 1990.

Saha, Barnali. "The Trauma and Tragedy of Partition Through the Eyes of a British Cartoonist: Reading Selected Cartoons by Leslie Illingworth." *New Horizons: A Multidisciplinary Research Journal*, vol. XV, Aug. 2018.

Saha, Barnali, and Anup Beniwal. "Laughter in the Communal: Partition Politics and Cartoons in Indian Press, 1946–1947." *ACADEMICIA: An International Multidisciplinary Research Journal* (ISSN: 2249–7137), vol. 9, no. 9, Sept. 2019, doi:10.5958/2249-7137.2019.00098.

Sampath, Vikram. "Gandhi Valued Sanitation More Than Independence. Modi's Swachh Bharat Is Fulfilling His Dream." *The Print*, 12 Apr. 2019, theprint.in/opinion/

gandhi-valued-sanitation-more-than-independence-modis-swachh-bharat-is-fulfilling-his-dream/220306/. Accessed 7 Mar. 2019.

Silver, Carole G. "'The Earthly Paradise:' Lost." *Victorian Poetry*, vol. 13, no. 3/4, 1975, pp. 27–42. *JSTOR*, www.jstor.org/stable/40001829.

Tanwar, Raghuvendra. *Reporting the Partition of Punjab, 1947: Press, Public and Other Opinions.* Manohar, 2006.

Tharoor, Shashi. "The Partition: The British Game of 'Divide and Rule'." *Al Jazeera*, 10 Aug. 2017, www.aljazeera.com/indepth/opinion/2017/08/partition-british-game-divide-rule-170808101655163.html. Accessed 7 Mar. 2019.

Tompkins, Matthew L., et al. Abstract. "The Phantom Vanish Magic Trick: Investigating the Disappearance of a Non-existent Object in a Dynamic Scene." *Frontiers in Psychology*, vol. 7, no. 950, 21 July 2016, doi:10.3389/fpsyg.2016.00950.

Wells, Paul. *The Animated Bestiary: Animals, Cartoons, and Culture.* Rutgers UP, 2009.

Williams, Howard, and McOwan Peter W. Abstract. "Magic in the Machine: A Computational Magician's Assistant." *Frontiers in Psychology*, 17 Nov. 2014, https://doi.org/10.3389/fpsyg.2014.01283. Accessed 7 Mar. 2019.

6

EXPLORATION OF INDIAN VISUAL PRACTICES FROM 1960 TO 1970

A Study of Indian Comic Books on Gandhi

Aparna Pathak

The study of visual culture is a very recent addition to the disciplines of research in India. Most of the researches that involve visuals pertain to studying the production of images in popular culture, iconographies, and perceptions. This scholarly interest in artistic representations further includes the study of visuals in the arena of cultural studies to understand the prevailing power dynamics and how meanings produced through the visuals are circulated as mass culture. The study of visual culture in the Indian context becomes all the more critical because, as Diana Eck remarks, "India is a visual and visionary culture, one in which the eyes have a prominent role in the apprehension of the sacred" (10). This affinity of visual culture with the sensory aspect of the eyes brings in the ideas of visuality and spectatorship, which aids in developing communication. In the print media, there has always been immense popularity of calendars, posters, and visual storytelling traditions in India, such as *chitrakatha*, all of which contributed to the rise of the comic book genre in post-independence India. For the scope of this paper, the focus is on two comic books based on the life of Mahatma Gandhi. *The Gandhi Story* by S. D. Sawant and S. D. Badalkar (1966) and the particular issues of *Amar Chitra Katha*, *Mahatma Gandhi I: The Early Days* and *Mahatma Gandhi II: Father of the Nation* (studied together and referred to as *Mahatma Gandhi* further on) published as a series in 1989 (reprinted in 2008).

Rise of Indian Comic Books

The rise of the comic book genre in the 1960s and 1970s was directly linked with several political and social factors including the feeling of disillusionment among the various sections of society leading to a severe distrust towards the government, slackened economic growth, and rising inflation.[1] It became an urgent matter of concern for the government to develop nationalist historiography that captured a pan-Indian imagination. The state took steps to promote readership and develop "national

DOI: 10.4324/9781003145479-9

modernity among children" by establishing initiatives like Children's Book Trust in 1957, Children's Film Society, and Nehru Bal Pustakalaya. However, these could not capture the Indian middle class's attention for reformist pedagogy because these attempts were presented with "abstract, internationalist notions of modernity" (Sreenivas 5).

Another pedagogic initiative by the Publications Division of India's Ministry of Information and Broadcasting was to introduce the comic book, *The Gandhi Story* in 1966. The Foreword of this official, a state-sponsored comic book, was written by Jawaharlal Nehru during the comic book production. He wrote,

> [t]his pictorial representation of the Gandhi story must appeal to children in India. The Gandhi story has become an essential part of our rich heritage from the past and is still influencing our present. I am sure the generations to come will wonder at this incredible story. It is well, therefore, that our children should get acquainted with it before they read more about it in books.
>
> *(iii)*

This comic book was published in English and translated into Assamese, Bengali, Tamil, Malayalam, Punjabi, and Hindi to achieve a pan-Indian readership. It would be incorrect to assume that it was the first-ever comic book to be published in India because, in the 1960s, American comic books such as *Tarzan*, *Mandrake the Magician*, and *Superman* were already popular among urban children.[2] However, it can be said that this was one of the first few comic books that were published in the Western form of comic book medium with an Indian subject matter.

In the late 1960s, Anant Pai introduced *Amar Chitra Katha* as an indigenous comic book to the Indian populace. The primary motive for establishing this was to reintroduce the traditions and refashion history and mythology to create a "national culture" (Sreenivas 40) and nationalist historiography based on heroism and charisma of heroes and outstanding personalities. These heroic narratives drawn from episodes of ancient, medieval, and modern India, along with characters and incidents of epical narratives founded upon a Hindu mythology, were presented as legends and simultaneously framed as a history of Indian culture. *Amar Chitra Katha* narrativized history as a re-installation of normative politics and took it into the popular domain. With *Amar Chitra Katha* (ACK), Pai pushed for educational content, and he established a heritage-based approach that was deeply rooted in the Indian culture. This approach localized the comics culture in an Indian tradition and quickly established a comic book national readership published in English and other regional languages of India. In her analysis of the ACK, Sreenivas argues "[t]he narrative composition of the series significantly contributes to the production of an 'Indianness' that is at once modern and traditional, contemporary and 'immortal'" (43).

It was Pai's attempt at refashioning history as a rich and glorious past. He presented a series of biographies of great personalities that glorified their heroism and charisma as a useful pedagogic tool. This knowledge of history and culture in the name of national pride and recreation is a direct example of excluding voices from below. When these early comic books started flooding the markets for middle-class consumption in the 1970s and 1980s, it was also a time when the Subaltern Studies Group started as an alternate strand in cultural politics. With the representation of national figures as revered, divine, and supernatural beings, the comic books aimed to create a middle-class sensibility that subscribed to specific ideas of selfhood and citizenship, valorizing Indian nationalism and normative power relations of the times.

What makes this rise of visual representation and dissemination in India's mass culture unique is the centrality of the iconography of various important figures. Mahatma Gandhi is the most iconic figure of modern India, and his iconography is complex and distinct in the sense that it began during his lifetime. Even after decades of his assassination, he continues to figure as an important personality for artists, cartoonists, and comic book authors globally, such as the Japanese artist Kazuki Ebine's manga comics, *Gandhi: A Manga Biography* (2011).

Influence of Indian Visual Culture

Both of these initiatives, the state-sponsored *The Gandhi Story* and the *Amar Chitra Katha* rendition, were urgent attempts to instill knowledge of the Indian freedom struggle and about the Indian heroes instead of the growing popularity of American superheroes. These early comic books borrowed heavily from traditional storytelling, *chitrakatha*, an ancient form of India's narrative practices. This art of *chitrakatha* has been immensely popular in Rajasthan, Gujarat, Maharashtra, and many other regions of India where *puranic* and local legendary tales were performed in the market places.[3] The story was narrated along with ritual singing and displaying of the painted scroll. The narrative was episodic throwing light on the critical instances of the hero's life. In the *chitrakatha* tradition, the folk hero is celebrated and idealized to the point of deification. It is an amalgamation of authentic incidents along with mythology and folklore (Sreenivas 54). The resemblance of the *chitrakathas* with the comic books of modern India is not limited to the displayed panels in scrolls but is visible in hero-worship and deification of the heroes. This idea of deification shall be explored later in this chapter in terms of spectatorship, gaze, and visual conceptualization.

The visuals of these early comic books follow realism. The iconic visuality of Hindu mythological characters and episodes are drawn from *Puranas*, and sketches of religious figures create a homogenous Hindu space by mass circulation and consumption. This mass circulation took place as early as the nineteenth century with the advent of the printing press in India. The important pioneer of this kind of visual representation was Raja Ravi Varma. His oil paintings that incorporated western influences set the stage for Indian realism and a unique aesthetic Indian sensibility to emerge.[4] This move towards a more Hindu-centric visuality was initiated by the lithographic press set up by him, "Ravi Varma Fine Art Lithographic Press" in Mumbai (then Bombay) in 1894. Even in the choice of content, these early comic books were influenced by the pre novelistic forms such as *dastan, kissa, itihasa* or the Sanskrit literary tradition. The typical features of these comic books, similar to traditional storytelling modes, are that no clear boundaries between myth and legend are elucidated. Hence, any form of history writing, as also in the case of these comic books, the biographies of the historical figures is a combination of myth and legend that differentiates them from the modern positivist sense of history. It "connoted a literary genre straddling both chronicle and fiction" (Sreenivas 86).

Going back to the visual influence of Raja Ravi Verma on these two early comic books, ACK artists used his realistic art as a reference to draw the characters of the comic books, their mannerisms, body language, expressions, and even the background. Many of the *Amar Chitra Katha* issues bear resemblances to Raja Ravi Varma's paintings, where the whole cover page captures the protagonist's image. "The Coquette" and "Mohini (Temptress)" – two of the most famous and detailed paintings of Raja Ravi Verma's realistic style – inspired similar renditions of realism in *Amar Chitra Katha's* cover pages of *Devi Choudhurani* and *Chandrahasa*.

Heroic Idealization Through Corporeal Representation

The corporeal representation of the protagonist on the comic book's cover sets the pace for the comic book's visuality. In most of these early comic books, since the content was sacred or historically significant, they were treated accordingly. As Sreenivas, in her study of *Amar Chitra Katha*, argues, "the poster-like cover illustration is an important means through which ACK centres the individual. The charisma/heroism of the hero(ine) sutures together the narrative within the cover pages as a binding agent" (66). In most cases, the hero is presented as a supernatural being. In *The Gandhi Story*, the artists have relied on photographs to illustrate the Gandhian figure realistically. When the reference has been a photograph, the artists have taken the liberty of presenting Gandhi as a larger-than-life figure. As Karline McLain says, "in many places they extend beyond the documentary imperative and open up space for the heroic idealisation of this historic figure through the employment of several visual tactics" (2014, 304).

The state and *Amar Chitra Katha* attempted to create a homogenized visuality through these early comic books that can be argued as powerfully Hinduized. The representation of Gandhi, especially in *The Gandhi Story*, directly corresponds to this kind of visuality, which plays a vital role in representing and disseminating the Indian culture. This heroic idealization of Gandhi can be perceived in the context of the Indian visual culture as one that is deeply rooted in the Hindu modes of visuality, majorly the concept, as E. Dawson Varughese explains, of "*darshan/darśan* and *drishti* (as ideas of 'seeing' and 'gazing')" (15). As Diana Eck, in her book *Darśan: Seeing the Divine Image in India*, writes "[h]induism is an imaginative, an 'image-making,' religious tradition in which the sacred is seen as present in the visible world – the world we see in multiple images and deities, in sacred places, and in people" (10).

The artists mould the cultural and visual consumptions through comic books to highlight this kind of visuality.

In *The Gandhi Story*, the creators have resorted to the visual tactic of drawing him at a hieratic scale. In one of the comic book's panels, Gandhi is drawn as addressing a crowd of Indians in South Africa (12). He is drawn as a figure of a supernatural size towering over fellow Indians. His towering figure is symbolic of a leader or a superhero that guides his followers. This tactic is used again to show him as a leader who guides the populace to strike against the discrimination they face; he is represented as a larger-than-life leader of the masses (17). As a superhuman figure, Gandhi's visual representation drawing him larger than life resonates with the aura created around his being. In the episode, when he is charged with seditious writing and pleads guilty, Gandhi is shown standing with full frontality shown to the reader giving him that hieratic stature (22).

It can also be argued that this frontality that is rendered to Gandhi's persona is used as a direct address by him to the readers. As Sreenivas argues, this frontality brings in a newer kind of gaze that is non-voyeuristic and "rules out identification with the image on the part of the viewer" (91). The creators intend to present Gandhi as a figure whose personality is to be revered. The use of this frontality confirms that particular response from the viewer. The comics creators have also used frontality when they want Gandhi's character to address the reader directly. Geeta Kapur argues that when an icon is represented through frontality, it is the "frontality of the word, the image, the design, the performative act. . . . This yield forms of direct address" (qtd. in Sreenivas 90–91).

S.D. Sawant and S.D. Badalkar seem to be breaking the fourth wall between the reader and the comic book by drawing Gandhi with a direct gaze focused on the reader (31). Even if it is in response to Mahadeo's concern over the village's lack of facilities, this direct address invokes a different kind of visuality. It invokes a direct engagement with the reader making it learn about sacrifice. This interactive gaze hints after the divine communication, and the direct address serves the pedagogical purpose that the comic book intends.

The representation of Gandhi in *The Gandhi Story* is an example of the aura created around the historical personalities. Even when the comics creators resorted to realism, they have been able to deify him and instill sacredness in the representation. In the elucidation of the juxtaposition of the sacred and realistic elements, this chapter explores Sreenivas' concept of "compromised realism." She says "realism is a constantly bargained commodity as it jostles with the demands of popular taste, local traditions and the dynamics of the market for sacred art" (71, 72). Usually, in film hoardings and posters too, the persona is constructed in larger-than-life proportions. This compromised realism adds to the texture of direct visuality and engages the viewer in a somewhat convoluted manner, not direct or flat but multi-layered.

This hieratic scale showing Gandhi as a larger-than-life figure in the comic book highlights the modality of gaze and spectatorship in the Indian context.

The idea of *darshan* is associated with the sacred in the Hindu religious context. However, this idea has been extended by the comics creators to formulate homogeneous Indian spectatorship. In a Hindu religious context, *darshan* is a basic form of worship whereby the devotee simply gazes upon the deity and, in turn, becomes the object of the deity's gaze. People take *darshan* of iconic objects, great humans, and even a landscape – in short, all things animate and inanimate that are believed to be imbued with divine power. It involves a visual communication that is established between the worshipper and the deity. Interestingly, this visual communication does not get limited to the sacred space and goes even to the public space, beyond the sacred. It is the most compelling aspect of this phenomenon, particularly from the perspective of art history and visual culture studies, as it is spectatorship associated with the divine, so it is the image that holds power when it is perceived in a particular context. Discussing the visuality in Indian culture, Varughese notes, "Without a direct translation in English, *darśan* is essentially the act of seeing wherein the meeting of the eyes connects the gazer, and the gazed upon in a multisensory moment of dialogue, both powerful and auspicious" (15).

This kind of *darshanik* gazing becomes central to the study of these comic books because Gandhi is, at times, deified by the comics creators representing him in a very auspicious manner that idealizes him to the level of the sacred. In her discussion of the deifying of the political figures such as MGR in Chennai Preminda Jacob also discusses Gandhi's persona and how people perceived him. She says, "A compelling demonstration of powerful political communication purely on the basis of the leader's image was afforded by M. K. Gandhi during the national struggle he led against the British imperial rule of South Asia" (241). She further remarks

> Gandhi understood that his visible presence was an opportunity for his followers to express bhakti (simple faith and religiosity). Moreover, he rationalized to ignore the crowd and . . . his writings or reading did not, in any way, diminish the people's desire to gaze upon him.
>
> *(242)*

This Hindu religious tradition of *Darshan* transcends religious boundaries to emerge as a secular form of veneration. The early Hindu rulers spun tales about legendary connections with Hindu deities. This fictive kinship associates the historical cults and royal families with gods and goddesses, making them no less than semi-gods. These rulers then presented themselves before the public and in the act of taking *darshan*, the public believed it or equated it with being in spiritual communication with the deity. This practice, however, was not confined to only Hindu rulers. Mughal emperors presented themselves before the public in the form of *jharokha darshan* on a balcony or a window for the public to gaze upon them (Jacob 246–47).

These cultural practices continue to figure in the popular imagination of the Indian people, and it is also reflected in the way important personalities are presented in the early comic books. In the comic books' visual realm, India, Indian culture, and influential personalities of the newly independent India are mainly presented through the logic of hero worship. Nandini Chandra says,

> What masquerades as a novel, different, and plural approach can be subsumed within the bourgeois genre of biographical narratives. Thus, the nation itself is identified in terms of an individual's inspiring life-narrative. Hero worship, an integral part of children's literature, is then put into life-narrative service designed to foster national feeling.
>
> *(5)*

As has already been argued in this paper, Gandhi was represented as a towering figure in *The Gandhi Story*. The deification can be seen in other instances where he is shown with a bright aura around him. One such case is when he is shown as a morally upright person who does not feel it ethically correct to keep gifts that he has been presented by his fellow Indians in South Africa (8). His determination is represented as a virtue and is glorified to represent him surrounded by an aura. This same effect is then transferred to "handmade sandals" gift that he sends to Smuts (Sawant and Badalkar 13). There are also two exact instances in the comic book that equate Gandhi with a god-like figure one of which is when Gandhi is drawn as collecting funds for the struggle to fight discrimination. This panel shows that Gandhi was revered as a saint or a god whose *darshan* seekers were always gathered in large numbers. The image shows women paying respects to Gandhi in the same manner as they would bow down in front of a deity (24).

This panel still visualizes him as a human who is deified. This deification is not an example of "compromised realism" because this represents the reality of that time. Even in the comic book's last panel, he is drawn as a celestial being looking over from heaven. Karline McLain has closely studied this last image as an influence of the avatar cycles that were famous during the early twentieth century. She says that the creators of this comic book have taken references from real-life photographs, and the last image of Gandhi with a child is also taken directly from one such photograph when Gandhi was sailing on the S.S. Rajputana in 1931 (47). She says that this image is drawn out of the historical context and directly corresponds to Gandhi's image with a child on the cover page. This kind of juxtaposition of the front cover with the last panel hints at the avatar cycles of that time and also reiterates the "closed loop of death and rebirth, and visually hinting that Gandhi – or at least his ideology – will live on in the next generation" (2014, 312). This comic book presents a prevalent narrative of Gandhi's life through its treatment of the visuals that appear to be influenced by the popular poster art of that time. With this treatment going beyond the official narrative of the life of Gandhi, the comic book serves two purposes – one, it appeals to the popular imagination, especially to the children; and in a manner that was already prevalent where Gandhi was frequently presented as a divine figure in the posters giving it an air of what Ramaswamy terms as "patriotic mythography" (Ramaswamy 236). And two, it creates an official account of Gandhi's life that was under much scrutiny by the Hindu nationalists.

While *Mahatma Gandhi* and *The Gandhi Story* share similar conventions of these early comic books, content-wise, both the comic books are episodic and take up similar instances from his life to represent these vignettes as a threaded biography. The comic books are written in a confessional tone, recounting incidents as episodes of realization of truth. Both of these comic books thread individual episodes from Gandhi's life that reflect on the importance of some virtue that the creators intend the readers to understand and incorporate in their life.

Memory and Memorialization

In terms of visual conceptualization, both comic books have dealt with Gandhi's figure in varied ways. While *The Gandhi Story* idealizes and deifies him, *Mahatma Gandhi* has a different approach. While studying multiethnic graphic narratives, Martha Cutter and Cathy J. Schlund-Vials argue that "integral to many multiethnic graphic novels is a re-seeing of history, and central to these revisionist works is an archival project of reassemblage" (5). While revisiting Gandhi's figure in these comic books, the artists have re-worked Gandhi's image as a subject of memory and memorialization in the context of popular culture and contemporary art.

Though ACK is known for representing many freedom fighters in larger-than-life projections, their comic book on Gandhi presents him as an ordinary human being. While comparing the two comic books might not be justified, *Mahatma Gandhi* can be compared with other issues by *Amar Chitra Katha*, where the protagonist is the centre of the focus visually as well. The issues on Gandhi, *Mahatma Gandhi I: The Early Days*, and *Mahatma Gandhi II: The Father of the Nation*, were published in 1989, nearly 20 years after the first publication of ACK comic books in 1970. McLain deals with the idea of a delay in the comic book's publication centred on one of the most celebrated personalities of modern India in her essay "Who Shot the Mahatma? Representing Gandhian Politics in Indian Comic Books." She writes, "as I studied the production of these comics at the comic book studio in Mumbai (Bombay) in 2001–2, I learned that Gandhi, who is best known for his technique of non-violent civil resistance (satyagraha), actually presented a formidable challenge to the comic book creators" (2007, 58).

The comics series has been publishing heroes and rulers like Shivaji, Rana Pratap, Prithviraj Chauhan, and Subhash Chandra Bose as active leaders engaged in fighting the enemy on the battlefield. It was a challenge to represent a rather less active (in the sense of physically engaged in a battle) figure who was the harbinger of peace in a comic book. Gandhi's portrayal is very ordinary when compared to other heroes. On the one hand, on the cover pages of *Subhas Chandra Bose: Born to Lead*, *Vikramaditya: Courage and Honour Win the Day*, *Shivaji: The Great Maratha*, and even *Rabindranath Tagore: India's Gentle Torch-Bearer*, the protagonist is the centre of focus visually. In the case of valiant heroes like Vikramaditya and Shivaji, along with many more, the hero is presented amidst a battle, captured in the glory of a fighter, and Subhas Chandra Bose is drawn in the very famous pose wearing the army uniform while soldiers hoist the national flag in the background. Even the cover page of Rabindranath Tagore's issue, who is not an "active" fighter published in 1977, shows him at the centre of focus while playing with children in the park.

On the other hand, Gandhi's issues of ACK show him as an ordinary citizen, among the many. In the first issue, *Mahatma Gandhi: The Early Days*, Gandhi is drawn burning the certificate along with fellow Indians, like any other person in the crowd of people, and the second issue, *Mahatma Gandhi II: The Father of the Nation,* captures Gandhi in what seems like one of the protest marches that he took out. Both these covers place him among other people as any ordinary citizen, as opposed to the valorized heroes of the *Amar Chitra Katha* franchise that gives the heroes the centre stage. These covers also visualize him as not even looking straight at the reader. It is almost as if Gandhi is drawn with an expression of guilt or remorse. This visualization calls to question the title given to him "Father of the nation," which is interestingly also the subtitle to the comic book issue.

While other heroes and leaders are not just textually presented but even are drawn in larger-than-life proportions, Gandhi's portrayal is diminished at many points in the comic book. During the entire comic book, there are instances where the textual and the visual do not correspond. This idea highlights W.J.T. Mitchell's argument about the text–image relations in a medium like comic books. He says that the interplay of text and image is not merely a technical question but also a site of conflict. He says it is "a nexus where political, institutional, and social antagonisms play themselves out in the materiality of representation" (90–91). On the last page of the first issue, an image of a gathering of a large crowd is drawn at the Indian National Congress session in Amritsar. This instance is marked when Gandhi was "established and acknowledged as a leader of the nation" (Dutt 31). In what looks like a stage, Gandhi is drawn as a very minute figure sitting with two more people. It is faintly drawn, and only because of his loincloth can one recognize him on the stage. Running contrary to the text that claims that he was established as a "leader" of the nation, the visuals tell a different story. This representation raises questions of visualization. He is the hero of the comic book, and in the last panel of the first issue, the reader is placed so far from him, barely even able to make out the figure of the Mahatma.

The most striking and significant difference between the two comic books is how they have dealt with Gandhi's assassination. *The Gandhi Story* identifies Nathuram Godse as the assassin and even pronounces his intentions. He followed the Hindu nationalist ideology and felt that Hindus were wronged when Gandhi asked India to pay 550 million rupees to Pakistan. The assassination incident is represented in a series of panels without any text (46, 47). Even though the visual representation shows the act of violence, the assassin's identification makes the whole act a condemnable act, as the official narrative of his assassination, and differs from the unofficial and populist ideas. This representation is, however, different from the one in *Mahatma Gandhi*. There, the assassination occurs in one panel without identifying the assassin (28, 29). This representation gives prominence to the act of violence rather than the actor. Karline McLain remarks about the identity of the assassin as marked with ambiguity as she says, "this issue neither exculpates nor blames Godse for his act, but instead leaves it up to the reader to decide whether Godse is a hero or a villain, whether his deed should be mourned or celebrated" ("Who Shot the Mahatma" 2007, 303). This version of the assassination corresponds to the popular Hindu nationalist allegiances.

Karline McLain also analyses *Amar Chitra Katha* issues and concludes that the comics series deliberately tries to depict the Jallianwala Bagh massacre as a causal reaction to Gandhi's call for a nationwide *hartal*. She studies this pattern not just in *Mahatma Gandhi* but also in other issues – *Rabindranath Tagore* (1977), *Bhagat Singh* (1981), and in *March to Freedom 3: The Saga of Indian Revolutionaries*. She remarks about this causal reaction recurrent in ACK series and about Gandhi's assassination,

> Images of the assassination in the G.D. Birla and Mahatma Gandhi II issues work – like images of the Jallianwala Bagh massacre – to again suggest a problem with Gandhi's philosophy: that non-violence is ultimately rewarded with violence. Whereas, the images of the Panjab massacre required an excess of text in order to 'explain' them – to causally connect the massacre with both Gandhi and the British – the images of Gandhi's assassination require the moderation of text in order to break the causal connection between Godse and the event.
>
> *(74, 2007)*

These representations put Gandhi in the position where he is directly held responsible for the violence in Jallianwala Bagh. It is also reflective of the political tension between the two perspectives in the national struggle for freedom. While one strand advocates for the non-violent ways as promoted by Gandhi, the other upholds the revolutionaries' violent path. This representation textually does not present Gandhi as responsible for the massacre but through the visual placement of him between the two panels of call for *hartal* and the massacre, visually places him at the centre as the cause of the massacre. On the contrary, *The Gandhi Story* recounts both these incidents, the *hartal*, and the massacre, that clearly state the reasons for the violence (19, 20). As a pedagogical comic book, it also draws Gandhi speaking about what *ahimsa* actually means to address the reader directly. Through this representation, the official narrative upholds Gandhi's philosophy of non-violence and tries to show the murky reality where the people and the British, both exercised violence.

Apart from the visuals created, there are so many images of Gandhi that were already popular at that time, and these images serve as direct references for the images drawn in the comic book, adding to the current visuality of the persona of

Gandhi. A person who himself never appreciated the deification and the hordes of people who gathered to take *darshan* was one of the most intensely photographed among the celebrated freedom fighters. He appointed some of his companions to keep himself from the *darshan* seekers. Gandhi asked Professor Kriplani particularly to help him, as he writes in his autobiography "For the time being he made it the end and aim of his life to save me from darshan-seekers. He warded off people, calling to his aid now his unfailing humour, now his nonviolent threats" (419).

Towards a National Historiography

In the newly independent nation-state, new modes of visuality contributed to developing a visual culture and re-installation of ancient and mythological narratives in the new media to educate the generation born in the independent nation.

Introducing translations in various languages, both the state-sponsored comic book and *Amar Chitra Katha*, encouraged a pan-Indian readership. Susie Tharu and K. Lalita argue about the rise of a robust middle class by asserting, "While it sought to centre the values of bourgeois individualism, it drew on nationalist sentiment 'to reshape a social Imaginary in which the nation is consolidated'" (qtd. in Sreenivas 22). One can say that through new initiatives such as a comic book depicting the life of Mahatma Gandhi, the state was attempting to create a public culture through the medium of the popular. In this context, 'public culture' is a term directly taken from Appadurai and Breckenridge, which they propose to be that "space between domestic life and the projects of the nation-state – where different social groups . . . constitute their identities by their experience of mass-mediated forms in relation to the practices of everyday life" (4–5). With these comic books, a new visuality is developed, reflecting the contemporary social reality. The difference in the visual representation of the life of the Mahatma in the two comic books discussed in the chapter, point towards different political orientations of the state-controlled narrative and the popular one endorsed and promoted by a commercial agency like the *Amar Chitra Katha*.

Notes

1 For more information on this, see Sreenivas (2010).
2 For more information on the early comic book publication in India, see Nandini Chandra (2008); Mandovi Menon (2017); Karline McLain (2009); Bharat Murthy (2009); Aruna Rao (2001); Ritu G. Khanduri (2010).
3 See Amresh Datta (1987).
4 See Kajri Jain (1997); Tapati Guha-Thakurta (1991).

Works Cited

Appadurai, Arjun, and Carol A. Breckenridge. "Why Public Culture?" *Public Culture*, vol. 1, no. 1, 1988, pp. 5–9.

Chandra, Nandini. *The Classic Popular: Amar Chitra Katha (1967–2007)*. Yoda Press, 2008.

Cutter, Martha J., and Cathy J. Schlund-Vials, editors. *Redrawing the Historical Past: History, Memory and Multiethnic Graphic Novels*. U of Georgia P, 2018.

Datta, Amresh. *Encyclopaedia of Indian Literature*. Sahitya Akademi, 1987.

Dutt, Gayatri Madan. Illus. Souren Roy, edited by. Anant Pai. *Mahatma Gandhi: Father of the Nation*, Kindle ed., Amar Chitra Katha, 1989.

Ebine, Kazuki. *Gandhi: A Manga Biography*. Penguin, 2011.

Eck, Diana L. *Darśan: Seeing the Divine Image in India*. Columbia UP, 1998.

Gandhi, Mohandas K. *An Autobiography: The Story of My Experiments with Truth*. Beacon Press, 1993.

Guha-Thakurta, Tapati. "Women as 'Calendar Art' Icons: Emergence of Pictorial Stereotype in Colonial India." *Economic and Political Weekly*, vol. 26, no. 43, Oct. 1991. pp. WS91–WS99. JSTOR, www.jstor.org/stable/4398221. Accessed 10 Nov. 2020.

Jacob, Preminda. *Celluloid Deities: The Visual Culture of Cinema and Politics in South India*. Lexington Books, 2009.

Jain, Kajri. "Producing the Sacred: The Subjects of Calender Art." *Journal of Arts and Ideas*, Dec. 1997, pp. 63–88.

Kapur, Geeta. *Mythic Material in Indian Cinema: Investigating Sant Tukaram and Devi*. Nehru Memorial Museum and Library, 1988.

Khanduri, Ritu G. "Comicology: Comic Books as Culture in India." *Journal of Graphic Novels and Comics*, vol. 1, no. 2, 2010, pp. 171–91, https://doi.org/10.1080/21504857.2010.528641. Accessed 13 Nov. 2020.

McLain, Karline. "'The Gandhi Story': An Official Indian Comic Book History of the Mahatma." *International Journal of Hindu Studies*, vol. 18, no. 3, Dec. 2014, pp. 291–325. *JSTOR*, www.jstor.org/stable/24713652. Accessed 9 Nov. 2020.

———. *India's Immortal Comic Books: Gods, Kings, and Other Heroes*. Indiana UP, 2009.

———. "Who Shot the Mahatma? Representing Gandhian Politics in Indian Comic Books." *South Asia Research*, vol. 27, no. 1, 2007, pp. 57–77, www.academia.edu/18617913/_Who_Shot_the_Mahatma_Representing_Gandhian_Politics_in_Indian_Comic_Books_. Accessed 10 Nov. 2020.

Menon, Mandovi. "A Complete Timeline: The Evolution of Comic Books in India (1926–Present)." *Homegrown*, 13 Mar. 2017, https://homegrown.co.in/article/21898/a-complete-timeline-the-evolution-of-comic-books-in-india-1926-present.

Murthy, Bharath. "An Art Without a Tradition: A Survey of Indian Comics." *MargMagazine*, vol. 61, no. 2, Dec. 2009, pp. 1–38, www.scribd.com/doc/26674355/An-Art-Without-a-Tradition-A-Survey-of-Indian-Comics-2008. Accessed 13 Nov. 2020.

Mitchell, W. J. T. *Picture Theory: Essays on Verbal and Visual Representation*. U of Chicago P, 1994.

Nehru, Jawaharlal. "Foreword." *The Gandhi Story*, edited by S. D. Sawant and S. D. Badalkar, p. iii.

Publications Division, *Ministry of Information and Broadcasting*. Government of India, 1966.

Ramaswamy, Sumati. "The Mahatma as Muse: An Image Essay on Gandhi in Popular Indian Visual Imagination." *Art and Visual Culture in India, 1857–2007*, Marg Publications, 2009, pp. 236–49.

Rao, Aruna. "From Self-Knowledge to Super Heroes: The Story of Indian Comics." *Illustrating Asia: Comics, Humor Magazines and Picture Books*, edited by John A. Lent, U of Hawaii P, 2001.

Sawant, S.D., and S.D. Badalkar. *The Gandhi Story*. New Delhi: Publications Division, Ministry of Information and Broadcasting, Government of India, 1966.

Sreenivas, Deepa. *Sculpting a Middle Class: History, Masculinity and the Amar Chitra Katha in India*. Routledge, 2010.

Tharu, Susie, and K. Lalita, editors. *Women Writing in India: 600 B.C. to the Present*. Vol. 2. Oxford UP, 1993.

Varughese, E. Dawson. *Visuality and Identity in Post-Millennial Indian Graphic Narratives*. Palgrave Macmillan, 2018.

7

GANDHI, THE NEW DIVINE

Gandhi Ethos in the Malayalam Socials of 1950 and 1960s

M.H. Ilias

Ashis Nandy stated four "Gandhis" survived Mohandas Karamchand Gandhi's death (1–4). Nandy wished to enumerate how Gandhi, in varying ways, continues to live on in public consciousness. According to Nandy, the first Gandhi who survived beyond the historical temporality of the man was the "Gandhi" of the state institutions, the figure who lives on in the symbols and icons of the Indian nationstate; a Gandhi who appears on the Indian currency notes or the pictures hanging on the walls of police stations, courts and other institutions of the government (1–3). The second Gandhi, according to Nandy, is the Gandhi of Gandhians, a benign presence in Indian public lore, who makes his presence felt via the formalized interfaith meetings, martyr's day celebrations, and seminars on Gandhian thought or conventions being held in various Ashrams/academia named after him across the nation to condemn the growing criminalization of politics or corruption in the country. For Nandy, the third Gandhi is a more vibrant one; Gandhi of the political anarchists who undermine the state's role in their scheme of thinking, and environmental and human rights activists at constant war against the state's inhumane developmental policies (3). According to Nandy, the fourth Gandhi is primarily a mythic or an "invisible Gandhi," an embodiment of values manifested chiefly through struggles against injustice (3–4). This chapter is an enterprise enquiring into how this fourth "Gandhi" – the *invisible Gandhi*– operates in different ways in Malayalam cinema. Taking cues mainly from the experience of the Malayalam films of the 1950s and 1960s, generally referred to as "socials," the chapter explores the constitution of *invisible Gandhi* through myths and images. Furthermore, the chapter explores what political and religious functions this invisible Gandhi serves in these films.

There are only two films (*Garshom* [1999] dir. PT Kunju Muhammed and *Yugapurushan* [2010] dir. R. Sukumaran) in the Malayalam language, having Gandhi as a primary character. However, there are umpteen numbers of films

DOI: 10.4324/9781003145479-10

that showcase his invisible presence. Numerous episodes from Gandhi's life and teaching have been featured throughout the history of Malayalam cinema, from the silent era to the current period, but often indirectly. In the 1950s and 1960s his life became a living story for many film-makers in Kerala as a didactic lesson to be continuously retold; fictional characters subtly adapted the Gandhian values within a contemporary framework. Gandhi's invisibility in Malayalam cinema takes various forms. These Gandhian forms are mainly the result of regional cinema's responses to Gandhi's charisma, ideas, moral values, teachings and practices.[1]

Viewers absorb movie meaning intuitively and instantly, and the story flows without the on-screen presence of Gandhi's specific persona. In some movies, Gandhi has been the theme of an individual or collective fantasy, often inserted into the film narrative to impart moral lessons. In the first few decades of India's independence, these films collectively shaped how Malayalis understood the postcolonial world, interpreted it, and became part of the cinematic imagination, profoundly influencing its politics and aesthetics. However, recent films have depicted Gandhi as a more complex and troubled figure in the context of a scathing attack on him by the Ambedkarite scholars for his alleged uncritical approach towards the caste system. *Papilio Budha*[2] (dir. Jayan K Cherian), a 2013 feature film, for instance, has direct remarks denigrating Gandhi; in the film a group of irate Dalit activists burn an effigy of Gandhi as a gesture of opposition to his contentious position on caste, conversion and cow protection. This film, which made a virulent attack on Gandhi, appeared when the Dalit critique of Gandhi was in the ascendance (Venkatesan and James).

Gandhians feature more recurrently in Malayalam films than in many other regional films from India. Nevertheless, their depictions are diffuse and vary in tune with historical, political and aesthetic changes. In the early films, they were shown as pacifists, friendly uncles, peace-loving neighbours or good mediators in quarrels, but politically brave and morally mighty. However, this image started fading in the 1990s as the Gandhians in the films of this period often became the target of crude caricaturing, especially for their idealistic life, artificial simplicity, impractical political ideas and avowed opposition to alcohol consumption. Interestingly, this period coincided with the decline of Gandhi's influence in the Indian public sphere due to the rise of a new middle class socialized in the neo-liberal consumerist culture (Scrase and Scrase). *Pavam Pavam Rajakumaran* (dir. Kamal), a film that released in 1990, for instance, has a new age Gandhian who efficaciously uses that image to cover up his "wrongful habits," including binge drinking. Another film released around the same period, *Simhavalan Menon* (dir. Viji Tampi), performed a crude caricature of Gandhians through the character of Hariprasad Menon – an aged person with high moral integrity upholding Gandhian values. The film, however, portrays him as "an endangered species," who likes only classical music, dislikes speed and cricket, insists everyone in the office speak no English and, therefore, remains peripheral to global energies.

There have been several films in the mainstream commercial cinema in which Gandhi features, though not as a character. Gandhi's influence has been profound in

Malayalam cinematic and aesthetic ventures, with his life and ideology represented mainly in the "socials" made in the 1950s and 1960s. It may not be necessarily expressive or visible, but it is manifested through the idea of compassion, simplicity or a sense of humanity. Analysing the experience of these films of this period, this chapter analyses Malayalam film's reception and understanding of Gandhi to examine how the circulation of Gandhi's moral and political philosophy could influence these films' political and religious settings.

Gandhi as Fantasy

In thinking about Gandhi in Malayalam cinema, we are faced with specific political and religious issues. First, there is Gandhi's image, which is constituted in the dominant public discourses. Subsequently, there is an image of Gandhi as a cinematic construct. There is a specific power in the image, which may not function as a mere social construct. This part of the chapter wishes to engage with representation and the matrix of social and political forces that impact the construction and circulation of Gandhi's images in Malayalam language productions. The image construction of Gandhi in Malayalam cinema is somewhat different, and it is precisely this difference that warrants a detailed study.

P.T. Kunjimohammed, a left-ideologically inclined diasporic film-maker, is perhaps the first to explore a "visible Gandhi." His film *Garshom* (means exile in Hebrew), made in the year 1999, tells the story of a frustrated left-ideologically inclined, Gulf returned protagonist who engages in a moral and ideological fight with the decline of values in Malayali society, that is symptomatic of the neoliberal reconfiguration of polity and economy in the postliberalization India. Gandhi appears in a fantasy sequence, consoles him, indoctrinates him of the ideology of anti-imperialism and lends moral support to his fight. Coincidently, the early 1990s, when *Garshom* was released, witnessed the disintegration of the Soviet Union, which opened up the possibilities for many new interesting ideological explorations in Kerala, especially among the Marxists (Chandran). The post-liberalization situation has been particularly interesting as the films of this period offered a revealing way of looking at how Gandhian values have been reimagined through addressing some developmental and human rights issues. The 1990s was also a time that marked unprecedented changes in Indian society. So, it is not surprising that historical figures from the past such as Gandhi and other regional social reformers and philosophers like Narayana Guru were reappearing in films like *Garshom* and *Olipporu* (dir. A.V. Sasidharan (2013). Social reformers and revolutionary leaders were being continually reimagined on the screen to respond to the daily crisis that ordinary Indian citizens were facing. This period also marked the beginning of an exciting and strange academic collaboration between Marx and Gandhi. This merger has spawned a tremendous amount of extraordinary movements and works that have, in effect, opened new fields of enquiry in Kerala's politics.

Nizhalkuth (dir. Adoor Gopalakrishnan 2002), a film set in the backdrop of pre-independence Travancore presents an invisible Gandhi so different from our textbook perception of a pacifist saint. Kaliyappan, an aging hangman in this film, fails to perform his duty but when he realizes that the condemned person is innocent, he leaves it to his Gandhian, freedom fighter son, Muthu to do the job. The son completes the job as an act of punishment of his father reminding him that all his prior executions have been a farce just like the current one. As part of his engagement with the national movement, the son weaves his clothes using *charkha*. The film closely follows the weaving of clothes and cuts it symbolically to the scene of weaving coir used for hanging in jail. A profound statement on capital punishment, this film reminds us of Gandhi's historical dilemma in effectively opposing Bhagat Singh's hanging (Gopalkrishnan 2014). This film also subtly subscribes to Gandhi's position that violence and non-violence are terms with contextual meanings, warranting nuanced understanding. Gandhi said "I do believe that where there is only a choice between cowardice and violence, I would advise violence (1920)." Endorsing Gandhi, *Nizhalkuth* states that there is no easy way to arrive at a stable distinction between the two when that distinction is so blurred.

Although Gandhi was seriously discussed and debated in Kerala's intellectual and academic circles only after the disintegration of the Soviet Union,[3] he has been simultaneously revered and reviled in Malayalam cinema since the very beginning. During the 1960s, Malayalam movies ignited Kerala society's most fundamental desire and hope of change through two personalities, Gandhi and Marx, and triggered emotional responses from viewers by reinforcing yearning that had lay dormant within them. Gandhi invoked an enormous amount of reverence as a champion of the anti-colonial cause in the early films, but as time progressed, films featuring invisible Gandhi emerged, granting characters a moral and religious power.

An influential body of literature on Malayalam popular cinema argues that the dominant conceptual framework that shaped the early Malayalam cinema's aesthetic modes was similar to other regional films in India (Pillai). This dominant conceptual framework was of the mythic-iconic mode, not of realism. In the films of the 1940s and early 1950s Malayalam cinema could not distinguish between reality and myth. It is also true that the mythical genre of Indian cinema had penetrated deep into the everyday life of ordinary people during the first few decades. As Chidananda Das Gupta argues, the mass audience of Indian cinema was deeply immersed in premodern viewing cultures and therefore was incapable of understanding and appreciating the rational-realist cinema (256–57). However, the experiences of the mid-1950s demonstrate a slightly different situation. Even as the mythical genre made many inroads earlier, this period marked a departure by introducing a neo-realistic visual aesthetic mode in the popular domain.

"Socials" with heavy ideological undertones constituted the bulk of commercial films in the 1950s (Pillai 271). To quote Meena Pillai, "The nascent Malayalam movies did not form part of the national formula to revive an Indian culture or to resuscitate a national or mythical ethos" (271–72). On its part, cinema halls offered a secularized space where strict notions of purity and pollutions or caste hierarchies' maintenance were not followed (Venkiteswaran 9–10). The virtual space it created was a modern one engaged in engendering narratives and grammar cutting across regional, cultural, caste and class differences (10).

Since Malayalam Cinema had maintained an umbilical relationship with literature from its initial days onwards, it could absorb the ripples that the new aesthetics of secular modernity and social realism produced in Malayalam literature from the 1940s (Venkiteswaran 9). The presence of left-leaning political theatres also had a tremendous influence on the nascent art form. Unlike regional cinemas elsewhere, Malayalam cinema was not steeped into the tradition of devotional films (Pillai 285). Kerala Peoples Arts Club (known popularly by its acronym KPAC), a politically motivated group of theatre artists, for instance, had shaped early Malayalam cinema by contributing a considerably huge number of actors, screenwriters and directors. Deeply influenced by the tradition of social realism, Malayalam cinema of the 1950s and 1960s brought the communities and classes previously kept outside the realm of literature and cinema into the centre (Venkiteswaran 9). Peasants, Dalits, fisherfolks, minorities – all previously side-lined made an appearance on screen for the first time.

The film-makers of the 1950s and early 1960s associated directly or indirectly with the left movement made an entry into the field with themes considered unconventional and not conforming to dominant societal codes (Radhakrishnan 35). The bourgeoning presence of such film-makers led to the valourization of realism, modelled along the line of "Soviet realism." Consequently, as Radhakrishnan notes, "a prominent binary between 'rationality' and 'irrationality' in terms of the role of cinema in the space of the social became more apparent" (35). From the 1970s, the narrative style that had been popular so far underwent a radical transformation. One can see that with the influence of "modernity" in literature, the "new wave" in cinema pushed the themes and people till then relegated only to the margins to the forefront (Venkiteswaran 9–10). The change was also a reflection of a major change in the social setting of Kerala. A new middle class emerged against the backdrop of land reforms, migration of the youth to major cities in India, and the decline of the joint family system, and with that, a change emerged that was central to the new narrative world. These movies' central themes revolved around either the upper/middle caste/class nuclear families or the movies that encapsulated such families' formation (Venkiteswaran 9–10). The conflicts within families, dreams and desperations of such families animated the film narrative (Venkiteswaran 9–10). While the issues, responses and resistances of different sorts were dealt with from the vantage point of the "social," the post-1970s witnessed an apparent shift – an individual's inner conflicts and sufferings gained the upper hand in narration. The themes shifted to existential issues and psychic conditioning of individuals from the earlier narratives that took inspiration from a face-off between the castes/classes and authorities' interests (10).

Socials in Malayalam cinema in the 1950s and 1960s had, of course, possessed some distinct features. Although the films belonging to this genre were products of modern Pan-Indian aesthetics of realism, they did not subscribe to its political content. They refused to wholly endorse the dominant narratives that valorize modern industrial life and belief in the triumph of scientific rationality. It is clear that transformations did not occur the same way or in the same direction, even within the realm of modernity. They instead reflected a slightly different and distinctly Malayali concept of realism, critiquing modernity for its alleged lack of humanity. The dynamics of neo-realism, which in other Indian contexts flourished in cordial terms with industrial modernity, have different significant expressions in Kerala.

That way, the films of the 1950s and 1960s stood for an idealism that Gandhi represented. The unwillingness of Malayali film-makers to appreciate genres highlighting the technological accomplishments of the modern nation was, in fact, not the endorsement of the inherited virtues of tradition, but the rejection of cultural values of the modern industrial life, that owed much to the influence of Gandhi (Joseph 26). Gandhian idealism became a major cultural determinant that Malayalam cinema was politically obsessed with since its early years. In the 1950s, even as the rest of India saw cultural productions being referred to and analysed in the context of the Nehruvian period; in Malayalam cinema, this was not so. If in the rest of India, the cultural artefacts were obsessed with a significant concern over the issues of modernization and the making of the new nation, Malayalam cinema picked Gandhian ethos as one of its central ideological premises. There was also a complex intermixing of modern values and Gandhian values as most of the socials of that period were deeply obsessed with themes such as love, simplicity, truth and non-violence as essential values to maintain and preserve in society.

The invisible Gandhi first appeared on the silver screen in the early 1950s, and the period interestingly had raised a set of questions expressing concern over the promise of material modernity and technological promise, an essential corollary of the former. It is a nice coincidence that *Neelakkuyil* (dirs. P. Bhaskaran and Ramu Kariat, 1954), one of the first neo-realist films in Malayalam cinema was also one of the first films to experiment with an invisible Gandhi. Some Malayalam cinema scholars have taken up *Neelakkuyil* as one of the early interventions of the Left aesthetics in Malayalam popular cinema (Joseph 26). Nevertheless, looking at the political sensibilities and aesthetic conventions, one can indeed see a not-so-loud play of an invisible Gandhi in it. This invisible Gandhi appears in the form of the village postman, Sankaran Nair, who adopts the boy child born to an unwed Dalit mother ignoring the protests of the caste-Hindu society, speaks vehemently of prevailing social injustices such as untouchability, denial of access of the lower-caste to the temples, structural disparities, caste-based atrocities.

Neelakkuyil (1954) suggests a symbolic effect of Gandhi's invisibility; Gandhi symbolically disembodies the village postman's character and assumes his voice to address the social inequalities. Disheartened by casteism's ill-effects, Nair resorts to Gandhi, saying that "God does not reside in temples, in which the backward castes are not allowed to enter in (Gandhi 336)." Coincidently, Nair's words resonate with Gandhi's famous speech at Vaikom in central Kerala favouring the lower classes' entry into Hindu temples almost three decades back.[4] Nair expresses anguish over disharmony and persistence of caste-based discrimination in Hinduism. That way,

Neelakkuyil marks a widespread appropriation of Gandhian thought as an Indian way of thought, albeit presented more subtly. On his part, the village postman represents a common Malayali fantasy of the 1950s revolving around the hope of a "modern Kerala," built necessarily as a casteless entity.

The invisible Gandhi of early Malayalam films is not political, but a Gandhi of the middle-class functioning as an inner voice and a moral guide. Although he has been concerned deeply about the shrinkage of the moral universe, decline of social values, increasing level of corruption and superstitious beliefs, this invisible Gandhi leaves many serious social issues of the period unaddressed. Analysing the political content of *Neelakkuyil*, Jenny Rowena argues that "simultaneous to engaging deeply with the questions of modernity and creating an ethical, moral space, Malayalam films of the 1950s and 1960s put forward an ideology based predominantly on middle-class Hindu morality" (34). The spaces belonging to the 'Other', especially Dalits and Muslims, were rendered entirely or partly invisible or insignificant.

Neelakkuyil was not alone; there were other instances of the same kind. *Newspaper Boy* (dir. P. Ramadas, 1955), another neo-realist production released after a year, expresses serious political concern over the ill-effects of modernity via narrating a low-income family's agony. The film, trying to address the ordinary Malayali on the street, shows the poor as a noble guy with inherent dignity and a character of significant moral superiority over the rich. As in the *Newspaper Boy*, in most of the social films of those days, Gandhi gives voice to the poor and marginalized, fantasizing about questioning or belittling authority figures, whether it is a filthy rich person, a corrupt politician or higher officials in the system. Heroes of these films are simple-hearted people influenced mainly by Gandhian ideology, holding the ideals of socialism, fighting against corruption and abstaining from materialistic pursuits like money. Many mannerisms and practices of the heroes were drawn personally from Gandhi. Interestingly, some male protagonists in this period's films were seldom shown as interested in wealth or turning away from it with a strong dislike. *Navalokam* (dir. V. Krishnan, 1951), a film released in the early 1950s based on a reformist story, is supposed to be the first film belonging to this genre. Besides discussing a plethora of issues lingering in the society such as child marriage, the enslavement of women, exploitation of labourers, using a revolt against the zamindari system in a village as the backdrop, this film set the prototype of a rigorously self-disciplined male protagonist with strong disinclination towards money, power and corruption, which many films appropriated in the coming decades in varying degrees.

Perhaps, more important than poverty and simplicity was the division between urban and rural spaces to the Malayalam film makers and their audience. The Malayalam film audience was overwhelmingly rural, so the early Malayalam films extolled rural values such as simplicity, self-reliance and honesty. The adoption of the Gandhian values of poverty as a virtue was taken more pragmatically by the Malayalam cinema. To reach the broadest possible audience, the film-makers undertook a careful selection of themes. These film-makers were often unwilling to risk filming themes that were too urban.[5] Reasserting the importance of taking a stand on social values, they rejected the trend of uncritically endorsing urban people's values and lifestyles in films.[6]

Although Gandhi himself was not directly against urbanization, his yearning for self-reliant villages with people living in honesty and simplicity defined ethos that remained strong in the Malayalam cinema. The villages where most of the Malayalis lived became a part of the popular imagination as being "authentic Kerala," while cities and towns were featured as "inauthentic" and often a "graveyard of moral values." *Nagarame Nandi* (dir. A. Vincent, 1967) valourized the Gandhian ideal of villages. Adopted from the plot of *Conquerors of the Golden City* (dir. Getin Gurtop, 1965), a Turkish production, this film narrates the poignant story of a family that migrates from a village to the city of Madras with a wish to lead a better life. This film reflects on the lure of city dreams and how its inseparable logic of greed crushes the innocent villagers' hopes. Urban–rural conflict had been a recurrent theme finding expression explicitly or subtly in most of the films of MT Vasudevan Nair, directed or scripted during this period and after. Three best examples of such movies that picturize villages, in opposition to urban spaces, as a milieu for warm and intense human relations and honest and innocuous individuals, have been *Murapennu* (1965), *Nizhalattam* (1970) and *Bandhanam* (1978).

Gandhi as Image

Although sentiments of anti-imperialism shaped notions of public ideology in Kerala of 1950s, Gandhi's positive reception in Malayalam cinema in the 1960s owes much to his stature as a religious reformer who launched a tradition of attacks on superstitious beliefs in Hinduism.[7] His reception as a religious reformer-figure shows how Malayali attitudes about Hinduism's reformist version structured his presence in Kerala.

Gandhi had visited Kerala five times between 1920 and 1937. Interestingly, the period that Gandhi visited the state had coincided with the peak of Hindu community's reform initiatives. Though the causes of the visits varied, during each visit he met with many scholars and activists who played an instrumental role in the Hindu social reform movement in the state, including Shree Narayana Guru, Mahatma Ayyankali and Swami Anantha Theertha. Each visit has generated a large corpus of literature and various forms of oral histories and local narratives. These narratives are particularly significant as his visits coincided with the emergence of several social movements within the Kerala society, including anti-caste movements. Gandhi had visited and experienced many seminal sociopolitical events of that time including Vaikom Satyagraha – a massive social protest against untouchability among various castes in Kerala's Hindu community.

Since the early spread of cinema coincided with the birth of the secular national movement and social reform movement in Kerala (Bhaskaran 26; Pillai 267), there was the need for reimagining popular culture that could cater to the ideological needs of the "newly liberated individuals" and mobilize them into a new political collective (Pillai 267). Many directors of the early Malayalam cinema, thus, eschewed the popularity of Gandhi's image as a social reformer in Kerala. Some, especially those of a liberal theological bent, felt that Gandhi fills a reformer-saint role. The experience of *Neelakkuyil* also demonstrated that modernity emerged in Kerala with a vital component of religious reform, which led to a situation wherein the film industry was forced to keep the values of religion intact. As it happened in Tamil films, religious values did not fade away with the rise of rational narratives of the Dravidian movement. By and large, Malayalam cinema failed to appreciate the cultural values of scientific rationality, modern industrial life and endorsed inherited virtues of tradition in the early 1950s. The prominent role of socials in the formation of modern Kerala, and the social films' ultimate icon, the modern autonomous self as an agent of social action, unlike in Hindi films and other regional films, can be seen not as a product of a Pan-India secular Nehruvian modernity, but as Kerala's specific phenomenon.

Most of the films of the 1950s also showed a reformed Hinduism in place of orthodox religion. The religion of rituals and customs also underwent a consistent change and presenting such rituals and practices in films showed in a way to teach people how they should be changed. Though there was open criticism of priesthood, superstitious practices and the deity cult were still followed, Malayalam films were rarely seen as anti-religious as those made in the highly politicized anti-Brahmanical context of the Tamil film industry. Although some have been criticized for engaging in superstitious or regressive practices, religiosity, especially simple devotion was highly valued.

With the emergence of Gandhi as an invisible icon, Malayalam cinema's view on religion was primarily transformed. During this period, the identity of a believer was not negotiated solely through the lens of modernity. Modernity's cultural hegemony and superiority made it difficult for a believer-viewer to accept it. In other words, Malayalam films of that period have never been anti-religious. Everyday religion was not completely avoided, notably ritual practices and temple visits in Hindu contexts and rituals of weddings and funerals in the Muslim context. Two major religious genres of mainstream Indian cinema – the epical and the devotional – were considered mainstream narrative techniques in the industry and operated strictly within the master narrative reform. Popular Malayalam cinema of the 1960s, thus, created a new way of imagining religious and spiritual practices in a more reformed and secularized way. Thus, invisible Gandhi made a dent in the superiority of secular modernity, which otherwise shaped the public ideology in the mainstream literature in Kerala.

Through several of his appearance on the title cards of the films and lithographic portraits hanging on the walls of the houses of ordinary people and public institutions, Gandhi was considered a person whose grace had triumphed and who was, as a consequence, eminent for his virtuous persona. What made Gandhi indeed a divine figure for Malayalam cinema was partly his images; his appearance with an aura in the photographs made him what many Malayalis expected in a saintly person. The saintliness of Gandhi was the result of collaborative work between the viewer and the viewed. The image of Gandhi with an aura seems to have been composed to give the film viewers' the chance to obtain his simultaneous *darshan*.

According to Christopher Pinney, *darshan* is a practice in which the devotee comes into visual contact with the deity's image and receives the divine's blessing (95–96). This practice has a spillover effect in the political field, where modern leaders like Gandhi provide *darshan*[8] to those who come into visual contact with him in the hope of gaining blessings. In visual representations, Gandhi was essentially different from others, endowed with a spiritual power to which ordinary mortals were not privy. It seems that Gandhi's charisma may not be derived solely from the dynamic bonding that Malayalis had with him. An array of cinematic editing techniques such as zoom in, pausing camera on Gandhi's face and eyes have also been used to enhance the viewing experience.

Gandhi's images moved further to become an object or a place not just for *darshan* but for a moral exploration for an ordinary viewer. The backdrop pictures of Gandhi at the police stations functioned as a solemnization of idealistic politics that does not exist in the real world. The heroes and heroines drew moral legitimacy for their actions from these pictures. However, such acts of gaining moral strength were not deeply political as they did not raise serious questions about social injustice or bring about radical social change. Instead, they were just acts of personal morality, which were based on those of religion. Analysing Gandhi's appearance in the Bollywood film *Lage Raho Munna Bhai* as a character, Rachael Dewyer argues that such a Gandhi is "not a political Gandhi, but a Gandhi who is an inner conscience and moral guide, as well as a fairy godmother who will help us to realize our dreams" (53).

Gandhi as "New Divine"

As discussed earlier, invisible Gandhi in Malayalam cinema of the 1950s and 1960s functions in two ways: political and religious. This part of the work focuses more on the divine aspects of invisible Gandhi. Looking at these films' plots, one can see that these films' common concern was to document the problems of the poor and marginalized people faced with mundane situations and crises, raising serious questions about God's existence and meaninglessness of religious belief. While the films of the previous decades (especially of the 1940s and early 1950s) served as the culmination of religious symbolisms and imageries of all significant religions crafted wonderfully in the film texts, the socials openly raised concerns over God and religious faith, revealing the meaningfulness of religious practices. *Aswamedham* (dir. A Vincent, 1967), a screen adaptation of a famous play with the same title, attempts to expose the futility of God and religious belief using the hopelessness of leprosy patients in a sanatorium as its central concern.

God's or saint's absence or withdrawal from humanity does not immediately amount to mere absence and non-existence, but it offers a space for the viewers to rethink God and saints' identity and provide them with an experience of recognizing the divine more genuinely. Such cinematic moments pointing to God's absence or saints in the usual scenario would not be comfortable for believers to tolerate. The films that featured Gandhi as an invisible presence, in a way, were replacing the usual godly and saintly figures with the hallowed figure of a Gandhi. Therefore, the socials did not present a complete rejection of religion but reflected a shift from the transcendental God towards an affirmed humanism, placing Gandhi at its centre.

The film-makers in the 1950s and 1960s came upon the idea of picking up Gandhian ethos in their cinema, presuming that Gandhi could be a better substitute for Raja Harichandra, Jesus or Mohamed in a more secularized world of socials.[9] Although Gandhi did not find a direct place in the texts of any of these films, the photographs of him served as a Christ-figure that shaped this world's moral and political universe. The replacement of saints by Gandhi provides the space to experience "divine" in alternative ways.

The imageries which the socials provide lead their audience to explore another area of divine existence, encouraging them to move from God to love, truth and non-violence, placing Gandhi as the symbol of all these. It is evident from these films that they invite their viewers to observe and experience the intense play of love, truth and non-violence in human relationships rather than thinking about a transcendent God. Withdrawal of God in the socials is not just the collapse of idols and figures that the human beings recognize as God, but it also involves a redefinition of the divine, making it a more profound and non-transcendent experience. In interpreting invisible Gandhi in the socials in this manner, one can say that the whole experience is not a profanation or complete removal of divine figures from the spheres of "sacred," but a replacement of them with more accessible forms of "divine."

More interesting is how Gandhi turned out to be the most popular image on the title cards of the socials overpowering even those of gods (Rajesh 29). Among the title card pictures of the 1960s, the most favourite was Gandhi's images with the *charkha* at his Sabarmati Ashram. The title of the film *Swayamvaram* (Adoor Gaoplakrishnan, 1972) apart from referring to the ancient practice of girls of marriageable age choosing a husband from among a list of suitors was an affirmation to one of Gandhi's beliefs about an individual's personal autonomy and his/her right to make own choices (Bhasakran 2010). This deliberate choice of Gandhi had not just a political function but also a religious function to serve. In the political mode, Gandhi's image on title cards, like that of any other national icon, serves to promote people's unity and singularity. In the religious mode, more than serving iconic functions, Gandhi's image reflects the quality of divinity; a sacred object is displayed reverentially for inviting viewers' "worshipful gaze." Gandhi's title card images sometimes became an alternative means of interacting with the divine in everyday life. While most of the viewers did not actually worship Gandhi's images, many did invest them with moral and spiritual significance in a variety of ways. Such images presented a very different vision of "modern Kerala" for believers and non-believers, who were alienated or offended by the religious symbols used in excess in the Malayalam films of previous decades, alike (Bhaskaran 28).

Certain films with title card images of Gandhi also endorsed the inclusive theology of him, *Sarva Dharma Sama Bhava*, with belief in one God that encompasses all

Gods rather than an exclusive one with belief in only one God. The film *Achanum Bappayum* (dir. K.S. Sethumadhavan, 1972), for instance, envisioned a multi-faith Kerala with the plot of an orphan Muslim child raised in a cross-religious setting by a Hindu man braving the wrath of his family and community. There were many films released between 1950s and 1970s, revolving around the themes such as cross-cultural mingling among Hindus, Muslims and Christians, interreligious romances and marriages, inter-faith dialogues, hassle-free conversions, visits of the places of worship of one community by the people of other community. The characters in *Rarichan Enna Pouran* (dir. P. Bhaskaran, 1956), for instance, represent a cross section of life and society in central Kerala; one can meet caste Hindus, Christians from central Kerala, Muslim from Malabar, migrant Brahmin communities from Cochin, all living in an inter-faith setting constituting a secular public imagined in cinema (Venkiteswaran 2011, 99–100). In the public space conceived by cinema, various local communities – Hindus, Muslims and Christians – who were identified by their diversity made their presence felt.

The role of religion remained not so visible and operative in most of these films, but deeply influenced by Gandhi, they proposed a slightly different variant of secularism emphasizing fraternity, religious pluralism, tolerance and sociability among various religious groups. Being equally respectful towards all the religions, these films believed in a doctrine that deep religious tolerance and diversity are not optional extras but essential for the society to survive. This vision of "modern Kerala" imagined through the socials using Gandhi as "divine icon" was, thus, premised not on a religious monolith, but instead on gestures of harmony and religious pluralism. It also resulted in the poor circulation of an Indian – predominantly Hindu – mythological symbols as symbols of modern Indian nationhood in Kerala.

Conclusion

Malayalam films made in the 1950s and 1960s remain a window to understand how Gandhi's image in its invisible form has been constituted in Malayali popular culture. While the cinematic representation of invisible Gandhi in the early 1950s was a direct rendition of the dominant national discourse, the films of the 1960s circulated a slightly different image of Gandhi. The films of the 1960s invested specific power in the image functioning, not as a mere social or political construct. Within the master narratives of socials, Gandhi's image served both secular and religious functions.

Although they were products of the same social realism, the Malayalam's socials did not follow the pan-Indian realist project of secularism and instead reflected an entirely different conception of religion and secularity. Similarly, unlike in the pan-Indian imagination, the "socials" in Kerala should not necessarily be understood as the expression of Nehruvian modernity. Many aspects of pan-Indian social realism were problematized by the films of this period; key among them was the conceptual relationship that the socials had with Nehruvian modernity that shaped the ideology of socials in other parts of India.

Various images of Gandhi – visible and invisible – were used to make him a substitute for "divine" in such films. One of this chapter's major efforts was to explore the ambivalence of secular/religious binary that the depiction of Gandhi represented during this period. Setting the ideals of Gandhi as the significant ideological premise in the socials, they profoundly transformed the very ground on which liberal, secular and other modernist projects were envisioned. Invisible Gandhi or using Gandhian ethos in films reaffirmed the need for an alternative way of approaching the role of religion, ethics and moral values in society and polity and exposed the failure of secular efforts to analyse religious practices that determine a modern state with a predominance of scientific thought and rationality at the core.

Gandhian ethos emerged as the central theme of the "socials" of the 1950s and 1960s. However, a refocusing of secularism away from the essential rejection of religious and moral values was majorly represented. They assumed a continued existence and importance of religious ideals even in a highly secularized setting. These socials inculcated the need to re-evaluate the basic assumptions of religion and secularism in Kerala's specific context, reflecting both the meaningfulness of religion in social and political affairs and the popularity of secular ideals. Making Gandhi a new divine, they envisioned a doctrine presupposing new concepts of religion, ethics and politics and new imperatives associated with them. The socials also challenged us to see God as love and truth, demanding the viewers to respond to this love and truth. They also showed us that God could be experienced beyond mere presence, and such experience is possible through love and truth.

Notes

1 Venkiteswaran, C.S. Film Critic, Personal interview, 2 June 2010.
2 The film, *Papilio Budha* known popularly as Budha Peacock, is derived from a butterfly species found in the Western Ghats region of Southern India. This film symbolically narrates the poignant stories of exploitation, betrayal and humiliation experienced by the Dalits of Western Ghats, equating it with butterflies' lives.
3 Gandhi seldom figured in the post-independence politics in Kerala; Aravindakshan sees the overwhelming presence of the left and the lack of legitimacy of Gandhians as the major reasons for Gandhi's poor reception in the political sphere. The disintegration of the Soviet Union and the resultant crisis in the left politics led to the emergence of a plethora of new ideological explorations and movements, mainly of environmental and human rights activists, placing Gandhi at the centre (Chandran).
4 As a gesture of solidarity, Gandhi visited Vaikom, a village in Kerala, the venue of a *satygraha* to allow lower-caste people in Hindu temples in 1925. During those days, the lower-caste Hindus were not even permitted to walk through the main roads leading to Hindu's places of worship.
5 Kamal. Filmmaker. Personal Interview. 8 June 2020.
6 Kamal. Filmmaker. Personal Interview. 8 June 2020.
7 Gopikrishnan, P.N. Script Writer. Personal interview. 8 June 2020.
8 Gandhi himself had trouble coping with his saintly image, what he called his "*darshan* dilemma" (Rudolph and Rudolph 115).
9 Gopikrishnan, P.N. Script Writer. Personal interview. 8 June 2020.

Works Cited

Bhasakaran, Guataman. *Adoor Gopalakrishnan: A Life in Cinema*. Penguin Books, 2010.

Bhaskaran, P. *Bahskarante Athma Kadha* (Malayalam). Mathrubhumi Books, 2015.

———. *Rarichan Enna Pouran*. T.K. Pareekutty, 1956.

Bhaskaran, P., and Ramu Kariat, directors. *Neelakkuyil*. Chandrathara Productions, 1954.

Chandran, Civik. "Foreword" *Gandhiyude Jeevitha Darshanam* (Malayalam), K. Aravindakshan, Poornodaya Publications, 1992.

Chatterjee, Partha. *Lineages of Political Society: Studies in Postcolonial Democracy*. Permanent Black, 2011.

Cherian, Jayan K, director. *Papilio Budha*. Silicon Media Kayal Films, 2013.

Dewyer, Raechel. *Picture Abhi Baaki Hai: Bollywood as a Guide to Modern India*. Hachette, 2014.

Gandhi, M.K. "Speech at Public Meeting at Vaikom March 10, 1925." *The Collected Works of Mahatma Gandhi*, Publications Division, Government of India, 1999.

———. *Young India*, 11 Aug. 1920, *The Collected Works of Mahatma Gandhi*, Publications Division, Government of India, 1999.

Gopalakrishnan, Adoor, director. *Nizhalkuth*. Joel Farges & Adoor Gaopalkrishnan, 2002.

———. *Swayamvaram*. Chitralekha Film Cooperative, 1972.

Gopalakrishnan, S. "Adoorinte Nizhalkuth: Panchaboothathile Soonyatha." *Bhashaposhini*, 6 Apr. 2014, pp. 66–69.

Gupta, Chitananda Das. *The Painted Face: Studies in India's Popular Cinema*. Roli Books, 1991.

Gurtop, Getin, director. *Conquerors of the Golden City*. 1965.

Joseph, Jenson. "Revisiting *Neelakkuyil*: On the Left's Cultural Vision, Malayali Nationalism and the Questions of 'Regional Cinema." *Thapasam*, Apr.–Sept., 2012, pp. 26–57.

Kamal, director. *Pavam Pavam Rajakumaran*. Cherupushpam Films, 1990.

Krishnan, V., director. *Navalokam*. Pappachan, 1951.

Kunju Mohammed, P. T., director. *Ghershome*. Janshakti Films, 1999.

Nair, M.T. Vasudevan, director, *Bandhanam*. Marunadan Movies, 1978.

Nandy, Ashis. "Gandhi After Gandhi After Gandhi." *The Little Magazine*, vol. 1, no. 1, 2000, pp. 1–4.

Pillai, Meena. "Cinema and Modernity in Kerala." *Beyond Bollywood: The Cinemas of SouthIndia*, edited by M. K. Raghavendra, Harper Collins, 2017, pp. 274–304.

Pinney, Christopher. *Camera Indica: The Social Life of Indian Photograph*. Chicago UP, 1997.

Radhakrishnan, Ratheesh. "What Is Left of Malayalam Cinema." *Cinemas of South India: Culture, Resistance and Ideology*, edited by Sowmya Dechamma and Elavarthu Sathya Prakash, Oxford UP, 2010, pp. 25–51.

Rajesh, M.R. *Malayalam Cinema Poster: Soundaryavum, Rashtreeyavum* (Malayalam). Kerala Lalita Kala Academy, 2011.

Ramadas, P., director. *Newspaper boy*. Adarsh Kalamandir, 1955.

Rowena, Jenny. *Themmadikalum, Thampurakkanmarum: Malayala Cinemayum Aanathangalum* (Malayalam). Subject and Language Press, 2011.

Rudolph, Lloyd I., and Rudolph Susanne Hoeber. *Postmodern Gandhi and Other Essays*. Oxford UP, 2009.

Sasidharan, A.V., director. *Olipporu*. Round Up Cinema, 2013.

Scrase, Ruchira Ganguly, and Timothy J. Scrase. *Globalization and the Middle Class in India: Social and Cultural Impact of Neoliberal Reforms*. Routledge, 2008.

Sethumadhavan, K. S., director. *Achanum Bappayum*. C. C. Baby, 1972.

Sukumaran, R., director. *Yughapurashan*. A.V. Anoop, 2010.

Tampi, Viji, director. *Simhavalan Menon*. Kilimanoor Chandran, 1995.

Venkatesan, Sathyaraj, and Rajesh James. "Casting Caste: Dalit Identity and Malayalam Cinema." *Economic and Political Weekly*, vol. 11, no. 49, 9 Dec. 2017, pp. 48–52.

Venkiteswaran, C.S. *Cinema Talkies* (Malayalam). D. C. Books, 2011.

———. *Malayalacinema Padanangal* (Malayalam). D. C. Books, 2011.

Vincent, A., director. *Aswamedham*. Supriya, 1967.

———. *Murapennu*. Sobhana Parameswaran Nair, 1965.

———. *Nagarame Nandi*. Roopavani, 1967.

———. *Nizhalattam*. Supriya Films, 1970.

8

FRAMING GANDHI

Nishat Haider

> You have given us freedom without using swords or shields,
> Oh saint of Sabarmati, you have performed a miracle.
> — (by the Hindi poet, Pradeep, for the 1954 film *Jagritii*,
> translated by the author [*The Awakening*])

The spectres of the Partition of the Indian subcontinent in 1947 and the assassination of Gandhi, as forms of originary national trauma, continue to haunt the postcolonial present, in both artistic and commemorative forms. Foregrounding the post-independence Hindi cinema, this chapter seeks to decode the representational matrix of Mohandas Karamchand Gandhi (1869–1948) by situating it within the ongoing debates on presentist regime of historicity and memory. Furthermore, the chapter describes the politics of mnemonic practices regarding the question of visual culture's capacity, or lack of it, to understand Gandhi and his legacy. Using Hall's explanation that films are best understood in relation to the "periods in which they were produced and consumed" (Hall 16), this chapter shall endeavour to map out the evolving afterlives of the image(ry) of Gandhi and its relationship to Bollywood. These afterlives are read as a response to political, socio-religious and economic transformations or shifts that have taken place in India. Although within the "visual reinscriptions and critical invocations of the twists of the nation's history, Gandhi's position as Bapu, a paternalistic force, has remained broadly unchallenged" (Sinha 116), an attempt will also be made to explore how the enunciations and framings of Gandhi and his values in Hindi cinema are deeply implicated in the negotiation of these shifts. This chapter brings together an assemblage of perspectives exploring the different cinematic memories of Gandhi and how these memories were constructed, reshaped and preserved in the national and cultural imaginary. Extending Christopher Pinney's argument that

DOI: 10.4324/9781003145479-11

to appreciate India, one must understand Indian films (28), the chapter reiterates that to comprehend Gandhi's changing images and his values within postcolonial India's competing discourses, it is important to examine Hindi films. Although there are filmic hagiographies, biopics and documentaries on Gandhi, this study is entirely premised on the enunciations of Gandhi and Gandhian values in post-independence Hindi films that serve as a rich archive of images to reinterpret his (Gandhi's) diverse versions and archetypes.

The Making of Mahatma: Gandhi and Cinema

Films are social texts and critical sites where "economic and political contradictions are contested and resolved . . . meanings are negotiated and relations of dominance and subordination are defined and contested" (Jackson 1). It is notable that Dadasaheb Phalke (1870–1944), referred to as the father of Indian cinema, "made explicit the links between film-making, politics and Indian statehood" (Ganti 9). While the historical figure of Gandhi has appeared in several films, Gandhi's low opinion of cinema was recorded in his interview with the Indian Cinematograph Committee (ICC 1927–28): "Even if I was so minded, I should be unfit to answer your questionnaire, as I have never been to a cinema. But even to an outsider, the evil that it has done and is doing is patent. The good, if it has done any at all, remains to be proved" (ICC). Post-independence, Hindi cinema emerged as the de facto national cinema of India (Ganti, 2004; Virdi, 2003) in which "something called 'India' becomes inscribed, in various ways, through representational practices . . . which endow that entity with a content, a history, a meaning and a trajectory" (Krishna 194).

From the distinctiveness of his position as the father of the nation, Gandhi's figuration in cinema has assumed multiple afterlives. Although Gandhi has been iconized "as a Bolshevik, a fanatic, a trouble-maker, a hypocrite, an eccentric, a reactionary, a revolutionary, a saint, a renouncer, a messiah, an avatar . . . likened both to Lenin and Jesus Christ," these various perceptions, however, settle into two major tropes in cinema after his death. Within India, he was the "Father of the Nation" and outside "an apostle of non-violence" (Markovits 13). With the largest number of films representing him than any other Indian historical figure, the question is what inspires film-makers to screen Gandhi and Gandhian notions even today? The most apparent reason could be that the subject of Gandhi as a visual entity and his memorialization in the nation's context resists historicization, maintaining "an easy slippage between the nationalist period and post-independence India as symbol of morality in public life" (Sinha 111). Although it is difficult to trace when Gandhi first appeared in the popular visual field, the image of Gandhi, as a foundational presence and symbol in the meta-narrative of modern India is continually re-invoked and reinscribed through cinema. And this continual presence of Gandhi links India's freedom struggle with present-day identitarian negotiations, ideological conflicts and encounters with corruption. Moreover, Gandhi's lasting image as a Mahatma shows him as a conduit between the terrestrial realm and the world of the Gods.

Based on the images of Gandhi in Hindi cinema, Rachel Dwyer divides films into three broad categories: (1) films in which Gandhi appears as a character, which includes historical films and biopics like Sir Richard Attenborough's *Gandhi* (1982) and Shyam Benegal's *The Making of the Mahatma* (1996); (2) films in which his ideas play a key role in the salvation of the hero/heroine. These includes other films like the Indo-Canadian film by Deepa Mehta's *Water* (2005), Kamal Haasan's *Hey! Ram* (*Oh, Lord*) (2000); (3) the "Gandhian ethos films" that raised Gandhian views indirectly. Oblique representation of Gandhi includes the controversial and long-banned film, *Nastik* (dir. I. S. Johar; 1954), *Do Aankhen Barah Haath* (dir. V. Shantaram; 1957) and *Naya Daur* (dir. B. R. Chopra; 1957). Other films based on the indirect representation of Gandhi include Ashutosh Gowariker's *Lagaan: Once upon a Time in India* (2001) and *Swades: We the People* (2004). Notably, Gandhi himself declared that his life is his message, and this idea is exemplified when it becomes difficult to differentiate the historical figure of Gandhi from Gandhism and Gandhian philosophy (Biswas 5). These films enable us to explore two kinds of historical engagements/negotiations. The first is the use of the cinematic text to understand or explain a specific historical moment. The second is to recognize the use of a nationalist agenda as part of the aesthetic ideology. This chapter, abjuring the truth claims of history, engages with "a twofold cultural and historical approach that, on the one hand, entails the introduction of contemporary interpretations into past narratives and, on the other hand, the application of those narratives to present-day political and cultural debates" (Lichtner and Bandyopadhyay 435). Drawing on films that mark high points and crucial turning points in the imag(in) ing of Gandhi, the next section of this chapter delineates cinema's trajectory as it reflects the ideals and narratives embodied by Gandhi and his worldview.

Imag(in)ing the Father of the Nation: The Trajectory of Hindi Cinema

Indian cinema grew up in the days of the nation's struggle for freedom, a movement predominantly led by Gandhi. The Gandhian philosophy of social reform, ethical and moral behaviour, peaceful coexistence and fight against corruption profoundly influenced Bollywood directors, screenplay writers and lyricists. Connecting his aesthetic work to the Indian independence movement led by Gandhi, who described swadeshi as the soul of swaraj (self-rule), Dadasaheb Phalke declared, "My films are Swadeshi in the sense that capital, ownership and stories are all Swadeshi" (qtd. in Mishra 13). Films such as Dwarkadas Sampat's *Bhakta Vidur* [*The Saint Vidur*, 1921], *Vande Mataram Ashram* [*The Vande Mataram Hermitage*, 1926], which was censored and briefly banned by the colonial authorities, and *Gopal Krishna* (1929) are exemplary of the swadeshi film tradition that sought to represent Gandhian anti-colonial nationalism. In one scene from *Bhakta Vidur*, a character "imprisoned . . . in his cell . . . is depicted spinning thread and wearing a Gandhi cap, both palpable symbols of nationalism" (Baskaran 2002). While in another, the saint Vidur appears "as Mr. Gandhi, clad in Gandhi-cap and khaddar shirt" (Rajadhyaksha and Willemen 244). Bhakta Vidur was Sampat's first politically subversive, pro-Gandhian patriotic film, made in the wake of the Rowlatt Act (1919), which foregrounded and perpetuated Gandhi's anti-colonial nationalist programme. This film was the first to be banned in India for the sole reason that it portrayed his personality. Censor Board restricted the film's screening with a report stating that "[w]e know what you are doing, it is not Vidur, it is Gandhi, we won't allow it" (Woods 98). Since Censor Board anticipated that it would incite people against the government, it was banned in Karachi, Madras and some other provinces (Pauwels 14).

With its wide popularity and reach, the Hindi film industry has become the "site of ideological production" (Prasad 9) that asserts the nation state's perspective and narrative within the cinematic imagery. The most important contribution of Hindi mainstream cinema is the portrayal of Gandhi as a saintly father who bequeathed to us a democratic nation-state "the bedrock of guaranteeing citizenship rights to masses of people of diverse provenances" which he "moulded with non-violence as his sole weapon" (Gupta 10). Gandhi's strategy of *Satyagraha*, a fight with moral and spiritual weapons, together with his definition of *Hind Swaraj* –the founding of an *ethical state* –provides "the blueprint for the Hindi film industry's depictions of nationhood" (Kripalani 133). Motivated by the socialist values and egalitarian ideologies of Gandhian philosophy, the progressive nationalistic directors, writers and actors belonging to the IPTA (Indian People's Theatre Association) from the 1940s onwards created films with a social message that not only showed solidarity with industrial workers and peasants (Khwaja Ahmad Abbas's *Dharti ke Lal* [*Children of the Earth*], 1946; and *Do Bigha Zameen* [*Two Acres of Land*], 1953), extolled the virtues of village life or rural utopia and denounced exploitative feudalism (Mehboob Khan's *Mother India*, 1957) and celebrated physical labour (the Gandhian ideal) over industrialization and mechanization (B.R. Chopra's *Naya Daur* [*The New Race*], 1957) but also framed other social problems (*Achuut Kanya* [*Untouchable Girl*], 1936; directed by Franz Osten). One also discerns "a strong desire to rebuild the nation" in films such as *Hum Panchii Ek Dal Ke* [*We are Birds On A Single Branch*], 1957, *Jagriti* [*The Awakening*], 1954, *Toofan aur Diya* [*Storm and Lamp*], 1956, and *Dhool ka Phool* [*Dust's Flower*], 1959, and *Dharmaputra*, 1961 (Kumar 2). Although there have been films on war with hyper-nationalistic overtones, but by and large, Hindi cinema, in a true Gandhian spirit, shows the ideal protagonist take up arms only for defending the national border. For instance, after the 1962 border war with China, Manoj Kumar's *Upkaar* [*Good Deed*], 1967) not only gave the popular song "*Mere desh ki dharti*" [*The Soil of My Land*] but also framed the slogan: "*Jai Jawan, Jai Kisan* [Hail the Soldier, Hail the Farmer]."

Talking about the general importance of the poetic imagination in the construction and understanding of nation, Alasdair MacIntyre says that one can comprehend the nation by a poetic register more completely (161). In fact, the

Hindi mainstream cinema, as a significant affective archive of national imaginary, epitomises the inextricable link between the state, the culture and the society. In the 1960s and the 1970s, Hindi films showcased post-independence euphoria and, simultaneously, the unease and concern bordering that euphoria. The 1960s and early 1970s were fraught with social movements such as the Naxalite movement, the women's movement, and especially, the political movement led by the veteran Gandhian socialist Jayaprakash Narayan, popularly known as JP. In this era, the films highlight the making and unmaking of Indian society's socio-economic aspects due to these movements that challenged the dominant vectors of Nehruvian developmentalism and its attendant undertakings of nation-making. In most Hindi mainstream films of this period, there is a loose assemblage, suitable compacts of evocative powers drawn, often haphazardly, from Gandhian values and ethics. These modules often organize narrative matters into binary expressions – religious/secular, country/city, traditional/modern, poor/rich and masculine/feminine – without resolving them in a progressive, dialectical way. The "retribution assemblage," for instance, "is frequently divided between two figurations, one linked to the legal order, and the other to criminal, lower-class forces. These sets often cast in the form of estranged brothers or friends working on opposite sides of the law, share a zone of filial affection where the administration of Dharma takes place" (Basu 19). This filial affection is evident in numerous films, from *Ganga Jamuna* (dir. Nitin Bose, 1961) to *Aatish* [*The Mirror*] (dir. Sanjay Gupta, 1994). These dualities (truth versus falsehood, rural life versus city, love versus lust, innocence versus knowledge, traditional values versus modernity) usually Western (Dissanayake and Sahai, 1988) appear in the popular Raj Kapoor films like *Aag* (1948), *Awaara* (1951), *Barsaat* (1949), *Sangam* (1964); *Satyam, Shivam, Sundaram* (1978); and Dilip Kumar's movies such as *Mela* (1948), *Deedar* (1951), *Daag* (1952) and *Naya Daur* (1957). At times "the body of the star itself has to be divided into twin assemblages – good/bad, dutiful/roguish, pacifist/militant – which are then reincorporated into a superset of justice" (Basu 20). This can be viewed in "the emblematic 'double role' films which are common in Hindi cinema" (Basu 20). Dilip Kumar plays the twin siblings in *Ram Aur Shyam* (dir. Tapi Chanakya, 1967), Sridevi in *Chaalbaaz* [*The Player*] (dir. Pankaj Parashar, 1990), or Salman Khan in *Judwa* [*Twins*] (dir. David Dhawan, 1997). This narrative function "allows a bucolic, often 'Gandhian' spirit of the nation to affectively share the face of the male star as the face of the Dharmic, with sad but necessary illegal/industrial agencies in an overall age of degeneration" (Basu 20).

The task of imagining India remains an ongoing plebiscite (a "daily plebiscite," the philosopher Ernst Renan anticipated), not just in everyday life but also in films. The kind of nation imagined in the 1950s differs from the one proffered in the 1970s or the 1990s. Still, in each of its phases, Hindi popular cinema remains adamantly focused on the Gandhian idea of a nation and actively engages in debating various national fantasies. In Indian politics, the 1970s exposed the waning of Gandhi and Nehruvian ideals, which manifested in the then Prime Minister Mrs. Indira Gandhi's centrist consolidation of power through the declaration of national emergency. The themes of surging corruption increased gaps between the rich and the poor, rising license raj consequently fracture Gandhi's unifying vision. During the 1970s, "when the very idea of India seemed to disintegrate, popular cinema more than any other form engaged the political unconscious of India in vital ways" (Joshi 7). For instance, the film *Amar Akbar Anthony* (dir. Manmohan Desai, 1977) "rewrites the trauma of Partition and the assassination of M. K. Gandhi as a manic reunification caper" (Joshi 95). The representations of a pan-Indian nationalism, the images of Gandhi, the charkha (Gandhi's spinning wheel) and various forms of divisions (rural–urban, religious, poverty and gender) are abundantly framed in Hindi films such as *Upkaar* [*Benefaction*] (1967) and *Roti, Kapada aur Makaan* [*Food, Clothes and Shelter*] (1974) with *Achut Kanya* [*The Untouchable Girl*] (1936). In Vijay Anand's adaptation of RK Narayan's *The Guide* (1965), what strikes us so forcefully is the metatext and the very forces that define the individual in a postcolonial capitalist world construct the subject of the male protagonist, Raju. Describing the ironic parallels with Gandhi (the Mahatma), Mishra says, "Yet the way in which Raju captures the imagination of Velan, the villager who reads even his confessional narratives as indicative of discourses that only enlightened individuals know, shows how in the culture the mantle of the Mahatma is thrust upon an individual despite the person's protestations" (46). Since Gandhi epitomized the authentic Indian self, Raju constructed a conception of the self that anticipated or echoed many of Gandhi's ideas of the Indian notion of self.

In recent years, the debates regarding the "politics of remembering and forgetting" Gandhi have underscored how the films construct or are constructed by the socio-political and economic environment. In the decade following economic liberalization in 1991, "the 'slum solidarity' that Nandy rhapsodizes gives way to a cinema screened far outside India's urban slums in suburban 'multiplexes' that disowned the poor as less amenable images of themselves and of India's" (Joshi 9). Subsequently, the Hindi films laid bare some of the fault lines of the Indian nation consequent upon the destruction of the Babri Masjid in 1992, the Mumbai riots of 1992–1993, the Gujarat carnage of 2002, and the rise of Hindutva politics. From the gaps in its national history and the elisions in representation that have emerged as a result of the nation's fault lines, Hindi cinema also highlights the nation-state's ongoing responsibilities. The two films in the new millennium that focus on the Mahatma's fictional, unsuccessful assassins are Kamal Haasan's *Hey Ram* (2000) and Jahnu Barua's *Maine Gandhi Ko Nahin Mara* [*I Didn't Kill Gandhi*] (2005). The film *Hey Ram* constructs a traumatized South Indian Brahmin male archaeologist's subjectivity through Saket Ram's (performed by Kamal Haasan) ordeal of witnessing his wife, Aparna's (portrayed by Rani Mukherjee) gang rape and murder at the hands of the rioting Muslims. Kamal Haasan's controversial film *Hey Ram* ingenuously projects a bold narrative of "Muslim bloodlust and Hindu trauma, juxtaposed with the notion of Mahatma Gandhi's politics of Muslim appeasement" (Ahmad 40). The title of the film *Hey Ram* is supposedly the last phrase uttered by Gandhi before he died.

Moreover, despite an ambiguous conclusion, these are the themes that "return as irreducible features of the historical memory relayed by the film" (Vasudevan 2920).

Signalling a fundamental shift in perspective on the consensus about leading figures such as Gandhi in a discourse about secularism, democracy and identity, Vasudevan underscores "the contradictory effects of the film, the distinct uncertainty that viewers experience when confronted with the inflammatory images and voices" (Vasudevan 2917). Saket Ram, a Hindu, now explicitly identified with exclusive victimhood, embarks upon a murderous plan to assassinate the Mahatma, his rage driven by the righteousness of acting on behalf of the Hindu victims and against Gandhi's policy of Muslim appeasement. Nevertheless, before its denouement can go wrong, the narrative reverts to asserting moral certitude, and another assassin, Nathuram Godse, kills the Mahatma, probably compelled by righteousness akin to Saket Ram's. According to the political psychologist Ashis Nandy, the "real" killers of Gandhi were the "insecure, traditional elite concentrated in the urbanized, educated, partly Westernized, tertiary sector whose meaning of life Gandhian politics was taking away. Gandhi often talked about the heartlessness of the Indian literati. He paid with his life for that awareness" (*At the Edge of Psychology* 87). Nathuram Godse was an acolyte of the "extremist nationalist" (Kumar 2015) V. D. Savarkar (1883–1966) who developed the Hindu nationalist political ideology of Hindutva. In court, Godse observed that Gandhi's doctrine of non-violence had "enfeebled the Hindus and emasculated a faith that would have to learn how to stand on its feet against the depredations of Muslims" (Lal 2). These critiques of Gandhi, however farcical they may be, continue to thrive, unleashing the haunting afterlives of Gandhi's legacy.

The film scholar Rachel Dwyer insists that "the specific melodramatic mode and requirements of the Hindi film are not well suited to the character of Gandhi" (370). Earlier in the essay, while talking about *Lage Raho*, Rachel Dwyer says, "Although Gandhi is back, it is not the historical Gandhi, a challenging and difficult figure urging the abandonment of consumerism, but a Gandhi of India's new middle classes" (353). Films like Rajkumar Hirani's films, *Lage Raho Munnabhai*[*Keep At It, Munnabhai*] (2006) and *3 Idiots* (2009) portray an India that is oblivious of Gandhian values and marked by a blatantly corrupt as well as increasingly unethical political system. These films depict a world of massive land grabs and avaricious global corporate forces that have gone out of control. These movies show a world where a son expels his inconveniently old parent and where the only possible option offered by Lucky, the real estate developer, to his victims is wads of money or a bullet. For the scholar Ashis Nandy, "Gandhian values are more like a potentiality incompatible with both classical and some aspects of the popular and can appeal to these sectors only under specific conditions" (Nandy, "The Lure of 'Normal' Politics" 167). *Lage Raho Munnabhai* selectively reclaims past Gandhian practices to articulate alternatives abstracted from history and the dense Gandhian philosophy as ruses to address a "New" India.

The engagement with the image of Mahatma in *Lage Raho Munnabhai's* allows him (Gandhi) "a second inning, and the figure has to appear as hallucination, a shadow of Gandhi's 'real' self that was incomprehensible even to those who knew him" (Joshi 129). Gandhi's appearance in *Lage Raho* offers a reminder to a new generation that "someone in this very country dared to experiment with another kind of politics, defying the academic and bureaucratic canons and, while this other politics might be taboo in the high culture of the Indian state, it still makes sense to millions in the world" (Nandy, "The Lure of 'Normal' Politics" 174). In an essay "Gandhi after Gandhi," Ashish Nandy distinguished between four Gandhis that emerged in popular representations after the death of the historical persona. While the first Gandhi is the Gandhi of the Indian state and Indian nationalism, the second Gandhi is that of the Gandhians, who, according to Nandy, "does not touch politics." The third Gandhi is the Gandhi of the "ragamuffins, eccentrics and the unpredictable" and is "more hostile to Coca-Cola than to Scotch whisky and considers the local versions of Coca Cola more dangerous than imported ones." Finally, the fourth Gandhi walks the mean streets of the world, threatening the status quo and pompous bullies in every area of life. Other critics, following Ashis Nandy's work on Gandhi, catalogue Nandy's four Gandhis and conclude, as Arunabhava Ghosh and Tapan Babu do, that *Lage Raho*'s "Gandhigiri is perhaps closer to the fourth variety of [Nandy's] Gandhi," who has been refashioned to become an "icon of popular culture" (5225).

In *Lage Raho Munna Bhai*, the putative ghost of Mahatma Gandhi makes pedagogical visits to a daft yet lovable rogue, played by Sanjay Dutt. He fakes being a Gandhi scholar to attract a female radio broadcaster and, in the process, finds himself espousing Gandhi's principles of *satya* (truth), *ahimsa* (non-violence) and *satyagraha* (*satya* –soul; *graha* –force) (Iyer 41; Moon 48–61) dubbed as "Gandhgiri." The film engages with Gandhi's advice to confront injustice with love, empathy and understanding which would save not only one's soul but also that of one's oppressors. So successful was the narrative deploying of those principles that, upon its release, the film roused actual Gandhigiri (Gandhi-ism) movements across India. The protagonist of the film Munna reinforces Mahatma's actual messages when he suggests, "stop bullying. Start Gandhigiri. . . . He said, if your enemy swears at you, smile back at him . . . if someone hits you on one cheek, offer him the other. This will reduce his hatred, and increase his respect for you." *Gandhigiri* becomes the presiding philosophy in the film espoused by Munna and his followers. A variety of subplots are happily resolved when characters adopt practices of truthfulness, non-violence and carefully constructed "*vinamrata*" [polite submissiveness], seemingly in keeping with the Mahatma's teachings. The protagonist's ruse succeeds, mainly because he receives help from an unexpected source – the Mahatma himself. Munna finds himself genially "haunted" by a walking, talking incarnation of the Mahatma; when Munna begins to lecture on Gandhism, it's the real figure behind him supplying the words to say. During Munna's lecture, someone asks him what should be done to a boy desecrating a Gandhi statue. Munna's instincts tell him to punish the boy, but Gandhi interrupts: "give him a stone and tell him to topple the statue. Bring down all my statues in the country. Remove my pictures from every wall. Erase my name from buildings, roads, currency. If you keep me somewhere, keep me in your heart."

Through Munna, Gandhi argues that honouring him with statues, imprinting his portrait on currency notes, or observing his birthday means nothing if no one remembers his actual message. Claude Markovits notes that Gandhi's image, while seemingly everywhere, now seems "more and more devoid of specific content. Although Gandhi remains a legitimizing image that no group or individual can dispense with, the more one tends to pay tribute to him, the less his message is taken seriously" (Markovits 62). This inability to engage with his philosophy renders Gandhi frozen in history and politically fossilized. Addressing the audience in the last scene, Gandhi says "I was shot down years ago. But three bullets cannot kill my ideology. . . . The choice is yours! Hang my picture on the wall, or think of my principles." Theorizing that Gandhi's ossified image might be a part of the problem, Ira Bhaskar suggests a dynamic engagement with Gandhian ethos. She says "an exorcism of our guilt" is the only way to "mobilize the memory of Gandhi to release his image from its ineffective place on the walls of Indian embassies and government offices into the light of contemporary political experience. She believes this will enable "Gandhism" to "become effective in marginalizing the forces that are destroying [nation's] plural and diverse fabric" (380). While recalling Gandhi with a picture/icon is virtually comparable to forgetting him in any real sense, but imbibing his philosophy in everyday life, on the other hand, as enunciated in this film, is concomitant to remembering him and learning from national memory. The message's presentation proved so appealing that audiences from all walks of life began practising "Gandhigiri" in real life, as a current popular spin on traditional Gandhism. For Munna, remembering Gandhi is sometimes not a choice; the Mahatma will return to haunt or help the new generation of Indians who are either oblivious of Gandhi's significance and philosophy or unwilling or unable to preserve or process his role in the nation's present.

The success and popularity of *Lage Raho* Munnabhai is a testimony to the fact that, notwithstanding the ascendancy of Hindutva and the glitzy allure of globalization, the spectre of Gandhi still looms large and haunts the Indian mass consciousness. The ghost of Gandhi that scriptwriters Rajkumar Hirani and Abhijat Joshi manufacture in *Lage Raho Munnabhai* is a device that offers its model of Gandhi's version of citizenship in the era of post-liberalization India when the people "learn to conduct his own version of passive resistance by offering his underwear to a corrupt pension officer demanding a bribe" (Joshi 129). The invocation of the ghost's cinematic device underscores the conflicted politics of memory and interweaves a spectropoetics of the violence of forgetting with a spectropolitics of redemption and quest for justice. In the film, Munna ruefully observes: "[h]e's [Gandhi] done so much for us. . . . And what have we done for him? Reduced him to a wall painting . . . we've ruined the country. If Bapu were around today, he'd say 'we found our country, but lost our people."

In one of the more curious manifestations, the film grounds Munna's hospitality to Gandhi's ghost within hermeneutics of the Benjaminian idea of "anamnestic solidarity" (*Illuminations*, 253). This solidarity is with the past and the other, necessitating recognition and compassion, protective care and assurances against degradation. For Benjamin, such solidarity "brushes against the grain of history" (Benjamin, *Illuminations* 257) and thereby subverts the view of history as the mere pastness of the past. If we consider Gandhi's image as a complex point of reference in the national imaginary and cultural memory, then the uncanny presence of Gandhi as "psychoanalytical listening" based on interpretations of the Hindi films entails a different role for spectators. The task of the spectator would then consist of "an identification of the concealed contents of the story (hidden deeper than its open and easily denoted theme), rendered dialectic by textual representation 'interiorised' in it in such a way as if it were the patient's memory" (Michera 152).

A cinematic engagement with Gandhi's alternative politics of ethics and his haunting legacies helps to situate the film in the gap between politics and ethics. Such an engagement can be understood as "an attitude or activity within the sphere of community, rather than a set of common principles or a narrative domain," which becomes "essential to the ordering of our lives together, and to the 'ensemble of human relations in their real, social structure' that we might call politics" (Berman 25). The spectators are not just passively absorbed in the film, instead s/he is an active interpreter (Rancière 37). The film presents a unique and powerful cinematic language for framing ruptures and silence wrenched out from the unconscious realm.

Conclusion

While the pervasive presence of Gandhi's icon(ography) in the national imaginary makes it very easy for most Indians to easily recognise his image, a lot of credit goes to the Hindi cinema for contextualizing Mahatma's philosophy/values and making it accessible and comprehensible to the masses across the Indian subcontinent. As Mei Li Badecker (2020) says, "Understanding Gandhi's legacy in the popular context is as important as appreciating his relevance in the political one" (145). The Hindi mainstream cinema has an intimate relationship with Gandhian values, nationalism and patriotism. The early Hindi mainstream cinema underscores Gandhi's preference for persuasion, self-reform and volition as ways of achieving distributional justice (Bose 79–90; Moon 133–35). These films also admire Gandhi's moral courage that brought forth a new method – rooted in non-violence, truth, virtue, dialogue, mutual respect and self-service – which proves to provide an effective avenue to solve modern conflicts. The film's male protagonist borrows Gandhian virtues, world views and ethical strategies to inspire the masses to lead good and virtuous lives. The socially responsible and engaged popular Hindi cinema and its discursive ecology reveal similarities and differences in its treatment of Gandhi and his morality across the decades. Rather than narrowing Gandhi's persona and the idea of "India," Hindi cinema continues to expand their understanding and scope, remaining the site where versions of the Mahatma and the nation are recuperated, performed and reworked. While a film like Jahnu Barua's *Maine Gandhi Ko Nahin Mara* has examined the lack of enthusiasm or indifference towards Gandhism in our society, the film has reformulated the term Gandhism and received tremendous acclaim is Raj Kumar Hirani's film *Lage Raho Munna Bhai*. The film appreciates Gandhi's moral courage that brought forth a new method – embedded in non-violence, truth, virtue, persuasion, dialogue, mutual respect and self-service – which offers a compelling prospect to resolve modern discords. The film is remarkable not only for its neologism "Gandhigiri" but also for its mixing of comedy with Gandhian praxis. *Maine Gandhi Ko Nahin Mara*, *Lage Raho Munna Bhai* and *Hey! Ram* suggests that if the partition of the Indian subcontinent's haunting legacies is to be resolved, then the competing/converging compulsions in the body politic construction must be reanalysed to recover and reconfigure Gandhi's role and relevance in Indian history and national consciousness.

Despite all-encompassing amnesia regarding traumatic events like Partition, the assassination of Gandhi, and "a reluctance in Bollywood to portray the terrorist as irredeemably evil and demonic" (Richter 494), two films (*Maine Gandhi Ko Nahin Mara* and *Hey! Ram*) show Gandhi's would-be assassins as part of the central narrative. This not only threatens but also consolidates cinema's imagined national community by enabling the audiences to act out and work through the originary trauma of patricide, the assassination of the father of the nation. Bollywood's appeal lies in capturing audiences by framing diverse aspirations and social responsiveness as cinema's defining feature that (re/de)constructs Gandhi. It nimbly evolves constellations of tropes and techniques to address them. With the altering Indian socio-economic and political landscape, the nature of the cultural ethos has also changed. The India of slumdogs living in overcrowded slums coexists alongside the millionaires inhabiting the decadent, luxurious and glittering high-rises. Hindi cinema continues to address and map out these changes. Bollywood has represented India as a flawed secular democracy marked by boardroom protocols of a market-dominated logic, economic liberalization and Westernization, unbridgeable economic disparities, infractions within the family that replace all human relations, loss of filial piety, sexual permissiveness and dissipation of conjugal steadfastness, sensibilities bereft of political, ethical and social responsiveness. However, Hindi films insist on reminding its viewers of the Gandhian virtues and his idea of India that inspired the state. Last but not least, the popular Hindi cinema remains a consistent form of critique and renewal that combines aesthetics and entertainment with Gandhian principles, morality and social responsiveness.

Works Cited

Ahmad, Sumaiya. "Presentation of Islamic Symbols in Indian Cinemas a Critical Study." *Journal of Islamic Studies and Culture*, vol. 2, no. 2, June 2014, pp. 33-54. http://jiscnet.com/journals/jisc/Vol_2_No_2_June_2014/3.pdf. Accessed 25 Feb. 2021.

Badecker, Mei Li. "A Modern Mahatma? Use and Misuse of Gandhi in Popular Culture." *M.K. Gandhi, Media, Politics and Society, edited by Chandrika Kaul (Palgrave Studies in the History of the Media)*. Cham, Switzerland: Palgrave Macmillan, 2020, pp. 143-157. https://doi.org/10.1007/978-3-030-59035-2_9.

Baskaran, T. "The Roots of South Indian Cinema." *The Journal of the International Institute*, vol. 9, no. 2, Winter 2002. quod.lib.umich.edu/j/jii/4750978.0009.206?rgn=main;view=fulltext. Accessed 20 Feb. 2021.

Basu, Anustup. *Bollywood in the Age of New Media: The Geo-Televisual Aesthetic.* Edinburgh UP, 2010.

Benjamin, Walter. "Critique of Violence." *Selected Writings Vol. 1*, edited by Marcus Bullock and Michael W. Jennings, Belknap Press, 1996.

———. *Illuminations.* London, England: Fontana P, 1992. Original Work Published 1968.

Berman, Jessica. *Modernist Commitments: Ethics, Politics, and Transnational Modernism.* Columbia UP, 2011.

Biswas, Sujay. "Gandhi's Struggle Against Caste and Untouchability in South Africa, 1893–1914." *South Asian Review*, 2020, pp. 1–16, https://doi.org/10.1080/02759527.2020.17 65069. Accessed 25 Feb. 2021.

Bose, Nirmar Kumar. "The Theory and Practice of Satyagraha." *The Meanings of Gandhi*, edited by Power Paul, East-West Center Book, The UP of Hawaii, 1971, pp. 79–90.

Dissanayake, Wimal, and Malti Sahai. *Raj Kapoor's Films: Harmony of Discourses.* Vikas, 1988.

Dwyer, Rachel. "The Case of the Missing Mahatma: Gandhi and the Hindi Cinema." *Public Culture*, vol. 23, no. 2, 2011, pp. 349–76, https://doi.org/10.1215/08992363-1161949. Accessed 20 Feb. 2021.

Ganti Tejasvi. *Bollywood: A Guide Book to Popular Hindi Cinema.* Routledge, 2004.

Ghosh, Arunabha, and Tapan Babu. "*Lage Raho Munna Bhai*: Unravelling Brand 'Gandhigiri'." *Economic and Political Weekly*, vol. 41, no. 51, 23–29 Dec. 2006, pp. 5225–27. Accessed 5 Feb. 2021.

Gupta, Dipankar. *From 'People' to 'Citizen' Democracy's Must Take Road.* Routledge, 2018.

Hall, Jeanne. "The Benefits of Hindsight: Re-Visions of HUAC and the Film and Television Industries in 'The Front' and 'Guilty by Suspicion'." *Film Quarterly*, vol. 54, no. 2, 2000, pp. 15–26, https://doi.org/10.2307/1213625. Accessed 20 Feb. 2021.

ICC (Indian Cinematograph Committee). 1927–28. Vol. 3. Oral Evidence of Witnesses Examined at Madras, Rangoon, Mandalay, Calcutta (One Witness), Jamshedpur, Nagpur, and Delhi, with Their Written Statements, Calcutta, Government of India Central Publication Branch.

Iyer, Rhagavan N. *The Moral and Political Thoughts of Mahatma Gandhi.* Oxford UP, 1973.

Jackson, Peter. *Maps of Meaning: An Introduction to Cultural Geography.* Unwin Hyman, 1989.

Joshi, Priya. *Bollywood's India: A Public Fantasy.* Columbia UP, 2015.

Kripalani, Coonoor. "Reviving Gandhi and the Utopia of Hind Swaraj in Popular Hindi Films." *Swaraj and the Reluctant State*, edited by K.B. Saxena, Routledge, 2021, pp. 133–52.

Krishna, Sankaran. "Cartographic Anxiety: Mapping the Body Politic in India." *Challenging Boundaries: Global Flows, Territorial Identities*, edited by H. Alker Jr and M. Shapiro, U of Minnesota P, 1996, pp. 193–215.

Kumar, Aishwary. *Radical Equality: Ambedkar, Gandhi, and the Risk of Democracy.* Stanford, California: Stanford University Press, 2015.

Kumar, Deepak. The Trishanku Nation: Memory, Self, and Society in Contemporary India. New Delhi: Oxford University Press, 2015.

Lal, Vinay ed. *Political Hinduism: The Religious Imagination in Public Spheres.* New Delhi: Oxford University Press, 2009.

Lichtner, Giacomo, and Sekhar Bandyopadhyay. "Indian Cinema and The Presentist Use of History: Conceptions of Nationhood in *Earth* and *Lagaan*." *Asian Survey*, vol. 48, no. 3, 2008, pp. 431–52, https://doi.org/10.1525/as.2008.48.3.431. Accessed 25 Feb. 2021.

MacIntyre, Alasdair. "Poetry as Political Philosophy." *Ethics and Politics: Selected Essays* Vol. 2. Cambridge: Cambridge UP, 2006, pp. 159–71.

Markovits, Claude. *The Un-Gandhian Gandhi: The Life and Afterlife of the Mahatma.* Anthem, 2004.

Michera, Wojciech. "The Image, the Crypt, the Interpretation." *Konteksty*, vol. 1, 2010, pp. 152–58. Accessed 22 Feb. 2021.

Mishra Vijay. *Bollywood Cinema: Temples of Desire*. Routledge, 2002.

Moon, Pendrell. *Gandhi and Modern India*. Norton, 1969.

Nandy, Ashis. *At the Edge of Psychology: Essays in Politics and Culture*. Oxford UP, 1990.

———. "Gandhi After Gandhi After Gandhi." *The Little Magazine*, vol. 1, 2000, http://vlal. bol.ucla.edu/multiversity/Nandy/Nandy_gandhi.htm. Accessed 20 Feb. 2021.

———. "The Lure of 'Normal' Politics: Gandhi and the Battle for Popular Culture of Politics in India." *South Asian Popular Culture*, vol. 5, no. 2, Oct. 2007, pp. 167–78. Accessed 27 Feb. 2021.

Nandy, Ashis, et al. *Creating a Nationality: The Ramjanmabhumi Movement and Fear of the Self*. Oxford UP, 1997.

Pauwels, Heidi Rika Maria. *Indian Literature and Popular Cinema: Recasting Classics*. Routledge, 2007.

Pinney, Christopher. "Introduction: Public, Popular and Other Cultures." *Pleasure and the Nation: The History, Politics and Consumption of Public Culture in India*, edited by Christopher Pinney and Rachel Dwyer, Oxford UP, 2001, pp. 1–34.

Prasad, M. Madhav. *Ideology of the Hindi Film: A Historical Construction*. Oxford UP, 1998.

Rai, A. "Patriotism and the Muslim Citizen in Hindi Films." *Harvard Asia Quarterly*, vol. 7, no 3, 2003, www.asiaquarterly.com/content/view/136/40/. Accessed 18 Feb. 2021.

Rai, Dhananjay. "Popular Hindi Cinema as Gandhi's Alter Ego: An Exploration in Respect of *Gandhi, My Father*." *Social Change*, vol. 41, no. 1, 2011, pp. 63–78, https://doi.org/10.1177/004908571104100103. Accessed 1 Feb. 2021.

Rajadhyaksha, Ashish, and Paul Willemen. *Encyclopaedia of Indian Cinema*. Oxford UP, 1994.

Ramaswamy, S. "The Mahatma as Muse: An Image Essay on Gandhi in Popular Indian Visual Imagination." *Art and Visual Culture in India 1857–2007*, edited by Gayatri Sinha, Marg Publications, 2009, pp. 236–49.

Rancière, Jacques. *The Emancipated Spectator*. Translated by G. Elliott. Verso, 2009.

Richter, Claudia. "The Ethics of Coexistence: Bollywood's Different Take on Terrorism." *CrossCurrents*, vol. 59, no. 4, Dec. 2009, pp. 484–99, doi:10.1111/j.1939-3881.2009.00094.x. Accessed 23 Feb. 2021.

Siegel, Lee. *Laughing Matters: Comic Tradition in India*. U of Chicago P, 1987.

Singh, Bhagat, et al. "The Philosophy of the Bomb." *SCRIBD*, www.scribd.com/doc/18623179/The-Philosophy-of-the-Bomb-Shaheed-Bhagat-Singh.

Sinha, G. *The Afterlives of Images: The Contested Legacies of Gandhi in Art and Popular Culture*. South Asian Studies, vol. 29, no. 1, 2013, pp. 111–29.

Vasudevan, Ravi. "Another History Rises to the Surface: 'Hey Ram' – Melodrama in the Age of Digital Simulation." *Economic and Political Weekly*, vol. 37, no. 28, 13–19 July 2002, pp. 2917–25. Accessed 21 Feb. 2021.

Virdi, Jyoti. *The Cinematic Imagination: Indian Popular Films as Social History*. Permanent Black, 2003.

Woods, Jeannine. *Visions of Empire and Other Imaginings: Cinema, Ireland and India 1910–1962*. Peter Lang, 2011.

PART III

The Construction of Self

Experimental Site of Praxis and
Its Discursive Limits

9

AN UNTOUCHABLE IN SEARCH OF AN *ASKETIC* GANDHI

The Religiosity of Postcolonial Political[1]

Dhritiman Chakraborty

> Real Kurukshetra is the human heart, which is also a *dharmashektra* (the field of righteousness). . . . Some battle or other is fought on this battle-field from day to day
>
> — M. K. Gandhi[2]

> In a political space where . . . the decisive elements reside more and more in men, in their decisions, in the manner in which they bring their authority to bear, in the wisdom they manifest in the interplay of equilibria and transactions, it appears that the art of governing oneself becomes . . . political.
>
> — M. Foucault (1986, 89)

> Who is the third that walks always beside you?
> There is always another one walking beside you
> Gliding wrapt in a brown mantle, hooded
>
> — T. S. Eliot's *The Waste Land* (1922)

Among the many concepts that assumed immense political significance during India's anti-colonial movement, *swaraj*, undoubtedly stands tall and distinct. It will not be an exaggeration to argue that the idea of *swaraj* shaped the heterogeneous political energies that we collectively identify as the "anti-colonial movement" with a conceptual solidity and a unifying force. It generated in the entire movement the necessary political energy to adequately address how to define the "postcolonial political," a political that unequivocally departs from all imperial concepts of power and subject formation. So, the idea of what we term as *swaraj* leads immediately to investigating the right self, the self-proper, which can undertake such a political act. The classification of this framework of the political entails the critique of colonial power. Also, it includes the opening up of new cartography of sociality that can

DOI: 10.4324/9781003145479-13

give birth to a whole new non-imperial, decolonized and non-majoritarian political subjectivity.

Swaraj does not merely imply political freedom; it directs us to a specific template of freedom that questions the very nature and boundary of autonomy. Swaraj brings forth a solid and differential understanding of self, one that relinquishes freedom to experience freedom. The idea of swaraj can be understood from what the first epigraph by Gandhi describes rhetorically as the perpetual "Kurukshetra" (trans. battle) occurring inside the heart. Therefore, swaraj amounts to refashioning of a postcolonial self, which is postcolonial in a definite sense of the term.

Ananya Vajpeyi, in her book *Righteous Republic* (2014), discusses this idea of the postcolonial subjectivity by outlining *swaraj* as being tied up with the historical quest of ascertaining the *swa* (self) upon which the *raj*, roughly glossed over as rule or domination, is instituted. She writes " 'self' thus is either the subject of rule, or the object of rule, or both the subject and the object at the same time" (ix). In swaraj's fascinating unravelling of the self's nature, Gandhi poses the contradictory nature of postcolonial subjectivity that simultaneously functions as subject and object. This contradictory relation perforce denotes a very nuanced understanding of politics that resonates with what in the second epigraph Michel Foucault identifies as the "art of governing oneself." It bespeaks of an aesthetico-political impulse that significantly echoes *satyagraha's* idea, an idea which will be discussed in detail later in the chapter. Even though Gandhi was writing from the immediate context of the anti-colonial movement with its limitations and restrictions, it led to a more concrete intervention in the dialectic between power and resistance.

On the other hand, for Foucault, the processes of subject formation over a long *duree* acquired its profound significance. He tried to understand the triadic working of power-subject-discourse formation that foreclosed on other possibilities of subjectivity. Through these diverse approaches that responded to two differential contexts – first, France's sociopolitical scenario post the 1968 student movements (Renaut 2000) and second, the political scenario of colonialism in India, Foucault and Gandhi offer us many seminal ideas which both intersect and yet remain abysmally disconnected from each other. These are not merely two epistemological traditions in contention with each other. On the contrary, this engagement between Gandhi and Foucault opens up the possibility of a dialogue for a more radical redefinition of politics categorized as micropolitical. A political that is always already microscopic in nature and molecular in form.

Consequently, this categorization of the political advocates a kind of self we need to become – which will always precede the kind of politics we can enact. This process of acquiring a "self-proper" to generate a politics in apposition to that self does not evince any causal ordering. It rather implies a mutually co-constitutive process. The question in the third epigraph "Who is the third that walks always beside you?" from T. S. Eliot's *The Waste Land* (1922), becomes extremely pertinent at this point. This invisible third as a possibility unravels in moments of crisis and restlessness. What this paper in specific grapples with is this idea of the "third."

And how does this invisible "third," secret and "hooded," and "wrapt in a brown mantle," manifests in an imagined encounter between Foucault and Gandhi in terms of their respective engagements with the question of subjectivity vis-à-vis the idea of political power.

Moreover, this emphasis on the "third" is not simply a numeric exercise; it instead looks for spaces that remain outside of the secular liberal understanding of politics. Further, this space of the third also refuses to see politics as a field of force between competing identities, their constitutive ambiguities, and the intersubjective formations. Instead, this space of the third revisits politics from its differential origin, without a singular metaphysical *arche*, an essence. This genealogical, originary understanding of politics destabilizes any given language of politics and looks for causalities that render the political possible in the first place. In contrast to origin/essence as grounding, originary thus unfolds the multiplicity of unity that underpins its existence. In this sense, originary looks to the future. It is futural as it marks the opening of differential politics.

If *Swaraj* can be interpreted as an "art of governing oneself," it would immediately open up the question of *"swa"* to its inextricable originary mooring in the concept of *being-with*, being-with-the-other, in being always minor, and in refusing to be the majority (Skaria 2016, 59). Therefore, Foucault and Gandhi's engagement promises a dialogue on how the "art of governing oneself" can lead to a self, which is always already non-sovereign. The idea of this non-sovereign self can only be sensed in the signs of its erasure. If Foucault tried to retrieve an *asketic* self from the foreclosed Greek traditions, Gandhi both owns up and disowns the self in his quest to experience freedom as *moksha* (salvation). Therefore, this dialogue[3] betrays continuity between refashioning selfness to giving birth to selflessness, from being ensnarled in selfhood to appear as a "lonely pilgrim finally."[4] The Gandhian paradigm of politics borrows from religion its core spirit – the eternal quest for *satya* (truth), the *satya-agraha* (the willingness to acquire truth). It also radicalizes secularism's central thrust for liberty and equality by extending it to "absolute equality" that significantly includes the non-human. The political struggle's paradigmatic feature unfolds a new terrain of politics borrowed from religion that enables one to relinquish all kinds of sovereignty.

Nevertheless, this paradigm of the political attains a unique sense of freedom, unmediated and unconditional. This freedom transports humans to the edge of all majoritarian thinking and, after that, redefines freedom from the position of the liminal, an otherness, a "third" space (Skaria 2015). Gilles Deleuze calls this process as leading to "minor," just as Gandhi identifies this process as putting limits, a willing condition of sacrifice without subordination (Due 2007, 49). Ajay Skaria (2016, 9) has impeccably put this point in the following words:

> Relinquishing sovereignty, satyagrahis must strive for equality of and with the minor. As that phrase suggests, the minor is never simply an individual – minority names here rather the community that perdures without sovereignty, and yet without submitting to majority or sovereignty.

Therefore, power is acquired in relinquishing sovereignty, sacrificing and securing freedom by "pure means" (Gandhi, *Hind Swaraj* 72). Put differently, this is the power of being able to dwell in powerlessness. It is politics in the sense that by exceeding politics, it becomes political.[5] It suggests both becoming political and becoming powerless, or refusing to be the subject of colonial power and, therefore, postcolonial and post-imperial. What is the nature of this power that one desires yet does not employ? Does this supposed passivity open up a new horizon of politics? Further, what role does religion play in framing this modality of politics?[6]

The new horizon of politics concerns asking questions related to the nature of religiosity of the postcolonial political that cuts through the binary of "Eurocentrism-Indigenism" (Menon 2019, 37). To further elaborate these points, this chapter will take recourse to a momentous scene of encounter in Mulk Raj Anand's fictional masterpiece, *Untouchable* (1935), to finally glimpse the possible opening of postcolonial political as the "third" space in politics.

Sauchalaya and the Politics of Caste in Anand's *Untouchable*

In 1935, after having edited and cut short as many as a hundred pages following Gandhi's suggestion, Mulk Raj Anand published his novel *Untouchable* (1935). It accounts for the hardship and stigmatized life of a sweeper boy named Bakha and his small family living in a shanty outside the town, Bulashah, located in a remote corner of North-West colonial India. By the time the novel opens, Bakha is already in his teens and is quite familiar with his daily work of cleaning toilets, sweeping streets and putting up an unperturbed face even when he is abused with a range of invectives. Bakha is quite dexterous in securing the loose ends of his teenage life. He is fond of playing hockey with his friends Chota and Ram Charan, and we are informed that all of them belong to the same caste. Bakha is also sometimes taken unaware of sudden eruptions of sensuous attractions to fellow local girl mates. In all, he is shown dealing remarkably well with the society, struggling and yet deriving his share of joy in between, until that "unlucky" and "inauspicious" day the novel sets to adumbrate (Anand 111).

It is a story of this single day, and Anand has left no stone unturned to make it as eventful as possible by packing it with all kinds of caste prejudices. Not surprisingly, Bakha and his family have been at the receiving end of all these series of events. Their collective victimhood only grows as the story reaches the final denouement where Bakha's "Indian day is over" (Forster), and he is placed in a labyrinth, at the threshold of newer and transversal possibilities. The narrator informs:

> He began to move. His virtues lay in his close-knit sinews and in his long-breathed sense. He was thinking of everything he had heard though he could not understand it all. He was calm as he walked along, *though the conflict in his soul was not over*, though he was torn between his enthusiasm for Gandhi and

the difficulties in his own awkward, naïve self. . . . A handful of *stars throbbed in the heart of the sky*.

As the brief Indian twilight came and went, a *sudden* impulse shot through the transformations of space and time. . . . 'I shall go and tell father all that Gandhi said about us,' he whispered to himself, 'and all that that poet said. Perhaps I can find the poet some day and ask him about his machine.' And he proceeded *homewards*.

(italics added; 148)

There is, however, a brief context to it, which makes this *homeward* journey significant. The entire story unravels between two public scenes. The first public scene befalls when Bakha is incriminated and stigmatized by a Brahmin for being "polluted" by his touch. The final scene occurs in a public meeting wherein Gandhi speaks at length of a possible roadmap to end stigmatization associated with caste prejudices and discriminatory behaviour. The first scene causes Bakha to realize his "Untouchable" self, and he kept on morbidly uttering "[t]hat's the word! Untouchable! I am Untouchable!" (43). In the second scene, he breathes a "handful of stars" with indistinct light glowing in his heart. In between these two scenes, Bakha is thrown out from his house after having spent the afternoon with his friends and deliberately withdrawing from his usual duties of cleaning public toilets to spare his self from the oppressive jolts of the Brahmin's revelation of his "polluted" being and its lingering after-effects.

However, his father, Lakha, finds no link in a sweeper boy being publicly humiliated and him not doing his duties, howsoever menial and dehumanizing. He vehemently scolded Bakha, "You, son of a pig! You, son of dog! Illegally begotten!" Bakha left his home, and "felt desolate and the fact dawned on him that he was homeless." A couple of hours back, in seeing his locality from a hilltop, he felt mortified how the indecency and filth covered the vicinity of his one-room thatched house, while the rest of the town was neatly structured. At one moment, "he didn't want to see his father, his brother" (90). We are told how the home was sort of "effaced" from the "map of his being" (Anand 108, 110, 90, 91). His father's vituperative abuses further stoked up this sense of alienation, and he resolved to leave home. It was liberation from all the squalor and dirt that filled his existence.

Escape from his home was an auspicious act of an inauspicious being. However, then, how do we read Bakha "proceeding homewards?" What made him reverse his plans and return to that inauspicious life? In between these two resolutions of "effacing" home and "proceeding homewards," we are informed that he came across a Christian missionary named Hutchinson. The latter explained how Christianity being devoid of caste hierarchization politics could release him from his stigma and agonies. However, the hymns and theological explanations sounded hollow to Bakha as his life in that shanty denied him even the breathing space to feel his being. Dejected, he walks off and reaches a sprawling field near the railway station where Gandhi was addressing a huge crowd. Bakha felt an immediate impulse to follow the crowd. He finally heard something that sounded soothing to his ears, long used to and embittered by coarse invectives. While he sat silently on a tree trunk, he turned restless within. However, a brief talk between a lawyer and a poet on how modern toilet equipment can truly free outcastes from their disrespectful cleaning works disrupted the spell. He felt equally inquisitive to know of this toilet equipment. However, he could not enquire. He then decided to return home and tell these things to no one but his father.

This decision on the part of Bakha undoubtedly marks an important event in the text. He was on his way back to his home, but this homecoming is characteristically different from all his previous homecomings. He is homeward, not homebound. Bakha's home, where he is supposed to return, is a different one, and the readers are shown how Bakha's understanding of his home has changed. This changed attitude is mirrored in the pressing need of Bakha to share the news of Gandhi with his father. Did he not previously doubt his father's ability to appreciate things other than servility (Anand 111)? Did he not know how his father thinks of servility as his duty, a moral obligation? Or, is it that after hearing Gandhi, he has acquired a new resonance of home where his "*swa*" (selfness in the world) can be accomplished?

Moreover, this new homecoming un-home[s] and un-ground[s] his earlier sense of home and reduces the tremendous feeling of claustrophobia that he initially associated with his home. What transforms his earlier idea about his home is the actualization of two possibilities. One possibility entails the idea of a modern toilet system, and the second possibility involves Gandhi's clarion call "May God give you the strength to work out your soul's salvation to the end." Bakha wondered: Salvation? The only salvation Bakha could think of was "shall I . . . be able to leave latrines?" (Anand 147). But what did God do to fulfil his wish? How could God enshrining *devalaya* be of any help to free him from the torment of *sauchalaya*? His previous wounds from a visit to a temple fester deep inside him. He was afraid of God. The narrator note, "the sense of fear came creeping into him. He felt as if gods were staring at him. They looked so real although they were not like anything he has ever seen on earth. They seemed hard" (55). What could be the relation between religion and Bakha's quest for liberation from *sauchalaya* (cleaning of toilets)? Would a possible connection redefine the current understanding of politics? Is Bakha therefore poised before a new frontier, a space of the "third"?

Gandhi and Foucault: From *Ascesis* to *Askesis*

In the preface to Gilles Deleuze and Felix Guattari's classic *Anti-Oedipus*, Foucault (1994) significantly emphasized a new mode of politics based on "de-individualization," by which he meant a reconstruction of the individual self, which is immanently achieved by recognizing, "[h]ow does one keep from being fascist, even (especially) when one believes oneself to be a revolutionary militant? How do we rid our speech, and our acts, our hearts and our pleasures, of fascism?" (1994, 108–09).

In a similar vein, in discussing "[g]overnmentality," Foucault again draws our attention to the remarkable transformation in the sixteenth century where a general "problematic of government" emerged, concerned more with "[h]ow to govern oneself, how to be governed, how to govern others . . . how to become the best possible of governor" (202). According to Foucault, the "government of the state" is distinguished from a more "general problematic of governance," which concerns one's immediate proclivities towards governing oneself. Therefore, it expands the question of governance to the intimate space of self and everyday living. Alternatively, Foucault thus broadens politics' scope, bringing it closer to what Deleuze identified as "micropolitics" (Bignall 2008; Widder 2012).

Bignall importantly informs, "Where macropolitics is a politics of form, micropolitics is a politics of transformation." Foucault did anticipate it when he writes about "several forms of government" (2008, 133), "multifarious and concerns many kinds of people- the head of a family, the superior of a convent, the teacher or tutor of a child or pupil" (205). At a fundamental level, this understanding transforms our basic assumption about identifying people residing in the domain of "political society." It problematizes the very premise that distinguishes "political society" from society in general. Because the question of governance or sovereignty is not concentrated in a given body or power edifice, it is dispersed and permeated across society. In their everyday life, people participate in this sovereignty multifariously.

One can find an uncanny resonance between what Foucault identifies as "micro-fascism" inhabiting in oneself and Gandhi's understanding of politics as self-transformation.[7] This transformation is an overcoming of this micro-fascist *himsa* by an intense and active act of passivity, *ahimsa*,[8] which Gandhi calls *satyagraha*. In an intense moment of active passivity, of willingly dispossessing all rights over possession (Gandhi called it *aparigraha*), one can become *satyagrahi* (Parekh 1989; Skaria 2015). After "sat," the suffix *"ya"* operationalizes the human quest for pure and ethical forms of living. It actualizes the subjective consciousness and thus inaugurates *swaraj* –a *rule over self*, to the fore. Swaraj produces the *satyagrahi*, a differentially political being that Gandhi called *tapashcharya* (1951, 100). On the other hand, Foucault emphasizes "care of oneself'– 'actions' exercised on the self by the self . . . by which one changes, purifies, transforms, and transfigures oneself" (1986, 10–11). This care of oneself marks the "ethical turn," an ethico-poesis dimension of political subjectivity, an "asketic potenza" to self-fashion and reproduces life in-against-and-beyond sovereignty. Foucault brings in the idea of *askesis* (self-disciplining) from his reading of Greek philosophy that became ascetic in Christian theology.

Askesis, instead of this transition from askesis to ascetic, argues for a transformative idiom of politics, politics of reaching out to truth, living in truth. Therefore, ascetic involves becoming committed to what, in postcolonial context, Gandhi means as *"sat"*(truth), where the means-end relationship gets converged into one. The adjective *"ya"* operationalizes this being into an *asketic* truth, not getting reduced to mere asceticism. Thus, the *ascesis* becomes *asketic* in Gandhi, an active religious force, a "soul-force" that thrives on *prem* (love) and *daya* (compassion). The distinction between the religion of love and the love of religion gets blurred. The Editor in *Hind Swaraj* (2019) informs that

> Passive resistance is a method of securing rights by personal suffering; it is the reverse of resistance by arms. When I refuse to do a thing that is repugnant to my conscience, I use soul-force.
>
> *(74)*

and

> Control over the mind is alone necessary, and when that is attained, man is free like the king of the forest, and his very glance wither the enemy.
>
> *(77)*

In trying to free oneself from the bio-political interpellations, this *asketic* subject then contemplates "governance of self," of that perfect moment in the chain of signification when bio-political mutates to bio-power. Ascetic Christian morality becomes *asketic* "practice and experience through which the subject carries out the necessary transformations on himself in order to have access to the truth" (Foucault 1986, 13). For Gandhi, this transformation to *asketic* involves the journey to "*sat.*" (the truth/essence of existence). These infinite ethical energies give birth to a constant "mobility of becoming," an idea of an emerging subject who willingly relinquishes sovereignty and reterritorialize his/her self in "the moral decision of not-having . . . in the knowledge that not-having is the only empirical condition that is available to all and hence the only mode of being equal" (Kumar 2011, 452).

In describing the functioning of bio-power, Jeffrey T. Nealon aptly observes, "[i]t is precisely at the intersection of biopower and everyday life that Foucault urges or teaches us to go looking for something we might call the ethical" (2007, 80). For Gandhi, this ethics resides in the experience of suffering, exposing oneself to the sufferer's pain. According to Aishwary Kumar, this experience leads one to be "slow, intimate, minute, and [relish] particular details of everyday existence" (2011, 456). Gandhi's understanding of ethical everyday uncannily resonates with Foucault's conceptualization of ethics as an everyday occurrence. The *sat* or truth is entirely immanent in these sudden encounters with the "other" in everyday life. In Gandhi's understanding, one lives in and by the truth. Akeel Bilgrami's (2003) observation in this regard is indeed instructive,

> Truth for Gandhi is not a cognitive notion. . . . It is an experiential notion. It is not propositions purporting to describe the world of which truth is predicated, it is only our own moral experience which is capable of being true. . . . And it is a mark of his intellectual ambition that by making it an exclusively and exhaustively moral and experiential notion instead, Gandhi was attempting to repudiate the paradigm at the deepest possible conceptual

level. His recoil from such a (cognitive) notion of truth, which intellectualizes our relations to the world, is that it views the worlds as the object of study, study that makes it alien to our moral experience of it, to our most everyday practical relation to it.

(4164)

However, two other points are germane to how one perceives the truth vis-à-vis politics. If truth is necessarily a moral response to living, how can it then be called politics? The question that, in specific, Ajay Skaria (2016, xvi) tries to explore in what he identifies as "unconditional equality" which both critiques and takes the liberal understanding of equality to its tensile strength and then breaks away to a new direction. But, is this quest for truth prerequisite to becoming *satyagrahi*, or does the absence of this knowledge continually propel the *satyagrahi* for newer quests that only cease in self-dissolution? Second, what is the exact nature of this truth on whom *satyagraha* is predicated? Is this truth accessible to people of all classes and castes, like Bakha or Uka whom Gandhi allowed staying in his Sabarmati *Ashram* despite knowing their lower-caste origin? Moreover, what kind of *agraha* for 'truth' can generate in Bakha the aspiration for *satya-agraha*? How can this *agraha* liberate Bakha from social stigmas? Further, why should Bakha even desire this political imaginary in the face of his complete loss of self?

In realizing himself as "Untouchable," has Bakha not virtually lost his sense of self? If somebody does not have a self and lacks the sovereign entity in the first place, can s/he at all aspire for a politics of self-transformation? Or does it mean in being seized by this impulse for transformation, not a transition, one acquires or regains a very different perception of self, self as *asketic* in opposition to the transcendental self? This understanding can lead to ontologically interpret and evaluate the more embedded forms of affirmative living. Bakha rethinks about his life, his friendship with Chota, the affection he received from Charat Singh, the disgust he felt inside the temple and the utter disrespect he experienced while receiving a meal from an upper caste household in the town. All these experiences flash in his mind as he listens to Gandhi. The narrator significantly observes:

> Bakha felt thrilled. . . . He loved the man. He felt he could put his life in his hands and ask him to do what he liked with it. For him he would do anything. He would like to go and be scavenger at his *ashram*.
>
> (italicized in original 138)

This realization radically opens up the opportunity of a complete dissolution of the dialectics that bound the relationship of Bakha with the other villagers. The realization indirectly hints at how Bakha can live an affirmative life, free from nihilist projections of *ressentiment* (Deleuze 2007, 119–120). Refusing to participate in the networks of domination, retrieving a sense of self and dignity as a "scavenger at his ashram," Bakha is poised at a radical possibility, the possibility of a complete exit from subalternity.

Bakha: A *Satya-agrahi?*[9]

At the beginning of the novel, we are told how Bakha is distinct in terms of his well-built physique, his ebony but shining skin and how he is "sensitive, with a sort of dignity that does not belong to the ordinary scavenger, who is, as a rule, uncouth and unclean" (Anand 8). Mark the word "rule" and how Bakha is already outside that rule or norm. This norm-deviant proclivity is further stressed when a little into the novel, the narrator highlights his "pioneering" (69) attributes ("He was a pioneer in his own way") and how he has the feature of "stoic in him" (84). But interestingly, despite his pioneering and stoical inclinations, he considers his friends "inferiors" (27). For a considerable period of that fateful day, Bakha pursues his dreams of getting a pair of "cast-off" trousers like the Britishers, in case the new ones are not coming by. The Britishers living in the cantonment appear to him embodying "the superior instinct of the truly civilized man" (85). In contrast, the Hindus are entirely unaware of how their practices, like wearing the sacred thread around their ears while urinating, their half-naked bodies except for the loincloth during worship or bathing activities invoke laughter. While listening to Gandhi, he felt "a queer sadistic delight staring at the beggars moaning for alms but not receiving any" (125).

Bakha, like most men, transpires a combination of these diverse, sometimes opposing instincts. His norm-deviant attributes cannot free him from the deep-seated assumptions of power that characterizes Indian society. He knows how to count upon whatever little social capital he has accumulated. With a minimal margin of error available to him, Bakha tries his best to secure social equilibrium. When he finally manages to reach the field riding on the "rushing stream of people," Bakha heard frantic chants like *"Mahatma Gandhi ki jai"* (Anand 126). Some say Gandhi is an *"avatar* of Bishnu" (128), while others keep on chatting "Gandhi will teach us the true religion of God-love which is the best *swaraj"* (129). Bakha then hears the word *"Harijan"* and "looked at Mahatma with a mixed feeling of wonder and fear" (133). Wonder because nobody ever describes them as *Harijan,* the "men of God." When Gandhi starts speaking, he feels an indelible ecstasy, but he cannot make out all that Gandhi said. He wonders, who is Gandhi? Was he their friend, or a *Mahatma,* a mythical entity beyond their reach?

Bakha wants to meet Gandhi and share his plights and anguishes. However, he cannot reach him, as a large swathe of followers surrounds Gandhi. It seems as if Bakha has finally reckoned an opportunity to wash off the "dirt" that defines his existence. However, as Gandhi gradually walks out wishing all, "[m]ay God give strength to work out your soul's salvation to the end," Bakha stands confused, interacting with himself, "What did that mean?" (147). It is twilight, and in that hazy light of the setting sun, Bakha fails to make out what Gandhi says. Does Gandhi mean that a scavenger would remain scavenger and seek purity in his works? Does he support the prospect of abolishing scavenging? Gandhi says he too sweeps his ashram, like other Brahmins inside his Sabarmati *ashram.*

But Bakha wants an immediate release from any of these prospects. The opacity of the evening symbolically corresponds with Bakha's bafflement regarding Gandhi's politics. Is not this state of confusion, a primary precondition to cultivate "*agraha*" for "*satya*"? Moreover, Bakha does say that he would not mind cleaning or sweeping if the stigma attached to it were taken away. The word "purity" lingers on in his ears "they have to purify themselves" (139). In a minute, Bakha feels as if he has understood Gandhi. However, in the next minute, it seems he has not. This constant trembling, this painstaking examination of what "constitutes purity," what knowledge of "*satya*" can ensure purity, reverberates in Bakha's mind for days to come.

In *Hind Swaraj*, it takes 20 chapters and a series of questions for the reader to derive a preliminary sense of *satyagraha*, *swaraj*, religion, civilization and passive resistance. In fact, towards the beginning, the editor tells the reader that his "views will develop of themselves in the course of this discourse. It is difficult for me to understand the true nature of Swaraj" (25). Gandhi had to indulge in countless experiments and revisions to formulate all his key ideas. He did not engage in the experiment for truth but *with* the truth. This replacement of "for" by "with" in his autobiography's title is immensely significant. Truth or "*sat*" is not predetermined; instead, it is arrived at by only walking with it. Moreover, this obscurity regarding what is *sat* will always disrupt the quest for *satyagraha*. In *Hind Swaraj*, Gandhi described *satyagrahi* as "fearless," a "warrior." Like a warrior who hails from the *Kshatriya* caste, he is ready to sacrifice his life, thereby constituting absolute equality by the immeasurable measure of "death."

This journey from "fear" to "fearlessness," from concrete wishes for material possessions to abstract and immeasurable "death," is the most intense and challenging one. In active participation in this extreme passivity, *satyagrahi* becomes the "the-embodied-moral-exemplar" (Dhar and Chakrabarti 2016). Bakha is, for the first time, exposed to these possibilities as he tries to walk down the abyss between being a subject of violence to overcome violence and thus emerge as a characteristic figure of non-violence. In this constant vacillation between having understood the ideal of non-violence and encountering violence that regularly rips apart such convictions, a passage will form across the abyss. The justice or equality[10] is not acquired or juridically imposed; it is practiced in the everyday encounter with violence, pushing inequality to its limit, in the assimilation of *satya* as the accomplishment of being.

Conclusion

While Mulk Raj Anand shows how Gandhi's words bring an immense change in Bakha, it also could not satisfy him entirely. Anand probably suggests by knowing and unknowing Gandhi, Bakha would possibly configure his own version of Gandhi. His "homeward" movement would take him searching for a home, which is his own or ownmost to his being. According to Suresh Sharma, "*Hind Swaraj* seeks to formulate: the meaning of human life and its possibility . . . self-sense and sense of the world" (2019, xii). Bakha's "Indian day" is over in that note of paradox. Because in the absence of self, the idea of "self-ness" remains elusive yet enticing. Bakha is both close to and yet abysmally distanced from *satyagraha*. Bakha might get freedom from toilet works and might improve his social status in the future, but can he, and this is what a Gandhian slant into the argument brings forth, achieve "*swaraj*"? Gandhi, therefore, pushes us to take politics one notch further. The imagined editor in "Hind Swaraj" (in chapter 14) says,

> The Swaraj that I wish to picture before you and me is such that, after we have once realized it, we will endeavor to the end of our lifetime to persuade other to do likewise. But such Swaraj has to be experienced by each one for himself.
>
> *(Gandhi, Hind Swaraj, 60)*

Bakha is placed in a similar kind of labyrinth. He is pushed to explore the question of "freedom" in all its multiple dimensionalities. If freedom from toilet cleaning does not lead to freedom from the nefarious binary that leads him to coercion, the political question will remain incompletely limited to "resentment," where the self is only conceptualised in terms of negation. What I want to argue, on the contrary, is that Bakha is looking for a politics of affirmation over negation, a politics of multiple becomings over the closed and narrow grid of identity fixtures. This essay began with the objective of finding a new language of politics that can both exposes the limit of secular-liberal understandings of politics and envisages a space of the "third," an outside space that momentarily unfolds in the interstices of binaries that underpin politics in institutional idioms. Do the binaries of secular-religious, objective interest-subjective choices, faith-reason stand opposed to each other, or are they only the two sides of the same coin? Does Bakha need to be an individual first to stake his claim to become a member of a secular, progressive public sphere? Will that resolve the tension between recognition (being a caste subject) and mobility (the improved class status)? In a world where binaries increasingly inhabit the same space, mobility and recognition can mean different things, and they do not need to be seen as opposed. There cannot be any one parameter to measure the varied demands for recognition. Bakha realizes that he can glimpse the problematic equations between binaries (Gandhi as mahatma/Gandhi as apologetic to caste structures). He can potentially understand the interconnection between equality as a social practice and equality imposed from the above as legal norms. But, where do they diverge, and why so?

Binaries are therefore remapped in Bakha's mind, just as he strives to acquire a self that neither the Brahminic rules nor the liberal norms concede. As this chapter has argued, his "homeward" journey is invested in these subtle complexities that importantly include a non-imperial, therefore postcolonial, quest for a liberated self (a new liberation theology in the making?). It transpires an *asketic*, not ascetic, modality of self as well as a very nuanced understanding of micropolitics in ethico-political terms. It evinces a new grammar of politics, which is politics in the sense we prioritize ethical considerations for painstakingly reconstructing a flexible, collective self that ends in discovering the plurality over an a priori essence (Bakha returns to his father, friends, sister and the shanty). Foucault has constantly been grappling with how violence, for example war, hates and sadism, found institutional forms, therefore normalization, in modern politics. He wanted to bring politics to its brink to bring forth what remains hidden to it as its dark, blind spot. Gandhi was also aware of it from the very beginning of his political activism. Hence, his attempt was to revamp politics from within, from those blind spots that many denied to see, therefore accepting blindness to the blind spot. When blindness gets doubled, it becomes even more destructive. Bakha's meeting with Gandhi is particularly significant as it introduces him to these blind spots rather early. In constantly orienting his own self to *askesis*, in encountering and being seized by the *sat-agraha* of existence, in appointing a rigorous vigilance over micro-fascistic inclinations, in negating and overcoming the resentment, Bakha can epitomize, as this chapter wants to argue, an affirmative dimension of postcolonial political, a "third" space of politics that solicits re-perspectivization of norms from norm-deviant, non-binaristic positions.

Notes

1 This prefacing of 'postcolonial' before the 'political' denotes two different, yet interconnected, ideas. First, it refers to the countless 'improvisations,' the non-normative, norm-deviant modalities at play in the making of politics in 'postcolonies' like India. The coordinates of this mode of politics were weaved around strategies of decentering and displacement of various universal categories, thus paving the way to what Dipesh Chakrabarty (2000) calls 'provincializing Europe.' Second, the 'postcolonial' also implies a more radical disjuncture, in epistemological and praxial sense. European epistemes, its dominant knowledge coordinates, are not just decentered; they are revised and even transcended. One can find the same phrase being used by Partha Chatterjee in describing the norm-deviant nature of politics in postcolony (2011, 19). According to him, politics in these spaces have been remarkably inventive in "piling up of exceptions" to different norms. Further, "[i]t is the theorization of these improvisations that has become the task of postcolonial political theory" (ibid.).
2 This quotation of Gandhi is taken from Chakrabarti and Dhar (2011, 27).
3 Another way of carrying out this dialogue could be how Gandhi's ideas can help us revisit some of the global concepts of politics. To refer back to the words of Dipesh Chakrabarty, we can think of this engagement as "exploring how this (European) thought- which is now everybody's heritage and which affects us all – may be renewed by and from the margin" (2000, 16).
4 This phrase was used by Gandhi in his diary from his Noakhali days. It is archived in https://archive.org/stream/lonelypilgrimgan00gand/lonelypilgrimgan00gand_djvu.txt.
5 Politics and political are not same. For a more comprehensive discussion on the difference between politics and political, see Marchart, 2007.
6 This particular point in regard to the question of religion in postcolonial politics is extremely pertinent in contemporary India. We have been witnessing a phenomenal (re)turn to religion due to backlash (Gudavarthy, 2019) to years of mumbling with secularism. An engagement with Gandhi from this perspective can open up a new vista of understanding our contemporary times.

7 The following line by Gandhi is quite illuminating in this context. He writes, "Without changing our life we may go on giving addresses, forming parties and hawk-like seize the game when it comes our way. This is no socialism. The more we treat it as a game to be seized, the further it must recede from us" (1951, 9)

8 *Ahimsa* is not merely the opposite of *himsa*; it instead walks with *himsa* to an extent and then transcends it by accepting death.

9 The hyphenated word 'satya-agrahi' emphasizes the suffix 'agrahi,' which precisely underlines the ethical dimension of this desire (agraha) for an immaterial entity called 'Truth.'

10 It is also important to remember these lines of Ajay Skaria. According to him, "Gandhi works within the terms of the proper, then even on the most generous reading he can only appear the way he does to Jawaharlal Nehru or, even more Dr. B. R. Ambedkar – as thoroughly unable to even recognize the demands for equality from the margins" (2016, 24).

Works Cited

Anand, Mulk Raj. *Untouchable*. Penguin, 2001.

Bignall, Simone. "Deleuze and Foucault on Desire and Power." *Angelaki: Journal of Theoretical Humanities*, vol. 13, no. 1, 2008, pp. 127–47. Accessed 28 Aug. 2017.

Bilgrami, Akeel. "Gandhi, the Philosopher." *Economic and Political Weekly*, 2003, pp. 4159–65. Accessed 7 Jan. 2018.

Chakrabarti, Anjan, and Anup Dhar. "Rajnitir Bhut of Bhabishyot" (The Present and Future of Politics). *Tepantor*, vol. 9, 2011, pp. 15–43. Accessed 7 Dec. 2013.

Chakrabarty, Dipesh. *Provincializing Europe: Postcolonial Thought and HistoricalDifference*. Princeton UP, 2000.

Chatterjee, Partha. *Lineages of Political Society: Studies in Postcolonial Democracy*. Permanent Black, 2011.

Deleuze, Gilles. *Nietzsche and Philosophy*. Translated by Hugh Tomlinson. Continuum, 2007.

Dhar, Anup, and Anjan Chakrabarti. "Marxism as Asketic, Spirituality as Phronetic: Rethinking Praxis." *Rethinking Marxism*, vol. 28, no. 3–4, 2016, pp. 563–83. Accessed 11 Feb. 2017.

Due, Reidar. *Deleuze*. Polity Press, 2007.

Eliot, Thomas Stearns. *Collected Poems 1909–1962*. Faber & Faber, 2009.

Forster, E. M. Foreword. *Untouchable*, by Mulk Raj Anand. Penguin, 2001.

Foucault, Michel. *The Birth of Biopolitics: Lectures at the College de France, 1978–79*. Palgrave, 2008.

———. *The Care of the Self, Volume 3 of The History of Sexuality*. Translated by Robert Hurley. Pantheon Books, 1986.

———. *Power – Essential Works of Foucault 1954–1984*. Vol. 3. Edited by James D. Faubion. Penguin Books, 1994.

———. *Security, Territory, Populations: Lectures at the College de France, 1977–78*. Palgrave, 2007.

Gandhi, M. K. *The Essential Writings*. Oxford UP, 2008.

———. *Hind Swaraj: A Critical Edition*, annotated, translated and edited by Suresh Sharma and Tridib Suhrud. Orient BlackSwan, 2019.

———. *Towards Non-Violent Socialism*. Edited by Bharatan Kumarappa. NavajivanPublishing House, 1951.

Gudavarthy, Ajay, editor. *Secular Sectarianism: Limits of Subaltern Politics*. Sage, 2019.

Kumar, Aishwary. "The Ellipsis of Touch: Gandhi's Unequals." *Public Culture*, vol. 23, no. 2, 2011, pp. 449–69. Accessed 7 Mar. 2018.

Marchart, Oliver. *Post-Foundational Political Thought: Political Difference in Nancy, Lefort, Badiou and Laclau*. Edinburgh UP, 2007.

Mbembe, Achille. *On the Postcolony*. U of California P, 2001.

Menon, Nivedita. "Beyond the Eurocentrism – Indigenism Binary." *Economic and Political Weekly*, vol. 54, no. 38, 2019, pp. 37–45. Accessed 5 Oct. 2019.

Nealon, Jeffrey. *Foucault Beyond Foucault: Power and Its Intensifications Since 1984*. Stanford UP, 2007.

Parekh, Bhikhu C. *Gandhi's Political Philosophy: A Critical Examination*. Springer, 1989.

Renaut, Alain. *The Era of the Individual: A Contribution to a History of Subjectivity*. Translated by M. B. DeBevoise and Franklin Philip. Motilal Banarasidas, 2000.

Skaria, Ajay. "Ambedkar, Marx and the Buddhist Question." *South Asia: Journal of South Asian Studies*, vol. 38, no. 3, 2015, pp. 450–65. Accessed 11 Oct. 2018.

———. *Unconditional Equality: Gandhi's Religion of Resistance*. Permanent Black, 2016.

Sharma, Suresh. Introduction. *Hind Swaraj: A Critical Edition*, annotated, translated, and edited, by Suresh Sharma and Tridib Suhrud. Orient BlackSwan, 2019.

Vajpeyi, Ananya. *Righteous Republic: The Political Foundations of Modern India*. Harvard UP, 2014.

Widder, Nathan. *Political Theory After Deleuze*. Bloomsbury Publishing, 2012.

10

REFORMULATION OF PUBLIC–PRIVATE DYNAMICS IN BENGALI WOMEN'S AUTOBIOGRAPHIES

Exploring Gandhi and Women's Activism

Bhaswati Chatterjee

Autobiography, according to Candace Lang, is a ubiquitous literary form found everywhere in all times and spaces. She further suggests that any writing can be adjudged as belonging to the autobiography genre, depending on how the reader engages with it (6). Lang's understanding of writing is an interesting observation as it presupposes that the autobiographical form of writing is not an enclosed structure; instead, it demands intensive participation from the reader. Taking this as the starting point for this essay, one can see how autobiographies can explore self and subjectivity issues, mode of expression and enunciation of personal and public matters. Its protean and dynamic nature in its inclusion of readers and the traversing of the trajectories of memory and myth-making allows autobiographies, memories and life writings to explicate the contradictory terrain of historico-political contexts. An autobiography relates the personal stories, memories of individuals and memories of events of great historical significance at a given period in time. In the words of one of the most influential critics of this literary genre, Philippe Lejeune, autobiography "is a prose narrative produced by a real person concerning his own existence, focusing on his individual life, in particular on the development of his personality" (193). However, this definition has not been able to explain the distinctive elements that have been observed in this genre. It is usually accepted that it is a self-written account of the significant events shaping one's life. Nevertheless, what makes autobiography interesting is the enunciation of a voice whose agency also becomes the agency of a community. That this genre is a highly mobile, and contentious literary terrain is registered by Jeanne Perreault and Marlene Kadar, who say that an autobiography is a form negotiating the political and social coordinates of gender, class and race through the "explicit presence of the subjected person (in voice, image, text) [to] expose and challenge oppression, trauma, and cultural norms" (5).

DOI: 10.4324/9781003145479-14

The autobiographical text is structured around the idea of "subject-formation" informed by understanding the subject's location in time and space (Freiwald 165). Women's autobiographies provide a useful analytical tool for feminist scholars enabling the "recovery" of women's voices from history. Women's subjectivity is negotiated with other social relations, which creates the political self of the narrator. Bina Toledo Freiwald states that the subject-formation entailed in this genre is defined by "ethical and existential concerns." In relation to others, the self's formation demands a critical understanding of the "self's location in the world" (165). Freiwald argues that this form of writing is always participatory, involving a sense of others, the place of belonging and a moment in time and space (165). Carolyn Steedman argues that as writing is always linked with subjectivity, the urge to reveal the self is part of the process of writing (25). Theorists argue that women's autobiographies are more collective than individual narratives, more about the self-in-society instead of the solitary self (Smith and Watson 1). Women's autobiographies are an exercise in dialogue and representing the "we" of the community, always inevitably plural in nature instead of singular. These autobiographical texts are the prime site for the "construction and the interrogation of the nation" (Freiwald 166). This chapter examines Gandhi's influence as reflected in specific autobiographies, and a monograph about the Noakhali incident written by three twentieth-century Bengali women that traverse colonial times' conflicting political formations and practices. All these autobiographies speak of an expansive feminine self where the individual self identifies itself with the broader moments of Bengal's history in the tumultuous days of the pre-independence period in tandem with the changing global scenario.

Gandhi, his very presence and philosophical teachings were significant to these women writers' fashioning of selves. Gandhi played an enormous role in their lives, and responding to his clarion call, they joined the nationalist movement and became social activists. Gandhian values and developmental strategies, his emphasis on developing rural areas through gram swaraj, sarvodaya and non-violence shaped their political world view. Gandhi creates "a new woman, a woman who could have strength, courage, patience, and a capacity for suffering, and thus become a symbol of non-violence and peace" (Patel 386). The emergence of these "new women" is vividly portrayed in the discussed autobiographies: Renuka Ray's *My Reminiscences: Social Development During the Gandhian Era and After* (2005), Ashoka Gupta's *In the Path of Service: Memories of a Changing Century* (2005) and her monograph *Noakhalir Durjoger Dineh* (Turbulent Days of Noakhali) (1999) and Phulrenu Guha's *Elomelo Mone Elo* (Haphazard Recollections) (1997).[1] All the authors were nearly contemporary, and their writings vividly portray their days with Gandhi as they transcend the "private" to enter the "public" domain, break new grounds and contribute to shaping India's new democratic state. Their writings provide an invaluable insight into a very significant period in the history of women's empowerment in India while also showing the contribution of Gandhi in emancipating and empowering women. Gandhi believed that women could be the arbiters of their fate, and this idea is articulated in various ways in the autobiographies discussed in this essay.

Bengali Women's Autobiography and Subjectivity

During the colonial period, the Bengali community witnessed the transformation that blurred the distinction between the home and the world – the *"ghar"* and the *"bahir."* The public space in Bengal underwent a crisis as women's role and subjectivity became instrumental in defining the idea of modernity. Sutanuka Ghosh explains that the autobiographical genre explicated a fractured self, straddling multiple worlds, occupying multiple subject positions (105). In the nineteenth century, while the reformers sought to introduce women's education to move away from the vestiges of the oppressive past, it also created a tension wherein women's educational reforms were believed to have led to a loss of tradition. This crisis in nineteenth-century Bengal foregrounded the issue of social and cultural issues besetting women's condition, to emerge as a complex political and social site of transformations. Bengali women started writing, and as Sumanta Banerjee estimated, 190-odd women authors from 1856 to 1910 produced about 400 works, including poems, novels, plays, essays and autobiographies. During the same period, 21 periodicals with which women were associated in an editorial capacity, primarily devoted to women's issues, were widely circulated in Bengal (Banerjee 160). The first autobiography by a Bengali woman was *Amar Jiban* published in 1868 by Rashsundari Debi. After Rashsundari Debi's publication, many Bengali women started writing about society's changing rhythms and their relationship with these historical and political changes. Most of these women writers wrote autobiographies that redefined women's history, enunciating its emancipatory potential.[2]

Partha Chatterjee has argued that in Bengal, by the end of the nineteenth century, nationalists had resolved the women's question by demarcating women's role into an "inner" domain where national identity was to be articulated and preserved. In this domain of familial and gender relations, the colonial state was not allowed to intervene. The relegation of women, family and gender relations to the inner domain, suggesting Indianness was a sign of emergent nationalism, symbolizing resistance to colonialism that was majorly associated with practices of Westernization and modernization. Dominated by the new patriarchy, Chatterjee could not identify an autonomous subjectivity of women during this period. To him, women's autobiographies, in contrast to males, were not the development of women's selves rather the social history of the "times" (139). It seems to engage more with the "facts of social history and the development of new cultural norms for the collective life of the nation" (Chatterjee 138).

While Chatterjee's arguments might be considered valid, it nevertheless fails to consider how these women autobiographical writers negotiated the conflicting social and political terrain of the nineteenth-century colonial Bengal. Tanika Sarkar argues that the autobiography, as a genre, confuses the boundary between the word and the world (9). The "word" and the "world," she argues, must be read together to comprehend an autobiography, as both are intrinsically related. However, textual production is derived from the world it inhabits, and the production of that world within the text, Sarkar elaborates, by default, is shaped by the text. The self's exploration, Sarkar opines, through the word cannot be complete without exploring the world that the self is a part of and is shaped by it (9).

While reading the first Bengali women's autobiography, Rashsundari's *Amar Jiban*, Sarkar finds that it underlines the "distance and the difference between the writing self and the written self, pointing out the temporal gulf, the development process that intervenes and ruptures the unity of the two" (10). Thus, in contrast to Chatterjee's view, Sarkar uses women's voices to restore women's agency in the nationalist struggle where women do not remain merely a symbol used by nationalists but represent an uncorrupted spiritual realm.

Women's Autobiographies of Twentieth Century: An Exploration of Social Change as a Dialogue With Gandhi

Rashsundari Debi was born in 1809. Nearly a hundred years later, Renuka Ray was born in 1904. By this time, Bengali women had traversed a long path, and the twentieth-century women came in contact with the magnificent personality of Mahatma Gandhi. Individual women's agency turned into a collective agency as they transgressed the space of the home, moved beyond the private into the broader space of public domain, the civic society. Gandhi made this transition possible and helped the emergence of the twentieth-century "new women." Renuka's own life took a significant turn when she came under Gandhi's influence and began to work under his guidance to spread awareness among women and help them overcome their poor, disempowering conditions. Later, she fought for women's rights, often facing opposition from her own party's male leaders. Ashoka, the civil servant's wife, was responsible for running a large joint family who chose social service as her calling. She became an active member of the All India Women's Conference, and her drive "to do something" for the nation was inspired by Gandhi's selfless work ideals. Gandhi inspired her to fight against communalism and work in the riot-stricken areas of Noakhali while simultaneously attending to her one-and-a-half-year-old daughter. Phulrenu, an erstwhile revolutionary, found in Gandhi's methods the true meaning of socialism. Throughout her life, as a politician and a social servant serving different positions in post independence India, Phulrenu joined Congress and participated in the nationalist movement and continued her responsibilities of relief and upliftment of women and children. These narratives become a window to the status and the condition of Bengali women in the turbulent days of nationalist struggle. Furthermore, these autobiographical narratives suggest how Gandhi helped them cross the "*lakshmanrekha*" (the boundary line that divides the home and the world) to enter the public sphere and work selflessly for women and other underprivileged sections of the society. The autobiographies explored in this chapter emerge as significant chronicles to navigate the conflicting, ambiguous terrain of politics, home, family, sense of identity and belonging.

While writing about Gandhi's view on women, Madhu Kishwar writes that Gandhi viewed women not as passive recipients of humanitarian initiatives but as active agents with a capacity for self-determination. Kishwar notes that Gandhi "helped women find a new dignity in public life, a new place in the national mainstream, a new confidence, a new self-view and a consciousness that they could themselves act against oppression" (1694). Radha Kumar similarly states that his "most important contributions were to legitimize and expand women's public activities in certain ways, extending the latter so that it cut across class and cultural barriers" (83). Gandhi made women's participation possible in the nationalist movement irrespective of their class, caste and religion. Women's myriad activities in the nationalist movement, social welfare activities, participation in the revolutionary movement and labour movements and many other public engagements led to a psychological victory, and the public opinion accepted that change was essential. In this changing socio -political landscape, women like Renuka, Phulrenu and Ashoka marched along with Gandhi. He had become the power behind women's emancipation, and women's participation in the nationalist movement brought about their emancipation. Gandhian values and developmental strategies shaped these women's political world views. Their writings show how this generation of women negotiated within the nexus of social relations and historical forces to construct an identity for themselves as political subjects.

The anti-Partition Swadeshi movement of 1905–1906 brought Bengali women in contact with politics for the first time. From the 1920s onwards, women of varying ideologies joined different political movements. Despite their ideological differences, these "new women" took an interest in the country's social and political condition and actively participated in the anti-colonial nationalist movement. They were the second generation of women who actively participated in public life, their mothers being the forerunners in various aspects. Participating in many social and political activities, articulating their views in journals and newspapers, these women saw the nation's transition from colonial subjugation to Independence. They availed colonial education and took politics and social activism as their profession. Joining politics at an early age, they later got involved in broader politics, organizing women, demanding legal rights for women and fighting for it. They moved into various public careers in politics, government and civil society in the post-independence period.

Renuka: The Beginning of a New Era

In her autobiography, Renuka, a noted leader of the women's movement and politician, explores a momentous history of Indian nationalism and the emergence of the new women in Bengali society. She presents a chronological narrative where she devotes a whole chapter "1920: The Dawn of a New Era," to describing Gandhi's influence on Indian national politics. This new era also narrates the influence Gandhi had on India's women, helping them transcend the middle-class normativity of femininity and accept new roles in society. Born in a progressive

Brahmo family that was "intensely nationalistic" and involved in Bengal's anti-partition movement (1905), she was familiar with Swadeshi's politics and praxis. Her grandmother, Sarala Ray's home was the centre for Calcutta's intellectual elite, a family with deep roots in Bengali culture despite being westernized. The Rowlatt Act[3] and the consequent Jallianwala Bagh massacre[4] aroused the nation to great fury, and Gandhi's call for non-cooperation found tremendous appeal among the students who left their school and colleges to join the movement.

She was only 16 when she met Gandhi, and as she says, "it changed my life" (Ray 14). Renuka and her friend Lalita, both first-year students at the Diocesan College for Women, were the two girls who decided to leave college to join the non-cooperation movement just before the Indian National Congress session of September 1920. Before the session, both these girls met Gandhi at Chittaranjan Das's residence who was Renuka's relative. She describes her first meeting with Gandhi vividly. He answered someone's query about the usefulness of non-cooperation to overthrow British authority, which had military might behind it.

Gandhi said, "[I]f we had the courage, determination, and self-restraint to follow the non-violent path, non-cooperation was the only way through which we could win freedom" (Ray 16). As they approached Gandhi hesitatingly, he asked them what they proposed to do after leaving college. Their prompt reply was "national work." He further asked if they thought they had enough training and were equipped and ready to work for the nation, to which Renuka and her friend Lalita eagerly replied that they were ready. To their dismay, Gandhiji felt that they needed a good deal of training before assuming responsibilities. He thought they should continue their studies and training and laid down a straightforward everyday routine. Renuka reiterates "our hopes of romantic deeds were rather dashed, and we were brought down to earth" (Ray 17).

To describe her first experience with Gandhi, she explains that "the small, fragile man had a magnetic personality, which drew all to him. However, that was not enough" (Ray 18), She remembers how much care Gandhi took of the younger generation who left their schools and colleges at his bidding. She realized that he could make men and women rise to heights of achievement, which they would never have guessed. To her, the 1920 Congress session marked the dawn of the Gandhian era. Elaborating Gandhi's appeal to the masses, she states that someone made a critical remark against Annie Besant during the session,[5] and there were loud murmurs throughout the pandal that grew louder and louder. It turned into a pindrop silence when Gandhi appealed to the vast assembly with simple language. "I am ashamed that any countryman of ours could thus stand up and decry one who had made India her home" (Ray 19).

After the session, before leaving for Shantiniketan, Gandhi entrusted them with the work to visit houses to rouse national consciousness among women and make collections for the Tilak Swaraj Fund. Thus, it was her first experience to participate in the nation's cause directly, an act of defiance against patriarchal norms and the colonial rulers. Gandhi ji was to address a large gathering of women after the Congress session. Renuka and Lalita were entrusted with the responsibility to get the women who were in purdah to come out and attend the meeting. As she recounts, this meeting was unique as it contained many women who for the first time abandoned purdah's seclusion and came out openly.

Speaking to women, Gandhi made it clear for the first time that he expected some unique understanding and appreciation of the Satyagraha movement from them (Ray 26). He appealed to them, many of whom had come out to a public meeting for the first time and were clad in festive garments and much jewellery only to donate their ornaments for the national cause. Women donated jewellery in large numbers. Renuka praises Gandhi's method as it effectively brought freedom to women from the "social bondage in which they had been enveloped through the centuries by action, not just by enacting some legislation" (Ray 27).

She could experience Gandhi's teaching and his way of life during her brief stay at Sabarmati ashram. Sacrificing personal comfort, Renuka enjoyed communal living and did not mind the daily chores she had to do. The ashram maintained a rigorous schedule, and she adjusted herself to it. When Gandhi went for a tour of the northern provinces, she returned to Calcutta to her parents. She intended to join Gandhi again, but meanwhile, the situation changed. Her parents wanted her to go to England for higher studies, and Gandhiji agreed with the decision. Gandhi replied that education in England was an education in a free atmosphere. "I trust, in a free atmosphere without becoming an anglicized girl, you will take full advantage of the education and come back well equipped to serve your country with courage and an independent outlook!" (Ray 29). Returning to India, she joined Gandhi's work of village reconstruction and welfare.

She became a close associate of Gandhiji and gave an insider's view of the historical events she witnessed. As an organizing member of the All India Women's Conference, she experienced obstructions from the patriarchal society while talking about women's rights. She actively participated in rescuing people during the Great Calcutta Killing of 1946. When Gandhiji decided to go to Noakhali to bring back sanity and help people get back to their homes, he asked Renuka to organize women volunteers from the AIWC and other social organizations to do relief work in the villages. "Our task was to help the people gain confidence and return to their homes because they were in hiding. As we walked from village to village, we would find them and take them back to Haimchar with us" (Ray 110). Her autobiography situates her in the transition period of Indian history, where women emerged as a collective entity and positions the narrator as an autonomous subject.

A staunch Gandhian throughout her life, Renuka asserts that the acceptance of Gandhiji's way of living raised the tone of politics. In place of Machiavellianism or even our ancient Chanakya's diplomacy, high moral and ethical standards became an integral part of politics (Ray 29). Her years spent as a student in Britain allowed her to examine many ideas about how societies should function and be governed. However, she did not find any system comparable to the Gandhian one. She remained a Gandhian all her life, committed to his ideals. Ray became a leader of the emerging women's movement in colonial India, demanding gender equality in an unequal society. She fought for women's rights and the rights of the underprivileged while holding different portfolios, thus participating in the making of the independent nation. Gandhi's influence on women could be summed up in her own words:

> It is acknowledged that Gandhiji turned the middle-class women to the nationalist movement. However, how significant the contribution of women was to the nationalist movement is not fully understood. For it was not merely the women who came in their thousands to join the non-violent fighters or those who gave the direction to the national aspirations of the women's movement but the tremendous influence they exercised in the homes that deepened dissatisfaction against British rule.
>
> (72)

Ashoka: From Home to the World

Ashoka, the daughter of a distinguished Bengali author Jyotirmoyee Debi and married to a civil servant, Saibal Kumar Gupta, was a housewife. Her autobiography is a narration of nine decades of turbulent changes in the life of a nation-in-making. It was also a period of evolution in gender relationships. In this changing scenario, the self-made ways of her social responsibilities as she stepped out of her home to do social service during the turbulent days of 1942–1943 Bengal famine and later riots of 1946 enabled her to fashion her subjective identity. Ashoka states "[t]hat was the first time in my life that I had a taste of freedom, of independence, which inspired me to serve my country. When I began to work for the country's welfare, I felt I was able to discover myself. I found my path" (Gupta 77). It was in this period that she came in touch with Gandhi.

A nationalist at heart, Ashoka followed the Gandhian ways even before she had the opportunity to meet him. In 1944 after Kasturba's death, Gandhi asked his followers to form the Kasturba Trust, dedicated to women's welfare. Ashoka was genuinely interested in being a part of it. She met the All India Women's Conference leaders like Sucheta Kripalini, Mridula Sarabhai and Aruna Asaf Ali and became associated with the women's organizational wing of the Indian National Congress. "I began to take their advice on how I could follow Gandhiji's guidelines." AIWC had done extensive relief work in Bankura during the famine days. Being an ardent follower of Gandhi, she named her third child Kasturi after Kasturba Gandhi, whom "we revered and who had passed away that year" (Gupta 86). Thus, she entered the public world, as did many contemporary Bengali women, creating a new space within the patriarchal social structure, challenging the existing gender binary.

The Noakhali riot of 1946 was a catastrophe in Bengal's social and political history, and every Bengali household was perturbed. It was a sequel to the Calcutta killings of 1946. The violence broke on 10 October 1946 when a series of massacres, rapes, abductions, forced conversions, looting and arson were perpetrated in the districts of Noakhali in the Chittagong Division of Bengal (now in Bangladesh) and Tippera. The scale of violence was unprecedented and took everyone by surprise. Mahatma Gandhi camped in Noakhali for four months in his effort to offer a healing touch to the distraught public.

Ashoka was at that time at Chittagong as her husband was posted there. AIWC, under the leadership of Nellie Sengupta, started rescue operations for the abducted women. On 7 November 1946, Gandhiji came to Chandpur, and on an impulse, Ashoka decided to meet him. At the station, she was informed that Gandhi was coming by a special steamer that would not come up to the jetty but would remain anchored mid-stream. She was so keen to see him that she got into a boat with her minor children and reached the anchored steamer.

> I still marvel at the steps that I took. I was so keen to see Gandhiji that I got into a boat with my group and reach the anchored steamer. I saw Arunangshubabu, someone I knew, standing by the steamer's railing and hailed him. He was very kind and got permission for my son and me to attend Gandhiji's prayer meeting on the steamer. We climbed onto the steamer and sat with the other members of the prayer group. I was so moved that I could not speak.
>
> *(Gupta 92)*

She got into the train that carried Gandhiji to Choumuhani. She describes that every compartment of that train was overflowing with people who had come to be with Gandhi; people who wanted to get a glimpse of Gandhi.

> We sat together with Mahatmaji and with his guidance came up with a plan of action. We decided first of all to allocate a worker who would cover a particular police station. Her work would cover all the villages under its jurisdiction. Thus, she would acquaint herself with the actual situation in the area and try to find out information about the abducted women from the locals. This was my first meeting with the Mahatma.
>
> *(Gupta, Noakhali 11)*

Ashoka's primary concern was to recover those abducted girls and bring them back to society. To continue her relief work, Ashoka decided to go to the Lakshmipur Police Station area. She made her camp in Tumchar, a Harijan village. Gandhiji himself camped alone at Srirampur village. As Ashoka remembers Gandhi's words,

> We must ourselves go and live in the villages. Before urging the villagers to return, we must show them the way. We must live in these villages with our small children and be prepared to face any situation even if it is dangerous. If you are not prepared for this, then you cannot ask the villagers to return. You will have to be their source of strength and courage. Till you are successful

in your mission there cannot be any talk of return. Therefore, think carefully before you decide to come forward for the work.

(Gupta, Noakhali 13)

Ashoka remembers how brilliantly Gandhi resolved the dispute between her and her husband as she decided to carry on the relief work in Noakhali. In an atmosphere of extreme communal hatred, she worked along with her one-and-a-half-year-old daughter keeping the other two minor children at home, which shows her commitment to the cause and dedication to Gandhian values. She decided to set up her camp in a Harijan village called Tumchar with her colleague Sneharani Kanjilal.

> I can never forget that by removing us from narrow, self-centered sphere of family life and flinging us into the world of social work, Gandhiji showed us how women could fulfill both our duty towards the family and responsibility towards society without creating a conflict.
>
> *(Gupta 103)*

Her autobiography gives a vivid account of the condition of Noakhali and the relief work after the carnage. About 33 different organizations were working in Noakhali and had been coordinated through Noakhali Rescue and Relief Committee. She tried to keep Gandhi informed about her activities.

> The few meetings I had with him, the hours spent in his company are unquestionably a treasured chapter in my own life. I was able to witness not just his moral strength and courage, but many other facets of his character, some amusing, some even disconcerting for us. Gandhiji was a stickler for discipline. His famous pocket-watch was a source of terror for all of us. Woe betides us if we were late for a task or an appointment scheduled for a particular hour! Similarly, his legendary passion for cleanliness also kept us on our toes.
>
> *(Gupta 99)*

Like Renuka, Ashoka, a mother of three children, a housewife, enjoyed the community's strict routine living in Gandhi's camp. Working collectively under a single leadership with a moral agenda was always enjoyable, as she realized Ashoka believed Gandhi never ignored anybody's problem, howsoever unimportant that person might be in social standing. She remembers that once Gandhiji heard that she would travel by foot from Bijaynagar to her way back to her own camp Tumchar, which was quite a distance, he was so pleased that his face emanated a glow. He asserted that to work in a village, Ashoka should live like a villager and become one of them. Then only she could gain confidence of the villagers, and her work would be successful (Gupta, *Noakhali* 26). Being the wife of a District Judge, she belonged to the privileged section of society, yet she was aware of the villages' conditions in East Bengal. Deep faith in Gandhian values helped her shook off her inhibitions and carry on her relief work, living and working among the stricken villagers. Before leaving for Bihar on 1 March 1947, where riots started in retaliation of Noakhali, Gandhi's advice had a lasting effect on Ashoka's mind. He said "[y]ou women must be like Mirabai. If like her, you truly believe that the path you have chosen is the rightful path, then you will also take everyone around you on that path. You will never look back" (Gupta 102). Till she left Noakhali in May, she did her job while keeping her little daughter by her side. Meanwhile, Partition was declared, and she returned to Calcutta. Society was changing forever, and she gave a first-hand account of this transition.

Phulrenu: The Emergence of a Leader

Phulrenu, a social activist and politician, was engaged with the social welfare programmes in various capacities. She was a parliamentarian who headed the Committee on Status of Indian Women, which produced the groundbreaking "Towards Equality Report." Her autobiography represents a generation where women availed education and strove to build a modern nation. She recounts the momentous changes that a colonized nation has passed through while gaining independence. These changes also affected women's life as they asserted their agency in an organized manner.

By the age of 15, she became a member of the revolutionary party *Jugantar*. Her parents sent her abroad for higher studies to get her detached from politics. When she returned to India after completing her PhD from Sorbonne, Paris, she joined the nationalist politics under Gandhi's leadership and remained a Gandhian till her last day. Being associated with AIWC, she participated in various social service programmes and held official positions in welfare boards, working towards uplifting women and children's condition. "Whenever I think of communal riots, inequality, I think of Gandhiji," she said (Guha 43). "When I first saw Gandhiji in a short dhoti and chaddar, as a child, I could not realize the reason of his attire. Being grown up, I realized that to penetrate among the poor Indians, he had to do so" (Guha 44). Once she met Gandhi in 1939, he advised her that no constructive work would be successful unless we understood people's condition. When Gandhi introduced *Nayi Talim*, Phulrenu was fascinated by it and attended its conferences also. She remembers Gandhi as a disciplined person who followed his routine punctually such as morning walks, meeting his visitors and spinning the *charkha*. Phulrenu attended several prayer meetings where Gandhi talked about building a human character. She observed his punctuality in every matter and tried to adhere to it in her own life.

Phulrenu met Gandhi several times. Though she was motivated by Gandhi's calling to work in Noakhali, she did not work in Gandhi's camp. She clarified that Gandhi had no scarcity of workers, whereas her service was more needed in those smaller organizations that were also doing relief work there. During the Bihar riots, she also met him when she delivered relief materials on behalf of the

All India Women's Conference. In her memoir, she explains why she had chosen the Gandhian path, even when belonging to the revolutionary party *Jugantar*. She was later associated with the Labour party. During the Second World War, she came in contact with the ex-members of the *Jugantar* party. While working with them, she got a clear idea of the Congress party's ideals and activities. She realized that socialism, equality in society, could be achieved if Gandhian ideology could be adopted wholeheartedly. The village reconstruction programme of Gandhi also attracted her, and she decided to join Congress. Phulrenu thought that he introduced *charkha* as he wanted people farming only once a year, not to remain idle for the rest of the time. She was convinced that Gandhi's idea of equality would be fulfilled one day, and that the Gandhian values will eradicate discrimination among people. Towards the end of 1945, Gandhi spent five days at Mahishadal, a small town at Midnapur, in connection with the opening of a *"sishusadan"* (children's house) under the auspices of AIWC's Save the Children Committee. Phulrenu spent these days with Gandhi, and according to her, it was a "unique experience" (Guha 45). Her life story allows us to analyse her performance as an autobiographical and political subject well defined by Gandhian values.

Conclusion

All these women made a career in the public world and participated in the process of nation-building. They were later awarded different responsibilities for their service. Their writings portray Gandhi as the liberator of Indian women, the saviour of the helpless downtrodden. His great sense of justice made him work towards all suppressed and oppressed sections of society. Gandhi's charisma helped these women to transcend the normative behaviour of femininity and enter the public domain. Renuka came in contact with Gandhi at a tender age while Ashoka, a housewife and mother, transformed herself into a social activist later in her life. Phulrenu was transformed from a revolutionary to a Gandhian once she realized the Gandhian way of life. All these women portray through their life narratives an entire generation of women who were ready to offer their services to better the nation. It was Gandhi who made this possible. Renuka, Ashoka and Phulrenu were the embodiments of the "new women." In Bengal, many women were influenced by the revolutionary ideology, and the communist ideology as political consciousness was high after the anti-Partition Swadeshi movement. Gandhi's ideology helped them break the social fetters and balance their private and public self.

Adapting from Benedict Anderson's idea of imagined community, Freiwald suggests autobiographies function "as privileged sites for both the construction and the interrogation of the nation" (166). As much as autobiographies register a sense of self-engendering simultaneously, they dramatize a collective subjectivity – an imagined space of mutual dialogues and deliberations. In these women's autobiographies, there is a constant negotiation and navigation of complex political and psychological realities of Partition, anti-colonial struggle and refashioning of gender identities. These autobiographies function as testimonies and confessions of a longing to transcend social, political and cultural boundaries. Autobiographies of Renuka, Ashoka and Phulrenu encapsulate solidarity of gender and "resistance to different forms of oppression" (Freiwald 166). These autobiographical writings allow the construction of a nation focalized through the eyes of these women. Their writings allow Gandhi's influence on women's activism during the turbulent period of the 1920s–1940s to be foregrounded and thus reformulate the conventional inscription of women as nurturers of the family, to be re-inscribed as material icons of economy, social and political symbol of education, politics and culture.

Notes

1 The translations of Ashoka Gupta's *Noakhalir Durjoger Dineh* (Turbulent Days of Noakhali) (1999) and Phulrenu Guha's *Elomelo Mone Elo* (Haphazard Recollections) (1997) are not available in English. The quotations used from Guha's *Elomelo Mone Elo* and Gupta's *Noakhalir Durjoger Dineh* have been translated from the original by me.

2 Srabashi Ghosh discusses Bengali women's autobiographies as a means to record changes in Bengali social and political life. According to Ghosh, these autobiographies, spanning two centuries, were a chronicle of women breaching the limits imposed on them to foreground issues of culture, religion, justice and ethics (WS88–96).

3 Rowlatt Act, the popular name for the Anarchical and Revolutionary Crimes Act of 1919, was a legislative council act seeking to detain the nationalists without recourse to legal machinery indefinitely.

4 Jallianwala Bagh massacre, also known as the Amritsar massacre, occurred on 13 April 1919, when Acting Brigadier-General Reginald Dyer ordered British Indian Army troops to fire their rifles into a crowd of unarmed Indian civilians who were protesting against the arrest of two nationalists Satyapal and Saifuddin Kitchlew. At least 379 people were killed, and over 1,200 other people were injured. Rabindranath Tagore relinquished his knighthood at this barbaric killing of innocents.

5 Annie Besant (1847–1933), a British socialist, theosophist, women's rights activist, writer, orator and educationist, is credited as one of the founders of Banaras Hindu University. She was an ardent supporter of Irish and Indian self-rule.

Works Cited

Banerjee, Sumanta. "Marginalization of Women's Popular Culture in Nineteenth Century Bengal." *Recasting Women. Essays in Colonial History*, edited by K. Sangari and S. Vaid, Rutgers UP, 1989, pp. 127–75.

Chatterjee, Partha. *The Nation and Its Fragments: Colonial and Postcolonial Histories*, Princeton UP, 1994.

Freiwald, Bina Toledo. "Gender, Nation, and Self-Narration: Three Generations of Dayan Women in Palestine/Israel." *Tracing the Autobiographical*, edited by Marlene Kadar et al, Wilfrid Laurier UP, 2005, pp. 165–188.

Ghosh, Srabashi. ""Birds in a Cage": Changes in Bengali Social Life as Recorded in Autobiographies by Women." *Economic and Political Weekly*, vol. 21, no. 43, Oct. 1986, pp. WS88–WS96. *JSTOR*, www.jstor.org/stable/4376267.

Guha, Phulrenu. *Elomelo Mone Elo*. All India Council for Mass Education and Development, 1997.

Gupta, Ashoka. *In the Path of Service: Memories of a Changing Century*. Stree, 2005.

———. *Noakhalir Durjoger Dineh*. Naya Udyog, 1999.

Kishwar, Madhu. "Gandhi on Women." *Economic and Political Weekly*, vol. 20, no. 40, 5 Oct. 1985, pp. 1691–702.

Kumar, Radha. *The History of Doing: An Illustrated Account of Movements for Women's Rights and Feminism in India, 1800–1990*. Kali for Women, 1993.

Lang, Candace. "Autobiography in the Aftermath of Romanticism." *Diacritics*, vol. 12, no. 4, 1982, pp. 2–16. *JSTOR*, https://doi.org/10.2307/465057.

Lejeune, Philippe. "The Autobiographical Contract." *French Literary Theory Today*, edited by Tzvetan Todorov, translated by R. Carter, Cambridge UP, 1982, pp. 199–222.

Patel, Sujata. "Construction and Reconstruction of Women in Gandhi." *Economic and Political Weekly*, vol. 23, no. 8, Feb. 1988, pp. 377–87.

Perreault, Jeanne, and Marlene Kadar. Introduction. "Tracing the Autobiographical: Unlikely Documents, Unexpected Places." *Tracing the Autobiographical*, edited by Marlene Kadar, Linda Warley, Jeanne Perreault, and Susanna Egan, Wilfrid Laurier UP, 2005, pp. 1–7.

Ray, Renuka. *My Reminiscences. Social Development During the Gandhian Era and After*. Stree, 2005.

Sarkar, Tanika. *Hindu Wife, Hindu Nation: Community, Religion, and Cultural Nationalism*. Indiana UP, 2001.

Smith, Sidonie, and Julia Watson. *Reading Autobiography: A Guide for Interpreting Life Narratives*. U of Minnesota P, 2001.

Steedman, Carolyn. "Enforced Narratives: Stories of Another Self." *Feminism and Autobiography; Texts, Theories, Methods*, edited by Tess Cosslett, et al., Routledge, 2000, pp. 25–39.

11

EXAMINING GANDHI'S DISAVOWALS AND RE-THINKING THE "EXPERIMENT" IN *THE STORY OF MY EXPERIMENTS WITH TRUTH*

Aishwarya Kumar

Introduction

Mohandas Karamchand Gandhi prefaces his autobiography *The Story of My Experiments with Truth* (2007) with an author's introduction in which he begins with two disavowals. He disavows the title of "Mahatma," and he disavows the act of writing a "real" autobiography. These disavowals come as a response to the doubts raised by his "god fearing" friend about the act of writing an autobiography (Gandhi *My Experiments* 13). He was aware of the fact that writing an autobiography entailed a struggle of reinventing the self and thus align with his political struggle; particularly, as he identified this genre as a "practice peculiar to the West" (13). This unnamed friend also draws Gandhi's attention to the authority of his words, reminding Gandhi that his ideas would evolve and that perhaps it would be better to write an autobiography at the end of one's life. Gandhi acknowledges these serious concerns but proceeds by outlining his objective:

> What I want to achieve – what I have been striving and pining to achieve these thirty years – is self-realization, to see God face to face, to attain *moksha*. I live and move and have my being in pursuit of this goal. All that I do by way of speaking and writing, and all my ventures in the political field, are directed to this same end.
>
> *(Gandhi My Experiments 14)*

The act of writing the autobiography is integral to the *being* of Gandhi, as Gandhi makes it clear. The autobiography is not an errant act or a departure from his pursuit of Truth. However, a few considerations help him integrate the act of writing the autobiography with his search for Truth. First is the disavowal of the title of "Mahatma." Gandhi remarks that the title of "Mahatma" won for his

DOI: 10.4324/9781003145479-15

experiments in the political field has "pained him" (Gandhi *My Experiments* 14). In the modernist vein, one could argue that Gandhi's disavowal to negate his authority allows his words to earn their literary authority. One could also argue that the disavowal is usual chicanery used by politicians to reaffirm their imminence more emphatically. However, those familiar with Gandhi's writings understand the philosophical import beyond the appearance of this gesture. Second is the repudiation of the practice of writing an autobiography:

> it is not my purpose to attempt a real autobiography. I simply want to tell the story of my numerous experiments with truth, and as my life consists of nothing but those experiments, it is true that the story takes the shape of an autobiography.
>
> *(Gandhi My Experiments 14)*

Tridip Suhrud notes in his essay "The Story of Antaryami" (2018) that Gandhi's distinction between a "real" autobiography and the one he writes is one of the "most creative transpositions of literary forms in Gujarati: in the original Gujarati, Gandhi introduced this difference through two forms, *Jivan Vrutant* (autobiography – or the chronicle of life) and *Atma Katha* (The story of a soul)" (Suhrud 48).[1] Suhrud claims that the "primacy of the experiments with Truth over the narration of the life story" gets blurred in the English translation but prevails in the Gujarati title – "*Satya Na Prayogo athva Atmakatha*" (49). Gandhi chooses the form of *Atma Katha* to emphasize his experiments and at the direction of his "Spirit" (Gandhi *My Experiments* 257). The "Spirit" or the "voice within" find repeated mention as the origin of Gandhi's actions, especially his fasts.

In this essay, one shall argue that Gandhi's disavowals are important literary strategies that help the reader think ethically. This essay would investigate the philosophical underpinnings of these literary strategies. Gandhi, as one observes, carefully traverses the precarious path of literary authority through his disavowals and invents an alternative to the form of autobiography that not only presents a narration of his life story but also educates the readers of his numerous experiments with Truth. Through a closer examination of the literary strategies and their philosophical significance, one would understand the vital concepts of truth, god and faith that form the "integral philosophy"[2] of Gandhi.

Atma Katha and *Jivan Vrutant*

Tridip Suhrud insists that Gandhi chose to write an *Atma Katha* rather than a *Jivan Vrutant* ("The Story" 48). *Atma Katha* means the "story of the soul," while *Jivan Vrutant* means the chronicle of life. It is the latter that Gandhi has in mind when he says that he does not want to attempt to write a real autobiography.[3] Gandhi further suggests that what he wishes to put forward is the story of his experiments with Truth that takes the "shape of an autobiography" (Gandhi *My Experiments* 14). Interestingly, in his rejection of autobiography as a chronicle, Suhrud shows that Gandhi also maintains a remarkable reluctance to present verified facts and corrected impressions.

The autobiography, published as a book only in 1927 and 1929, first came out as separate chapters in *Navijivan*, and its English translation was published in *Young India* over the course of 166 weeks. This serialized publication allowed the readers to write to Gandhi if they felt misrepresented, or there were some factual errors in reporting. Gandhi, however, expressed strong reluctance to incorporate any suggestions and make corrections. There are two instances that Suhrud points out that puzzle any reader of Gandhi's autobiography ("The Story" 51). First is the episode involving Gandhi's meeting with Sister Nivedita. Gandhi's first impressions of Sister Nivedita were of amusement, and he uses the adjective "volatile" to describe her. When the chapter was published, Gandhi received a strongly worded response from *Modern Review*, an English language monthly magazine in Calcutta. They took exception to Gandhi's use of the adjective "volatile" and the suggestion of "splendour" to describe her. Gandhi published the correspondence with the magazine in *Young India*. However, he refused to incorporate the suggestions. Gandhi remarked with a slight mockery that the "impressions of mind" should not be taken seriously (quoted in Suhrud, "The Story" 51).

The second instance of Gandhi's reluctance to make changes is even more astounding. HSL Polak, a close ally of Gandhi in South Africa, was sent the autobiography for proof-reading. Polak reported factual inaccuracies and expressed his concerns about the unfair representation of his wife, Mrs Millie Polak, and Sjt Mansukhlal Naazar. Despite their close association and shared struggles in South Africa, Gandhi did not consider it fit to make changes to the autobiography. Suhrud notes that Gandhi would willingly publish letters and correspondences about misrepresentations and errors but would never incorporate those suggestions even if he admitted to making errors. Gandhi considered the "Spirit" to be the prompter of the narrative (Gandhi 257). The story was prompted by the voice, which had the sole authority over the narration. There is also a related claim that Gandhi makes about the form of autobiography being inadequate histories. This concern is raised primarily because the author cannot be relied on to narrate his history even if he maintains an objective distance towards his reflections on his life.

By foregrounding his unreliability as a narrator and an author, Gandhi is gesturing towards conceptual assumptions that he wishes the reader to take cognizance of while reading his autobiography. An examination of these conceptual assumptions about form and authority would lead one closer to the central concept of Truth that shapes Gandhi's idea about "experiments."

Mahatma and His Authority

> "A name makes reading too easy"
> – Michel Foucault, "The Masked Philosopher" (1980)

The French newspaper *Le Monde* published an interview with the French philosopher Michel Foucault in 1980, in which Foucault chooses to conceal his identity. In the interview Foucault claims the nature of contemporary consumerist culture involves reading and thinking as having been encumbered upon by the writer's celebrity status. While responding to the question of why he chooses anonymity, Foucault replies: "since you don't know who I am, you will be more inclined to find out why I say what you read; just allow yourself to say, quite simply, it's true, it's false. I like it or I don't like it. Period" (321).

Western thinkers have widely studied the crisis of authority[1] that Foucault discusses. Soren Kierkegaard is perhaps one of the most important names in this list. He wrestled with the question of authority and tried to demystify the power of the author's signature. As a practice, Kierkegaard wrote under pseudonyms that did not have "an *accidental* basis in (his) person . . . but an *essential* basis in the production itself" (Kierkegaard, *Concluding Unscientific Postscript* 527). The pseudonyms, Kierkegaard believed, helped him withdraw from the act of communicating ideas. Kierkegaard also wished that all one knows about the author of *Fear and Trembling* or other works written under pseudonyms is what the text chooses to reveal. This strategy might seem like a definite success in foreclosing the possibilities for readers seeking preexisting moral positions from authors whose authority is derived from outside the text. However, as Jonathan Lear points out in the essay "Ethical Thought of J. M. Coetzee" (2007), this strategy fails the moment Kierkegaard chooses to come out of the shadows to claim authorship of these pseudonyms in "A First and Last Explanation" – a short piece that one can find at the end of the *Concluding Unscientific Postscript* (1992):

> My pseudonymity or polyonymity has not had an accidental basis in my person . . . but an essential basis in the production itself. . . . I am impersonally or personally in the third person a *souffleur* [prompter] who has poetically produced the authors, whose prefaces in turn are their productions, as their names are also . . . what and how I am are matters of indifference. . . . Therefore, if it should occur to anyone to want to quote a particular passage from the books, it is my wish, my prayer, that he will do me the kindness of citing the respective pseudonymous author's name, not mine.
>
> *(Kierkegaard, Concluding Unscientific Postscript 527–28)*

In coming out of the darkness to claim authorship of the pseudonyms, Kierkegaard reverses his pseudonyms' authority from the autonomous productions to himself. As a result, it is complicated to take Kierkegaard's "wish" seriously in the present time. If one observes closely, Gandhi's repudiation of the title of "Mahatma" is not to negate the "authority of his words" that precedes the book and engender an obsequious reading of his autobiography. It is instead to relocate his authority. Gandhi is alert that his readers would be susceptible to affirming his principles as their own without any scrutiny or examination. The act of disavowing the title retracts the legitimacy of authority from the 'self' and places it on the validity of his experiments. The experiments earn Gandhi his authority:

> I claim for them (experiments) nothing more than does a scientist who, though he conducts the experiments with the utmost accuracy, forethought, minuteness, never claims any finality about his conclusions, but keeps an open mind regarding

them. I have gone through deep self-introspection, searched myself through and through, and examined and analyzed every psychological situation. Yet I am far from claiming any finality or infallibility about my conclusions.

(Gandhi My Experiments 15)

Gandhi's choice to efface the title of Mahatma is an attempt to realign the reader's engagement towards an education that is transformative. More importantly, it defers the author's tendency to provide legitimacy and the readers to seek knowledge in the customary understanding of the author–reader relationship. In Book VII of the *Republic*, Plato describes the famous allegory of the cave. Along with the allegory, he provides perhaps one of the most enduring statements on education. Education, Socrates argues, is not putting "sight into blind eyes" but turning the soul towards the light (Plato 518c–d):

> the power to learn is present in everyone's soul and that the instrument with which each learns is like an eye that cannot be turned around from darkness to light without turning the whole body. This instrument cannot be turned around from that which is coming into being without turning the whole soul until it is able to study that which is and the brightest thing that is, namely, the one we call the good.
>
> *(Plato 518d)*

Socrates carefully distinguishes the purpose of education from a mere "implantation of knowledge" to "turning the soul" (Plato 518d). The distinction between "turning the soul" and "implantation of knowledge" is fraught with the dangers of overlaps. Plato, for one, was the first culprit of this convolution, and as a result, he misdirected the path to the study of the good. He reinstated the authority of the philosopher by alluding to the allegory of the cave. Plato argues that only the philosopher travels outside the cave and can distinguish between the shadows and the objects.[5] However, Socrates held the primacy of the "instrument of the eye" over the philosopher's authority to educate. There is a similar assumption in Immanuel Kant's account of rational agency.[6]

The rational agency or the instrument of the eye forms the basis for Gandhi's experimentation with truth. Gandhi resists the acts of disclosing secrets of an examined life. Instead, he provides instances of the application of his principles (Gandhi *My Experiments* 15). However, there remain those who read Gandhi as providing unalterable moral principles and who see Gandhi as a herald, undermine his attempts to climb down from the pedestal and earn due authority through his experiments. They use the conclusions of these experiments as the necessary key to the purported transformation. A reader can easily bypass the foregrounding of the experiments over the results in the absence of the foreclosure of comprehending Gandhi's findings. In other words, the method of arriving at the conclusions can still be secondary to the moral principles generated.

Gandhi does it in a similar fashion of disclosure as Kierkegaard, except his revelations do not demystify the *souffleur* or the prompter. Gandhi claims that the prompter in his case is the "Spirit" (*My Experiments* 257). Gandhi refers to the Spirit as the "voice within" or the "small, still voice" that dwells within ("In Search" 23).[7] Gandhi effectively vacates the position of the self as the souffleur and thus delegitimizes his authority. The experiments stand on their own merits as Gandhi seemed to be prompted by an unknown source that one cannot bear witness to outside Gandhi himself.

Madness of the Voice Within

Another instance of Gandhi being prompted by the "voice within" was the occasion of the 21-day fast for self-purification in May 1933. Gandhi described the inner dialogue to his fellow prisoner Sardar Vallabhbhai Patel, in great detail:

> [it is] as if for the last three days I were preparing myself for the great deluge! On many occasions, however, the thought of a fast would come repeatedly to my mind and I would drive it away . . . but the same thought would persistently come to my mind: "If you have grown so restless, why don't you undertake the fast? Do it." The inner dialogue went on for quite some time. At half-past twelve came the clear, unmistakable voice, "You must undertake the fast." That was all. Gandhi knew that his invocation of the inner voice beyond comprehension and also beyond his capacity to explain. He asked: "After all, does one express, can one express, all one's thoughts to others?"
>
> *(qtd. in Suhrud, "Truth Called" 11)*

Suhrud reports that many of his fellow prisoners were not convinced of his claim of hearing the inner voice: "It was argued that what he heard was not the voice of God, but it was hallucination, that Gandhi was deluding himself and that his imagination had become over-heated by the cramped prison walls" ("Truth Called" 12). Patel tried to dissuade him from fasting and disagreed with his reasons to fast. Rabindranath Tagore, on the other hand, believed that Gandhi was risking his life for a cause that only served him (if it served him at all), and the risk of losing him could hurt the nation badly that required his leadership (Suhrud, "Truth Called" 14). Gandhi was convinced because of faith that the inner voice that he was witness to was the voice of God in so far as he was completely subordinated to it: "[s]uch a moment of total submission transcends reason" (qtd. in Suhrud, "Truth Called" 12).

It renders Gandhi in a Don-Quixote like situation, and two questions open up for the observers: Does Gandhi see monsters where none exist? Is he tilting at the windmills, as the phrase goes? Or does Gandhi see *invisible* monsters? The monsters that *we*, like others, cannot see. In any case, Gandhi admits that the grip of this voice remains beyond the scope of reason and thus incommunicable to those who do not believe him. There is, however, an interesting formulation of God as Truth that develops in Gandhi's admissions about the voice. This Truth, Gandhi said, "was not only truthfulness in word, but truthfulness in thought also, and not only the relative truth of our conception, but the Absolute Truth, the Eternal Principle, that is God" (*My Experiments* 15).

Truth as God could reside within the body of oneself but remain in the dark, unknown to oneself. Gandhi tried to reach the voice by dwelling within himself and by holding onto the voice. This theological explanation of finding the Truth as God, Gandhi, defined as *moksha*, is a quest to know himself. The quests are inseparable, and one cannot be achieved without achieving the other. In making God or Truth both reside "within oneself" and "outside of reason," Gandhi opens up questions about the problem of knowledge.

Truth as God: The Unknown–Known and Nothing

Slovenian Philosopher and Psychoanalyst Slavoj Zizek, speaking on Donald Rumsfeld's three formulations of the relationship between the known and the unknown,[8] adds his fourth formulation:

(1) "Known-knowns" are things that we know, and we know that we know them, that is, facts that we know.
(2) "Known-unknowns" are things we know that we do not know, that is, facts that we do not know. These facts still exist within the horizon of knowledge.
(3) "Unknown-unknowns" are things we do not know that we do not know. These facts exist beyond the horizon of knowledge, and we do not know them.
(4) "Unknown-knowns" are things we know, but we do not know that we know. These are facts made unknown to us by our own mechanisms.

Of interest to our discussion on Gandhi's conception of God residing within oneself but unknown to one are categories 3 and 4. While Rumsfeld used "unknown-unknowns" to describe the threat of Iraq's weapons of mass destruction, to cite dangers that are unknown to the world that essentially exist as "secrets."[9] These "secrets" are cryptic and want to be hidden. For instance, take the story of Vlado Clement is and his hat as told by Milan Kundera in *The Book of Laughter and Forgetting* (1982). Vlado Clement is and Klement Gottwald were present on the balcony of the Baroque Palace in Prague, from where Gottwald harangued the newly independent nation of Bohemia. In a moment of comradery, Clement is took off his fur hat and put it on Gottwald's head. Kundera writes "on that balcony, the history of Communist Bohemia began. Every child knew that photograph, from seeing it on posters and in schoolbooks and museums" (3). However, later, Clement is was charged with treason and executed, and soon the propaganda systems erased Clement is from all photographs: "Ever since, Gottwald has been alone on that balcony. Where Clement is stood, there is only the bare palace wall. Nothing remains of Clement is but the fur hat on Gottwald's head" (3). The fur hat on Gottwald's head is a key to the crypt of history that the propaganda machinery wishes to erase. It is a secret that desires to be hidden and which Kundera suggests determines the "struggle of man against power" (3). Gandhi's conception of God as Truth can be understood as a crypt that Gandhi strives to unlock. However, the readers of Gandhi are increasingly assured that God for Gandhi remains unknowable.

Gandhi's God as "Truth" is not hidden from him under the force of any visible and known power. It is a secret, if it is a secret at all, that wants to be revealed. The story of Melquíades and the parchment from Gabriel Garcia Marquez's *One Hundred Years of Solitude* (1970) sheds light on the nature of a secret that wants to be revealed. The mysterious gypsy, believed to have magical powers, lived with the Buendia family over generations, both when he was alive and afterwards as a ghost. The parchment written in Sanskrit was deciphered by Aureliano Babilonia, the last descendant of the 100-year-old family of the Buendias. The script of Sanskrit is Devanagari, a peculiar form of writing. Here, the alphabets are written below the line, unlike the Roman script where the alphabets are written over the line. The secret of the parchment is one that wants to be revealed. In the absence of any knowledge of the Devanagari script, the parchment exists as nonsense, gibberish and nothing. It requires knowledge of a different language and a different script, which also necessitated a different way of reading and *seeing*. Like the monster of Quixote that was invisible to those watching him tilt at the windmills, it is important to consider the ontology of this very *thing* as not merely absent, but present as well as absent.

Martin Heidegger, in "What is Metaphysics?" (1929), opens up the problem of knowledge that is fundamental to understanding the problem posed above. "Nothing" denotes for Heidegger, the "negation of the totality of being" (97). The logic of integral negation cannot merely achieve it (in the number system, the negation of the whole number one is simply negative one denoted by a minus sign "−." Therefore, the negation of 1 is −1). The being of absence, as Heidegger suggests, can thus be only explained in negative terms (97). As Heidegger suggests, the negation of the totality of beings represented by the number zero in the numerical system shows a lapse in the way Truth was enumerated. Reason in post-Enlightenment thought was predicated on this understanding of ontology. The conviction spurred scientific discovery that everything knowable can be known, and everything that is unknowable exists as "secrets" and can thus be deciphered. For those who see him as a critique of post-Enlightenment thought, Gandhi seem to ignore the buttoning of pursuit of truth with a theory of Truth as "Nothing."

Akeel Bilgrami, in the essay "Gandhi, the Philosopher," argues:

> Truth for Gandhi is not a cognitive notion at all. It is an experiential notion. It is not propositioned purporting to describe the world of which truth is predicated, it is only our own moral experience which is capable of being true. This was of the utmost importance for him.

(4164)

Bilgrami suggests that Gandhi's apparent rejection of truth as a "cognitive notion" integrates epistemology, morality and politics. He argues that Gandhi symbolically conveyed this idea by spinning cotton (4164). The act of spinning cotton becomes evidence of Gandhi's integral philosophy – of making *something* out of nothing. Truth exists for Gandhi not as a fully graspable entity but presents itself only in glimpses and "small still voices." In search of this Truth, one cannot rely on instruments of reason but take a leap of faith to know of its presence. Gandhi too responded with a similar diffidence when he suggested that the only proof of God telling him to fast would be affirmed in his survival at the end of the ordeal.

There is an important understanding of faith that begins to take shape in Gandhi's steadfastness towards Truth – described as God. The pursuit of Truth would lead Gandhi to come face to face with God, philosophically argued as coming face to face with Nothing. Johannes de Silentio, Soren Kierkegaard's pseudonym, gives a crucial exposition of faith in *Fear and Trembling*, in which he suggests that the final stage of Faith is preceded by a stage of "infinite resignation" (*Fear and Trembling* 37). Kierkegaard bases his ideas on his interpretation of Abraham's story in Genesis, in which God asks Abraham to sacrifice his son Isaac, and Abraham sacrifices his only son to honour God's command and his faith. Abraham emerges as the "father of faith" and a symbol of steadfast devotion. In the moment of uncertainty caused by God's reckless demand, Abraham comes face to face with the absolute limit of knowledge. This event engenders in him anxiety about the future that he assuages by relying on his faith in God.

It is ironically a fuller realization of the injustice in God's demands that produces a will to proceed with the sacrifice. The predicament of Abraham and his resolution towards it defines the notion of Christian faith for Kierkegaard. However, on the obverse side of this formulation stands science. Kierkegaard's notion of faith is crucial to understand the true face of scientific inquiry. Zizek argues that faith lends more to objectivity than obfuscating it. In an anecdote about the German physicist Neils Bohr, he points out Bohr's reply to a friend's question about a horseshoe hanging at his house's door. Bohr tersely quipped about the horse shoe that "I have been told that it works even though you don't believe in it" (quoted in Zizek 51). It is a specific gesture towards an awareness of the limits of knowledge based on a scientific inquiry. For instance, the principle of falsifiability suggests that one can never be sure to know if all crows are black, even if one has only seen black crows. Statements become axioms when one delimits observations. It is important to remember that axioms stand on willing disbelief of witnessing an aberration. Objectivity is built on the bridge between conviction generated from consistent observations and the elemental doubt about their consistency.

It is here that the space for faith opens up, in the face of never being able to close down on the possibilities of determining axioms. Gandhi's experiments with Truth begin from this point of absolute faithlessness. Gandhi is never sure of ever coming face to face with God in the mortal life, yet he proceeds to pursue it doggedly. As a result, what Gandhi leaves behind are methodological interventions in grappling with the unknowable Truth. His diffidence about these experiments being effective is essentially his diffidence about their universality. Gandhi instead suggests that these experiments are universalizable, claiming that "instruments for the quest of truth are simple as they are difficult. They may appear quite impossible to an arrogant person and quite possible to an innocent child" (*My Experiments* 16).

Conclusion: Experiments and the Writer

In examining the Heideggerian notion of "Nothing" to understand Gandhi's idea of Eternal Truth or God, one opened important methodological question about Gandhi's experiments in the spiritual realm. One also found Gandhi's remarkable resistance to making corrections in his autobiography as his attempt to resist the form of autobiography as a chronicle. By making *atma* the author of his story and delegitimizing his authority, Gandhi makes a final gesture towards an ethical strategy. This facet of his writings is not often acknowledged. There are substantial studies on Gandhi's political philosophy and praxis, but very few look into his literary innovations. Through this paper, one has argued that Gandhi's literary strategies have improved upon the existing known strategies of producing ethical thought. Kierkegaard's failure, according to Lear, lies in claiming authorship of the pseudonyms that marks the end of their autonomous existence and his ethical strategy (248). Gandhi, on the other hand, does not invent pseudonyms and alter egos. He claims authorship of the autobiography is guided by a voice from within, the voice that can be variously understood as the voice of conscience, God or Truth. The second strategy to defer authority comes in the form of withdrawing the veracity of his reflections. Gandhi takes ownership of his impressions and reflections by refusing to correct apparent inaccuracies and misrepresentations. This ownership is primarily a move to efface his authority and remind the readers of his reflections' fallibility and reassess their engagement with the autobiography.

Socrates, who is paid great homage in the ideas of Gandhi,[10] was very sceptical of the practice of writing. Socrates never wrote anything; his ideas are communicated to us through Plato, one of his students. Lear argues that Socrates believed that writing by its very nature defeats ethical thought:

> People can read the words, think they know what's at stake, pass the words along to others who think they are being taught – all without friction. There is a mimicking of ethical thought: the reading, reproduction, and transmission of "ethical arguments" that make no difference to how anyone lives.
>
> *(248)*

Gandhi heeds to the dangers of transmitting ethical thinking without the "friction." In *Hind Swaraj* (1909), we see him experimenting with the dialogue form to allow the reader to synthesize ideas from the page while the author Gandhi hides behind the interlocutors. However, as Lear points out with reference to Plato's works, the form of dialogue fails in how the opinions and principles are laid out for readers to choose from without a foregrounding of the dialogue. In *The Story of My Experiments with Truth*, Gandhi makes headway in his attempt to foreclose the possibility of the reader choosing principles according to taste. The reader is entangled in a dialogue with Gandhi, as Gandhi submits to the voice within.

As Gandhi's god-fearing friend recognizes correctly, the practice of autobiographical writing has Western roots, especially those of confessions. It is difficult to extricate a narrative of the self from the binds of a confession or reconstruct the image of one-self. However, Gandhi uses this medium, well aware of its confessional pulls, to create his "self in the image of his method" and reveals not the Mahatma but the source of authority that earns the title – his methods (Erikson 636). In contemporary times, Gandhi's experiments in the spiritual realm and autobiographical writing serve as a belated gift of modernity, an exposition on the methodology of communication.

Notes

1 While *AtmaKatha* translates from Gujarati and Hindi as the story of the self, Surhud uses the word *Atma* with *Atmaa* interchangeably to point out the underlying philosophical significance that re-establishes the relationship of the soul with the self and the self with authority.

2 Akeel Bilgrami (2003) introduces the idea that Gandhi's philosophy can be called integral philosophy as it integrates his commitments in the political field and his spiritual endeavours.

3 Jawaharlal Nehru makes a similar admission in the preface of his autobiography *Toward Freedom* (1936) about his authority. However, his diffidence comes as a response to the doubts about legitimacy of his "personal narrative" as a historical survey of past which he suggests lack the objectivity of a historical observer. He instead claims his autobiography to be complementary to historical accounts. Interestingly, contemporaneous to both Gandhi and Nehru, B. R. Ambedkar's autobiographical memoir *Waiting for a Visa* (1990) takes a different approach to the subject of authority. In the absence of historiography of Dalits, the "personal narratives" become extremely important. There is no room for diffidence in Ambedkar's disclosures. For Ambedkar, the purpose behind writing an autobiography was to familiarize readers with the oppressive face of untouchability. Unlike Nehru's doubts against his autobiography's legitimacy as historiography, Ambedkar's personal narrative stands as a testimony to the absence of Dalit history.

4 In her essay "What is Authority?" Hannah Arendt calls the modern condition the crisis of authority, where metaphysical sources of authority in politics, religion and tradition have disappeared engendering experiences of alienation.

5 Central to Plato's arguments against art and literature is the cave allegory. The cave houses prisoners that have been chained to a wall since their births. These prisoners have only seen shadows of objects passing behind them, leaving them unable to distinguish between shadows of things and the thing itself. The allegory opens an elaborate discussion on the nature of representation and the related problem of knowledge (Plato 514). Plato defines the role of philosophy as educating the prisoners by "turning their soul" towards the light (518c-d). Plato's arguments from the cave allegory have paved the way for thinking about the nature of fiction and its fraught relationship with philosophy.

6 In the essay, "The Politics of Recognition," Charles Taylor considers Kant's notion of dignity to have been instrumental in shaping the modern politics of equal recognition. The underlying assumption in Kant's notion of dignity is that humans are rational agents capable of determining their lives (41).

7 Gandhi makes several such references to the "voice within" when talking about 'Truth as God.' His correspondences with interlocutors through *Young India* provide ample

evidence. See *In Search of the Supreme* (1961), published by Navjivan Publishing House in three volumes.

8 Donald Rumsfeld, the U.S. Secretary of Defense in 2002, gave the much-publicized statement about the relationship between the known and the unknown concerning the lack of evidence against the Iraq government for possessing weapons of mass destruction. Zizek responds to Rumsfeld's philosophical formulations on the nature of knowledge by pointing out the missing category of the "unknown-known" (Zizek "What Rumsfeld"). His response was published as an article in the magazine *In These Times* titled "What Rumsfeld Doesn't know that he knows about Abu Ghraib" (2004).

9 Gayatri Spivak defines the two kinds of secrets in her discussion on the idea of "ethical singularity" in the Preface of *Imaginary Maps* – "secrets that do not want to be concealed and secrets that want to be revealed" (Spivak xxv).

10 Phiroze Vasunia writes about the influence of Socrates on Gandhi's conception of *satyagraha*. Gandhi first encountered the figure of Socrates in Plato's *Apology* while imprisoned in South Africa. He later translated *Apology* in Gujarati while still in prison and remained deeply engaged with Plato's works through the rest of his life (Vasunia 175). See Vasunia (2015).

Works Cited

Ambedkar, B. R. "Waiting for a Visa." *Writing and Speeches*, edited by Vasant Moon, vol. 12, Dr Ambedkar Foundation, 2014.

Arendt, Hannah. *Between Future and Past: Six Exercises in Political Thought*. Viking Press, 1961.

Bilgrami, Akeel. "Gandhi, the Philosopher." *Economic and Political Weekly*, vol. 38, no. 39, 2003, pp. 4159–65. *JSTOR*, www.jstor.org/stable/4414080. Accessed 10 Sep. 2019.

Devi, Mahashweta. Translator's Preface. *Imaginary Maps*, by Gayatri Chakravarti Spivak, Routledge, 1995, pp. XXIII–XXX.

Erikson, Erik H. "Gandhi's Autobiography: The Leader as a Child." *The American Scholar*, vol. 35, no. 4, 1966, pp. 632–46. *JSTOR*, www.jstor.org/stable/41209414. Accessed 21 Sep. 2019.

Foucault, Michel. "The Masked Philosopher." *Ethics: Subjectivity and Truth*, edited by PaulRabinow, The New Press, 1994, pp. 321–28.

Gandhi, M. K. *In Search of the Supreme*. Navjivan Publishing House, 1961.

———. *The Story of My Experiments with Truth*. Penguin, 2007.

Heidegger, Martin. "What Is Metaphysics?" *Basic Writings: From Being and Time (1927) to The Task of Thinking (1964)*, edited by David Farrell Krell, Harper Collins Publishers, 1993, pp. 89–110.

Kierkegaard, Soren. *Concluding Unscientific Postscript*. Translated by Howard V. Hong and Edna H. Hong, 2 vols. Princeton UP, 1992.

———. *Fear and Trembling/Repetition*. Translated by Howard V. Hong and Edna H. Hong, 6 vols., Princeton UP, 1983.

Kundera, Milan. *The Book of Laughter and Forgetting*. Translated by Linda Asher. Rupa, 1982.

Lear, Jonathan. "The Ethical Thought of J. M. Coetzee." *Wisdom Won from Illness*, Harvard UP, 2017, pp. 244–65.

Lippit, John. *The Routledge Guidebook to Kierkegaard's Fear and Trembling*. Routledge, 2016.

Marquez, Gabriel Garcia. *One Hundred Years of Solitude*. Penguin, 1970.

Nehru, Jawaharlal. *Toward Freedom*. John Day Company, 1941.

Plato. *Plato Complete Works*. Edited by John M Cooper. Hackett Publishing Company, 1997.

Suhrud, Tridip. "The Story of Antaryami." *Social Scientist*, vol. 46, no. 11–12, 2018, pp. 37–60. *JSTOR*, www.jstor.org/stable/26599997. Accessed 10 Sept. 2019.

———. "Truth Called Them Differently." *India International Centre Quarterly*, vol. 38, no. 2, 2011, pp. 1–15. *JSTOR*, www.jstor.org/stable/41803998. Accessed 10 Sept. 2019.

Taylor, Charles. "The Politics of Recognition." *Multiculturalism Examining the Politics of Recognition*, edited and introduced by Amy Gutman, Princeton UP, 1994, pp. 25–75.

Vasunia, Phiroze. "Gandhi and Socrates." *African Studies*, vol. 74, no. 2, 2015, pp. 175–85, www.tandfonline.com/doi/citedby/10.1080/00020184.2015.1045722?scroll=top&needAccess=true. Accessed 9 Jan. 2020.

Zizek, Slavoj. *First as Tragedy Then as Farce*. Verso, 2009.

———. "What Rumsfeld Doesn't Know That He Knows About Abu Ghraib." *In These Times*, May 2004, https://inthesetimes.com/article/what-rumsfeld-doesn-know-that-he-knows-about-abu-ghraib. Accessed 23 Oct. 2019.

———. "Why Only an Atheist Can Believe." *YouTube*, Uploaded by Ippolit Belinski, 13 Mar. 2017, www.youtube.com/watch?v=8Kck_YJQEvs&t=215s.

12

GANDHIAN ENVIRONMENTALISM AND ITS LIMITS

A Reading of C. K. Janu's "Autobiographical Testimonio"[1] *Mother Forest*

P. Rajitha Venugopal

With rampant manifestations of global climate change, the environment is among the most compelling concerns of our times. There are several protests against issues of environmental degradation all over the world, inviting urgent attention and action from authorities and people. In the context of environment as well as resistance movements, MK Gandhi is one global icon who is looked up to by all as an inspiration and a model. Gandhi's importance comes from the novelty of resistance techniques he introduced, such as satyagraha, ahimsa, civil disobedience and fasting to fight the colonial oppressor. Gandhi's *swaraj* and village economy concept has also inspired economists and environmentalists who emphasize discrete use of natural resources.

This chapter attempts to understand Gandhian environmentalism through a reading of C. K. Janu's *Mother Forest: The Unfinished Story of C. K. Janu* (2004) and her "unfinished" struggle to regain the lost lands and ecosystem for her community.[2] Janu is an Adivasi activist and a political leader from Wayanad, Kerala. Janu's life and work embody in her fight for land and ecological rights of the Adivasis of Wayanad,[3] a blurring of boundaries between the personal, the communitarian and the political. *Mother Forest* is a narrated testimonio, transcribed by Bhaskaran in Malayalam and published in 2003 and translated into English in 2004 by N Ravi Shankar, in the aftermath of two resistance movements under Janu's leadership in 2001 and 2003.[4] *Mother Forest* provides a glimpse of Janu's political life. The text and the political struggle are significant in understanding Indian environmentalism and Gandhian modes of struggle from the perspective of Adivasis. While Gandhi's organizing capability, outreach and popularity had a significant impact, many contemporary grassroots movements of marginalized groups for rights assertion do not receive much media attention or public support and are often suppressed. Given this difference, this chapter inquires about the relevance and problems of Gandhian environmentalism in contemporary times.

DOI: 10.4324/9781003145479-16

Gandhi in Indian Environmental Discourses

Gandhi is often regarded as "the patron saint of Indian environmental movement" (Guha "Mahatma" 112) for his influence on environmental movements like Chipko Andolan and Narmada Bachao Andolan (NBA).[5] Gandhi's environmental thought is synonymous with his rejection of Western culture and proposal of a robust, self-sufficient swaraj as he "anticipated the damaging effects on nature of the industrial economy and the consumer society" (Guha, *Environmentalism* 29). Deriving his criticism of industrialism from reading Western authors like John Ruskin, Edward Carpenter, Henry Salt and William Morris, it could be said that Gandhi's sense of "tradition" and environmental thought developed from English Romanticism's opposition to industrialism. But, Guha refutes the influence of English Romanticism on Gandhi by arguing that Gandhi's vision of Indian villages was practical. Unlike English poets and artists, Gandhi's rejection of industrialism was based not on poetry but on political economy (*Environmentalism* 34). Gandhi's idea of swaraj was based on the binaries inherent in Indian civilization as opposed to Western civilization and the city as opposed to the village. His sympathies for the Indian village can be seen in his words: "[t]he blood of the villages is the cement with which the edifice of the cities is built" (qtd. in Guha, *Environmentalism* 31), and he envisioned empowerment and development of the villages. In the scheme of these binaries, Gandhi attributed all "goodness and virtue" to a monolithic idea of Indian civilization and the countryside. Though he strongly cautioned against communal tensions (*Hind Swaraj* 45–49), it can be said that he overlooked the social hierarchies in the Indian society by shifting the focus to fighting the colonial oppressor, who was perceived then as the larger and immediate enemy. But this country/city binary is far removed from an organic understanding of the functioning of Indian society. In his vision of the ideal village, Gandhi assumed the village commons as accessible to all (Guha *Environmentalism* 32) while that was hardly the reality.

A hitherto unexplored aspect of Indian environmentalism, namely the naturalization of casteism in Indian society reinforced and justified with mystification of Indian tradition is investigated by Mukul Sharma in *Caste and Nature: Dalits and Indian Environmental Politics* (2017). Sharma calls this tendency eco-naturalism, an approach by which the Indian society is considered pristine, natural and a given. This pristine image is then disrupted and corrupted by Western influence and needs rectification and restoration. Regarding the "commons," Sharma exposes that the access to the commons in Indian villages have always been categorically demarcated by caste system, and Dalits have been denied access to natural resources in their localities.[6] In the colonial context, the access to the commons was determined both by casteism and by colonial administrative regulations.

Gandhi, Malayalam Literature and Adivasi Concerns

Gandhi and Indian national movement have had a massive influence on mainstream Malayalam literature, especially in the poetry of pre-independence era. Critics and literary historians note that the tides of nationalist movement and the progressive social reforms in Kerala, known as *Navothanam* (Renaissance), together have helped the society of Kerala become more dynamic and democratic (Vasanthan 222–23). The most popular reference to Gandhi in Malayalam literature is perhaps the one elatedly made by Vaikom Muhammad Basheer, when he remarked he *touched* Gandhi when the latter visited Kerala[7] (Asher 111). On the contrary, a recent reference to Gandhi in Malayalam literature is in Narayan's novel, *Kocharethi* (*The Araya Woman*, 1997),[8] which traces the story of three generations of an Adivasi (Araya) family and community from early decades of the twentieth century during the colonial rule, through the independence of the nation, to the decades post-independence. By illustrating the transition of this community to modernity, *Kocharethi* becomes a significant text – being the first published novel by an Adivasi writer in Malayalam and providing a view of independence and colonial modernity from a tribal perspective.

While Gandhi seems to have perceived the Indian society in terms of country/city binary, and assumed that the commons were accessible to all (Guha *Environmentalism* 30–33), *Kocharethi* illustrates the Arayas' experience of the forest, forest produce and the forest policies of pre-independent times. It offers perspective about the different levels of exploitation faced by the Arayas as the produce they cultivated in the forest were often confiscated by the colonial officers, representatives of the local King and the board members of a nearby temple, all of whom claimed ownership to the forest. All the while the Arayas were easily tricked, manipulated and cheated by these different powerholds.[9] It is in one such instance that the reference to Gandhi appears, when the Araya men overhear people talking about "Congress" and "freedom struggle" and about someone called "Kanthi." Unable to comprehend the discussion, they wonder if "Kanthi" was their "new king"? (161–63). In this fictional reference, the author implies: a major political transformation happening in the mainstream society, the alienation felt by Adivasis in the forest, their remoteness of positioning in the new political formation and a detachment of inconsequence and their invisibility irrespective of whoever their "king" is. The different levels of exploitation in this reference illustrate the conflict over the commons and the difference in approaches to the forest, between Adivasis on one hand and mainstream society and State (both colonial and postcolonial) on the other hand. The Adivasis, who have been living in the forest, have always perceived it as a space that is not owned by any stakeholder but one that provides for and sustains their lives. They have had a relationship of ritualistic reverence and harmonious co-existence with nature until when outsiders arrived, conceived it as "private property" and laid their claim to it.

Through colonial forest policies, designed on the scientific forestry method for optimal utilization of natural resources for commercial use, the colonial State consolidated its custodianship of the forest, thereby denying indigenous communities their customary rights to the forest. Guha notes that "[w]hen a comprehensive Indian Forest Act was enacted in 1878. . . the government was warned by a dissenting official, that the new legislation would leave 'a deep feeling of injustice and resentment among the agricultural communities'" (*Environmentalism*

56). Madhav Gadgil and Guha (both environmental historians in the Gandhian tradition) have extensively discussed the conflict over the commons, between tribals and colonial authorities, in *This Fissured Land* (1992) and *Ecology and Equity* (1995). Interestingly, they have not quoted Gandhi's views on this issue. Similarly, Vinay Lal expresses uncertainty about this lacuna in Gandhi's perception about the environment, in his article "Gandhian Ecology."[10] The post-independent administration continued the legacy of colonial policies in drafting the National Forest Policy of 1952, as "it reinforces the right of the state to exclusive control over forest protection, production, and management" coupled with "rapid expansion of forest-based industry . . . (whereby) the demands of the commercial-industrial sector have replaced strategic imperial needs as the cornerstone of forest policy and management" (Gadgil and Guha *This Fissured Land* 163). With this background, the chapter analyses *Mother Forest: The Unfinished Story of C.K. Janu*, which illustrates the significance of forest in Adivasis' lives, the loss of the forest, the subsequent sense of loss of identity, and the need for the struggle for sustenance.

Gandhian Resistance and Janu's Resistance

In Gandhi's political vocabulary, satyagraha is of paramount importance as a resistance method, which he defines as the truth force *versus* brute force, and as the soul force *versus* body force or violence of the oppressor. Satyagraha and passive resistance, Gandhi believed, could appeal to the moral consciousness of the oppressor (*Hind Swaraj* 66–81).[11] Satyagraha has been lauded as Gandhi's "alternative to the traditional theory of revolution" (Parekh, n.p.) and as the epitome of his "tenacity in the pursuit of truth" (Bilgrami 7). Gandhi's vision of a self-sustained village economy remained an unachieved dream postindependence because of the demands and challenges faced by the newly independent nation. Yet, despite the continuation of the spirit of the colonial forest policy in postindependent India to the disadvantage of peasants and tribals, there is a re-emergence of "Gandhism" in the environmental discourse with movements like Chipko and NBA. Although there is a long history of peasants' resistance against colonial rulers, Gadgil and Guha call the postindependence environmental struggles as satyagraha, to refer to the non-violent nature of their resistance ("Ecological Conflicts" 409). Within this framework, C.K. Janu's struggle for redistribution of lands for the landless Adivasis may also be termed as Satyagraha in Gandhian terms.

In 2001, Janu organized many Adivasis of Wayanad for a major protest called *kudilketti samaram* (hut-building protest) in front of the Kerala State Secretariat in Thiruvananthapuram for 48 days. This protest culminated in an agreement whereby the government conceded to their demands to initiate redistribution of lands to the landless Adivasis. Two years later, in 2003, following the failure of the government's promises made in 2001, and following several starvation deaths, Janu led the Adivasis to occupy the Wayanad Wildlife Sanctuary and Reserved Forest in Muthanga. This occupation was a way of protest and assertive reclamation of lands that were alienated from them. She organized around 300 Adivasi families, of 2,000 men, women and children, to occupy and form settlements in the Reserved Forest. After over a month, they were met by gruesome police action and firing that reportedly killed one Adivasi and left many badly injured. They were tortured, traumatized and charged with several cases of violation of law, leading to their increased alienation and distrust of the government. This was for "illegal encroachment" of Adivasis into the Reserved Forest area from where they had been once forcefully evacuated and displaced.

The same forest had been declared as a Wildlife Sanctuary in 1973.[12] Janu notes that, before this forest became a wildlife sanctuary, it was a "common land that the *Paniya, Thenkurumar,* and *Vettakuravar*" had inhabited for generations (Interview with Raj 443). So, through this protest, the Adivasis had come into a confrontation with the State to reclaim a space that had been rightfully theirs. From this example, one can question the situation of Gandhian means of satyagraha in postindependent India. This instance also problematizes the State's approach towards the protection of natural resources and its attitude to indigenous communities living on these natural spaces. Further, the State's idea of conservation appears contradictory, self-defeating and questionable in light of Janu's description of the condition of the forest when they went to occupy it for the protest: "except for bamboo groves on the roadside, the land (was) barren . . . the ecosystem of Muthanga had already been destroyed. . . . There used to be a river named *Mamanalam*and a stream called *Chellithodu.* Both these have now run dry" (444). She recounts how they tried to revive the land through their traditional methods of cultivation and the waterbodies by planting "the *pandanus* along the banks of these two streams to restore the water flow." Before beginning their protest, they also revived and worshipped at the "sacred groves that had fallen into bad state in and around Muthanga" (444). These words testify the wide gap between the State's idea of conservation and the indigenous communities' approach to their ecosystem, which they hardly call "conservation."

Further, Janu explains the Alienated Land Act of 1975 which was amended in 1995 and thereby made unfavourable to the Adivasis. As per the Act of 1975, "all land transfers before 1961 were to be annulled and land was to be returned to the Adivasis" (439). The Act also safeguarded the land rights of Adivasis, with the mandate that subsequent governments should implement it without amendments. However, in 1995, an Amendment was made according to which "only land which was alienated after 1986 need to be restored" (439). But by this time, the Adivasis had lost almost all lands.

Conflicts between the indigenous communities and the State over forest rights existed even in pre-independence times. Post-independence, the problems got an added ecological edge because of increasing scarcity of resources. Gadgil and Guha divide the population of India into three groups based on their socio-economic conditions and resource management: the omnivores, the ecosystem people and the ecological refugees (*Ecology and Equity* 4). The omnivores are the small minority who are the beneficiaries of economic development and environmental degradation; ecosystem people are the vast majority of rural India whose lives depend on the natural environment; ecological refugees are those erstwhile ecosystem people who are displaced from their natural habitats due to economic activities and who "live on the margins of islands of prosperity" (4).

In *Mother Forest*, the displacement of Adivasis from being ecosystem people to ecological refugees is clearly traceable. In the first part of the book, Janu recounts life in the forest through her childhood memories. The affinity of their lives with the rhythm of the forest is writ large, though there are references to working on the fields of the feudal landlords. She mentions that when there was no work on the landlords' fields, the Adivasis would work on their own lands and cultivate *thina, chaama, payar* and other varieties of food crops for their sustenance. She elaborates on the lost self-sufficiency of the Adivasis as with the loss of forests and the threat of false cases slapped against them for entering the spaces that had been hitherto "commons." This in turn, led to acute food shortages due to the loss of cultivable lands and thereby to unprecedented starvation deaths. With their displacement to "colonies" their lives got confined to the houses in the three or four cents of land that they had been allotted (432–33). Here, she indicates the removal of Adivasis from their natural spaces due to the new forest laws, and the rehabilitation/displacement, which is officially referred to as "colonization." The government-allotted settlements where Adivasis are relocated/displaced to are called "colonies," which are essentially cramped spaces. Unlike their erstwhile lives in the forest where they were free to cultivate their choice of crops, grains and vegetables, in the colonies they cannot cultivate and must buy supplies from the market. Thus, their traditional food culture is also disrupted. Squabbles and arguments erupt in these colonies, which Janu later understood, were because of the dislocation and the dire material situations for survival. Through several interactions with the families in the community, Janu concluded that "[o]nly when the physical and the economic circumstances of the Adivasis change can they develop independent thinking or produce a vision of their own" (435).

The second part of *Mother Forest* begins with the line: "Mother Forest had turned into Departmental Forest" (30). Janu identifies the early signs of alienation when barbed wires appear and the Adivasis' entry into those areas becomes "trespassing." She also marks the rise of a new class of landlords, the migrant settlers from outside Wayanad, who came looking for comparatively inexpensive property. The Adivasis gradually lost their lands because they had no documents, and the new migrants were able to make documents to prove their "ownership" of their lands.

The deprivation of Adivasis' lands was also the outcome of some historical factors that determined the transformation of land ownership in Wayanad. There was a huge influx of migrants from southern parts of Kerala to Wayanad during the 1940s and 1950s. As part of the *Grow More Food* campaign, following the food shortage in India during these years, people were encouraged to migrate to geographically suitable areas and other fertile lands to cultivate more food (Mochish 38). Then with the ascension to power of the first democratically elected Communist government in 1957, the land reforms legislation was introduced with the motto of "land to the tillers." Narratives of Kerala's development[13] have been much celebrated purportedly for bringing about social equity and high standards of living through social development rather than economic development. However, both the land reforms and Kerala's development experience have been topics of much contention and debate. Dalit activist and critic, Sunny M. Kapikkad, notes that land reforms had many loopholes that largely helped upper caste families to save their lands from confiscation and that the beneficiaries of the reforms were the middle castes. Dalits and Adivasis have been excluded from the benefits of land redistribution and have been rehabilitated to the "colonies" (478). Large plantation estates since colonial times and the State's Reserved Forest areas were excluded from the purview of land redistribution. Despite the existence of several laws for the protection of Adivasis' rights to land, there was little effect as land grabbing was a persistent challenge, whereby new migrants took advantage of the vulnerable condition of Adivasis and seized their lands through fake documentation. Further, the palpable experience of casteism is extremely high in people's attitudinal behaviour towards many Adivasi groups in Wayanad. The cumulative discontent among deprived Adivasis about the denial of social justice is evident from the fact that Wayanad has been the hub of several land struggles by different groups of Adivasis, both before and after Janu, to regain their rightful lands.

Janu notes the difference between two approaches to land – one in which individuals *own* the land as "property," proved by documents; and the other in which the people feel indebted to the land in a more communitarian and spiritual sense, which is not recorded in documents. Yet, she registers the changing times and realizes the threat of not having documents as she notes, "A growing number of our people were becoming landless and homeless. And the land was acquiring more and more survey numbers. Since we never knew how to find out or remember the survey numbers, there were many among us who lost their lands because they were unable to prove their ownership" (*Mother Forest* 40–41). Thus, the Adivasis become wage labourers on their own lands.

Meanwhile Wayanad's geography transformed with the State-owned reserved forests, sprawling tea and coffee plantations owned by big industrialists, booming tourism industry capitalizing on the breath-taking beauty of Wayanad and a burgeoning real-estate industry – all of which led to increased displacement and marginalization of Adivasis. This shows how the omnivores, that Gadgil and Guha define, have created a class of ecological refugees in Wayanad. Deprived of their lands, and left with meagre wages, Janu remembers that earlier they had cultivated crops such as *thina, chaama, kappa, kaachil* and *chena*. Now, bereft of land, they must buy everything from the market: "When our people try to buy something, there is no money. And there is no work. There is no work on the land. Land is a commodity for sale and other deals. It is in this situation that we felt, we must have some land of our own to keep hunger away" (32).

The protests led by C.K. Janu stand out from the other environmental movements in India. Gadgil and Guha identify three ideological trends in Indian environmentalism: The "Crusading Gandhians" who emphasize on moral imperative and restraint from consumerism; the "Ecological Marxists" who focus on resource accessibility and "Appropriate Technologists" who seek to reconcile "modern and traditional knowledge to fulfil the needs of social equity, local self-reliance and environmental sustainability" ("Ecological Conflicts" 419). One environmental movement where these three approaches successfully coincided is the Chipko movement, according to Gadgil and Guha. However, the Adivasis' movements led by C.K. Janu may be beyond any of these ideological trends, as it is a different kind of protest caused by the stark reality of starvation deaths in Adivasi communities for want of lands to cultivate. Further, Gadgil and Guha enlist the common protest methods used by environmental groups in India. These include the following, in the order of intensity and severity of the protest: *Pradarshan, Dharna, Gherao, Rasta Roko, Jail Bharo* and *Bhook Hartal* ("Ecological Conflicts" 409–10). Guha notes that "these methods were perfected by Mahatma Gandhi in his battles with British colonialism" (*Environmentalism* 146). In the context of Janu's protests, the most pertinent one to be discussed is the *bhook hartal* (hunger strike), defined as follows:

> Whereas the other forms of protests highlighted above are characteristically collective, the *bhook hartal* is most frequently the preserve of *one charismatic figure*. The fast unto death by a *widely respected popular leader* is a *coercive technique* to compel the state to yield, in *fear* of the consequences of the leader succumbing to the fast.
>
> *("Ecological Conflicts" 410, my emphasis)*

One of the most historic of Gandhi's *bhook hartals* is the one that led to the Poona Pact in 1932.[14] It worked as a *coercive* technique that compelled Ambedkar to yield, to save the life of the *charismatic* leader. Since *bhook hartal* has great moral value within the Gandhian methods of resistance, it is important to probe its relevance in the case of subaltern struggles. The Adivasis that Janu had organized had been battling a situation where there was no land to cultivate the kind of food related to their food habits. There was no money to buy rations. Children and mothers were malnourished. When they protested in front of the State Secretariat as well as in Muthanga forest, they did not observe hunger strike, but they protested by building hutments, implying their right to live. Fasting cannot be a political tool for a group of people fighting starvation deaths. The high ethical value attributed to *bhook hartal* only indicates a vast chasm in society between people who can relinquish their food as a matter of choice and those who starve for lack of any other choice.

Gandhian environmentalism exposes its limits in front of such cases, whereby neither the mode of satyagraha fetches any audience in terms of authorities, civil society or media, nor does its most effective political tool, the *bhook hartal*, prove to be fruitful. This point is further elucidated in Arundhati Roy's article "Ahimsa" which begins by referring to a group of Adivasis in Madhya Pradesh fasting for compensation and rehabilitation for lands taken away for the Narmada Valley project: "Today is the 23rd day of the indefinite hunger strike by four activists of the Narmada Bachao Andolan. They have fasted two days longer than Gandhi did on any of his fasts during the freedom struggle. Their demands are more modest than his ever were" (Roy, n.p.) because they are demanding the government to implement its own policy of distributing land to Adivasis whose lands have been taken for construction of the dam. Despite the 23 days of hunger strike, the government had not responded. These men were not "charismatic" leaders who were widely respected, nor did anybody fear for the consequences of them succumbing to the fast. Later in the article, Roy notes that this is not just a fight for compensation but one for the "survival of India's greatest gift to the world: non-violent resistance. You could call it the Ahimsa Bachao Andolan" (Roy, n.p.). In such instances, it is, thus, seen that there is a state-sponsored, systematic and legitimized *himsa* on the people who are protesting the *ahimsa* way.

The Limits of Gandhian Environmentalism

Though products of different times and contexts, Gandhi's satyagraha and Janu's satyagraha are similar to the extent that they are non-violent in nature and just in their cause. Yet, in both cases, the non-violent struggle was met with violence from the part of the oppressor. The oppressor in the case of Gandhi was the colonial power and that in the case of Janu is the State – an entity that came into being through non-violent struggle. While Gandhi's satyagraha in the colonial context is a nationalist endeavour, Janu's satyagraha in the post-independent context is considered as a challenge to the State.

Among some successful Gandhian environmental struggles in post-independent India, Guha and Gadgil include (a) Chipko Andolan, which was led by the Gandhians – Sunderlal Bahuguna and Chandi Prasad Bhatt; (b) the protest against the Bedthi project in Uttara Kannada led by prosperous Brahmin orchard owners who could lobby with politicians and bureaucrats, and get the project cancelled and (c) the Save Silent Valley movement in Kerala to stop the hydroelectric project to preserve the biodiversity of the forest.[15] This was led by the Kerala Shastra Sahitya Parishad, a left-leaning organization, with massive support of cultural doyens like writers, teachers, social activists and students ("Ecological Conflicts" 398). The subject positions and leadership in these successful movements include followers of Gandhian thought, Brahmin landowners and cultural elite and intelligentsia. These examples indicate that *who* leads the struggle, is an important factor in evoking prompt and effective response. In fact, the Save Silent Valley movement and the Muthanga struggle (2003) can be compared to see the wide disparity in terms of the interest of the civil society. In the case of Silent Valley biosphere conservation, the involvement of the cultural elite was reverberating, as passionate speeches were made, pamphlets were circulated and poems were written. Such levels of public support or discourse was absent in the case of Muthanga struggle.

Regarding leadership and subjectivity, Gandhi had strong social support and international attention during the national movement. As part of his resistance to British imperialism, he invoked narratives of superiority of Indian civilization and tried to project the idea of a united people proud of its ancient culture. Any factor antithetical to the idea of a *united* people was perceived as counter-productive to Gandhi's project of national movement. In the post-independence context, it is pertinent to ask the question – can the Gandhian politics and resistance methods be used to fight against any oppressor, even if it is the nation-state? The idea of the nation-state assumed such central importance in the post-independence period that the larger narrative then was that of nation-building. This sentiment is also evident in the National Forest Policy of 1952 according to which the State retains the power over forests, to conserve them as resources for industrial development. In this concept of development, the marginalized sections of the nation, Adivasis being among the worst-affected ones, have been expected to sacrifice and make way for, what Arundhati Roy calls, "the greater common good,"[16] that is, the interest of the nation.

As seen in CK Janu's protests and in many other similar cases, the State has been non-responsive, indifferent or repressive. The nation-state, with the validity that a procedural-democratic system provides, assumes the legitimacy to be indifferent to such movements or even to stamp them as anti-national. Thus, movements for self-assertion of right to livelihood by these communities often fail to make an impact, and the State's response works as a containment strategy of pushing them into passivity and effacement. Just as the narrative of a united people was used for the freedom struggle, the ruling class in the post-independence period is always keen to project the nation-state as a harmonious space. Any kind of counter narrative from grassroots movements, even in the form of demand for constitutionally guaranteed protections, are considered as anti-national. Thus, this chapter raises the question – is it possible to re-articulate the Gandhian means of non-violent resistance with an understanding that the nation is not a harmonious finished product, but a process that is perpetually in the making and involves continuous negotiations between competing claims and antagonistic forces? Rather, hypothetically, had Gandhi been alive today, would he still be considered a Mahatma leading popular movements?

Conclusion

The Gandhian environmental ethic is often expressed in his words as "the world has enough for everybody's need, but not enough for one person's greed" (2007, 52). Post-independent India has been developing at the cost of a large section of invisible people at its fringes. While the benefits of development are reaped by a small minority, the people at the fringes pay the price in terms of displacement, deprivation and misery, particularly in the event of ecological disasters. This disparity in the experience of ecological disasters reflects Rob Nixon's idea of "slow violence" that is unleashed by a small group of rich and powerful people in their indiscrete exploitation of the environment for their profits, by putting into peril the lives of a large majority of poor people of the world. Nixon observes that such violence is often not counted as violence because the effect is not seen/felt at the time of exploitation and because the affected ones are always the poor people at the margins of society (2–3).

This chapter illustrates that there is an implied romanticism and selectiveness in glorifying Gandhian environmentalism. It effectively blunts the vigour of self-assertion of marginalized communities, thereby making them invisible, to perish in neglect and apathy. Gandhian environmentalism largely serves the ethos of traditional intellectuals and the struggles they choose to endorse. Janu's protests and struggles, on the other hand, emerge as instances of subaltern environmentalism because it is led by an organic leader. What lie outside the purview of celebrated Gandhian environmentalism are the myriad "unfinished" struggles of many tribal, Dalit and other marginalized communities in different parts of the country fighting against multiple levels of oppression and exploitation, including the State and neo-imperial forces.

Notes

1 The term, testimonio is borrowed from Rekha Raj, when she used it in her introduction to an interview with C.K. Janu, published in *No Alphabet in Sight*, edited by Susie Tharu and K. Satyanarayana, Penguin, 2011, p. 429.
2 Although there have been several instances of land struggles led by Dalits and Adivasis in Kerala, Janu's 'kudilketti samaram' and Muthanga struggles are the most famous ones. Another famous land struggle was the Chengara land struggle led by Daltis and Adivasis by occupying the Harrisons Malayalam Plantation estate in 2007.
3 Wayanad district in north Kerala has the highest number of tribal populations in Kerala. The Adivasis of Wayanad belong mainly to eight communities – Adiya, Kattunaika, Kurichya, Mullukuruma, Paniya, Tachanaada, Vettakuruma and Kada. These groups are highly heterogeneous and differ in language, culture, lifestyle, occupation and socio-economic status. Kurichyas fare better than the other Adivasi communities in that they own lands. Many of them are educated and have government jobs. While Adiya, Paniya and Kattunaika are among the most backward groups of Wayanad tribes, Janu belongs to the Adiya community, which means slave. For more details, see https://kirtads.kerala.gov.in/tribals-in-kerala/, Accessed 25 August 2020.
4 A 48-day protest in front of the Kerala State Secretariat in 2001 and occupation of Muthanga wild life sanctuary in 2003.
5 Chipko movement, which began in 1970, is considered one of the most important protests for environmental conservation in post-independent India. Chipko, in Hindi, literally means 'to hug,' and the movement entailed women in the Garhwal Hills of the Himalayas, in Uttarakhand hugging trees to protest deforestation. Narmada Bachao Andolan (Save Narmada) is a movement against the construction of dams across the Narmada River which flows through Madhya Pradesh, Maharashtra and Gujarat. Sardar Sarovar Dam is one of the largest dams across the river. The dam construction has endangered the lives of many Adivasis, peasants and rural population living in the Narmada valley in these states. These movements are deemed Gandhian as their leaders upheld Gandhian mode of nonviolent resistance.
6 For more details, see chapters 1 and 2, *Caste and Nature: Dalits and Indian Environmental Politics*, Oxford UP, 2017.

7 Of Gandhi's five visits to Kerala between 1920 and 1937, the second one was to participate in Vaikom Satyagraha, a protest movement demanding that Dalits be allowed to use the public roads around the Vaikom temple. Vaikom Satyagraha (1924–1925) was being organised by leaders like T.K. Madhavan, K.P. Keshava Menon, K. Kelappan and others. Following the Kakinada meet of the Indian National Congress, where these leaders convinced Gandhi and the Congress members about the importance of eradicating untouchability, Gandhi visited Vaikom to extend his moral support for the struggle. The struggle against caste-based discrimination and injustice had already begun in Kerala in the early years of the twentieth century and was at its peak during the Vaikom Satyagraha. It is interesting to note that Gandhi visited to 'participate' in the satyagraha and not to 'lead' it. It is after this visit that there is a conspicuous turn in Gandhi's writings about 'Harijans' and the question of caste.

8 Narayan is the first published Adivasi writer in Malayalam. Kocharethi was published in 1997 and won the Kerala Sahitya Akademi Award for the best novel in 1998. The Arayas in the novel refer to the Mala Araya community of Adivasis who live in parts of Idukki, Kottayam and Pathanamtitta districts in southern Kerala.

9 See Chapters 8–12, Kocharethi. Translated by Catherine Thankamma. Oxford UP, 2011.

10 Vinay Lal. "Gandhian Ecology." UCLA http://southasia.ucla.edu/history-politics/gandhi/gandhian-ecology/, Accessed 25 August 2020.

11 See Chapters 16 and 17, Hind Swaraj. Navjivan Trust, 1938.

12 www.forest.kerala.gov.in/index.php/wildlife/2015-03-16-09-50-24/2015-06-26-09-04-29/wayanad-wildlife-sanctuary, Accessed 25 April 2020.

13 Land Reforms legislation was one of the most radical ideas introduced by the first government of Kerala under EMS Namboothiripaad. The legislation mandated an upper ceiling for the possession of lands by individual families and redistribution of surplus lands to the landless peasants. This was meant to end the feudal structure and ensure more socioeconomic equity in society. After much contentions and amendments, the Land Reforms Act was implemented from 1 January 1970. Kerala model of development refers to the achievements of the state by which its living standards are compared to those of developed countries based on the indices of literacy, education, public health, low infant mortality and high life expectancy.

14 Poona Pact is a historic agreement regarding electoral seats to the provincial legislature of the British India government in 1930. The British Prime Minister Ramsay MacDonald had agreed to give separate electorates for depressed classes to the legislative assembly. Gandhi was against this reservation of separate electorates. He undertook a fast until death in jail to revoke the decision of separate electorates. His protest was successful, and the decision of reservation of separate electorate for depressed classes, which Ambedkar had wanted for political representation, was revoked.

15 The Chipko movement in the Garhwarl hills of the Himalayas started in 1971 and went on for years and even a decade with different results. The most eventful incident of this movement was when the women led by Gaura Devi hugged the trees to resist the loggers from cutting the trees in 1974. The Bedthi Hydroelectric project had commenced in the late 1970s, and the protests against it have happened through 1980s and 1990s. The Save Silent Valley Project started in 1973 against the construction of the hydroelectric project on Kunthipuzha river and went on till 1985 when Silent Valley was declared as a National Park.

16 Arundhati Roy. "The Greater Common Good." Outlook. 24 May 1999. www.outlookindia.com/magazine/story/the-greater-common-good/207509, Accessed 25 April 2020.

Works Cited

Asher, R.E. "Vaikom Muhammed Basheer: Freedom Fighting Into Fiction." *South Indian Horizon*, 1997, pp. 107–25.

Bilgrami, Akeel. "Gandhi, the Philosopher." *Economic & Political Weekly*, vol. 38, no. 39, 27 Sept. 2003, www.epw.in/journal/2003/39/special-articles/gandhi-philosopher.html. Accessed 15 Oct. 2020.

Gadgil, Madhav, and Ramachandra Guha. "Ecological Conflicts and the Environmental Movements in India." *Environmental Issues in India: A Reader*, edited by Mahesh Rangarajan, Pearson, 2007, pp. 385–428.

———. *Ecology and Equity: The Use and Abuse of Nature in Contemporary India*. Penguin, 1995.

———. *This Fissured Land: An Ecological History of India*. Oxford India Perennial, 1992.

Gandhi, M.K. *Hind Swaraj*. Navjivan Trust, 1938.

———. *The Story of My Experiments with Truth*. Penguin, 2007.

Guha, Ramachandra. *Environmentalism: A Global History*. Allan-Lane, 2014.

———. "Mahatma Gandhi and the Environmental Movement." *Environmental Issues in India: A Reader*, edited by Mahesh Rangarajan, Pearson, 2007, pp. 111–28.

Janu, C.K. *Mother Forest: The Unfinished Story of C.K. Janu*. Transcribed by Bhaskaran, translated by N. Ravi Shanker. Kali for Women &Women Unlimited, 2004.

Kapikkad, Sunny M. "Beyond Just a Home and a Name." *No Alphabet in Sight*, Penguin, 2011, pp. 474–85.

Lal, Vinay. "Gandhian Ecology." *UCLA Social Sciences MANAS*, http://southasia.ucla.edu/history-politics/gandhi/gandhian-ecology/ Accessed 25 Apr. 2020.

Mochish, K.S. "Public Action and the Print Media in Kerala: A Historical Analysis, 1923–1965." *Social Scientist*, vol. 42, no. 1/2, Jan.–Feb. 2014, pp. 37–62.

Narayan. *Kocharethi*. Translated by Catherine Thankamma. Oxford UP, 2011.

Nixon, Rob. *Slow Violence and the Environmentalism of the Poor*. Harvard UP, 2011.

Parekh, Bhikhu. "Gandhi's Legacy." *Gandhi Sevagram Ashram*, www.gandhiashramsevagram.org/gandhi-articles/gandhi-legacy.php. Accessed 15 Oct. 2020.

Raj, Rekha. "We Need to Build Huts All Over Kerala, Again and Again." Interview with C.K. Janu. *No Alphabet in Sight*, Penguin, 2011, pp. 429–51.

Roy, Arundhati. "Ahimsa." *Outlook*, 13 June 2002, www.outlookindia.com/website/story/ahimsa/216044. Accessed 25 Apr. 2020.

Sharma, Mukul. *Caste and Nature: Dalits and Indian Environmental Politics*. Oxford UP, 2017.

Vasanthan, S.K. "Swatantra Samaravum Malayala Sahityavum" (Freedom Struggle and Malayalam Literature." *Nammude Sahityavum Nammude Samoohavum. (Our Literature and Our Society)*, *Volume II: 1901–2000*, Kerala Sahitya Akademi, 2000, pp. 222–60.

PART IV

Gandhian Presence in Intimate and Public Spheres

Reflections on Corporeality, Ethicality and Society

13

THE MISSING/DIVERGENT INSCRIPTION OF THE GANDHIAN BODY

Examining Corruption in Shrilal Shukla's *Raag Darbari*

Indrani Das Gupta

Body and its attendant values of corporeality, physicality and embodiment have long been verbalized as potent sites of political and personal subjectivity, as being shaped by socio-cultural registers, and as illustrative of a material signifier defining the nation state. Since the time of Plato, the Greek philosopher, the corporeal body has been identified with the "anthropomorphic analogy of *body politics*," exemplifying the broader philosophical, cultural and social meanings circulating in the society (*emphasis in original*; Rosenberg and Fitzpatrick 1). This discourse of body politics became hugely popular in India in the twentieth century with Gandhi's idea of embodiment. Gandhi's version of corporeality as a cultural tool in consonance with political will and psycho-cultural emancipation has long been noted (Godrej, par. 1, 2010). From being couched in the discourse of spirituality and theology grounded in narratives of health, dietary regimes and controlled sexuality, a sound body in Gandhian teachings emerges as an indispensable pre-requisite to building an ethical, robust nation. If Gandhi's idea of the body operates in a given historical moment as a critical tool of understanding the interplay of ethics, politics and individual will, its subsequent disruption at a later historical moment can prove to be an interesting study of how socio-political and cultural values evolve.

Moreover, this invariably leads us to locate the Gandhian body in a world of mutating values – in a world where the perversion and distortion of the body's earlier moment of the inscription are seemingly possible. As this chapter explores, the misrepresentation of values inscribed on the body at a given historical juncture throws light on the nation-state's failure. The various discourses surrounding the Gandhian body shall be employed in this chapter to address the miscarriage of justice and the corruption inherent in India's newly born postcolonial nation-state, encapsulated in Shrilal Shukla's award-winning novel *Raag Darbari* (1968). Through the exploration of Gandhi's understanding of the body as a central site of political possibilities and framed in terms of Sudipta Kaviraj's framework of

DOI: 10.4324/9781003145479-18

postcolonial state as "strange travesties" ("Modern State" 47), the disintegration of the postcolonial Indian nation-state is demonstrated via the analysis of Shukla's novel.

The chapter, divided into three sections, reads Shukla's novel as a disintegration of the Indian state's broader values and as analogous to the undermining of the principles and ethos of the Gandhian discourse. In the first section, a mapping of the body from the late nineteenth century to the first half of twentieth-century colonial India is provided. In its description of the rise of Indian wrestling, this introductory section affords a cultural-historical backdrop to Gandhian body politics. The second section introduces the Gandhian body as the leading site of the performance of the political ideology of non-violence. This section further demonstrates Gandhi's notion of asceticism premised on the body as a means to inculcate the idea of *swaraj* (self-rule). Swaraj emerges as equivalent to Gandhi's idea of bodily health/spirit, and where dietary regimes function as symbolic of a somatic truth intervening in the processes of history. The last section builds upon the earlier two sections of the chapter to posit Shukla's novel and its narrative of corporeality as enunciating India's newly born postcolonial nation-state as a veritable site of corruption through its inversion of Gandhian body politics.

Building the Body and Nation-Building in Nineteenth-Century Colonial India

The "body," as an embattled site, emerges as not only a means of self-expression but also is found implicated in the paradigms and practices of power, knowledge, subjectivity, identity, and politics. As James H. Mills and Satadru Sen enumerate, the body operates as the most important "analytical tool in colonial and postcolonial studies" (1). The significance of the body is underlined by Kathleen Canning "as a site of intervention or inscriptive surface" (500), where the colonial state inscribes its power politics. Additionally, the positioning of the state machinery as the dominant mechanism of colonial India subsequently gave rise to the numerous struggles of nationalist intent. Most of these nationalist struggles sought to reclaim the inscribed body from the colonial matrix of power. These contestations focused on how the "allegorical problem" of the body (Canning 500) developed in the last two decades of the nineteenth century as the central foci of power relations in the mechanisms of colonialism in India.

In the aftermath of the First War of Independence (1857), the move from the mercantilist and commercial institutions to administrative and bureaucratic structures of the colonial state led to a massive restructuring of the society, identified by Manu Goswami in her book, *Producing India* (2004) as the beginnings of "territorial colonialism" (8). The introduction of railways, telegraph and other technological changes, education systems, and the introduction of the colonial state initiated new understanding of time, space and polity. However, this was not all. As Deane Heath argues, the inauguration of the colonial state made possible newer ways and methods to comprehend individual subjectivity (9). After the sepoy mutiny of 1857, the colonial state "set about enumerating, demarcating and classifying colonized people" (9). This taxonomical classification premised on the body performed the exotic otherness of racial differences. To this end, David Arnold's *Colonizing the Body: State Medicine and Epidemic Disease in Nineteenth-Century India* (1993) shows in his readings of historical documents how the Indian body materialized as a site "of a colonizing process" (7). This systematic classification, or to use Canning's phrase "body as method" (500), extended to categorize specific native communities as effeminate (Bengali community) and few other communities as brave and virile (Sikhs and Gurkhas communities). The inevitable reorganization of the military set-up and the consequent translation of this taxonomical categorization post-1857, is rightly asserted by Gavin Rand as having, led to "a reflection of the irreducible alterity of the Indian people" (4). The enumeration and classification of the natives' premised on their bodies established the colonial state as "a form of surveillance and control." This taxonomical system was a classic instance of Michel Foucault's idea of bio-governmentality – where to govern was "to structure the possible field of action of others" (qtd. in Wakankar 45).[1]

Consequently, the body became enmeshed in a discourse of an uneasy alliance between the colonial West and the colonized East. Mills and Sen's observation that "the body was at the heart of colonial encounter" (2) registers how the classification of the natives' body performed the negation of the individuality of the colonized subjects in the modernization process. Nevertheless, the colonizers' practice of emasculating the natives' bodies inevitably occasioned a rejoinder, as John Rosselli identifies, by the natives whose "sense of degradation was especially physical." Rosselli affirmed that this "sense of physical degradation" inspired the nationalists to embody masculine strength and thus to counter the "self-image of effeteness" (122). The pejorative representation's internalization, Subho Basu and Sikata Banerjee argue, "impinged on the consciousness of Bengali Hindus who from the late nineteenth century engaged in a political project of recovery of physical prowess through a physical culture movement" (477). From the natives' initial response to these deprecatory representations of their body as one of tacit acceptance to the recognition of a felt need to improve their body both physically and morally, the last two decades of the nineteenth century and the early twentieth century saw a horizon of expectations being defined by the "physical" resurrection of the natives. While Bankim Chandra Chatterjee's novel – *Anandamath* (1882) valourizes martial strength, Swami Vivekananda's writings moved beyond the ideas of physical strength and martial prowess to include notions of, as Basu and Banerjee state, "muscular" spirituality" (482). This "muscular" spirituality entailed a discourse defined by loss, decline and degeneration, which impinged on the natives' body in the early years of the anti-colonial struggle. However, this discourse of loss inexorably led to the growth of nationalist sentiments informed by a need to invigorate the present by reinventing the indigenous, "authentic" past premised on physicality. In this space of lack and its inevitable renewal, we see the re-emergence of the rural, ancient sport of Indian wrestling.

Parallel to the rise of swadeshi nationalism in the first decade of the twentieth century, the mushrooming of *akhadas* (gymnasiums) and physical culture fairs all over the province of Bengal became widely visible.[2] However, the encouragement of physical culture was not couched merely as a retort to taxonomical classifications instituted by the British. Ashish Nandy argues that Indian wrestling needs to be defined as an alternative paradigm of masculinity. He suggests that the "main threat to the colonizers is . . . that the colonized will in . . . trying to redeem their 'masculinity'" not become "the counter player of the rulers according to the established rules" but by discovering an "alternate frame of reference within which the oppressed do not seem weak, degraded, and distorted men" (175–76).

To elaborate on this alternative frame, one needs to examine the set of new practices that encased wrestling since its renewal from the last two decades of the nineteenth century. According to Joseph Alter, wrestling's popularization can be read in the confluence of ideas either cast in the language of the new or in the encapsulation of wrestling in the mythical past's idiom, materializing it "as a way of life" (*Wrestler's Body* 6). In the words of Alter, the meteoric rise of Indian wrestling from the late nineteenth century to the early twentieth century can be interpreted as a "nationalist project" "in order to reform India and rebuild national character in terms of hypermasculinity" ("Body, Text" 21). Wrestling surfaces as a symbol, an expression of a moral, righteous citizen whose very body, apart from its way of life, as Alter notifies, "takes on nationalistic overtones as it comes to symbolize ethical reforms" ("Hanuman" 127). Unlike "professional wrestling," whose analysis was undertaken by Roland Barthes within the rubric of myths, an Indian wrestler "models himself on a particular conception of ascetic self-discipline" to provide "the wrestler [with] a unique sense of self" ("Sannyasi" 317). The most crucial feature of Indian wrestling, according to Alter, is practising *brahmacharya* or celibacy. For him, both celibacy and Ayurveda medicinal practice, considered as essential components of the practice of Indian wrestling, are identifiable with a "state of equilibrium and balanced existence" ("Heaps of Health" 549).

Gandhi's notion of the body can be read following the system of meanings promulgated by this revival of wrestling and the physical culture movement during the late nineteenth century and the early twentieth century, particularly in Bengal.[3] The second section of this paper presents the Gandhian system of body signification and how it embodies an essential feature of his ethical system of political resistance.

Gandhi's Somatic Nationalism: A Study of "Biomoral" Subjectivity and Truth

Though Benedict Anderson traces the origins of the construction of nation with the beginnings of print capitalism, it should also be seen as inclusive of, in the words of Joseph Alter, "bodies, embodied acts, and both commonplace and elaborate forms of social practice" ("Body, Text" 19). Following Gandhi's injunction that "a perfectly moral person alone can achieve perfect health" (CW 2:50), this second section of the chapter examines the close correlation of health, diet, *brahmacharya* and the bodily health of a nation.

To diagnose Gandhi's position and value in the nationalist project, Alter suggests we read his teachings and socio-political programme by understanding "his faith in the biomoral imperative of public health" ("Gandhi's Body" 302).[4] In the letter to Shankerlal Banker, Gandhi foregrounds his mode of political resistance as grounded in the remodelling of one's body:

> It is easier to conquer the entire world than to subdue the enemies in our body. And, therefore, for the man who succeeds in this conquest, the former will be easy enough. The self-government which you, I and all others have to attain is in fact this. Need I say more? The point of it all is that you can serve the country only with this body.
>
> *(qtd. Alter, "Gandhi's Body" 301)*

This extract from Gandhi's letter highlights that body disciplining involved a political, social and psychological dimension. This letter also demonstrates Gandhian politics of body dynamics as inclusive of the framework of political activism, and as refashioning individual subjectivity in parallel to civic society's public transformation. Body, as this letter suggests, is aligned with political redefinition.

Many scholarly studies have examined Gandhi's idea of physicality and embodiment in terms of his wider philosophic and political discourses on *ahimsa* (non-violence) and *satyagraha* (truth-force; soul-force). Since his early days as a practising lawyer in South Africa, Gandhi's dietary experiments with vegetarianism embodied, Srirupa Prasad states, political action (94).[5] For Alter, Gandhi's nationalism was closely intertwined with "his personal experiments with dietetics, celibacy, hygiene, and nature cure and his search for Truth; between his virtual obsession with health, his faith in non-violence, and his program of sociopolitical reform" ("Gandhi's Body" 302). Sudhir Kakar's book *Intimate Relations: Exploring Indian Sexuality* (1990) provides a fascinating overlap of Freudian psychoanalysis and Gandhi's explanation of celibacy. Parama Roy's "Abstinence: Manifestoes on Meat and Masculinity" explores the trajectory of Gandhi's turn towards vegetarianism from his meat consumption experience in London in terms of internalizing his understanding of non-violence and as straddling the terrain of modernity and tradition. His practice of vegetarianism also, as Roy argues, was an alternative modality to contend with the "gendered character" of body politics (63). Rebecca Brown has defined Gandhi's spinning wheel (*charkha*) not only as a political act of resistance against the British's exploitative practices but also as redefining the gender norms prevalent in political discourses of the mid-twentieth century. More importantly, Brown identified the *charkha* as "reinforc'[ing] the centrality of Gandhi's body, his experiments in relation to masculinity and his revaluing of feminine and masculine norms through his own persona" (98). Kakar suggests that Gandhi's importance to food and diets in his autobiography is a displacement mechanism from his preoccupation with genital sexuality (91). However, Alter argues that Kakar's psychological approach distances Gandhi's "biomoral" experiments from its colonialist politics and the nationalist struggle for independence. Alter rejects the analogical derivatives of Gandhi's emphasis on *brahmacharya* as merely a spiritual project and framed solely within the practices of Hinduism lacking political and social intent (*Gandhi's Body*, 5).[6] Instead, Alter claims Gandhi's somatic projects were closely aligned with "questions of morality in colonial India [that] also denoted a particular logic of modern public health" ("Gandhi's Body" 303).

Interestingly, unlike the focus of Indian wrestling and the popularity of the physical culture movement in Bengal to the project of constituting hyper-masculinity, Gandhi's somatic nationalism sought to move away from body-building and ideas of visible masculinity to emphasize only its frame of signification.[7] As Rebecca Brown states, "he sought to equate a steely, strong physique not with an overly muscled, violent body but one borne of self-control, vigour and devotion" (98). It is in this practice of self-regulation and self-disciplining that the Gandhian principle of *brahmacharya* takes birth. Often understood as celibacy, *brahmacharya*, according to Veena Howard, "meant a comprehensive control of the senses and was laden with ethical, religious, and mythical connotations." Howard explains that Gandhi's connotation of *brahmacharya* "held the promise that a collective self-control by the masses would shatter oppressive structures of violence" (xi). Howard's explanation of the Gandhian vision of brahmacharya as "ascetic activism" defines a political action underscored as a psycho-ethical quality and as rendering a service to the nation, an ideological act identified as challenge and resistance to hegemonic powers.

Drawing upon the study of the centrality of Gandhi's body politics as being structured in a framework that is inherently political, social, ethical and spiritual predicated on the vectors of colonialist and nationalist politics, this last section of the paper shall explore the perversion of Gandhian body politics in the postcolonial Indian novel, *Raag Darbari*.

Gandhi's "Biomoral" Practice: Outline of a Political Practice in *Raag Darbari*

As a recurrent subject of history, politics and culture, corruption has been a characteristic problem faced by all government systems since antiquity. Among the vast body of fictional representation on corruption, one of the finest literary expressions is found in the Hindi novel *Raag Darbari*.[8] Published in 1968, Shrilal Shukla's novel *Raag Darbari* (trans. Gillian Wright 1992), the winner of the Sahitya Akademi award in 1970, captures in its earthy, warm and rustic flavour the portrayal of, as Gillian Wright states, "an absolutely correct description of village politics" (v). The realistic details of numerous political agencies' functioning and the description of government officials located in a North Indian village enable this novel to rank even several years after its publication as a cult classic.

This chapter's premise in using the ethos of Gandhi's body dynamics as the most significant discourse to rethink the discursive constitution of the nation-state rests on two central characters within the novel. One of the characters is Vaidyaji, a power broker, a local state official and an ayurvedic doctor. The second character is Ranganath, his nephew, who is pursuing his doctoral research in the city. Ranganath's coming to the village of Shivpalganj to recover his health with the help of medicines prescribed by his uncle propels the narrative thread forward. Vaidyaji is the central locus of the political structure of post-independence 1950s India, the nodal point within the novel where corruption is pre-eminently visible. He is the principal actor embodying the site of distorting the state welfare schemes like education, village council and local cooperative bodies.[9] Most critical studies have concentrated on the character and working ethos of Vaidyaji to reveal the corruption that has seeped into the fabric of the Indian political and social milieu. However, the portrayal of Vaidyaji as a health giver has not been considered in any critical readings of the novel to date.

This interesting trivia about Vaidyaji being a health practitioner and Ranganath seeking to improve his health provide the entry point for the Gandhian discourse on health, national identity and political regeneration to surface as a critical theoretical framework. As we saw in the second section of this chapter, referring to Gandhi's book *Key to Health* ([1948] 1992), that recognizes the appeal of a healthy body as the "key" to "a complex reform strategy," Alter notes that the "dreary details" in Gandhi's book "is not so much [inclusive] of pedantic obsession [instead figures as] the key [to] the potential of a great nation" ("Gandhi's Body" 305). Documenting bodily health as illustrative of political and psychological action, Gandhi sought to locate the performance of serving one's country in practising body activism sustained by truth, individual freedom and social justice. However, the events panning out in Shukla's *Raag Darbari* contorts this idea of health.

Instead of a healthy individual being analogous to a healthy nation, Vaidyaji's guidance on developing good health corresponds to corruption of all kinds; like, nepotism, factionalism and the manipulation of power running rampant in Shivpalganj. The representation of corruption in this village, as Akhil Gupta states, redefines the nation-states understood previously as mere "culturally embedded imaginaries" ("Narrating" 175). The description of the political system of democracy in rags (Shukla 135), poor being reduced to a condition of complete destitution, explains the novel's background and encapsulates the idiom of the postcolonial nation-state. Also, the image of the diseased "democracy" in need of help runs parallel to the inversion of the ethos of Gandhi's notion of bodily health understood as a moral schema.

Shukla's novel is set in an obscure village of Northern India, Shivpalganj, probably located in and around Eastern Uttar Pradesh where, in the 1960s, Shrilal Shukla was posted as an Indian administrative officer. Shukla states the novel's context as located at the "edge of a town," where "beyond it [is] the ocean of the Indian countryside" (1). This evocative beginning is the start of the roller-coaster ride of the fiercely competitive world of corruption where, as Francesca Orsini maintains, "it is vital to know the rules to survive, and words are more likely to dissemble meaning than convey it" (88). The grotesque background of this village also provokes a reconceptualization of the philosophical postulations on the rural–urban divide. Located at the "edge of the town," the context of the novel collapses the dichotomy between rural and urban to postulate it as Rajagopalan proposes "rural-urban continuum" (61). Even as the novel inaugurates the village life as full of "fresh air" that would help Ranganath to "get well" (Shukla 46), the life in this village resembles what happens outside its precincts. Shukla writes,

> In just a few days Ranganath began to feel that Shivpalganj was like the great Hindu epic, *Mahabharata* – what was to be found nowhere else was there, and what was not there, was to be found nowhere else. He realized that all Indians are one, and everywhere are minds are alike. . . . As Ranganath realized this his faith in Indian cultural unity was reaffirmed.
>
> *(47)*

The rural locale is represented neither as a den of misery and exploitation nor as an image of rustic simplicity; instead, it is merged and conflated with the urban landscape's ethos. The philosophy that holds for this terrain and its unique characters is "encroachment." As Shukla enumerates on this philosophy, "when you find empty land on your borders, grab a few feet of it when no one's looking" (25). This encroachment is a metaphoric figuration of how borders collapse, how truth and lies merge, and where both innocence and immorality blend to represent the fundamental values of life and health as having lost their potency.

The idea of encroachment inevitably recalls Veena Howard's examination of Gandhi's ascetic activism as a mode of political participation and transformation, which involved self-control, self-discipline, the principle of renunciation and non-possession (40–45). Gandhi, according to Howard, "aimed to develop a living strategy in which renunciation and activism, spiritual liberation (mokṣa), and political freedom (svarāj) were understood to be compatible, rather than antithetical" (41). In Gandhi, the body appeared as a site where the boundaries between the public and the private domain dissolved thus redefining the values identified with socio-political contexts. If the blurring of boundaries between the self and the nation, private and the public, ethical and political, and individual and society serves as the foundational thought of Gandhi's political activism; in Shukla's novel, this integration of the rural–urban sphere, the conflation of the public and private sphere embodies a merger of corrupt political institutions with Gandhi's somatic civic activism.

An urban-educated young man, Ranganath's arrival in the village is mainly positioned within the debates centring around physical fitness, control of diet and as continually being framed as an outsider. The subject of health that emerges as a predominant concern with Ranganath's entry registers the metaphor of corruption as a debilitating, perverse health issue. Gandhi's ideas about perfect health and the sound body were found on his criticism of Western allopathic medicine. He termed this Western form of healing, a perfect mechanism to supervise and subdue the natives (Alter "Gandhi's Body" 310). He was simultaneously sceptical of ayurvedic practice because, as a mode of "healing [it was] outside the reach of every man," being an example of "upper-caste medicinal healing" (309–10). Instead, Gandhi suggested a natural mode of healing that inculcated a balanced lifestyle in opposition to "the undisciplined lifestyle of gastronomic excess and erratic habits which in his view caused illnesses" (CW 4: 373). In "General Knowledge About Health," published serially in 1913, he writes: "{our} subject is not how to exist anyhow, but how to live, if possible, in perfect health" (qtd. Alter, "Gandhi's Body" 309). Ranganath's conscientious following up of the daily routine set by his uncle, Vaidyaji, runs parallel to the images of defecation that litter the pages of this novel, to evoke a picture of a landscape that is filled with heaps of rubbish. In addition, this conjures a world where discipline and lack of self-control are two sides of the same coin.

Gandhi believed that a dedicated dietary regime and adherence to the life of a brahmacharya, observing vegetarianism and appropriate hygienic practices could seemingly capture the distinguishing characteristic of swaraj. However, in Ranganath, an educated citizen practising healthy somatic practices – we encounter the debasement of individual agency. Suraj Rath's construction of Ranganath as an ethical hero frustrated and trapped in an immoral landscape, I argue, does not hold (50). This ethical hero formulation remains unsupported by a lack of evidence, as Ranganath only finds escape in his illusory speeches in an imagined coffee house with his friends (Shukla 147). In this world, speeches that are too unreal, and dramatic gestures that are invariably false are all Ranganath can muster.

Further, Ranganath's subsequent glowing health because of his uncle's treatment includes the daily concoction of bhang comprising of "almonds, raisins and pistachios" (Shukla 31).[10] This bhang mixture dramatizes the hollowness of the rhetoric of building the nation, reducing it to only forming the body. The Gandhian diet of vegetarianism was a means to inculcate compassion and challenge racial prejudices (Devanesen 321–22). Ranganath's eventual escape from the villages' brutal in-fighting for power is the failure of political idealism. If Gandhi's "science of diet," according to Alter, "provided the means by which to effect moral change on a large, demographic scale" (306), in the character of Ranganath, the discourse of health and disciplining of the body through strict dietary regimes loses the potentiality to embody "progressive freedom [in a world defined by] triple curse of [the] economic, mental and moral drain" (Gandhi CW 70).

The distortion that marks the "biomoral" body politics is found charted in other vectors of the postcolonial nation-state as well. The education system and ethos of governance are underscored in Ranganath's figure where, as Suraj Rath rightly affirms, the signifiers of idealism and hope which sustained Nehru's education policy are disassociated from its evasive signified (50). Ranganath's growing fascination with his daily routine functions as more of an extensive commentary on the education system whose only preoccupation is a self-obsession with health. However, health like education lacks its strength and remains merely a mechanized version of curing ills, building a muscled body and indulging in an assortment of specific treatments. This description of conscientious observance of regulated diet and controlled exercise recalls Gandhi's dietary fads without its ethical effectiveness and political power.

The title of the novel, *Raag Darbari*, points to the complicated Indian classical melody "raag," sung for the magnificence and glory of the court, "darbar." However, the "raag" in the title of this novel refers to various fraudulent schemes being hatched at the court/darbar of the local leader, Vaidyaji – the main protagonist in this narrative of corruption. Termed by the Sub-Inspector as "the climate of the village" (Shukla 174), Vaidyaji is the brains behind the (mis)management of the farmers' cooperative union and the local College and who, during the novel, stamps his authority on the village council (albeit illegally) by placing his henchman, a lowly worker called Sanichar as the village headman. The introduction of Vaidyaji, the ayurvedic practitioner as who "was, is and will remain" (28) is vividly described through the practice of celibacy apart from the rhetoric of good health and disciplining of the body. Shukla writes:

> In Vaidyaji's opinion the greatest harm caused by the loss of chastity was that after losing it, a man no longer remained fit to lose it again. . . . He described a rather strange physiology from which he calculated that you have to consume several tons of food to produce a few ounces of "essence"; "essence" is converted into blood, blood into something else, and in this way finally one drop of semen is created. He proved that it doesn't cost as much to build an atom bomb as it does to produce one drop of semen. . . . One on side flowed rivers of milk and honey; on the other rivers of semen.
>
> *(29–30)*

This invocation of celibacy is reiterated in Vaidyaji's firm belief that the loss of chastity is the root cause of all evil (Shukla 29–30). The previous passage closely corresponds with Gandhi's evocation of celibacy; however, there is a difference. Gandhi described brahmacharya in his article "What is brahmacharya?" printed in *Young India* (5 June 1924) as the "search [for] Brahma [truth]," and thus, in its most ordinarily accepted sense, the "control in thought, word and action, of all the senses at all times and in all places" (qtd. Lal 105). Vinay Lal describes brahmacharya as "the elimination of all desire, [that] was to be obtained by diving into, and realizing the inner self: and it is this spiritual discipline that furnished the non-violent resister with true armor" (105–06). Simultaneously, Howard's framework of "ascetic activism" immediately places the body within the rubric of control and discipline and is irrevocably understood as negating sexual impulses.

In Gandhi, the categorizing of brahmacharya in the idiom of "sober," "chastity," "purity," "humility," and "the all-sufficing cause of service of some dear one or of the country" (qtd. Alter "Gandhi's Body" 306) suggests an intense devotion to a cause greater than the individual. The vow of brahmacharya that Gandhi took in South Africa during the ongoing Zulu rebellion suggests the war-like insistence on this mode of living (Alter "Gandhi's Body" 318–19). Furthermore, the act of sexual renunciation emerges as the key to end all violence and to embody the truth of living. Brahmacharya, enmeshed within the various discourses of national and cultural identity, health and non-violence, appears in Gandhi's politics to "withstand disease" (1958, 71). At once, connected with social reform and upliftment of the marginalized, brahmacharya develops in Gandhian vision as a repository of moral action and distinguishes truth as an embodied practice. Vaidyaji's opinion of the immorality of losing one's chastity, on the other hand, reveals the "disjuncture between "common sense" assumptions about the way the state works and the experience of the state from a perspective of those on the receiving end of its programmes" (Anjaria 4798). The loss of chastity is now reduced to an advertisement "A Message of Hope for Youth" (Shukla 58). Shukla explains this "hope" as "referring to a tablet which looked like a pellet of goat shit, and which as soon as it reached the stomach, sent electricity coursing through their veins" (30). As a degraded farce, the fall from grace of celibacy's rhetoric demonstrates the misuse and mismanagement of the institutions of the postcolonial state. This recapturing of the past's glory is merely an imitative gesture, which fails to reconcile with the present dynamics. Ayurveda, which Vaidyaji postulates as a synonym for Vedanta, the ancient mode of Hindu knowledge, roughly translates into factionalism, where "all want to capture each other's position" (Shukla 74). Like the blurring of boundaries between the rural and urban landscape, the sanctity of state institutions is marred with the duties of public office translating into private interests. Whether it is winning the local college elections or the village council through strong-arm tactics, Vaidyaji's eventual takeover of all institutions like the gram panchayats and educational institutions is constantly reified by the memory of Mahatma Gandhi (Shukla 29, 142, 161, 202). This love for power and position subverts the Gandhian mode of renunciation espoused through disciplining of the body and bodily desires. The "filth," the piles of rubbish and stench that colour every page of the novel (Shukla 315), mark a disappointing end to the hope and idealism of the policies of the central and most significant institutions like the village councils (panchayats), local College and farmers' cooperative unions of the postcolonial state. These inversions of the values of Gandhian somatic activism portray the world of expanding state village politics and democratic institutions at the end of the Nehruvian era as a failure and as woefully inadequate.

The site of the embodied ideal, the body, emerges as the key signifier to counter-challenge colonizers' might. However, in this novel, as Badri's figure shows, the body is simply a symbol of decline and immorality. Badri manages to have his way only on account of his "no-nonsense presence," and not because his body reflects sound judgement, intellectual ability and moral values. This decline in the self-sufficiency of the body is unlike what sustained and provided political ammunition to the debates surrounding the popularization of wrestling during the nineteenth century. Wrestling's highly textured meaning is also underscored in the precincts of the akhara or wrestling pit. The boundaries of this sacred terrain (akhadas) are elided and transformed to the drawing room of Vaidyaji, the site of abuse of power. This frequent melding of boundaries demonstrates the discordant notes in the metanarrative of nationalism and marks the state machinery's eventual deterioration.

Interestingly, Gandhi was against "brute strength," which he felt was a common theme practiced in many regional gymnasiums *(akhadas)*. However, Gandhi did consider it unfortunate that the country was only filled with "rickety bodies of young men" (CW 32: 444). Gandhi, when inaugurating gymnasiums (CW 34:411; 71:135), insisted on the need to move away from brutish power espoused by wrestlers and sought to draw a metaphysical, political connection to Lord Hanuman, the presiding deity of celibacy and the sport of wrestling. If Gandhi defined the "physical strength" of Hanuman as framed in the "manifestation of his devotion to Ram and a derivative consequence of celibacy, [and] not an end in itself" (Alter "Gandhi's Body" 312), the references to Lord Hanuman in Shukla's novel (9, 84, 184) is only a measure of the grotesque values in the social, cultural and political life of the postcolonial nation-state.

Conclusion

Gandhi's body politics devoid of its power in this novel demonstrates a separation between imagination and idealism. Shivpalganj is not a pastoral idyll, as illustrated in Ranganath's escape. Instead, the town symbolizes a vast gulf between the somatic culture and the body politic. To a certain extent, the only character who follows the path of righteousness is Langar – a lame figure, further underscoring the inadequacy of somatic asceticism to revitalize the nation-state. The irony of Langar fighting a righteous battle where bribery and other forms of corruption have drenched the whole society is Shukla's most biting invective against the malice of immoral practices. The only response to Langar's struggle against the rottenness pervading the judicial system is the presence of "dogs, pigs and piles of rubbish in whose company he had set out to fight a righteous war against officialdom" (Shukla 103).

The novel represents the Gandhian discourse of bodily health as interrogating the production and invention of "nation" cut off from the rhetoric of the past and also being disassociated from the present. Gandhian somatic-ethical idealism, which is continually invoked in the novel, albeit in its deflated form, shows the chasm between the institutional ethos of the nation-state and its collective identity. If the vibrancy and the promise of the early years of India's independence are deflated to give way to automatization of the democratic policies then, this "inversion" of the intended ideals of the institutions of the nation state identifiable with the rhetoric of Gandhi's corporeal activism is no more than a deadening practice.

Notes

1 Michel Foucault in *The Birth of the Clinic* (1973) speaks about the convergence between political ideology and those of medical technology to "allow the formation of an accurate, exhaustive, permanent corpus of knowledge about the health of the population" (38–9). This 'permanent corpus of knowledge about the population' is what Foucault explains as the operation of governmentality, understood as the efficient management of subjects. Furthermore, medicinal knowledge premised on the body played a crucial role in manifesting this idea of governmentality in colonial India.

2 Rabindranath Tagore's family in Jorasanko, Calcutta, instituted "Hindu Melas" or gatherings that ran consecutively for 14 years – from 1867 till 1880. The "chief preoccupations of the organizers of the melas were to encourage a culture of physical prowess" (Chowdhary 21). Read Skikata Banerjee's translation of Sarla Debi Chaudhurani's *The Scattered Leaves of My Life: An Indian Nationalist Remembers* (2011) for a detailed description of Sarla Debi's role in the revival of martial arts and such martial organizations.

3 Joseph Alter in his book, *Gandhi's Body: Sex, Diet, and the Politics of Nationalism* (2000), stated, Gandhi's body politics was more grounded in ideas of health and private quotidian practices. This framework of body as defined by healthy practices constituted the discourse of satyagraha and struggle towards political emancipation as not an exotic gesture but as an instance of experiential living.

4 Alter's categorization of the Gandhian somatic activism as 'biomoral' relates to the close relationship between the individual and the collective identity, the body framed by ethical praxis, and healthy corporeality combined with spiritual acts. Biomoral practice is defined as a mode of resistance and an authentic moral practice to usher in a positive change.

5 See also Roy 2002; L. Gandhi 2008.

6 See Parekh 1989; Susan and Llyod Rudolph 1983.

7 According to Alter, an understanding of Gandhi's body politics being distinct from the ethos of wrestling needs to be problematized. From 1918 onwards, Alter argues that there was a distinct belief in Gandhi "to define militant" nonviolence in terms of "manliness," "virility" and "a strong physique" ("Gandhi's Body" 312).

8 The study of Shukla's novel is undertaken following Akhil Gupta's seminal work on corruption, outlined in his book titled *Red Tape: Bureaucracy, Structural Violence and Poverty in India* (2012). Gupta enunciates corruption as giving rise to "popular knowledge about the state" (76). Terming corruption as a "structural violence" (ibid.), Gupta defines it using the semantic field inaugurated by its Hindi equivalent, *bhrashtaachaar*. Gupta explains "bhrashtaachaar as refer[ing] simultaneously to activities that may be illegal, violate societal norms . . . [and as] invoke[ing] the moral obligation of ruling elites and upper classes to look after the poor and indigent" (80). Gupta's notion of corruption as a legal, political and moral irregularity is analogous to, I argue, the Gandhian discourse of body politics.

9 See Raina. "Nehru on Education," for a detailed description of Nehruvian India built upon education, village politics and educational development (1993). And Sudipta Kaviraj's *The Enchantment of Democracy and India: Politics and Ideas* (2011) on planning reforms initiated by Nehru.

10 The mention of bhang recalls the strict dietary regime followed by Indian wrestlers. According to Alter, bhang was understood as a divine restorative and, thus, casts the art of wrestling in metaphysical overtones (*Wrestler's Body* 1992).

Works Cited

Alter, Joseph S. *Body, Text, Nation: Writing the Physically Fit Body in Post-Colonial India*. Mills and Sen, pp. 16–38.

———. "Gandhi's Body, Gandhi's Truth: Nonviolence and the Biomoral Imperative of Public Health." *The Journal of Asian Studies*, vol. 55, no. 2, 1996, pp. 301–22, JSTOR, www.jstor.org/stable/2943361.

————. *Gandhi's Body: Sex, Diet, and the Politics of Nationalism.* U of Pennsylvania P, 2000.

————. "Hanuman and the Moral Physique of the Banarsi Wrestler." *Living Banaras: Hindu Religion in Cultural Context,* edited by Bradley R. Hertel and Cynthia Ann Humes, State U of New York P, 1993, pp. 127–44.

————. "Heaps of Health, Metaphysical Fitness: Ayurveda and the Ontology of Good Health in Medical Anthropology." *Current Anthropology,* vol. 40, no. 1, 1999, pp. S43–S66. *JSTOR,* www.jstor.org/stable/10.1086/200060.

————. "The 'Sannyasi' and the Indian Wrestler: The Anatomy of a Relationship." *American Ethnologist,* vol. 19, no. 2, 1992, pp. 317–36. *JSTOR,* www.jstor.org/stable/645039.

————. *The Wrestler's Body: Identity and Ideology in North India.* California UP, 1992.

Anderson, B. *Imagined Communities: Reflections on the Origin and Spread of Nationalism.* Revised ed., Verso, 1991.

Anjaria, Ulka. "Satire, Literary Realism, and the Indian State. Rev. of Six Acres and a Third, by Fakir Mohan Senapati, and Raag Darbari, by Shrilal Shukla." *Economic and Political Weekly,* vol. 41, no. 46, 2006, pp. 4795–800. *JSTOR,* https://www.jstor.org/stable/i401939.

Arnold, David. *Colonizing the Body: State Medicine and Epidemic Disease in Nineteenth-Century India.* U of California P, 1993.

Barthes, Roland. *Mythologies.* Translated by Annette Lavers. Noonday Press, 1991.

Basu, Subho, and Sikata Banerjee. "The Quest for Manhood: Hinduism and Nation in Bengal." *Comparative Studies of South Asia, Africa and the Middle East,* vol. 26, no. 3, 2006, pp. 476–90. *Project Muse,* https://muse.jhu.edu/article/207576.

Brown, Rebecca M. *Gandhi's Spinning Wheel and the Making of Modern India.* Routledge/ Studies in Asian History, 2010.

Canning, Kathleen. "The Body as Method? Reflections on the Place of the Body in Gender History." *Gender and History,* vol. 11, no. 3, 1999, pp. 499–513, https://doi.org/10.1111/1468-0424.00159. Accessed 30 Dec. 2014.

Chaudhurani, SarlaDebi. *The Scattered Leaves of My Life: An Indian Nationalist Remembers.* Translated by Sikata Banerjee. Women Unlimited, 2011.

Chowdhury, Indira. *The Frail Hero and Virile History: Gender and the Politics of Culture in Colonial Bengal.* Oxford UP, 2001.

Devanesen, Chandran D. S. *The Making of the Mahatma.* Orient Longman, 1969.

Foucault, Michel. *The Birth of a Clinic: An Archaeology of Medical Perception.* Pantheon Books, 1973.

Gandhi, Leela. *Rethinking Gandhi and Nonviolent Relationality: Global Perspectives.* Routledge, 2008.

Gandhi, Mohandas K. *The Collected Works of Mahatma Gandhi.* 80 vols, The Publications Division, Ministry of Information and Broadcasting, Government of India, 1958, pp. 158–80.

Godrej, Farah. "Gandhi's Body, Pain, and Suffering in Environmental Discourse." Conference of the American Political Association, Washington, 2–5 Sept. 2010, https://ssrn.com/abstract=1669831.

Goswami, Manu. *Producing India: From Colonial Economy to Nationalist Space.* U of Chicago P/Chicago Studies in Practices of Meaning, 2004.

Gupta, Akhil. "Narrating the State of Corruption." *Corruption: Anthropological Perspectives,* edited by Dieter Haller and Cris Shore, Pluto Press, 2005, pp. 173–93.

————. *Red Tape: Bureaucracy, Structural Violence and Poverty in India.* Duke UP, 2012.

Heath, Deane. *Purifying Empire: Obscenity and the Politics of Moral Regulation in Britain, India and Australia.* Cambridge UP, 2010.

Howard, Veena R. *Gandhi's Ascetic Activism: Renunciation and Social Action*. Suny Press, 2013.

Kakar, Sudhir. *Intimate Relations: Exploring Indian Sexuality*. U of Chicago P, 1990.

Kaviraj, Sudipta. *The Enchantment of Democracy and India: Politics and Ideas*. Permanent Black, 2011.

———. "The Modern State in India." *Politics and the State in India*, edited by Zoya Hasan. Sage Publications, 2000, pp. 37–63.

Lal, Vinay. "Nakedness, Nonviolence, and Brahmacharya: Gandhi's Experiments in Celibate Sexuality." *Journal of the History of Sexuality*, vol. 9, no. ½, 2000, pp. 105–36, www.jstor.org/stable/3704634.

Mills, James H., and Satadru Sen. *Confronting the Body: The Politics of Physicality in Colonial and Post-Colonial India*. Anthem-Wimbledon, 2003.

Nandy, Ashis. *The Intimate Enemy: Loss and Recovery of Self Under Colonialism*. Oxford UP, 1983.

Orsini, Francesca. "India in the Mirror of Word Fiction." *New Left Review*, vol. 13, 2002, pp. 75–88, www.eprints.soas.ac.uk.

Parekh, Bhikhu. *Colonialism, Tradition and Reform: An Analysis of Gandhi's Political Discourse*. Sage Publications, 1989.

Prasad, Srirupa. "Gandhi's Moral Politics and Plague in South Africa." *Medicine and Colonial Engagements in India and Sub-Saharan Africa*, edited by Poonam Bala, Cambridge Scholars Publishing, 2018, pp. 88–106.

Rajagopalan, C. "The Rural-Urban Continuum: A Critical Evaluation." *Sociological Bulletin*, vol. 10. no. 1, 1961, pp. 61–74. *JSTOR*, www.jstor.org/stable/42864580.

Rand, Gavin. "'Martial Races' and 'Imperial Subjects': Violence and Governance in Colonial India, 1857–1914." *European Review of History*, vol. 13, no. 1, 2006, pp. 1–20. *Taylor and Francis Online*, https://doi.org/10.1080/13507480600586726.

Rath, Suraj Prasad. "Carnivalized Public Corruption: Old Feudalism and New Democracy in *All the King's Men*, *Wise Blood*, and *Raag Darbari*." *Comparative American Studies*, vol. 8, no. 1, 2010, pp. 39–56.

Rosenberg, Emily S., and Shanon Fitzpatrick. Introduction. *Body and Nation: The Global Realm of U.S. Body Politics in the Twentieth Century*, edited by Rosenberg and Fitzpatrick, Duke UP, 2014, pp. 1–15.

Rosselli, John. "The Self-Image of Effeteness: Physical Education and Nationalism in Nineteenth-Century Bengal." *Past and Present*, vol. 86, 1980, pp. 121–48. *JSTOR*, www.jstor.org/stable/650742.

Roy, Parama. "Meat-Eating, Masculinity, and Renunciation in India: A Gandhian Grammar of Diet." *Gender and History*, vol. 14, no. 1, 2002, pp. 62–91, https://doi.org/10.1111/1468-0424.00252. Accessed 16 Jan. 2015.

Rudolph, Susanne Hoeber, and Lloyd I. Rudolph. *Gandhi: The Traditional Roots of Charisma*. U of Chicago P, 1983.

Shukla, Shrilal. *Raag Darbari*. 1968. Translated by Gillian Wright. Penguin, 1992.

Wakankar, Milind. "Body, Crowd, Identity: Genealogy of a Hindu Nationalist Ascetics." *Social Text*, vol. 45, 1995, pp. 45–73. *JSTOR*, www.jstor.org/stable/466674.

Wright, Gillian. Introduction. *Raag Darbari*. By Shrilal Shukla Translated by Wright. Penguin, 1992, pp. v–xi.

14

GANDHI, ABSTINENCE AND POLITICAL FREEDOM

Reading Saadat Hasan Manto's *"Swaraj Ke Liye"*

Baran Farooqi and Disha Pokhriyal

Introduction

> "The very purpose of marriage is restraint and sublimation of sexual passion."
>
> —(Gandhi *The Conquest of Self* 79)

> "I feel humans must remain humans. If a couple wants to curb their carnal passion, let them. But the entire human race? For God's sake!"
>
> —(Manto *Swaraj Ke Liye* 188)

The Conquest of Self (1943) is a compilation of Gandhi's observations on celibacy, his attempts at following an ideal *brahmacharya* and his vision of how men and women could contribute to personal and political freedom through the realization of conjugal abstinence. Gandhi tries to counter the various fears and failures about balancing conjugality and political commitments, many of which were primarily his own and were often shared and contested by his followers and comrades. *The Conquest of Self* reveals how Gandhi constantly makes and breaks his self and his ideas and engages with the praxis of personal and political struggles.

While these ideological tussles have found space in a range of fictional and creative narratives, one story comes closest to the lesser discussed Gandhian dilemmas about sexuality, identity and politics. *Swaraj Ke Liye* (translated as *For Freedom's Sake*), written by Saadat Hasan Manto and originally published in the anthology *Nimrud ki Khudai* (1950), counters Gandhi's views on celibacy and sexuality. *Swaraj Ke Liye* looks at the contradictions within Gandhi's practices of disciplining the individual body to achieve a political ideal and sees conjugal abstinence not as an opportunity for self-evolution but as a hindrance to the political involvement and spiritual development of individuals. In the introduction to his translation of Manto's stories, Muhammad Umar Memon writes, "Manto knew too well that

DOI: 10.4324/9781003145479-19

most humans live and breathe in the obscuring haze of contradictory impulses and that certainties – the arbiter of human behaviour so predisposed to doling out reward and punishment – are the prerogative only of ideologues, whether religious and political" (xiv). Manto reveals the schisms in Gandhi's discourse that emerge when the redirection of sexual energies is turned into a contorted compulsion, with men being prescribed control and women being prescribed self-effacement. This paper will study the story in the backdrop of *The Conquest of Self* to highlight how Manto captures Gandhi's struggles to identify the troubling passions of lust and carnality, primarily in the realm of conjugality.

The Ideal and the Real: The Fraught Landscape of Marital *Brahmacharya*

Gandhi's autobiography, *The Story of my Experiments with Truth* (1927), mentions his experiments with conjugality, lust, marital pleasures and filial duty following his marriage to Kasturba at the age of 14. The instance of his father's death, Gandhi documents in the *Autobiography*, leads to a "double shame" (24) and provides the first step in Gandhi's journey towards conjugal abstinence. With a 16-year-old Kasturba expecting a baby and his father being bed-ridden, Gandhi vacillates between sustaining a loyal devotion to his parents and a carnal lust for his wife. He writes "every night whilst my hands were busy massaging my father's legs, my mind was hovering about the bed-room – and that too at a time when religion, medical science and common-sense alike forbade sexual intercourse" (25). And on one such critical occasion, as he slips away from the father's room to wake up Kasturba and indulge his desires, he gets the message of his father's demise. Gandhi writes about "this shame of my carnal desire even at the critical hour of my father's death, [which] demanded wakeful service" (25). An indelible "blot" on his character, Gandhi finds himself to be a "lustful, though a faithful, husband" (26). Exploring further in his *Autobiography*, Gandhi asks "Did my faithfulness consist in making my wife an instrument of my lust? . . . To be fair, I must say that she was never the temptress" (172). Since the child eventually born could not live for more than four days, Gandhi reiterates that "let all those who are married be warned by my example" (26).

In the *Autobiography*, Gandhi states that in 1906 he finally decided that only the elimination of the feeling of desire towards Kasturba can be the first step towards his "vow of renunciation" (173). Even though this decision existed within the realm of marriage, Gandhi writes "I had not shared my thoughts with my wife until then, but only consulted her at the time of taking the vow. She had no objection" (174). With his way cleared out, he begins to discover in *brahmacharya* the roots of his Satyagraha. For Gandhi, the strength emerging out of conjugal abstinence was much purer than the joy one would get out of relishing the so-called "naturalness" of sexual pleasure. Only through the attainment of a complete control on the self could one even begin to engage with the questions of political freedom and planning a mass movement. Gandhi writes, "*Brahmacharya* does not mean that one may not touch a woman, even one's sister, in any circumstance whatsoever. But it does mean that one's state of mind should be as calm and unruffled during such contact as when one touches, say, a piece of paper. . . . He has to be free from excitement in case of contact with the fairest damsel on earth as in contact with a dead body" (*Conquest of Self* 44). He connects his ideal of *brahmacharya* with the state of conjugality. A man's experience of bodily purity was marked by resistance to temptations and controlling their hunger and lust. Gandhi declares, "*Brahmacharya* means control of the senses in thought, word and deed" (*Autobiography* 176). In his essay on Gandhi and celibacy, Vinay Lal writes "[Gandhi] would dictate letters to his secretaries, or conduct other important business, while his body was being massaged, and he thought nothing of putting his arms around the shoulders of friends, associates, and even visitors. He kept a minute record of the food ingested by him, and his bowel movements were of as much concern to him as the negotiations for Indian independence. Gandhi's attentiveness to matters of sexuality, hygiene, nutrition, and the presentation of the body was his way of injecting the body into the body politic" (86). In his pursuit of developing the inner soul-force to sustain an external political struggle, Gandhi saw indulgence, sexual or dietary, as a disruption of the harmony existing both within an individual's bodily fluids and in his/her commitment to wider political participation.

This is visible in the way Gandhi pays attention to man's material/physical world in comparison to the physicality of a woman, except when the latter is seen as an aberrant, inducing lust in men through adornments and make-up. Control and avoidance are primarily the responsibility of men, while women must learn to recognize the power of their virtue and purity. Since women are visualized as conscience keepers, any signs of a woman recognizing her beauty are to be erased. Gandhi gives women the responsibility of deciding how they wish to be understood by the society. Women must choose whether their emphasis should be on looks, physicality or pleasure, these categories being necessarily isolated from each other. A woman must be wary of the appeal her sexuality can generate and be wise enough to choose self-effacement and an enforced simplicity. Adornment is seen as a continuation of the oblique indulgence in sexual play that Gandhi fears ensue between the man and woman, husband and wife. A man could only deal with this aberration by focusing within, maintaining an inner composure and chanting the *Rama-nama* (the name of Rama). Gandhi wanted people, individually and collectively, to struggle with a process of evolution, located mainly in the realm of marriage, through the practices of *brahmacharya* and mutual abstinence. At the individual level, for men, it is about controlling their lust towards women who could be potentially threatening. For women, whose sexuality Gandhi does not discuss much of, it is about transforming into a higher, purer, virtuous self. "Married should remain like the unmarried," writes Gandhi, "like brothers and sisters, free from all sensual desires. Regarding all women as mothers, sisters, daughters is in itself elevating . . . it widens the family and love grows after wiping out the sensual element" (*Conquest of Self* 21).

Young Men and Modern Juliets: Epistles on Celibacy, Family and Progeny

Gandhi continuously received observations and complaints from people about what they perceived as "unnatural" and beyond-human means to claim Swaraj for the country. *The Conquest of Self* includes excerpts from letters admonishing Gandhi for his "perversions" and asking about the possibility of love being the basis of marriage. One such letter reads "[f]rom your writing I doubt if you understand the young mind. What has been possible for you is not possible for all young men. I happen to be married. I can restrain myself. My wife cannot. She does not want children but she does want to enjoy herself. What am I to do? Is it not my duty to satisfy her?" (213). Gandhi reverts and asks "Is he sincere when he says he can restrain himself? Has the animal passion become transmuted in his case into a higher passion, say, for service of fellow beings?" (213). Gandhi prescribes that if the man's emotions were sincere, he should explain to his wife "the physical effects of union without the desire for procreation. Let him tell her what the vital fluid means. Let him further engage his wife in healthy pursuits and strive to regulate her diet, exercise, etc., so as to still the passion in her" (215). There is another letter which gets into the details of Gandhi's views concerning progeny and places it in the Indian context of the desire for a male offspring. Since Gandhi mandated that "cohabitation in marriage should only be for the purpose of begetting offspring, never for sensual gratification" (68), the letter addresses the dilemmas this prescription had created. The writer notes "I am being slowly forced to the view that sexuality is man's primitive nature, (and) self-control is a cultivated virtue. . . . But I am not prepared to condemn it (sexuality) as a heinous sin or to regard a husband and wife who cannot help their nature as fallen creatures to be treated with cheap pity or highbrow contempt" (69).

Some letters, made available in *The Conquest of Self*, echo the early twentieth century debates in India on birth control and how the introduction of contraceptives was changing the sexual dynamics of the youth. A young man strongly rebukes Gandhi "[y]ou want everyone to become moral in order to change the world. . . . I do not see you pointing out to your capitalist and landlord friends the great injustice and harm they are doing by making huge profits at the expense of labourers and tenants, while you are never tired of castigating young men and women for their moral lapses in sexual matters." The letter further states, "Since the invention of contraceptives the sexual basis of the institution of marriage has been knocked down. . . . You will, perhaps, be shocked at these ideas. I would here venture to ask you not to forget your own youth when judging the present-day youth. You were an over-sexed individual given to excessive indulgence, which seems to have created in you a sort of disgust towards the sexual act, and hence your asceticism and the idea of sin" (217). Gandhi's response was drawn from learnings from his own life. He shares, "I awoke to the folly of indulgence for the sake of it even when I was twenty-three years old, and decided upon total *Brahmacharya* in 1899, i.e., when I was thirty years old" (219). On the issue of birth control, he writes "the coming in of contraceptives has changed the ideas about sexual relations. If mutual consent makes a sexual act moral whether within marriage or without, and by parity of reasoning even between members of the same sex, the whole basis of sexual morality is gone and nothing but 'misery and defeat' awaits the youth of the country" (218).

Gandhi had to consistently address birth control questions and the availability of contraceptives/preventive mechanisms in the market. In *The Conquest of Self*, Gandhi writes, he found the use of contraceptives as breeding recklessness instead of supporting his idea of "self-realization through self-control" (121). He writes "I am afraid that advocates of birth control take it for granted that indulgence in animal passion is a necessity of life and in itself a desirable thing . . . Any large use of the methods is likely to result in the dissolution of the marriage bond" (118). In his responses to Margaret Sanger, the leader of the Birth Control Movement, Gandhi emphatically notes, "When a husband says, '[l]et us not have children, but let us have relations,' what is that but animal passion? If they do not want to have more children, they should simply refuse to unite. Love becomes lust the moment you make it a means for the satisfaction of animal needs" (124). Gandhi felt that the country was not capable of caring for the current population: "Self-indulgence with contraceptives may prevent the coming of children but will sap the vitality of both men and women perhaps more of men than of women" (30).

These correspondences voiced concerns that many of Gandhi's comrades and companions had about his experiments with sexual abstinence, sharing with women the intimate details of his dreams, sleeping alongside younger women, taking open baths and declaring his explorations as guidelines for those living with him and participating in the freedom struggle. Gandhi's responses to the previous questions followed along the lines of sexual morality. He saw marriage as the basis of societal structure and emphasized truth, instead of desire, as the basis of everything one does for oneself and the country. Moreover, Gandhi felt that it is his utmost moral responsibility to write and engage with these letters, to guide the people of the country who continue to be inundated with literature that presents a counterview. He dismisses such prevalent writings and says, "a man in the grip of the sensual desire is a man without moorings. If such a one was to guide society, to flood it with his writings, and men were to be swayed by them, where would society be?" (*Conquest of Self* 47).

Saadat Hasan Manto could very much be this man "without moorings," as Gandhi said. Political yet sensual, Manto's writings look at people and humanity with all their feelings and failings. In one of his essays, published in 1990 in *Mantonama* and translated by Muhammad Umar Memon as *The Short Story and Matters of Sex*, Manto writes, "Bread and stomach, man and woman–these are correlations that go back to the beginning of time. Eternal. Which of the two is more important, I can't say . . . It is as evident as daylight that all of world literature is the product of just these two relationships" (*The Short Story* 423). He feels that women who actively seek to exercise their own sexual choices appear to have been put out of the question by Gandhi. One does see that when Gandhi talks of man relinquishing the sexualized gaze over the wife/women, he only rarely sees women as actively recognizing and identifying with their sexual needs. In talking about the roles of modern girls and ideal wives, Gandhi very clearly states that a "woman must cease to consider herself the object of man's lust. The remedy is more in her hands than the man's. She must refuse to adorn herself for men including her husband, if she will be an equal partner with man. I cannot imagine Sita ever wasting a single moment on pleasing Rama by physical charms" (*Conquest of Self* 194). If a woman does indulge herself, she will choose to become, in Gandhi's words, "Juliet to half a dozen Romeos," only to be troubled further by these Romeos if she continues "painting herself and looking extraordinary" (224).

Manto's writings show that he was aware of the rebuttals and retaliation to the Gandhian solutions. He reveals the outrage among women to the girls-as-Juliet response. These women admired Gandhi but were piqued by his insensitive insight. Manto addresses this in an essay, translated as "Beautiful Girls will be Harassed" by Aakar Patel in *Why I Write: Essays by Saadat Hasan Manto* (2014). Manto responds to Gandhi's image of women as Juliet and writes, "The other day Gandhiji wrote of the educated girls of India saying, 'each of these Juliets has a hundred Romeos behind her.' At this there was such an extreme reaction in Lahore that the heavens trembled. Ms Mumtaz Shahnawaz and other girls gave a strong response to Gandhiji. For many days, even veiled women wrote essays in Indian papers against this half-covered man" (*Beautiful Girls* 33). In giving details about what followed, Manto shares that Gandhi asked the boys to keep their gaze down while walking in the bazaar, asking them to "wear a hood so that your eyes don't light upon the faces of young girls. Thus, you'll hold on to your virtue. Gandhiji's hold on India is intact. But alas, his essay had little effect on India's young men" (*Beautiful Girls* 33). Amidst this perennial discursive conflict between abhorrence/abstinence and consumption/consummation, Gandhi as an experimental leader and Manto as an experimental writer are engaged in difficult dialectics.

Freedom for/from Whom? Reading *Swaraj Ke Liye*

Manto's story weaves together two sets of ideas. One looks at Gandhian politics, celibacy, its connection with Satyagraha/Passive Resistance and the critique of politico-religious spaces like the Ashram being used for such experiments. The other talks about the possibility of the existence of harmonious man–woman relationships, going against the Gandhian discourse of erasure, and sublimation of female sexuality, and establishing Manto's affirmation of sexual desire. Set in the early twentieth-century Amritsar, when "the dread, tinged with sadness, which had hung in the atmosphere since the bloody incident at Jallianwala Bagh had completely disappeared and a dauntless fervour had taken its place" (*Swaraj* 170), the story and its characters are realistic and robust, brimming with vitality and life even as they work around the necessities of life.

The narrator, who seems to be Manto, is an observer of all that is happening in the lives of those around him, especially Shahzada Ghulam Ali, Nigar and Babaji.

Ghulam Ali is a young "half-baked revolutionary" rousing local people to resist and protest against the British, thanks to his participation in some political rallies. Nigar is the comrade-in-arms and love of Ali's life "a beautiful confluence of the Muslim namaz and the Hindu *aarti*" (174). Manto's Babaji is learnt, intelligent and god-fearing, with obvious similarities to Gandhi. He is everybody's leader, a raw and earthy man who often visits Amritsar, believes in singing *bhajans*, giving *darshan* to his abundant followers and accepting the hospitality of the richest jeweller of the city. As a "major figure" and an active influencer of the politics of his times, Babaji is "a political riddle that even the brainiest government functionaries could never hope to solve" (175). He displays "an unassailable conviction that he could not be dislodged, not even by the worst earthquake, from the summit on which the world had placed him" (176).

The story dwells on the impact of Babaji's widespread discourse around married *brahmacharya* on the lives of Ghulam Ali and Nigar. His aura draws Ali, Nigar and the narrator to partake of his *darshan*. Ali wants to marry Nigar and keenly desires that Babaji should bless his wedding. Babaji agrees and not only does he infuse in Ali a passion to serve the country, safeguard the self and nurture belief in the non-sexual companionate marriage, but he also probes Ali and Nigar about their commitment. "Sometimes . . . one is obliged to change the decisions one has made," Babaji reminds them. But nothing deters Ali from taking the pledge to live in a non-sexual marital companionship with Nigar. He also vows not to bring slave children into this world until the country attains independence. "Until India wins her freedom, our relationship will be entirely like that of friends" (*Swaraj* 183), remarks Ali. Babaji blesses them and reveals that "although few people ate solely out of the need to stay alive, they alone knew the true meaning of eating" (183). The profundity of the idea of observing a celibate marriage overwhelmed not only Ali but also the entire marriage gathering, as they listened to Babaji talk about the purity of marital life, "the true joy of marriage as something above and beyond the bodily union of husband and wife" (183). Ali was "drinking in every word" and upon his turn, speaks "non-stop in a voice weighed down by emotion." In keeping up the image of an ardent fighter and making lofty promises before Babaji, he is entirely oblivious to the feelings of Nigar. She sits with a confused and visibly shaken face, unable to fathom how this pledge would ever be implemented. "He was like a drunkard," Manto writes in *Swaraj* "who keeps pulling out note after note without any idea of how much he is spending and then suddenly finds his wallet empty" (184).

Dilemmas of Conception and Contraception

Gandhi defined a precarious territory for couples who married and continued to serve in the freedom struggle. He suggested that couples be more of friends and companions and relinquish the carnality of marital relationships. Radha Kumar recounts how Gandhi had even discouraged Sucheta Kriplani from marrying J.B. Kriplani. He became "unhappy and restless" because she like many others would "just get embroiled in the family and household" (84). Sucheta stood her ground, got married and had to take the vow of *brahmacharya*. In her work on Gandhi and the fusing of political power with bodily asceticism, Veena Howard writes that "because Gandhi linked his accomplishment in the perfection of his practice of *brahmacarya* to success in his non-violent methods to free India, most interpretations of this unconventional enterprise present it as a desperate move to quell the conflagration of violence . . . by testing his own sexual control" ("*Rethinking Celibacy*" 23). Gandhian politics, undoubtedly, regards the body as a kernel of each political strategy. "I have not a shadow of a doubt," claims Gandhi, "that married people, if they wished well to the country and wanted to see India become a nation of strong and handsome full-formed men and women, would practise perfect self-restraint and cease to procreate for the time being. . . . It is easier not to do a thing at all than to cease doing it" (*Conquest of the Self* 43).

Manto keenly perceives how the desire to be part of the struggle for freedom leads Ali to an unexamined subscribing of the ideals of abstinence and becoming an impassioned groom promising to safeguard both his wife and the motherland. As the days of high-strung political rhetoric dwindle, with "the listlessness, the exhaustion" (*Swaraj* 184) spreading all over the country and independence continuing to be a dream, the story shifts to an unexpected meeting between the narrator and Ali. The narrator has moved to Bombay from Amritsar and one evening visits a shoe store that does not sell "any rubber footwear at all" (185). Upon inquiring, the owner is none other than Shahzada Ghulam Ali. Their conversations reveal Ali's journey from a political firebrand to a common family man. For Ali, now a father of two sons, "the past four, five years have been pure bliss" because he has "completely forgotten the days when this thing about being a leader had gotten into my head" (187). The narrator probes more to know what transpired in Ali's life and what happened to his announcement of not fathering kids until India's independence. "I felt that with that declaration my head had started to soar upwards until it touched the sky," remarks Ali. "However, when I got out of jail, the painful realization slowly took hold of me that I had curbed a vital part of my body and soul, that I had crushed the prettiest flower in my garden between my palms" (189).

Ali's impulsive decision to allow his marriage to be governed by extraneous vows and principles undercuts the very idea of Swaraj, of being able to decide how we must govern ourselves. Ali confesses to the narrator that this unnatural pledge of a non-sexual companionate marriage till India's independence was brutal curtailing of a natural desire under pressures to achieve a political victory. The ebb and flow in Ali's narrative shows a distant, critical perspective on the politics around the freedom struggle and the repercussions of this politics in the lives of common people. Writing on the politics of celibacy, Vinay Lal notes that this "zealous advocacy of celibacy, and Gandhi's insistence on recommending celibacy even to married couples is construed as evidence of his irrational and almost monstrously insensitive view of 'human nature'" (80).

Gandhi vehemently supported his position on what was deemed as an "unnatural" marital celibacy. He says "I can affirm, without the slightest hesitation, from my own experience as well as that of others, that sexual enjoyment is not only not necessary for, but is positively injurious to health. All the strength of body and mind that has taken long to acquire is lost all at once by a single dissipation of the vital energy. It takes a long time to regain this lost vitality, and even then, there is no saying that it can be thoroughly recovered" (*Conquest of Self* 37). The preservation of the vital fluids of men and the sexuality of women is seen by Gandhi as paving the path for Passive Resistance. Passive resisters, in the *Hind Swaraj* (1938), are defined as those who "observe perfect chastity, adopt poverty, follow truth and cultivate fearlessness. . . . He whose mind is given over to animal passions is not capable of any great effort . . . a passive resister can have no desire for progeny" (97). He believed that action generates a thought and that thought can be the source of impurity of the mind. He writes "[s]elf-restraint and not indulgence must be regarded as the law of life, if we are to accept and retain the sanctity of the marriage tie" (*Conquest of Self* 119).

Manto uses Nigar and Ali's life to cast a sharp look at this ideal of abstinence, while connecting the reader with Ali's experiences with "rubber" to negotiate the pledge. As they struggle to find a way out, Ali and Nigar surreptitiously begin to use condoms and establish conjugal intimacy. Nigar continues to harbour longing for a child but is considerate towards Ali's desire of remaining steadfast to his vow. After an initial phase of satisfaction, this use of contraception feels artificial to Ali. He finds himself and Nigar turning into "rubber dummies." The artifice of the vow and the plasticity of contraception creates around Ali's mind "a thin rubbery web" (*Swaraj* 190). The revulsion towards the unnaturalness of the vow and the contraception reaches its peak when Ali begins to hate not only his body but his very being. He wrestles to emerge out of this abnormal and artificial universe wherein he feels trapped and dehumanized. Ali derives only aversion, instead of pleasure, out of this piece of "rubber," "a used sheath" (190), a hateful object which turned him into a "dried-up, shrivelled-up piece of sinew, all my desires smothered." He is unable to find any support in Babaji's discourse, even as he wants helplessly "to grab my affliction in my two fingers and toss it away" (191). He only finds a way when he reads in the Hadith that procreation is an inevitable component of marital life and that is when the pledge and self-control is flung aside.

Ali's revulsion to rubber encapsulates his critique of the pledge and his disgust towards a mode of politics which rests on "show business." Ali's realizes that there exists a normal desire for sexual intimacy and progeny after marriage which is in stark contrast to the improbable ways in which Babaji envisages couples to stay together and fight for the country's independence. He shares with the narrator that "it's no bravery to fight nature, no achievement to die or live starving . . . this is show business" (*Swaraj* 191). There is pretence in the use of rubber, just like in taking the pledge. It drained all vitality out of Ali and Nigar's life and led to an awakening of the grand artifice on which the freedom struggle hinges. Ali is emphatic about this recognition when he says "the reason India hasn't gained freedom is precisely because she has more showmen than true leaders. And the few leaders she does have are going against the laws of nature" (191). Even though

Gandhi had envisaged the dilemma which Ali undergoes, his political frame found no solution in it. There existed a double bind: pledge to not have children till the country attains freedom and the inability to share a genuine marital sexual desire despite the use of contraception.

The story, through Ali, asks how valid it is to gain political "freedom" premised on eliminating a personal, natural and conjugal "freedom." The inauthenticity of Babaji's clarion call for celibate marriage echoes with the dissatisfaction Ali eventually feels on using contraception. Both methods work against a holistic human desire that exists between men and women. "A person should stay the way God made him," says Ali when he talks of reformers who are too concerned with artificialities to understand "natural human weaknesses" (*Swaraj* 188) because they are busy shaving their heads, wearing red ochre clothes and smearing their body with ash. Babaji's discourse, based on a higher ideal and premised on a beyond-human sense of control and effacement, can only push people to lead lives which can barely resemble living in its true sense. Ali asks the narrator "What do you think? Doesn't every effort that India has made to free herself look unnatural? . . . Why have we failed to achieve freedom"? The reason lies in the way "we conduct our politics and live our sham lives. Lives in which we deceive others, and ourselves even more" (188).

With this discourse resounding in their minds, Gandhi's followers, like Ali, were living an unreal life, Gandhi's narrative of abstinence falls flat. Ali vehemently proclaims at one moment in his story that "whoever attempts to go against nature is bound to come to grief" (*Swaraj* 189). How could curbing of a stronger, natural freedom lead to the attainment of another? Could this usher in a harmonious freedom? In associating himself deeply with Babaji's way of life, Ali and Nigar missed the meaning of their own marriage. Ali calls his journey along these "tortuous byways" as an inherently paradoxical way to help the country become free, even as they were imprisoning their own selves. Ali calls this deceptive political leadership which imposes non-human demands upon the followers and thrives on a façade of self-control to fight the foreign enemy when all one is doing is fighting his/her natural impulses. Denial and diversion of sexuality creates a new form of perversion, which plays with the natural flows and desires of human life to fashion "a politics that stops faith and candidness from being born." This political ideal, Ali tells us, has essentially "blocked the womb of freedom" (191).

Spaces of Struggle: Living and Longing in the Gandhian Ashram

Veena Howard has observed that

> a study of Gandhi's *brahmacarya* as a linear theoretical approach to gender issues presents contradictions: his language of mixed sexualities; his striving to become a woman and a eunuch, while at the same time boasting the value of semen control; and his yearning to acquire the miraculous powers

traditionally associated with this practice, while simultaneously defying the
traditional rules of sex segregation.

("Rethinking Gandhi's Celibacy" 5)

Gandhi created the Ashram as an arena of experimental living and testing
Brahmacharya among young men and women. Manto critiques this politics which
bases itself on the principles of acute control and aversion to the basic human
sexual need through the character of Kamal, a *panditayin* (brahmin woman) who
sings *bhajans* before Babaji and has expressed her resolve to stay celibate by joining
his Ashram. Exceedingly beautiful, brimming with youth, and "a just opened bud
from the vale of Kashmir" (*Swaraj* 176), the narrator feels that even the khadi
saree could not diminish her intrinsic sensuality. The narrator is intrigued by the
contentment which Babaji derives out of the *bhajans* and patriotic songs being sung
by Kamal because he has "frozen like an idiot" (*Swaraj* 176) and finds in himself an
awakening of the desire to kiss this woman, and if impossible, rush back home to
make love to his maidservant. He wonders at this contrast between his raging desire
and the "elderly man's granite confidence and serenity" (*Swaraj* 176), as he listened
to a youthful woman's voice.

Manto uses Kamal's decision to join Babaji's Ashram instead of getting married
to highlight how women were willing to undergo self-effacement and erase their
sexual personas. In Kamal, we have a woman who still has youthfulness and beauty
which she, for no given reason, is willing to sacrifice at the altar of the freedom
struggle and in the life of the ashram. It must be mentioned here that Babaji had
also invited Nigar to join his ashram because he knew about the impending arrest
of Ali due to his political participation and the loneliness Nigar would feel. Manto's
narrator, through his desire for Kamal, senses the urgent need to take these women
away from this self-induced drudgery and the prevalent notions of discarding and
concealing sexuality to participate in public service or the freedom struggle. This
invitation to the Ashram, to live a life devoid of pleasure and desire, was part of the
Gandhian principle of self-denial and suffering to surpass the baser human desires.
For Gandhi, *brahmacharya* and non-violence were inextricable. He wrote, "Non-
violence is universal love. When a man proffers all his love to a woman or a woman
to a man, what can remain with him or her for others? Neither of them can look
upon the whole world as his or her family. They have already a world of their own.
This is a great obstacle in practising universal love" (*Conquest of Self* 20).

Radha Kumar gives another version of this extended yet restrictive notion
of loving when she writes that "those who joined the Sabarmati Ashram were
doused with buckets of cold-water morning and evening to dampen their passions;
married people were expected to live sexless lives and the unmarried were neither
to marry nor fall in love" (84). For Manto, a movement which is driven by the
dream of independence and equality, but where living and working together entails
an inhuman curbing and disciplining of desires, will never be a healthy, happy and
holistic movement. Ghulam Ali voices his disgust of the same when he says in the
story, "I can't understand why none of these contemporary reformers can see that

he's disfiguring humans beyond all hope of recognition. . . . You want to make him a God, while the poor thing, he's having a hard time just holding on to his humanity" (*Swaraj* 188).

For Manto, Ashrams are a paraphernalia, an unnecessary display of celibacy and a brutal fostering of the practice of sublimating sexuality. He finds these spaces repulsive, emaciated and dry. This sentiment is expressed even towards "*vidyalayas, jamat-khanas, takiyas* and *darsgahs*" (*Swaraj* 179). These set-ups are incapable of fostering fulfilment and vitality because they are "as blanched and lifeless as the udders of a cow from which even the last drop of milk has been squeezed out" (*Swaraj* 179). Manto finds in the inhabitants of the Ashram certain beastliness in spite of their regular prayers, a body still parched and repulsive as they "reeked of perspiration" despite bathing, rotten breath and "no trace of good nature and freshness" (*Swaraj* 179). Veena Howard states that in the consolidation of the Ashram, "Gandhi utilized his authority as a religious leader to draft a constitution that negotiated the boundaries between the sacred and secular, the religious and political, and the individual and the community" (*Gandhi's Ascetic Activism* 141). For Manto, these are restrictive spaces teaching people to curb their most basic and most natural impulses, negation of everything beautiful and desirable and especially detrimental to a woman's emotional and physical well-being. How could these cloisters with their aversions and censorships about the body ever give energy and vitality to the freedom struggle?

Conclusion

Swaraj Ke Liye takes up the most debated and critical arena of Gandhi's world – his thoughts about sexuality and his relations with women – an area which Gandhi intensively wrote about and was experimental for its time. Gandhi's contention is whether to view conjugality as passion or devotion, and what men and women can do to transcend sexual desires and transform political involvement into a higher ideal. Manto's story, in responding to Gandhi, raises significant questions: Are the ideas of free-will, and political and sexual freedom, self-driven or collectively defined? What could have been the more human/sustainable way of doing politics? Must abstinence be the sole path to realize Passive Resistance and Satyagraha? *Swaraj Ke Liye* shows that in erasing or struggling with natural human sexual desire, the grand political design of freedom and liberation can only be a bland, impotent reality, described by Ghulam Ali as "a politics that stops faith and candidness from being born" (191).

The story has Manto's clear stance of humans as desiring subjects, which makes him question the need felt by Gandhi to structure his desire for freedom on the foundations of control and revulsion. There are also certain realizations, via the tribulations of Ali. His journey tells us that the trials of being publicly visible and managing revolutionary movements calls for beliefs which might verge on the eclectic, with the individual willing to fail and try again. The story is an examination of what is natural politics and unnatural desire, and how body and sexuality play a larger role than we choose to believe in the worldviews sustained by politics and literature. It tells us that each individual has their own idea and journey towards freedom and evolution. One can never prescribe the routes, but only suggest. *Swaraj Ke Liye* is a reflection on the possibilities of a confluence between the twin streams of a Gandhian ambivalence towards sexual pleasure, and the vigorous critique of this unnatural denial of sexual agency by Saadat Hasan Manto who firmly places a throbbing and desiring human self at the heart of his story.

Works Cited

Flemming, Leslie A. "Manto Bibliography." *Journal of South Asian Literature*, vol. 20, no. 2, 1985, pp. 152–60. *JSTOR*, www.jstor.org/stable/40872787. Accessed 20 Oct. 2019.

Gandhi, M.K. *An Autobiography or The Story of my Experiments with Truth*. NavajivanTrust, 1927.

———. *The Conquest of Self*. Compiled by R. K. Prabhu and U. R. Rao. Thacker and Company, 1943.

———. *Hind Swaraj or Indian Home Rule*. Navajivan Trust, 1938.

Howard, Veena R. *Gandhi's Ascetic Activism: Renunciation and Social Action*. State U of New York P, 2013.

———. "Rethinking Gandhi's Celibacy: Ascetic Power and Women's Empowerment." *Journal of the American Academy of Religion*, vol. 81, no. 1, 2013, pp. 130–61, www.jstor.org/stable/23357879. Accessed 20 Oct. 2019.

Kumar, Radha. *The History of Doing: An Illustrated Account of Movements for Women'sRights and Feminism in India 1800–1990*. Zubaan, 1993.

Lal, Vinay. "Nakedness, Nonviolence, and Brahmacharya: Gandhi's Experiments in Celibate Sexuality." *Journal of the History of Sexuality*, vol. 9, no. 1/2, 2000, pp. 105–36. *JSTOR*, www.jstor.org/stable/3704634. Accessed 20 Oct. 2019.

Manto, Saadat Hasan, and Aakar Patel. *Why I Write: Essays by Saadat Hasan Manto*. Edited and Translated by Aakar Patel. Tranquebar Press, 2014.

———. "Beautiful Girls Will Be Harassed." *Why I Write: Essays by Saadat Hasan Manto*, pp. 32–42. Edited and Translated by Aakar Patel. Tranquebar Press, 2014.

Manto, Saadat Hasan, and Muhammad Umar Memon. *My Name Is Radha: The Essential Manto*. Translated by Muhammad Umar Memon. Penguin Random House, 2016.

———. "The Short Story Writer and Matters of Sex." *My Name Is Radha: The Essential Manto*, pp. 422–425. Translated by Muhammad Umar Memon. Penguin Random House, 2016.

15

GANDHI AND PEASANT ORGANIZATIONS IN COLONIAL INDIA

A Reading of Satinath Bhaduri's *Dhorai Charit Manas*

Bharti Arora

The making of nation and nationalism in India has been a dominant, glorified and hegemonic project. In the process, it often erases the plurality of personal and/or political registers whereby people make sense of, negotiate, or even contribute to this project of the nation. Satinath Bhaduri[1] (1906–1965) calls this ambiguity out in *Dhorai Charit Manas* (1949–1951, translated in English as *Dhorai Charit Manas* 2013) as he unfolds Gandhian nationalism's canvas. The novel betrays the affectations of nationalism's dominant strain to illustrate how it could not address caste/class, gender, communal and regional inequalities. The Gandhian ideals of truth, non-violence and *satyagraha* were systemically appropriated by the nation game,[2] which demanded the sacrifice of poor and marginalized people at the altar of national independence. G. Aloysius, in his book *Nationalism without a Nation in India* (1998), affirms in this context that such strategies of inducting the poor in the nationalist movement homogenized their disparate contexts and arrested their potential to challenge premodern forms of culture–power fusion. This fusion was "unequal, hierarchical, and legitimized by Brahminic tradition as well as the present collusive, colonial power structure" (59). He further emphasizes that this mobilization was carried out within a specific religio-moral discourse against their current educational concerns, social mobility, diversification of occupation and political agenda (197). Thus, the masses were mobilized for a purely emotional effect to aid the Congress elite in their nationalist assertions with respect to the British.

The chapter examines Satinath Bhaduri's *Dhorai Charit Manas* to highlight the caste- and community-based procedures whereby the nationalist consciousness was built and expanded across colonial India under the aegis of Gandhi and the Congress, 1920 onwards. Bhaduri's wide-ranging experience of participating in the anti-colonial movement enabled him, to borrow from Ipshita Chanda, "to understand the complex power-play between groups and factions" (ix). He painstakingly documents his growing despair at what he felt were "machinations disguised as

DOI: 10.4324/9781003145479-20

public service" (Chanda ix) in the novel, highlighting how these could distort the dream and character of independence for millions of its emergent citizens. Mapping the epic structure of *The Ramayana*, *Dhorai Charit Manas* presents the life-narrative of Dhorai, a new age Ram, who learns to perceive the social, cultural and political complexities of the colonial world through a tenuous lens of Gandhian/nationalist morality. Chanda observes "Satinath conceives of him [Dhorai] as the prototype of Rama, human yet rising above his human limitations if the occasion demands: this may well be Satinath's dream for the future, a dream outlined during the long labour that gave birth to India" (xi). The novelist weaves an intricate and multi-layered narrative to illustrate the procedures of this labour.

The novel, originally written in Bengali, highlights a fractured cultural milieu of Jiraniya (Purnea district in Bihar), where only a small section of *pravasi* (non-resident) Bangalis, "Babubhaiya of the town" (1) speak Bengali. They hold all the lucrative posts in the administration. Bhaduri deploys Bengali language and community as self-reflective tools to probe the unequal contexts of language, culture, caste–class and gender chiefly inhabited by the lower-caste Tatmas, the Dhangars and the Koyeri peasants. Chanda argues, "This is a Bangla novel that spontaneously overcomes the barrier of and even satirizes bhadralok refinement, the obstruction of bhadralok identity and the refusal to accept the limitations of the language to dictate the limitations of the material of life" (xv). Doing so also interrogates the dominant socio-cultural, religious and gendered contexts that feed into the nation's meta-narrative and/or nationstates.

The paper is divided into three sections. The first section deals with the varied registers of the Tatmas' political awakening concerning the dominant nationalist and Gandhian morality. The second section highlights how the extant nodes of solidarity among the lower-caste masses were affected by and negotiated the nationalist unity constructions. The final section critiques the caste/and class biases embedded in the Congress' and/or Gandhi's attitude towards poor and peasants, affecting their land ownership rights.

"Political Awakening" of the Tatmas[3]

Bhaduri foregrounds the nodes of systemic transformation under colonial rule, which led to the emergence of a new structure of aspirations among people. Dhorai is born in a lower-caste community called the Tatmas or Tantrimachatri, who earn their living by thatching roofs and sieving out sand from uncemented wells. Dhorai's father dies, soon after his birth, leaving Dhorai under the care of his mother Budhni. However, she too abandons Dhorai so that she could marry Babulal "the chaprasi, the orderly, of the Baichermen of the Distiboard" (14). She leaves Dhorai at a holy place inhabited by Baoka Baoa, a speech-impaired ascetic, who raises Dhorai within the same village community where Budhni lives with her new husband. In a way, the new order of "Baicherman" and the premodern socio-cultural and hierarchical ascriptions co-exist.

Even as the current order aspires towards "homogenisation of power within culture" (Aloysius 59) by allowing a widow to remarry, it demands that her son from previous marriage be abandoned on the grounds of illegitimacy. Thus, the new order synchronizes with the traditional segmentations and premodern ascriptions in varied ways, affecting the emergence of an egalitarian national political community. Moreover, this new community does not offer any legitimate space to the already destitute people like Baoka Baoa and Dhorai. As Aloysius argues, the emergent national community was predicated on a sense of continuity, albeit in a modernized form, of premodern ascriptions of hierarchy. This continuation proved detrimental to the varied aspirational contexts among the masses (59).

Gandhi's entry to the nationalist scene further arrested these contexts as he sought to mobilize the masses within a specific religio-moral discourse of the Non-Cooperation and Khilafat movements, diverting them away from "their own autonomous or semi-autonomous political agenda" (Aloysius 220). Shahid Amin takes this point further, assessing the spread of the Congress movement and nationalist consciousness among the masses under the aegis of Gandhi. He asserts that the spread of Gaurakshini Sabhas (Cow Protection Leagues), the rise of the Nagari Pracharini (Hindi propagation) movement, setting up of Hindi literary journals and Hindu social reform in the 1910s significantly propounded the message of *swaraj* and nationalist activity in Gorakhpur in the period up to 1919–1920. Even as the non-cooperation and Khilafat movements advocated Hindu Muslim unity, and Muslim leaders played a significant role in these agitations, the inception and perception of the nationalist movement were rooted in the ideas of Hindi–Hindu movement, community, nation and gaushalas. In this religious atmosphere, the "mythopoeic imagination" (Amin 292) of the masses activated when they learnt about Gandhi's agitation at Champaran and his sympathies for the poor and peasants. This proved crucial to popularizing and cementing his image as a God-like persona or mahatma.

The novel, however, is interested in probing deep into the political efficacy of such an awakening. Bhaduri suggests that the lower strata, comprising the Tatmas and the Dhangars, had a certain consciousness of their deprivation vis-à-vis upper-caste Babubhaiyas even before Gandhi's arrival on the political scene. Even as the said resistant consciousness sought to make sense of Gandhi's God-like stature, it was not always expressed within the dominant purview of religion or what Amin calls "patterns of popular belief and ritual action corresponding to these" (331). Bhaduri highlights the variegated ways in which the Tatmas negotiate the popular discourses and rumours about Gandhi. Their first encounter with Gandhian glory happens when Babulal brings the news of Bangali Babu-Master Saheb's resignation from his government job as a teacher because "he has become a follower of Ganhi Baba" (31). Gandhi is described as "Bada guni aadmi (sorcerer),[4] he has renounced meat-fish and intoxicants. He hasn't married. And he goes around completely naked" (31). However, this does not have any significant impression on the Tatmas, who wonder about Master Saheb's plight as a Gandhian, "Bangali Babus are too fond of their prawn curry. Can Master Saheb tolerate so much takleef, such hardship? Must have accumulated some land or property" (31).

This incident betrays the unequal contexts of caste, class and gender between the Tatmas and the Bangali Babus of Jiraniya. The strain is reiterated in the novel at multiple junctures, exposing how Gandhi's first perception was not that of a Messiah or leader of the masses but the classes. Second, the incident also reveals how Tatmas' encounter with Gandhi's merit(s) may not necessarily be located within the dominant context of reverence or nationalist awakening. The talk among the Tatmas expresses their doubts about the longevity of austerity. Their sense of wonder and awe at Master Saheb's ease in giving up non-vegetarian food may border on humour but evokes a deep experiential interface with the Gandhian project. Bhaduri suggests how the actual contexts of hunger and hardship faced by the Tatmas equip them to negotiate and represent their sharp insights into class and caste violence vis-à-vis the privileged contexts of Bangali Babus. This political awakening precedes the dominant discourse of nationalism contingent on what Aloysius has termed "the Gandhi- Event" (190).[5]

Likewise, there are numerous instances in the novel that juxtapose the actual hardships of the Tatmas vis-a-vis the "polysemic nature of the Mahatma myths and rumours" (Amin 294). By doing so, the novel problematizes the dominant perception of the masses as childlike, whose "tryst with nationalist destiny" could only be facilitated by the elite political intermediators of the Congress party. In one of these instances, the Tatmas are so overwhelmed to discover a "murat, an outline" (33) of Gandhi on a pumpkin that they perceive it as a testimony to Gandhi's magical powers. However, Bhaduri portrays the irony embedded in this sudden revelation of Gandhi. His God-like stature is as fragile as the outline etched on a perishable pumpkin. Soon after mahantji/priest of the Thakurbari temple refuses to enshrine this pumpkin in the temple, "it is not right to keep Ganhi Baoa's murat in a Thakurbari which has the murat of Ram Sita" (34), the mystical trance of Baoa and others is broken. They are forced to confront their lack of resources and wealth vis-à-vis the rich, who seem to have complete control over deciding which God is worthy of a temple. Baoa muses, "Only if we had money like the foreigner sahibs, the middle class Babubhaiya, the ruler, Raj Darbhanga, we'd have made a place of worship for Ganhi baoa" (34). We come across a series of such incidents, whereby the Tatmas accept, negotiate and even outrightly reject/dismiss the popular discourses on Gandhi. This active dialogic process offers a glimpse into how the Tatmas apply deep cognition to understand Gandhi. Thus, Bhaduri's novel challenges the dominant political discourses of the period whereby the likes of Tatmas were allotted a limited role on the stage of nationalist performance. According to Amin, "To behold the mahatma in person and become his devotees were the only roles assigned to them, while it was for the urban intelligentsia and full time party activists to convert this groundswell of popular feeling into an organized movement" (291).

Nevertheless, the non-cooperation movement, launched under Gandhi's aegis, ushered in a new political scenario, witnessing numerous incidents of opposition against zamindars/landlords. The masses were so inspired by the idea of *swaraj* that they assumed it would bring them freedom from the clutches of "those power relations deemed inviolable until then, such as British/Indian, landlord/peasant, high caste-low caste, etc." (Amin 312). However, as Amin argues, this incipient political awakening proved counterproductive at times. The peasants broadly understood *swaraj*⁵ in material terms [*Ramrajya* – where Indians would have a separate existence without the British presence, non-violence (not using lathis and looting baazars), self-purification – giving up of meat, liquor and ganja/smoke – spinning the wheel, achieving freedom from oppression]. These terms indirectly facilitated a personalized and culturally specific perception of *swaraj*.

Amin builds this argument further, highlighting the role played by caste sabhas under the influence of the non-cooperation movement thus, "[t]he evolution of the Pipraich Sudharak Sabha [in Gorakhpur city] at about the same time indicates how those who were actively involved in the promotion of Hindu culture could be promptly induced to espouse the cause of Non-Co-Operation" (298). Unfortunately, this mode of politico-cultural awakening severely affected the extant patterns of inter- and intra-caste solidarity among society's lower strata.

In the novel, Bhaduri foregrounds this aspect when the Tatma panchayat, too, approaches the idea of *swaraj* in terms of their personalized caste and communal contexts. They look forward to transgressing the limitations of their caste status by maintaining cleanliness, giving up liquor, and ensuring that "one day a month, all the jhotaha [women] are to bathe and become paak saaf" (37). The panchayat also declares Sunday to be observed as a holiday so that the community could stay at home and clean their houses. However, the panchayat's impositions have warped consequences for the ordinary Tatmas. Dhorai gets worried that they would have to give their Sunday earnings up "[d]on't cut into our stomachs, Mahato. The earnings on Sunday are our real income" (37). His assertion of the actual contexts of hunger and misery challenge the spectacular narrative of Gandhian morality, which systematically clouded these contexts within vague rhetorics of sacrifice and austerity. In doing so, Dhorai claims his right to democratize the village panchayat's otherwise hierarchical structure "[t]he nayeb-Mahato are amazed at this juvenile's gall. Such a little boy, and he has the presumptuousness to speak at the panchayati!" (37). It is also noteworthy that the panchayat's perception and response to the *swaraj* rhetoric are opposed to ordinary Tatmas.

This instance in the novel further reveals how Dhorai's assertions have a strong potential to arrest the possible damage, which could be caused by Gandhian mobilization around the traditional axis of caste/community as it affirmed the importance of the local and regional elite therein. Aloysius rightly affirms, "Gandhi was acutely sensitive to the traditional pattern of power-spread within the communities and exploited this to the maximum. He never approached the masses directly but always through the regional and local elite, who in the process tended to gain importance, which they then owed to the supreme leader" (221). Thus, the political will and assertion of the caste panchayat, in the novel, not only betrays the life patterns of the Tatma community but also indirectly strengthens the traditional social order.

Disguised in the moral vocabulary of self-purification, the ideal of cleanliness reeked of, what Muralidharan suggests "a patronizing attitude of Gandhi towards those at the bottom of the ascriptive hierarchy" (21). In one of his letters addressed to Jawaharlal Nehru, Gandhi expressed his views on the ideal village thus:

> My ideal village still exists only in my imagination. . . . In this village of my dreams the villager will not be dull – he will be all awareness. He will not live like an animal in filth and darkness. Men and women will live in freedom, prepared to face the whole world. There will be no plague, no cholera and no smallpox.
>
> *(qtd. in Mukherjee 36)*

Gandhi's idealization of the countryside indirectly suggests that it has been a place of inequality, filth, disease and darkness. The villagers are so used to living in these deplorable conditions that it is pertinent to "teach them the value of cleanliness."

Muralidharan also quotes Gandhi's exchange with two members of the depressed classes in the early 1920s, "They should give up drinking, refuse to eat leftovers, stop eating meat and, though for the sake of service, engaged in the most uncleanly work, remain clean and worship God. All this is for them to attend to. Others cannot do it for them" (20). The novel exposes the marginalization of lower-caste people vis-à-vis these 'nationalist' self-purification drives. Dhorai wonders how Ganhi Baoa, who otherwise belongs to his group and sympathizes with the poor, can "cut into their stomach?" (37). Unlike the Tatma panchayat, Dhorai is discerning and therefore questions the veracity of the self-purificatory drive, which indirectly throws the Tatmas at tender mercies of the caste panchayat.[7] By doing so, he also questions the caste biases embedded in nationalist politics, which sought the support of ordinary masses and peasants to attain *swaraj* but did little to ensure their social liberation.

Scholars like Swaminath Natarajan (*A Century of Social Reform* 1959), David Hardiman (*Peasant Nationalists of Gujarat* 1981) and Ghanshyam Shah ("Traditional Society and Political Mobilisation" 1974) have underscored how this "religio-millenial nature of the Gandhi -Event . . . did not prove beneficial to the political advancement of the country in general and did a lot of harm to the struggles against the traditional order in particular" (Aloysius 196). The deployment of vague concepts like sin and truth further distorted the perception of *swaraj*, "It was sinful to co-operate with the government, not to support Khilafat, not to work for the abolition of untouchability, etc. Gandhi went about as a religious preacher . . . peddled to the masses as a miracle-worker who could conjure up Swaraj from out of nowhere" (Aloysius 196).

Bhaduri's novel challenges these aspects of the "Gandhi-Event" by showing how the ground reception of Gandhian principles has a differential impact on people belonging to a specific community and across the varied caste, class, gender and religious contexts of society.

More to the point, Dhorai's consciousness about the inequitable class and caste structure makes him question the constructed nature of Gandhi's divinity. His first encounter (*darshan*) with Gandhi's persona does not evoke any sense of *bhakti* (devotion). His lack of a beard, spectacles and soothing soft skin strikes not an image of a saint but an upper-caste middle-class Babubhaiya "Dhorai sees, he [Gandhi] is perhaps shorter than him, even, but so 'laram thanda,' soft and soothing. Dhorai has heard that, if you eat ghee you begin to look like that. But what kind of saint is he, without a beard?" (74). What he and others in his community "dislike the most about this sant aadmi is that he is partial to wearing glasses like the urbane babubhaiya" (74). Dhorai and his fellow Tatmas do not accord Gandhi a divine status. The novel punctures the mythmaking procedures around Gandhi, subtly hinting at his mortal existence. The fact that Gandhi appears more like a Babubhaiya betrays the elite character of the nationalist movement. The incident further problematizes the logic and structure of the circulation of specific images that project Gandhi as a powerful and/or divine figure.

Gandhi's preference for frugal clothing, khadi and charkha are constructed as markers of his immense potential to sacrifice himself for *swaraj*. Seema Bawa ("Power and Politics of Portraits, Icons and Hagiographic Images of Gandhi" 2018), who has worked on Gandhi's official and popular iconography, describes how Gandhi's body becomes a site of his personal and nationalist politics. She states "Gandhi's dhoti or later his loincloth firmly establish him within an Indian discourse, partly nationalist, partly traditionalist, while the disrobed body partakes of both renunciation and identification with the deprived masses" (61).

Alternatively, the novel identifies Gandhi's Godliness as an offshoot of his class alliances and privileged location, which are otherwise outside the reach of the Tatmas. They display a deep understanding and dismissal of these personality markers vis-à-vis their unequal caste status and exploitation at the hands of Babubhaiyas. By so doing, the novel problematizes the dominant rubric of Gandhi's *darshan* whereby, in Amin's words, "the task of the janta is to congregate in large numbers, feast eyes on the Mahatma, count themselves lucky and . . . return to their inert and oppressed existence" (305). Thus, Bhaduri critiques extant scholarship on representation and what falls under the rubric of politics itself.

Re(defining) Truth and Non-Violence: Towards Empathy and Forgiveness

On a similar note, the Dhangars tribe in the novel does not give in to Gandhi's charisma. They are descendants of the untouchable Oraons, and most of them have converted to Christianity. Bhaduri describes how their *aachar* (practices), rituals, life contexts and habitus are entirely different from the Tatmas. When Mahato and Charidaar ask them to give up pigs and chickens (42), the Dhangars respond that they earn "their living by selling pig's meat and chicken's eggs to the foreign sahib-mem. If Ganhi baoa cuts into our stomachs, may he remain yours alone. And pachai is needed for our pooja, we can't give it up" (42). This dialogue highlights the ambiguous combination of the religious and political elements in constructing the Gandhian discourse on *swaraj* and its differential impact on different groups of people, who are often "related antagonistically within the traditional social structure" (Aloysius 191). The moral and political authority presumed by people like Mahato and Charidaar was no different from the Congress volunteers' power-driven motives, who often mediated the Gandhian narrative for their benefit. As Aloysius and Amin illustrate, these volunteers and Ashram members often acted as propaganda machines for Congress politics. Thus, the constructive programmes intended for the moral regeneration of society at large were deeply entwined with a "ruthless pursuit of monopoly, political power" (191).

However, it is interesting to see how Bhaduri deploys the discourse on satya (truth) to validate the Dhangars' customary practices in a uniquely Gandhian way. Selling and eating non-vegetarian food, using liquor for ritualist procedures comprises the Dhangars' everyday sustenance. Since *satyagraha's* objective lay in dismantling the coercive state apparatuses and "recovery of individual autonomy within a framework of civil society" (Muralidharan 12), the Dhangars have all the rights to assert their *satya*/truth based on their community habitus. This incident interrogates the majoritarian bias embedded in the nationalist movement and expands the scope of *satyagraha* for the readers. In the words of Muralidharan:

> Different ideas of truth can coexist, as they should. But none should cross the threshold of civilised discourse and end in violence. That was the final test that Gandhi set for the truth-value of any belief. If it impelled the adherent into an act of violence against a fellow being, then it could not aspire to the status of truth.
>
> (12)

Thus, Bhaduri suggests that the customary practices and livelihood patterns of the Dhangars make them equal stakeholders to the discourse of *swaraj*. Thereby, he also liberates the conception of *swaraj* from its dominant caste and community contexts.

The novel explores alternative ways of social and communitarian bonding among people who may or may not draw their lives from caste and/or religion. Dhorai's act of joining the Dhangars in the construction work of the pakki (metalled road) is one such instance whereby he forges bonds across caste and religion. It further expands his consciousness to accommodate and accept people's narratives belonging to different castes, communities and regions. "The road goes from one end of the world to another. . . . A shadowy picture of the enormity of the country emerges in his mind. He understands in a rudimentary fashion, that there is a relation between his road-making and the coming and going of so many people" (82). Partha Chatterjee (*The Politics of the Governed* 2004) locates Dhorai's bond with the Dhangars and the construction of the pakki, a marker of colonial modernity, within the teleological conception of history. According to Chatterjee, Dhorai learns to forge a sense of belonging to the emergent nationstate based on new vistas of citizenship and rights-based discourse (12–13). However, as the novel reveals, this political consciousness is not purely an offshoot of the national regeneration.

The pakki (concrete) road facilitates the coming together of heterogeneous communities, expanding Dhorai's capacity to empathize with their diverse reasons to traverse the road. "Some carts come laden with corn, some people come in carts to fight a court case, and some people come to get patients seen by doctors" (82). Dhorai learns to extend his kindness to each of these concerns. He also warns people about the impending fine if their bullock carts go over the road's metalled part, unlike Shanichara, who threatens the cart driver and pockets the money (80). Thus, Dhorai's emergent bond with these diverse communities of travellers is indicative of his urge towards what Aloysius has called "homogenization of power (in the sense of even distribution) within culture" (59). According to Aloysius, "homogenization of power within culture" comprises varied forms to "shake off the yoke of ascriptive bondage, under the emerging modern political structure" (60). He further asserts, "The awareness of the changing power relations seems to have dawned upon the lower rungs of the hierarchy. These were communities who at one time, had been most exploited, and hence were sensitized to possible escape routes" (59). Dhorai's act of forging affirmative bonds with such disparately located communities of people stands in opposition to the traditional caste- and community-based structures of hierarchy and social organization.

Alternatively, the Tatma panchayat's decision to burn Baoa's *thaan* and punish Dhorai for his transgressions betrays the panchayat's allegiance to community sensitive identities. The novel problematizes such communal allegiances that seek their fulfilment in and through retributive mechanisms. It underscores the need to alter the extant equations of caste and class in India as the very "constitution" of postindependence India was at stake. Bhaduri suggests, in this context, how Gandhian ethics of *satyagraha* and ahimsa could prove as viable tools for modifying and (re)forging the identity-based politics. For instance, when the senior Daroga interrogates the Tatmas about the fire incident, Baoa and Dhorai remain quiet, "what's done is done, it is not right to keep alive quarrels with people of your own caste" (69). It is noteworthy that Baoa invokes the same community bonds, albeit in the Gandhian way, to forgive his fellow Tatmas who had burnt his *thaan*. He becomes an exemplar in the spirit of a *satyagrahi* as he prefers forgiveness to retribution. Akeel Bilgrami, in his essay "Gandhi, the Philosopher" (2003), quotes Gandhi on ahimsa thus: "Ahimsa is not the crude thing it has been made to appear. Not to hurt any living thing is no doubt part of ahimsa. But it is its least expression. It is hurt by hatred of any kind, by wishing ill of anybody, by making negative criticisms of others" (4161). Thus, Baoa displays his generosity and an ability to perceive the importance of *satyagraha* at a complex level.

In another instance, Baoa muses over the possibility of leaving Dhorai for spending the rest of his life in Ayodhya. He also wonders why Gandhi and his disciples are close to Muslims when they have "changed Ramchandraji's temple in Ayodhya into a mosque, a masjid" (139). However, Baoa can separate moral judgement from criticism in this context. His religious temperament and conscience expand the idea of divinity for him. Baoa realizes that God's benevolence does not reside in a fixed territorial space, "yet how is Ramchandraji still so benevolent towards them [Muslims]?" (139). This spirit of perceiving things in their entirety makes him conclude that Muslims are equally worthy of divine benevolence.

Gandhi wished to tap this heterogeneous version of religiosity, which was already embedded in India's living cultures and could be substantially improvised and dovetailed with his lessons on non-violence. Bilgrami further argues "Take the wrong view of moral value and judgment, and you will inevitably encourage violence in society. There is no other way to understand Gandhi's insistence that the *satyagrahi* has not eschewed violence until he has removed criticism from his lips and heart and mind" (4162). In this context, we witness how Gandhi played a crucial role in sowing the seeds of a secular nation state.

Speaking on the fundamental rights resolution during the Karachi Congress, 1931, Gandhi emphasized that "religious neutrality" is an "important provision" (qtd. in Muralidharan 17) of the emergent nationstate "Swaraj will favour Hinduism no more than Islam, nor Islam more than Hinduism. But in order that we may have a State based on religious neutrality, let us from now adopt the principle in our daily affairs" (17). Bhaduri's Baoa successfully decodes and imbibes this message, as explained previously.

Years later, when the Partition plan materializes despite Gandhi's forceful opposition to it, he concludes that the nation has failed the principles of ahimsa and *satyagraha*. As Sudhir Chandra (*Gandhi: An Impossible Possibility*) informs, "Precisely when their 30-year-long *satyagrah* movement based on truth and ahimsa was bringing them independence, people were descending into savagery. How could *satyagrah* have brought forth such a fruit? In what depths had lain repressed such cruelty and violence" (47). The novel published immediately after independence not only casts an ironical glance at the partitioned reality of 1947 but also alerts us to being morally conscious of the call of ahimsa. Baoa, like Gandhi in this context, seeks to erase the difference between "we" and "they" as he chooses forgiveness over revenge. His conscience is aligned with Gandhi's lessons on ahimsa and satya "All I say is that no individual can save his religion by becoming a sinner, through deceit or by oppressing others. This applies to Hindus as well as Muslims" (Gandhi, qtd. in Chandra 64).

Peasant Consciousness Within (Without) the Gandhian Framework

In the second part of the novel, Dhorai moves to Bishkandha where he engages with the Koyeris. The dominant framework here happens to be land "[n]o one ever talked of land in Tatmatuli. . . . But the ambience is different here [Koyeritola]. Here, joys, sorrows, jokes, tamasa, gibes, and insults are all related to farming and the landlord" (175). Bhaduri narrates that most of the peasants in Koyeritola are adhiar (share croppers) of the Rajputs. They have also been working as servants in the Rajput households for generations. "Legally, the owner of all the land in these parts is Raj Darbhanga" (175). The caste divisions dominate the land ownership patterns in Koyeritola as most of them are exploited by zamindar Bachchan Singh (Babusaheb).

While Dhorai sang Bidesia songs in Tatmatuli about "mahatmaji's salt-making" (174), Bilta sings songs about the exploitation of the Koyeris by the landlord, "The zamindar's sipahi has come to collect tax, rey bidesiya/My elder brother-in-law has been taken away this morning, rey bidesiya/He's tied up to a stake in the indigo-factory, rey bideshia" (173). Interestingly, even as the last of indigo factories have been wound up in this part of Bihar by the 1920s, they still find their reference in Bilta's songs. This reference to the indigo factory is a key to understanding the exploitative zamindari system of Bishkandha and ways in which the rural tenure holders and communities were rendered landless.

Aloysius relates that the premodern ascriptive hierarchies find newer, alternative modes of expression during colonial times. Unlike precolonial India, where land was a site of convergence between "hierarchical interdependent interests and rights of different rural communities" (Aloysius 41), the British rule ushered in a phase of consolidation of private property rights for the privileged castes and landowners. The British needed capital and personnel to maintain their rule over India. This requirement made the British join hands with local elite, zamindars, moneylenders and landlords of different localities. "Far from upsetting the existing order of superordination and subordination, British rule tended to act as a freezer on the social structure by sharing the new legal and moral authority" (40). Thus, the Koyeris do not perceive any difference between their exploitation at the hands of zamindars like Bachchan Singh and the wreckage caused by a previous generation of British indigo planters.

The political and economic affirmations of the Koyeris are deeply entwined with their subordinated contexts. Dhorai, who has become an outcast after severing his ties with Tatmas, plays a significant role in foregrounding these subordinated contexts and concerns of the Koyeritola. For instance, when a famine strikes Bishkandha, Dhorai encourages all ryots to get together and claim their rightful share of paddy from their zamindar Bachchan Singh. The political consciousness which was hitherto nascent in Dhorai gets manifested in this act of empathizing with the Koyeris. He reaches out to them, despite knowing that the Koyeris look down upon his Tantrimachatri caste. By doing so, he remains consistent with his commitment to overcoming the traditional caste and community-based modes of social organization "[w]here he had his roots, even there he did not shy away from clashing with the panch, the village elders, so being afraid here [Koyeritola] is out of question" (198). Thus, the alliance between Dhorai and the Koyeris is not predicated on abstract community-centric notions of mutual interdependence but approximates, to borrow from Kavita Punjabi (*Unclaimed Harvest* 2017), "a unique politics . . . rooted in concrete intersubjective experiences and the responsibilities of the process of caring for another that embodied and concretized the ethic of justice and the claiming of rights" (122). This act of solidarizing differences based on care ethics offers a counternarrative to the overwhelmingly dominant framework of nationalist unity and politics of appropriation launched under Gandhi's influence.

It is also noteworthy that Dhorai's effort to support the Koyeris against Bachchan Singh's oppression is located outside the influence of Gandhian discourse. Seeking to penalize the Koyeris for their audacious demand of paddy share, Bachchan Singh files a lawsuit against them for the unpaid taxes. He even replaces the Koyeri peasants with people from the Santhal neighbourhood. However, the zamindar's retributive action does not dampen the Koyeris' spirit to fight for their rights. Instead, they too approach Ramnuvaj Munshi, a clerk in the Jiraniya court, to learn "how much it will cost to fight a case, a mukkaddama, against Babusaheb" (204). The Koyeris do not even consider offering *satyagraha* against Bachchan Singh.

It is essential to engage with Gandhi's perspectives on the peasants' movement in this context. Even as he enthusiastically took the case of peasants up against Britishers in the agitations of Champaran and Kheda, Gandhi subsequently towed the Congress line, advocating a balance between the interests of the zamindars and peasants. He did not encourage the peasants to launch the non-cooperation movement against zamindars and withhold taxes/rent from them. Gandhi (*Young India* 1924) asserts, "The Kisan Movement must be confined to the improvement of the status of the kisan and the betterment of the relations between the Zamindars and them . . . and scrupulously abide by the terms of their agreement with the Zamindars whether such agreement is written or inferred from custom" (741–42). Thus, Gandhi's agitation favouring Champaran peasants against British Indigo planters was structurally different from ways in which he dissuaded the peasants from offering *satyagraha* against their local landlords and zamindars.[8]

In the novel too, Gandhi does not figure in the Bidesia songs of the Koyeris. *Satyagraha* has no major implications for them. Alternatively, the Koyeris are inspired by other extant models of agitation, which were more pertinent to challenging their oppressive contexts. As Ranajit Guha illustrates in *Elementary Aspects of Peasants Insurgency in India* (1983), the poor peasants deeply discerned the collusion between *sarkar* and *zamindar* and the procedures that led to their exploitation at every level in colonial India. Guha records ways in which the peasant consciousness found expression in "activities of rural masses known as revolt, uprising, dhing, bidroha, ulgulan, hool . . . and so on" (4). The peasants were already familiar with diverse ways of reacting to the colonial and/or feudal oppression, becoming "the makers of [their] own rebellion" (Guha 4). Thus, Gandhi was neither the first nor the only leader of peasants. The peasants could organize themselves against the British planters and adopt appropriate strategies to fight for their cause. These strategies did not hesitate to deploy violence when required and raised awareness about the exploitative relations through newspapers and court cases.

The novel engages with the intricate patterns of nationalist mobilization, illustrating how it sought to discount multiplicities of caste, community and gender in the guise of a religio-moral discourse. This nationalist mobilization becomes clearer through Bhaduri's account of the Assembly Elections of 1937 and how the Congress inducted the poor in its propaganda on the issue of "Ramrajya" and "bote/vote" (244). Congress volunteers convince Dhorai and the Koyeris to vote for the Congress ministry in the name of Gandhi, "It was through an act of God that he [Dhorai] learnt from the Bolunteers that the meaning of 'bote' is that you have to put a letter into the white post box in reply to Mahatmaji's letter. As soon as he receives the letter, Mahatmaji knows whether you want Ramrajya or not" (247). The foundation of Ramrajya is contingent on the assurance that Gandhi and the Congress would make relevant laws to decrease taxes and "put the zamindars in their place" (247). The Koyeri peasants are also told that as per the new law "no 'adhiadaar' will give the zamindar his share of crop without a receipt. The zamindar gets eighteen seers by weight and you get twenty-two. Not half and half" (254).

This vision, of a world free of Bachchan Singh's exploitation, is so powerful that it brings together the hitherto exclusive groups of the Koyeris and the Santhals. They have been continuously pitched against each other by zamindar Bachchan Singh to serve his interest. "That very night, the Koyeris and the Santhals get together on the field before the monastery. The crop is ready in the field. That is why Mahatmaji has sent the kanoon, the law as soon as possible" (256). Even as the promise of Ramrajya makes them aspire towards socio-cultural equality, its thick religio-moral vocabulary affects their negotiations vis-a-vis the zamindar on equal terms. The Congress' stratagems ensure that the zamindars like Bachchan Singh also stand benefitted from the grand narrative of Ramrajya, facilitating them to appropriate the role of farmers. "Bolunteer has come just now, with a paper from Collester saheb. It says in the paper that Babusaheb is a "kisan (farmer). The eighteenth-twenty-two law will not be valid for his adhiaars" (258). Aloysius rightly affirms in this context, "The lower caste masses have had millennia-old traditions of struggle against the oppressive Brahmanical division of labour. However, lack of any change in material and economic conditions often prevented these struggles from spreading beyond the realm of philosophy and religion" (226).

Sahajanand Saraswati (*The Struggle of My Life* 2018) also informs us that the Assembly Elections and Tenancy Reforms carried out by the first Congress government (1937–1939) betrayed the cause of peasantry by ensuring that the zamindar candidates emerged victorious. "The Congress ministry entered into pacts with zamindars, not once but twice. They even managed to give legal sanction for the seizure of the standing crops of peasants. Even laws meant to help the peasantry were couched in such ambiguous wording that zamindars rendered them useless and inapplicable" (311). In the novel, the Santhal peasants' demand for a receipt unleashes a series of retributive measures, "a chain of thana police begins. . . . No one got a receipt; three santhals were sent to jail . . . they were accused of taking someone else' crop by force" (258). Thus, the peasants end up becoming parts of a mob that has to be suitably punished for forcibly taking away the land of Bachchan Singh, a fellow peasant. Sahajanand Saraswati further expresses his disappointment at the Congress' tendency to see kisan struggle as an aberration, an obstacle to achieving political independence. He relates an incident when Bihar premier (Shri Babu) asks him to be cautious of these mobs (peasants):

> There was a time when he used to call the peasants as 'mass' and now he had started calling them 'mob'. For these Congress leaders, poor peasants were always a 'mob'. In between they had referred to peasants as 'mass' because they had vested interest in getting their support. Now they had once again become a 'mob' for them.
>
> *(313)*

Anupama Roy (*Gendered Citizenship* 2005) takes this argument further, asserting that the nationalist leadership only concerned itself with the aspect of self-determination, seeking political representation and equality alongside the colonizers. They consistently betrayed what Roy terms "their Brahminical-feudal, sectarian character" (193) when it came to representing the social and economic concerns of the vast majority of social groupings (peasants, tribals, workers, marginalized communities and women) in the country. Social questions were seen as "divisive" (193), and the Indian national movement's (spearheaded by the Indian National Congress) primary objective was to attain political independence.

This conservative nationalist strategy had disastrous implications for women peasants and their land ownership rights. In the novel, the Koyeri women peasants are shown as disadvantaged because of their claim to land inheritance and ownership. Some of these women are also forced to work in the Rajput houses as maids, making them vulnerable to sexual threats. In such circumstances, the novel reveals how difficult it is for widows like Mosammat to retain their rights over land. Bachchan Singh manoeuvres to dislodge Mosammat from her land ownership, branding her a witch and throwing her out of the clan (240). Adrienne Cooper's (*Sharecropping and Sharecropper's Struggles* 1983) and Kavita Punjabi's research on the Tebhaga movement in Bengal in 1930–1950 reveals the cultural, non-economic, sexual implications the sharecropping system had for both women peasants and women who worked from home, assisting their peasant husbands. The landlord's ownership of land extended to exercising control over peasant women's sexuality, reducing them to commodities in the process. Thus, Bachchan Singh's manoeuvrings activate the extant structures of cultural, patriarchal and gendered biases, betraying women peasants' vulnerability.

However, this instance in the novel contradicts the actual historico-political instances of political mobilization among women under the radical influence of the Kisan Sabha in Bihar from the 1930s. Kaushal Kishore Sharma ("Women's Participation in the Peasants' Movement in Bihar"1981) documents how women had gained immense confidence to fight for their rights under the aegis of the Kisan Sabha. "They could come out of their houses but what is important is that they organised themselves in groups to face the onslaughts of the henchman of the Zamindars" (Kishore Sharma 484). Alternatively, Mosammat succumbs to the dominant structures of her caste without a sign of protest. "Even when she was to leave her husband's homestead, she does not scream her lungs out in sorrow. She does not even abuse her caste community" (242). One can attribute an important purpose to Bhaduri's historical oversight: his interest in highlighting the nationalist movement's dominant gendered contexts, wherein women had limited scope to assert themselves as political beings.

As Bhaduri highlights, these women were either *darshan* seekers of the mahatma or cooks who prepared delicious meals for the Congress volunteer lest he is arrested by daroga and "will have to eat jail food" (274). Under Gandhi's aegis, women were called upon to participate in political campaigns like the non-cooperation and civil disobedience movements and spread the message of *satyagraha* and non-violence. This newfound liberation in the nationalist movement could not politically emancipate them.[9] Thus, the Congress' and Gandhian claim of representing the entire nation has to be problematized in the wake of discriminatory practices towards women, peasants and masses. Such treatment also betrays that any motif of their assertion and political awakening outside the nationalist movement's dominant religio-moral vocabulary was severely discouraged. "This meant wresting the masses away from their own agenda of destruction of the Brahminical social order and reducing them to the level of political show-pieces in the power bargain" between the British on the one hand and native elite on the other hand (Aloysius 221). Political mobilization in this context resulted in the exploitation of the masses.

As the paper has shown, Bhaduri's novel works against these assumptions of nationalist glory by consciously recovering the poor's voices and political agency. It highlights how this recovery assumes multi-directional perspectives, which could strongly counter the metanarrative of the colonial-nationalist institutions of power. Bhaduri probed the disparate caste, class, communal and gendered contexts among lower castes and landed elite in colonial India, suggesting how their political mobilization was not contingent on Gandhian methodology of passive resistance. The poor already had a certain consciousness about their deprivations vis-à-vis the British empire as well as the immediate ruling caste-class structure, which sought to manoeuvre their rights and claims to equality. This reading becomes important as it challenges the dominant understanding that the Congress government, both before and after the independence, represented the peasantry's cause. In doing so, Bhaduri undergirds a differential axis of identity formation, which encompasses categories of political empathy on the one hand and redistributive justice on the other hand.

Notes

1 Satinath Bhaduri was born to Indubhushan Bhaduri, a well-to-do barrister, in Purnea, Bihar. He studied law but later gave it up to join the Congress. However, he soon grew disillusioned by the Congress after it came to power in the United Provinces in 1946. He eventually joined the Socialist Party in 1948. Bhaduri's wide ranging experience of participating in the anti-colonial movement enabled him, to borrow from Ipshita Chanda, "to understand the complex power-play between groups and factions" (ix). He painstakingly documents his growing despair at what he felt were "machinations disguised as public service" (Chanda ix) in *Dhorai Charit Manas*, highlighting how these could distort the dream and character of independence for millions of its emergent citizens.

Some of Bhaduri's major works comprise *Jagari* (1946), *Gananayak* (1948), *Chitragupter File* (1949), *Achin Ragini* (1954), *Aparichita* (1954), *Sangkat* (1957) and *Alok Dristi* (1964). He was awarded the Rabindra Award for *Jagari* in 1950.

2 I borrow this phrase from Benjamin Zachariah's book title *Playing the Nation Game: Ambiguities of Nationalism in India. Yoda Press,* 2011.

3 The narrator describes the Tatmas as "weavers by caste. . . . They had come to Jiraniya as a group from Roshra village in Darbhanga, driven by the bidding of their stomachs" (Bhaduri 2). [However], "they usually don't weave clothes or accept that they are weavers" (2). Instead, they exhibit a streak of upwards social mobility as they ask for land to build houses on. "If there is enough at home for one meal each day, they don't go out looking for work" (2). Aloysius describes the rejection of one's caste affiliations as an attempt to "shake off the yoke of ascriptive bondage, under the modern political structure" in colonial India (60). In fact, the Tatmas struggle for their right to wear the sacred thread, later in the novel, thereby refusing to perform traditional labour for the upper caste communities (Bhaduri 75).

4 Ipshita Chanda says in the translation of the novel that "guni aadmi" refers to a sorcerer (Gandhi as a miracle man/sorcerer 31).

5 Aloysius describes the Gandhi-Event as a conglomeration of several socio-historical factors ranging from the manoeuvrings of the Congress and its volunteers to represent Gandhi as a spiritual leader. The colonial rulers also played a considerable role in magnifying the Gandhian image. The outstanding support of Gujarati and Marwari business communities that Gandhi alone enjoyed and the multiplicity of local interpretations of the Gandhian national message also played a massive role in representing Gandhi's mythopoeic constitution (190).

6 The non-cooperation movement's objective was not simply to withdraw active consent from the colonial rule, but to awaken the society's moral power. Gandhi called upon people to exercise self-restraint, leading morally ethical and responsible lives:

> The power to control national life through national representatives is called political power. Representatives will become unnecessary if the national life becomes so perfect as to be self-controlled. It will then be a state of enlightened anarchy in which each person will become his own ruler. He will conduct himself in such a way that his behaviour will not hamper the well-being of his neighbours. In an ideal state there will be no political institution and therefore no political power.(qtd. in Mukherjee 36)

7 Amin suggests that these panchayats were based on an extant model of religious organizations like Gaurakshini sabhas and caste panchayats, betraying a seamless connection between religiosity and an incipient political consciousness (294).

8 Pushyamitra's *Neel Ka Daagh Mita*-1917 (2018) puts Gandhian strategy concerning the peasants in perspective. He cogently states that Gandhi never launched a peasants' movement in Champaran. Gandhi's research on and survey of the situation in Champaran was conducted in an independent researcher's capacity, without Congress' support (113). He was threatened with charges of sedition and forced to leave Champaran subsequently. However, Gandhi refused to accept the administrative orders, turning Champaran into a political laboratory to evolve the idea of *satyagraha* and civil disobedience. Gandhi wrote letters to the local administration, met with British officers, and frankly sought their assistance in conducting the Champaran survey. He said he had done nothing against the law by seeking assistance from the government. Congress does not figure in this moral equation between Gandhi and the peasants. Pushyamitra clarifies that the Congress was so occupied with the "dream" of achieving independence that it did not want to waste their energies on this minor issue of the Champaran peasants.

9 Radha Kumar in *The History of Doing* (1993) relates how, according to Gandhi, the experience of pregnancy and motherhood, especially qualified women, to spread the message of peace and non-violence. Gandhi created the mother's image as a repository of

spiritual and moral values as a preceptor for men (82). More to the point, even though he had called upon women to participate in the civil disobedience movement and *satyagraha*, he restricted their activity to mass picketing of liquor shops, drug shops as to him, women were prime victims of their husbands' endorsement of such shops. It was a matter of moral purity in personal life. Salt, on the other hand, was an issue related to economic hardships Indians endured under British rule, so it was an issue relevant to public life and not considered suitable for women (83).

Works Cited

Aloysius, G. *Nationalism Without a Nation India*. Oxford UP, 1997.

Amin, Shahid. "Gandhi as Mahatma: Gorakhpur District, Eastern UP, 1921–22." *SubalternStudies*, vol. III, Oxford UP, 1984, pp. 288–348.

Bawa, Seema. "Power and Politics of Portraits, Icons and Hagiographic Images of Gandhi." *Economic and Political Weekly*, 5 Feb. 2018, pp. 54–61. Accessed 10 Aug. 2020.

Bhaduri, Satinath. *Dhorai Charit Manas*. Translated by Ipshita Chanda. Sahitya Akademi, 2013.

Bilgrami, Akeel. "Gandhi, the Philosopher." *Economic and Political Weekly*, 27 Sep. 2003, pp. 4159–65. Accessed 20 May 2020.

Chanda, Ipshita. "Preface." *Dhorai Charit Manas*. By Satinath Bhaduri. Translated by IpshitaChanda, Sahitya Akademi, 2013, pp. vii–xxiv.

Chandra, Sudhir. *Gandhi: An Impossible Possibility*. Translated by Chitra Padmanabhan. Routledge, 2020.

Chatterjee, Partha. *The Politics of the Governed: Reflections on Popular Politics in Most of the World*. Columbia UP, 2004.

Cooper, Adrienne. *Sharecropping and Sharecropper's Struggles in Bengal, 1930–1950*. K.P. Bagchi, 1998.

Gandhi, M.K. *Young India (1919–1922)*. S. Ganesan, 1924.

Guha, Ranajit. *Elementary Aspects of Peasant Insurgency in India*. Oxford UP, 1983.

Hardiman, David. *Peasant Nationalists of Gujarat*. Oxford UP, 1981.

Kumar, Radha. *The History of Doing*. Kali for Women, 1993.

Mukherjee, Rurangshu. "Gandhi's Swaraj." *Economic and Political Weekly*, 12 Dec. 2009, pp. 34–39. Accessed 15 Dec. 2019.

Muralidharan, Sukumar. "Religion, Nationalism and the State: Gandhi and India's Engagement with Political Modernity." *Social Scientist*, vol. 34, no. 3/4, 2006, pp. 3–36. Accessed 10 Aug. 2020.

Natarajan, Swaminath. *A Century of Social Reform*. Asia Publishing House, 1959.

Panjabi, Kavita. *Unclaimed Harvest: An Oral History of the Tebhaga Women's Movement*. Zubaan, 2017.

Pushyamitra. *Jab Neel Ka Daag Mita: Champaran-1917*. Rajkamal Prakashan, 2018.

Roy, Anupama. *Gendered Citizenship: Historical and Conceptual Explorations*. Orient Blackswan, 2005.

Saraswati, Sahajanand. *The Struggle of My Life: Autobiography of Swami Sahajanand Saraswati*. Translated and edited by Ramchandra Pradhan. Oxford UP, 2018.

Shah, Ghanshyam. "Traditional Society and Political Mobilisation: The Experience of BardoliSatyagrah (1920–28)." *Contributions to Indian Sociology*, no. 8, pp. 89–107. Accessed 10 Aug. 2020.

Sharma, Kaushal Kishore. "Women's Participation in the Peasants' Movement in Bihar." *Proceedings of the Indian History Congress*, vol. 42, 1981, pp. 482–87. Accessed 10 July 2020.

INDEX

Note: Page locators in *italics* denote figures.

For Product Safety Concerns and Information please contact our EU
representative GPSR@taylorandfrancis.com
Taylor & Francis Verlag GmbH, Kaufingerstraße 24, 80331 München, Germany

www.ingramcontent.com/pod-product-compliance
Lightning Source LLC
Chambersburg PA
CBHW071547110726
47908CB00007B/2027